THE LOCAL ORIGINS OF MODERN SOCIETY

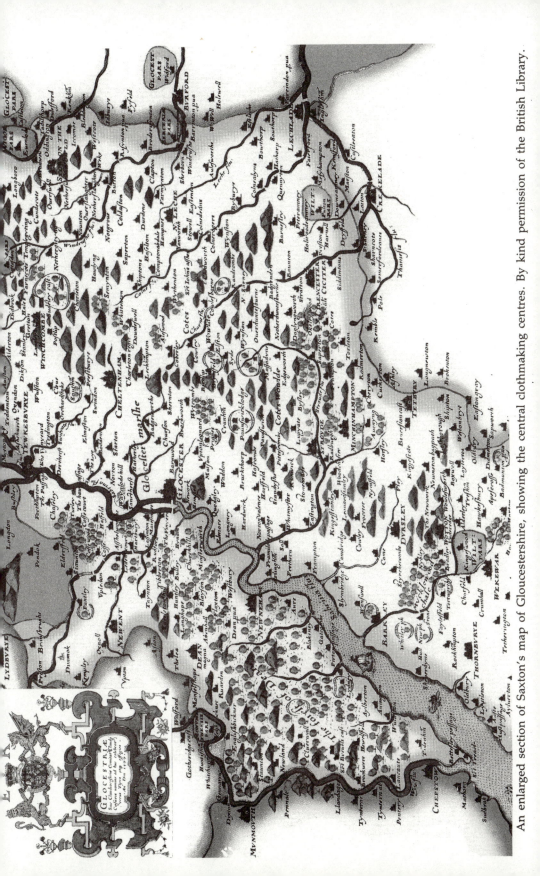

An enlarged section of Saxton's map of Gloucestershire, showing the central clothmaking centres. By kind permission of the British Library.

THE LOCAL ORIGINS OF MODERN SOCIETY

Gloucestershire 1500–1800

David Rollison

London and New York

First published 1992
by Routledge
11 New Fetter Lane, London EC4P 4EE

Simultaneously published in the USA and Canada
by Routledge
a division of Routledge, Chapman and Hall Inc.
29 West 35th Street, New York, NY 10001

© 1992 David Rollison

Phototypeset in 10 on 12 point Palatino by
Intype, London
Printed in Great Britain by Clays Ltd, St. Ives plc.

British Library Cataloguing in Publication Data
Rollison, David
The local origins of modern society:
Gloucestershire 1500–1800.
I. Title
303.4

Library of Congress Cataloging-in-Publication Data
Rollison, David
The local origins of modern society : Gloucestershire 1500–1800 /
David Rollison
p. cm
Includes bibliographical references and index.
1. Gloucestershire (England)–History. 2. Gloucestershire
(England)–Social conditions. I. Title
DA670/G5R65 1992
942.4′1–dc 20 91–41500

ISBN 0–415–07000–7

Dedicated to the memory of my father, Peter Herbert
Rollison, born Eastbourne, England, 29 June 1923, died
Sydney, Australia, 6 January 1973

CONTENTS

Acknowledgements — xiii
Note on sources, method and perspectives — xvi
Introduction Country capitalism — 1

Part I Cradles of change

1 CRADLES OF CHANGE: THE MANUFACTURING DISTRICTS — 21

2 TRAILS OF PROGRESS: THE REORIENTATION AND INTENSIFICATION OF TRAFFIC, 1600–1800 — 45

Part II Neighbourhood to nation

3 PROVERBIAL CULTURE — 67

4 TYNDALE AND ALL HIS SECT — 84

5 NEIGHBOURHOOD TO NATION: THE TROTMANS: A MIDDLE-RANK KIN-COALITION, 1512–1712 — 97

Part III Two revolutionaries

6 'SMALL THINGES AND GRANDE DESIGNES': A REVOLUTIONARY'S HISTORY OF THE ENGLISH REVOLUTION — 123

7 CUNNING MAN AND QUAKER: JOHN ROBERTS OF SIDDINGTON ST MARY — 164

CONTENTS

Part IV The multitudes around us

8 COMMUNITY AT THE BORDERS: MOCKERY AND
   MISRULE IN AN EIGHTEENTH-CENTURY INDUSTRIAL
   VILLAGE   199

9 'A CONCATENATION OF VICIOUS HABITS':
   A SEASON OF RIOTS AND A PUBLIC DISCUSSION,
   1738–41   219

10 LASTING PREJUDICES: LANGUAGES OF
   SOCIAL DISCRIMINATION   247

   Notes and references   265
   Index   310

LIST OF TABLES

1.1 Occupational specialisation and population growth in Gloucestershire market towns, 1551–1801   28

1.2 Population of Stroudwater parishes, 1551–1831   30

1.3 Occupations in Stroudwater in 1608   30

1.4 Occupations at Dursley and Wotton-under-Edge in 1608 and c. 1690   33–4

1.5 Gloucester diocese probate values in the cloth industry   42

2.1 Lechlade's changing occupational structure, 1608–1706   49

xi

ACKNOWLEDGEMENTS

The 'Country Capitalism' project, of which this and my previous publications are part, is not a conventional English county study. The basic research, however, was and continues to be done at Gloucester, which is blessed with rich archives and a team of archive workers who make working there a pleasure I always look forward to. I would like to thank Brian Frith, Kate Haslem, Vickie Thorpe, Tom Bowers, Paul Evans, Averil Kear, Graham Whitehead, Arthur Rigby, Stan Wood, Nicholas Kingsley, Julie Courtenay, Brian S. Smith, David Smith and Margaret Richards at the Gloucestershire Records Office; Neville Chapman, Jill Voyce and Rosealeen Lane at the Gloucester City Library. Albion Urdank has been my closest colleague since I began work at the GRO in January 1979; Albion, Brian Frith, James Horne, Andrew Foster, the late John Wyatt and his wife Eileen, Nick Herbert and John Jurica of the Gloucestershire *Victoria County History* were the best 'graduate school' I could have wanted.

Working on (a) British History, and (b) Early Modern History in Australia in the 1980s and 1990s would have been a lonely and thankless business without the biennial conferences of the Australasian Medieval and Early Modern Historians Association to look forward to. I am especially grateful to Vivien Brodsky, Patricia Crawford, Christopher Hill, Barry Reay, the late Ron Neale, Joan Thirsk, Sybil Jack, John Morrill, Amanda Whiting, Alison Wall, Christopher Haig, Colin Davis, David Sabean, Conal Codren, Lyn Martin, Roger Hainsworth and Wilf Prest. Thanks also to David Phillips, Paul Turnbull and members of the Australasian Modern British Historians Association; Ian Harris; Des Crawley, Dean of the Faculty of Arts and Social Sciences at the University of Western Sydney (Macarthur), for supporting my applications for research funds, and making it possible for me to travel to conferences and seminars in Australia, New Zealand, Britain and America to test my ideas; John Morrill, for his broad-minded support, hospitality and encouragement at a time when it mattered a great deal; Anthony and Belle Low, John Garrod and the staff, fellows and postgraduate students of Clare Hall; the late Trevor Aston and Paul Slack, past editors of *Past and Present*, and 'Reader 5', whoever s/he is.

The following have commented on early drafts of parts of what is published here and offered valuable comments: Vivien Brodksy, John Morrill, Colin Davis, Joan Thirsk, Christopher Hill, Trish Crawford, Paul Slack, Andrew Moore, Andy Wood, Michael Frearson, M. B. Rowlands, Mark Kishlansky, Richard Trexler, Wilf Prest, Ian Harris, Ronald Hutton, Christopher and Annie Lee, Michael Keane, Des Crawley, the editorial board of *History Workshop Journal*, Christopher Haig, Steve Hendrick, Alan Gilbert, John Adamson, David Phillips, Barry Smith, John Stevenson, John Walter, Adam Fox, Albion Urdank, James Horne, Andrew Foster. These are valued critics. If I have managed to be clear, accurate and honest about what I am saying, it is largely owing to their responses, and those of audiences at conferences and groups at seminars. Friendly debate and controversy are the lifeblood of any craft. Lack of them signifies stagnation.

Keith Wrightson read the entire, sprawling penultimate manuscript of this book and wrote ten pages of closely typed comments and suggestions in December 1990. It has been a privilege to share a little of the excitement generated at Cambridge by students associated with the Cambridge Group, Keith Wrightson, John Morrill, Bob Scribner, Margaret Spufford and Patrick Collinson. Since my first tentative visits to consult the library of the Cambridge Group in 1979, to the six months I spent as a Visiting Fellow at Clare Hall with my family in the second half of 1990, the connection has grown without my knowing it. I hope the interdisciplinary Early Modernist Group survives the current generation of postgraduate students, and would like to thank Paul Griffiths, Adam Fox, Andy Wood, Mick Brightman, Mike Frearson and all the members for making me welcome at its meetings.

I would also like to thank Jim and Doz Jones, Roger Janes, Bruce and Allison Johnson, Gail and Roger Macdonald, Rosemary and Roy Lawrence, Adrian and Rose Hall, Paddy George, Humphrey Price-Jones, Ann Osborne, Stephen and Julie Rollison, Lesley and Louis McLaughlin, Paula and Trevor Hammett, Ceridwen Iles, Dot and Ken Short and Britt Meyland-Smith.

My mother and father taught me whatever appreciation of the variety, subtlety and moral influence of historical landscape I have, and much else. This book is dedicated to the memory of my father, who died in 1973. My mother and step-father, Bill Job, made it possible for me to pursue this long-term obsession with people who died hundreds of years ago, and I thank them for their love, generosity and understanding. Christine Rollison encouraged me to go to university in the early 1970s, and supported me while I did it; she and our sons

ACKNOWLEDGEMENTS

Ben (b. 1974) and Dafydd (b. 1978) have been at the centre of my life throughout the researching and writing of this book. I would like to thank them for their love all these good years, and for sharing it with me.

NOTE ON SOURCES, METHOD
AND PERSPECTIVES

The primary sources, printed and written, are mainly located at the Gloucestershire Records Office and the Gloucester City Library. Precise references to the sources used for these studies appear in the notes to each chapter.

The first, 'structural', stage of the research, begun in 1979, involved a complete survey of the local records of Gloucestershire relating to population, economy, wealth distribution, religious affiliation and social structure. A discussion of methodology (including examples of forms designed for transcribing information, and the maps onto which this information was transferred) and a full list of sources can be consulted in Rollison, 'Intensification' pp. 554–667, 'Appendices, Sources and Bibliography'.

The structural stage mapped out long-term trends. Chapters 1, 2 (in part) and 9 belong to that phase, although the material has been considerably reworked. The remaining chapters concern work done since 1981, the intention of which was to relate changes in culture, *mentalité* and ideology to the structural changes examined in the first stage. Further studies will follow.

INTRODUCTION

Country capitalism

When one has grasped the full diversity of England as a whole, then much of the dynamism in the kingdom's economic and social development in the sixteenth and seventeenth centuries may be seen to have come from localised changes, setting up a chain of reactions and interactions between neighbouring, varied, but closely-interdependent, regions and communities. Each and all of them became increasingly reliant on the others, as first one and then another was more insistently, and then permanently, drawn into the mainstream of commercial marketing.

Joan Thirsk[1]

The nature of individuals depends on the material conditions in which they are produced. It also presupposes the intercourse of individuals one with another. The form of intercourse is again determined by production.

Marx, *The German Ideology*[2]

1

These studies explore focal points in the transformation of English society and culture as it occurred in one English region between 1500 and 1800. The transformation began with the rise of industries in the countryside, a phenomenon which gradually restructured English society. The everyday lives of individuals, households, neighbourhoods, communities and classes were transformed. The pace of life was altered, and interconnections multiplied, horizons expanded and orientations changed. Experiences varied from place to place and person to person, the process was uneven, but however we describe it there was a massive aggregate effect which has shaped the everyday forms and expectations of all societies, everywhere in the world. The world is what it is today because of what happened in the most dynamic parts of the world in the sixteenth, seventeenth and eighteenth centuries. Gloucestershire was one of those parts.

Industrialisation was not a sudden watershed that occurred between 1750 and 1850. England was the first industrial nation, but it was not suddenly transformed in the late eighteenth and early nineteenth centuries.[3] The coming of industrial capitalism is best understood as a gradual process, an evolution not a revolution.[4] It was an epochal collective construction, the work (never equally apportioned) of at least fifteen generations beginning in about 1300. It was a remarkable social transformation, but, measured against the conventional time-scales of English historiography, it was a process of very slow and gradual change. We should abandon the jargon of revolutionary transformation and see instead a long process of industrial, commercial, social and cultural *intensification*.[5]

The seeds of intensification were sown by the gradual migration of manufacturing industry, above all clothmaking, from the regional cities and boroughs of Norman-Angevin England to the small towns and villages of districts like Gloucestershire's Stroudwater Valleys and Vale of Berkeley. The transfer of production from town to rural district took place in the fourteenth and fifteenth centuries. By 1500 large-scale manufacturing for national and international markets took place largely in rural districts. 'Cradles of Change' (Chapter 1) describes the structural impact of large-scale clothmaking in central Gloucestershire from the late middle ages to the early nineteenth century.

The rise of industries in the countryside had a gradual but discernible impact on the wider, regional and national cultures.[6] As the populations of the industrial archipelagos grew – more mercurially and, in the long term, twice as fast as neighbouring agricultural districts – they generated increasing traffic in goods and people into and out of their districts. 'Trails of Progress' (Chapter 2) explores intensifying links between the hot-spot (manufacturing) localities and the wider world, initially with reference to the recorded locations and number of carriers and 'badgers' (small-time middle-men, mainly in the food trade), then by using the richer information relating to traffic and communications in the eighteenth century taken from advertisements and notices in the region's leading newspaper, the *Gloucester Journal*, founded in 1723. The *Journal* itself, and the eighteenth-century network of provincial newspapers of which it was a conspicuously successful example, was also a symptom of the general process of intensification, and a distinct force for change in itself.[7]

'Trails . . .' is about 'traffic'. Today, the word refers most commonly to 'the passing to and fro of persons, or of vehicles and vessels, along a road, railway, canal, or other route of transport'. Between 1500 and 1800 this meaning was intertwined with another, 'the transportation of merchandise for the purpose of trade; hence trade between different or distinct communities; commerce'.[8] In early modern England 'the passing to and fro of persons, etc.' signified what we, more abstractly, call 'commerce'. 'Traffic' was the substantive face of 'trade'. It was also its pejorative face, surviving today in our 'trafficking', which we usually reserve for illegal forms of trade.[9]

In 1550 Gloucestershire had a population of about 75,000. Between 1550 and 1600 it rose to about 95,000, to 120,000 in the 1670s, 128,000 in 1712, 161,000 in 1779, and 210,267 at the time of the first national census in 1801.[10] In 250 years population tripled, about the average for England and Wales as a whole. This alone implied change in social relations and organisation in the 300 parishes, 30 market towns and 3 parliamentary boroughs of the county. But there was more to it than absolute numbers. 'A relatively thinly populated country with well-developed means of communication has a denser population than a more numerously populated country with badly developed means of communication'.[11] *Intensification*, in this context, means growing population *plus* increasing traffic.

The process had affective consequences. Significant changes in size and routine movement, if sustained, will bring about changes in individual and collective psychology. If people stand still, no matter how many of them there are, there will be no collisions, coalitions and conflicts – no dynamism. Sustained increases in numbers and movement mean that a culture will have to develop new ways of dealing with strangers. Interpersonal interactions intensify geometrically as a result of increasing population plus increasing traffic. One of the reasons modern people don't think and behave like their ancestors five centuries ago has to do with intensification in this sense.[12]

The term 'intensification' is an attempt to make sense of detailed historical evidence in terms of a long historical transition as envisaged by Marx and other grand theorists, and like the great structuralist historian, Fernand Braudel. 'Intensification' is an attempt to see the history of an English county as a process of accumulation and evolution. The first two chapters focus on the production of the bricks and mortar which went into the construction of the 'great arch', as E. P. Thompson once described the rise of bourgeois civilisation in England.[13]

'Proverbial Culture' (Chapter 3) examines the culture of the middle rank of Gloucestershire's Vale of Berkeley through its dialect and proverbs, as written down by John Smyth of Nibley in 1639. This unusual source provides us with a substantial case of Ong's observation that oral cultures are 'utterance collecting', and enables us to study the preoccupations and tendencies of one culture of this sort. The sayings give us access to the mental world of the settled, proper-

tied, landholding middle rank of a highly commercialised rural industrial district just before the civil wars. They highlight its patriarchal
traditionalism, and show us what it took for granted. They describe
a community that had much in common with English communities
everywhere, but which was also identifiably unique, a highly specific
ongoing dialogue between language and landscape that gave the district an idiom all its own. The local landscape served as a 'memory
palace'. The dialect and proverbs reveal the intimate links that existed
between culture and specific location in the pre-nationalist era. They
were recorded at a time when such links were being weakened by the
relentless forces of intensification.

'Tyndale and all his Sect' (Chapter 4) returns to the forces which
were weakening the links. It sketches the career of one of those
renegade priests who, instead of peddling the official line of the established Church, translated and interpreted Holy Scripture in terms of
assumptions derived from the circumstances of his native district, the
Vale of Berkeley. Tyndale represented – and projected via the printed
word – the explosive implications of a highly commercialised manufacturing district. The same theme is continued in the saga of Tyndale's
neighbours, the Trotman family, but this time the expansive aspects
of Tyndale's life are stretched across seven generations, only gradually
filtering into consciousness. Tyndale's genius lay in the fact that he
concentrated into one highly articulate lifetime, cultural forces which
were to take many generations before they were taken for granted as
'normal' dimensions of human experience. His career foreshadowed
the much larger social and cultural transition of which the trans-
generational Trotman story is much more typical.

'Proverbial Culture' is a study of the oral dimension of life in the
Hundred of Berkeley before the civil wars of the 1640s. *Berkeley Hurns*
(the Anglo-Saxon variant for 'Hundred', often used by the man who
wrote down the proverbs, John Smyth of Nibley) was part of the
central Gloucestershire clothmaking region. Chapters 3–5 rely heavily
on the powerful and detailed notes and writings of John Smyth of
Nibley. They focus on Smyth's *countrey* (a contemporary term which
generally meant something like the modern 'district' or the French
pays) in the Vale of Severn between the Reformation and the English
Revolution, so a few introductory remarks about the history of the
district are in order.

In earlier centuries it was the barony of Berkeley, but Smyth of
Nibley, who knew it and its history intimately, usually called it the
'Hundred'. In the fifteenth century the power and competence of the
household which had ruled it since the mid-eleventh century was in
decline. The period of domination by the Fitzharding lords Berkeley
lasted from 1150 to 1490. The estate was mismanaged and neglected

in the fifteenth century, the lords were not able to prevent the depredations of plundering armies during the Wars of the Roses, the
family lost the respect of the Hundred, and in the 1490s William
Marquis Berkeley bartered his inheritance with Henry Tudor in
exchange for courtly favours and titles. The estate was restored to the
family on the death of Edward VI, and Henry the seventeenth lord
Berkeley havocked his patrimony with a few years of bastard feudal
display. John Smyth of Nibley began to take over the affairs of the
Berkeley estate in the late 1580s. Between then and 1643, when he
died, he worked out the history of the district from the muniments of
the barony and the kingdom (he often made research trips to the
Tower of London), and from long association with its yeoman-elders,
his peers and contemporaries.

The Tyndales were one of the leading yeoman families in the
Hundred of Berkeley in the time of the Henrician Reformation. Their
influence had declined by the time Smyth came to live there (they were
promoted into the gentry), but for one generation Edward Tyndale was
the most powerful man in the district, and his younger brother William
was the most notorious heretic in the kingdom. Tyndale envisaged
and did much to construct a Bible written in the language of his kin
and neighbours at home, the *wevers* and *plowmen* whose spoken language he kept in mind when translating Christian scripture into English. 'Tyndale and all his Sect' explores points of contact between
Tyndale's ideas about religion and church/state polity and how things
were actually run in the district he grew up in, the Hundred of
Berkeley. Tyndale's was also a national vision. Wotton-under-Edge
Grammar School and Oxford ensured that his Vale of Berkeley dialect
was sharpened and clipped into something less broad, and thus comprehensible anywhere in England. That said, the greatest influence
on Tyndale's life and thought was not Oxford, even less Cambridge
(although he seems to have had more to do with Cambridge men in
his maturity, they being more radical). I also question the proposition
that Tyndale was seminally influenced by Luther. In certain areas his
and Luther's backgrounds were similar. Tyndale was less a peasant
than Luther. He came from a *countrey* in which manufacturing was
the chief employer of labour. Another heretic Tyndale brother, John,
the youngest, was a *cloathman*, organising production in the Vale and
selling the product in London.

'Neighbourhood to Nation' (Chapter 5) focuses on the history of
Tyndale's neighbours and relatives-by-marriage, the Trotmans. It
explores the kinship dimension of intensification: the 'rise', but more
accurately the geographical, social and intellectual expansion, of a
single family of the middle rank from the purchase, in 1512, of a
fulling mill at Cam in the Vale of Berkeley, to the occasion of a

marriage, in 1712, by which the two main branches of the family, both descendants of the clothier who purchased the fulling mill two centuries earlier, now members of the squirearchies of Gloucestershire and Oxfordshire, were united. The chapter describes seven generations of what Eric R. Wolf calls a 'corporate kin coalition', accumulating wealth, land, status, experience and new world-views: it transposes a yeoman-gentry genealogy onto the map of the 'trails of progress' outlined in Chapter 2, and in doing so describes one of the most important ways in which middle-rank families of the period between the Reformation and the civil wars slowly accumulated nationalist experience and perspectives. Again the underlying theme is the expansionist implications of involvement in the organising and merchandising branches of the cloth industry. In Tyndale's case these implications were represented in a single life, in the case of the Trotmans they are seen as a process of accumulation over seven generations.

'Small thinges and grande designes' (Chapter 6) is an historical critique of John Corbet's explanation of the civil wars in Gloucestershire, published in 1645. Corbet was probably the originator of the 'middle-class' interpretation of the English Revolution, and saw 'the middle ranke' as 'the only active men' in the resistance to and defeat of the royalist invasion of the country, which eventually centred on the siege of Gloucester. The study involves a close reading of his text, measuring the accuracy of his highly controversial interpretations in the light of other contemporary evidence. The chapter includes a set-piece study of the Gloucestershire elections to the Short Parliament ('Weavers and Shepherds'), which I suggest mark a parting of the ways. I conclude that Corbet's 'middle ranke' interpretation, while generally correct, needs qualification in the light of the agency of the class he called 'the vulgar multitudes' in stimulating and driving on resistance, and of the shrewd and above all determined leadership of the army officers.

The most dynamic agencies of change, 'structural' and 'cultural', 'religious' and 'political', originated in districts and neighbourhoods which contemporaries rightly regarded as highly exceptional, given the predominant modes of production and communication at the time. Similarly, historians looking back on the whole society, the nation-state that emerged over several centuries, conclude that radical hot-spots like these were statistically exceptional. The protoindustrial districts were exceptional in a quantitative sense. They were unusually densely populated. Also consequential was the extraordinary energy they radiated, measured by traffic in goods, people and ideas. Tyndale projected the vernacular culture of the middle rank of the Vale of Berkeley onto a national state; he was an agent in the construction of the theatre: a nation-state dominated by respectable middle-class property-holders. Kin-coalitions like the Trotmans continued the work. Originally agents of local manufacturing, then Common Lawyers who, like John Smyth of Nibley, adhered to Ancient Constitution ideology, then revolutionary merchants like Throgmorton Trotman (1590–1663), and, finally, the somewhat effete squires of the early eighteenth century who took everything the past generations had constructed for granted.

Every major theme and turn in the history of the region – Lollardy, Protestantism, Puritanism, Dissent and Nonconformity, the rise of the middle rank as a decisive force in local and national affairs, the Parliamentarian cause, the rise of a market economy and, paradoxically, opposition to it in the form of persistent 'moral economy' campaigns, industrial riots and disputes, and the appearance of trade unions – had its roots in the 'rural' manufacturing districts. The case studies of middle-rank consciousness and ideology in Chapters 3–7 explore ideas emerging from specific lives lived in specific localities, before the ideas had been assigned the convenient general labels by which we know them, and debate them, today: 'protestant', 'puritan', 'congregational', 'presbyterian', 'independent', 'radical'. Each represents a highly specific conjuncture of the process of intensification located in a particular place and time. Each is part of an attempt to deconstruct English history in order to do justice to the extraordinary diversity of English culture, without entirely dissolving the structural continuities outlined in Chapters 1 and 2.

'Cunning Man and Quaker' (Chapter 7) is a study of the radical individualism of another revolutionary, the yeoman John Roberts of Siddington St Mary (1620–83). It explores the effect of the experience of the civil wars on the consciousness of a particular individual, and the ways the Quakers can be said to have left the corporate bodies of the old world (the household, the family, the parish) and entered the modern world, and at the same time radically deconstructed the power discourses of the modern world. The revolution of the long sixteenth century (roughly, from the birth of Tyndale, c. 1490, to 1649) saw a dispersal of economic, religious and political legitimacy from the great secular and ecclesiastical lordships of the middle ages, into the households and nieghbourhoods of the middle rank. The most powerful and dynamic loci of the long sixteenth century were the household, family, neighbourhood and *countrey*. These were made powerful by the Protestant sensibilities and ideologies, epitomised in the work of Tyndale.

Yet all the while these loci of production were assuming ideological, religious and political significance, the trade which intensifying production implied was eroding them, bringing larger national and international contexts forward as the most important practical contexts. The eschatology of men like Tyndale, the sixteenth-century Trotmans and John Smyth of Nibley was radically congregationalist/communitarian. Their world-view can be likened to a series of concentric circles radiating out from the personal soul in its relationship with God, to the household, extended family, neighbourhood, *countrey* and commonwealth. Where it is possible to study this *mentalité*, as in the richly documented case of John Smyth of Nibley, each 'circle' melts gently and imperceptibly into the next. The individual soul will, finally and alone, have to answer to God for the life it has led. But the final interrogation, determining whether the soul will dwell for eternity in the realms of the prince of light or darkness, concerned the person's behaviour in the household, family, neighbourhood . . . , and so on.

Quakers like John Roberts deconstructed the neighbourhood, household and family-centred conception by locating the spirit of God exclusively in the self, the inner light. The god that failed in the English Revolution was the god of the independent Congregationalists as conceived, originally, by Tyndale (which produced many variants, all of which focused legitimacy on the gathered people of the neighbourhood led by the neighbourhood elders). Congregationalist ecclesiology and ideology were a transitional form, a product of the early stages of the rise of industry and trade, experienced as crisis in the manufacturing localities. Its dynamic radicalism derived from the need to reformulate community hierarchy and discipline, and to establish the absolute legitimacy of the class of men (the landed middle rank, predominantly yeoman) invested by tradition and everyday practice with authority in the localities. As the experience of this class became increasingly extra-local, finally national, the Congregational emphasis inevitably lost its radical edge. Roberts' radical individualism was an intuitive recognition of its failure. 'Cunning Man and Quaker' describes one man's life-long practical critique of all the institutions of the old regime.

Roberts returned from service with Cromwell in the late 1640s, married a member of the Tyndale family, and, in 1655, was 'discovered' by Richard Farnsworth, one of the founders of the Society of Friends. In 1660 he was described as the leader of the Gloucestershire Quakers, and from then until his death in 1683 he was an active and radical critic of the secular and religious establishments in the region. Roberts was regarded by his neighbours as a 'cunning man' or 'wizard', and they often came to him for advice on their problems. Cunning people and Quakers shared a radically empirical mentality, which Roberts exemplifies. They also shared a conviction that observation and experiment were of limited social value, because they can reveal only what is possible, not what is right and desirable. Many courses of action and many conclusions may emerge from a particular set of circumstances. Only inner light, the result of a process of internal meditation perceived as communion with God, could enable a person to decide which of many conclusions or courses of action to pursue. In this way I suggest that Quakerism, like Tyndale's Protestantism, was a refinement of indigenous (though not unproblematical) common sense. This chapter is an attempt to deconstruct the inner light of one Quaker.

The effort to reconcile love and loyalty for particular localities or *countreys*, for specifically local cultures, with the broadening horizons necessitated by manufacturing, trade and traffic is a recurring theme in these studies, which are organised in a broadly chronological way. I have exercised licence with Chapters 3 and 4: the proverbs on which the study of oral culture in Chapter 3 is based were written down 103 years after Tyndale was strangled and burned in 1536. A few of the proverbs are specifically stated to have come into use in the generations after Tyndale. Readers who prefer to maintain the chronological sequence can read these two chapters in reverse order.

The distancing impact of print and literacy on the consciousness of the middle ranks is one theme. Contempt for towns and trade, and celebration of the virtues of agrarian self-sufficiency, are most explicit in the thought of John Smyth of Nibley. Disdain for the 'vulgar multitudes', the emerging industrial proletariat, is the strongest unifying thread between otherwise rather different thinkers. Tyndale, Smyth, the proverbial culture of the middle rank, John Corbet, the Trotmans, John Aubrey (Chapter 10) and, less obviously, John Roberts despised industry as an activity fit only for people who had no other means of sustaining themselves. Contemporary descriptions of this class ranged from Shakespeare's 'many-headed monster', Corbet's 'vulgar multitudes', Smyth's 'slaves in nature though not in lawe' to Aubrey's distinction between primitive 'aborigines or indigenes' and the blue-blooded heirs of Roman and Norman civilisation.

In the sixteenth and seventeenth centuries the experience of the middle ranks became national and international, through the agencies of travel and traffic, and through printed material diffused along the 'trails of progress'. There is an almost caste-like aversion in their contempt for the landless classes, a sense that all physical labour other than tillage is the function of an inherently impure class of people. The middle ranks of Tudor–Stuart England were proud of their ability to conceive, finance and organise projects that employed the poor. They took for granted that they could run the country better than all the lords and kings in the world, because for the most part they actually did organise most activities at the grass roots (where 95 per cent of the population lived), where it counted. In modern eyes they can seem very conservative revolutionaries. Traditions passed on orally from the past, documented by John Smyth of Nibley, preserved the memory of the brutal anarchy unleashed on the Vale in the fifteenth century by lords who no longer held the reins of power in their own barony. War disrupted production and trade more, even, than famines and epidemics of bubonic plague and other such diseases. From the generation of William Tyndale to that, a century later, of John Corbet the power and confidence of the 'middle ranke' (as Corbet called it in 1645) grew to a point where it was ready to fight and defeat the armies and evil advisers of the king, Charles Stuart.

Royalists and Parliamentarians, however, shared a desire to distance themselves from the dirty world of industrial work, thus defining themselves as being 'above' it. Industry was an evil necessity; their own view of the matter was that clothiers and merchants selflessly put themselves at the service of the poor, and were even prepared to fight and die in defence of the poor against their enemies, the disdainful and selfish lords who would use the king to further their desire to 'rule their neighbours like vassals', as Corbet put it. Crown loyalists retorted that Parliamentarians were short-haired hypocrites whose real aim was to profit from the industry of the poor without interference from men who were born to rule and carried civilisation in the blood. Civilisation meant real as against feigned concern for the welfare of inherently inferior classes. That this polarisation of collective opinion travestied the complexity of motives and circumstances was less consequential, in the long term, than the fact that both sides embodied contempt for the landless labouring classes, albeit differently expressed and formulated. The English civil wars were the culmination of a long struggle about who should rule the landless proletariat and how.

John Corbet saw the civil wars as a struggle between the middle rank and the magnates, and regarded the 'vulgar' or 'necessitous multitude' as a passive agency, committed to either side according to the rank, occupation and constitution of its local masters. He admitted that it had decisively affected Gloucestershire's resistance; perhaps, initially, inspired it. But its middle-rank employers grasped, maintained and led its cause to victory. In everyday life the middle rank employed and maintained the labouring poor, and understood their cause better than the poor understood it themselves. His was the middle-rank interpretation of the events of the early 1640s, published in 1645. As he saw it, he wrote *for* the poor, but was very definitely not a member of any multitude. He was a solid Protestant individual, voicing the case of others like himself. It was the function of the congregation of the elect to order and discipline the multitudinous masses.

The ability of the middle rank to pose a genuine challenge to Caroline absolutism, indeed its very existence as an alternative ruling-class bloc, was premised on the rise of rural manufacturing. Rural manufacturing entailed travel in search of raw materials and markets, which gradually generated an interconnected national and international market. This entailed new world-views linking problems associated with organising and disciplining new kinds of communities at home, characterised by large numbers of landless industrial workers, with the broadening horizons entailed by routine travel. The 'rise' (and 'expansion') of the Trotman family illustrates an important agency in the creation of the nation and the constructing of a market culture: kinship. It describes a process of accumulation in which an at first highly localised 'kin-coalition' colonised London and planted its influence on the continent and in Virginia.[14] This gradually accumulated experience, coupled with the increasing literacy of the middle ranks, and the intensification of the print revolution, generated physical and intellectual distance from the still-localised contexts and cultures of the majority of working people.

Chapters 8 and 9 are two probes into the mental and material worlds of the emerging working class. We explore the alternative values and the historical agency of working people, the 'multitudes' or 'aborigines' disdained, in their different ways, by Tyndale, Smyth of Nibley, Roberts and Aubrey. 'Community at the Borders' (Chapter 8) is a grassroots study of everyday 'Brechtian class-struggle' in the poorest and least respectable village in the region; it relates a scandal which erupted in 1713 to a Feast of Fools revel held in the same village every year, and shows that the attitudes represented in the former were celebrated annually in the latter. The revel was initiated by a ceremony accompanied by the incantation of a psalm, which was written down in 1784 by an interested observer. The words of the psalm point to the weavers' dreamtime, a golden age in which all people were roughly equal. Its egalitarian utopianism, I suggest, is an inherent, structural element in English working-class cultures, though not the only and not always the dominant one. Carnival, in this context, was more about metaphors of levelling than of turning the world upside down.

'A Concatenation of Vicious Habits' (Chapter 9) describes the class-riven turbulence of a region transformed by the process described in the earlier chapters. It focuses on what was perhaps the first 'condition of England' or 'two societies' debate to take place on the public stage created by the emergence of a national Press. The chapter explores the significance of the riots which occasioned the debates, to the extent that contemporary records allow it, through the eyes of the participant workers, and (an easier matter) through the eyes of rival parties of the new ruling class, the Land and Trade 'parties'. By means of actions and debates such as these, the new class structure of English society, a function of long-term interconnected structural and cultural developments, was cemented in place by another product and cause of those same processes, the mass media.

These 'thickish descriptions' of the people of one of England's most highly industrialised regions during the transition from feudal–tributary to capitalist civilisation in England are concerned with the nature of the relationship between inherited, or 'structural', circumstances and culture, the ways those circumstances are interpreted, represented and communicated. The structure/culture dichotomy is too crude, for cultures are also structured by abiding idioms, metaphors and myths which shape the fluid historical surfaces of individual and collective consciousness. My final chapter, 'Lasting Prejudices', is concerned with the conjuncture, in the seventeenth century, of three systems, or languages, of social discrimination which remain important elements of English culture today. The problematical dialectics of social matter and collective mind are under scrutiny throughout the book. Of all the modern discourses which relate to this problematic, one of the most interesting and important is the Information Technology question.

2

For most of the period covered by this book written language was a highly imperfect net cast across a predominantly preliterate subject population by the institutions of class domination and their agents.[15] England was an outpost of one of the great agrarian civilisations. From its origins some six thousand years ago in Sumer, agrarian civilisation used writing, in the form of sacral scripts like Sanskrit, Mandarin Chinese, Arabic and Latin, to store and legitimise particular kinds of knowledge about the communities under control.[16] For millennia, written language was the hegemonic technology *par excellence*. It was the chief instrument of ideological control, as the arts of war were the instruments of physical domination.

And then, between the fifteenth and nineteenth centuries, there took place an extraordinarily powerful movement from below. People hitherto defined as subjects of the State and established church began to appropriate the communications technology which had for so long been used as an instrument of expropriation. This movement, at first, involved an intensification of the value attached by ordinary people to literacy and written texts. Its leaders, invariably condemned by the authorities as heretics, proclaimed that the great written texts of civilisation were so important that everyone should be able to read and study them. It became a moral, religious and practical duty to learn to read and to appropriate and interpret texts.[17]

The nature and consequences of this revolution in the mode of social communication are controversial topics. The sacred texts of the great agrarian civilisations were undoubtedly treasuries of ethical wisdom which could be and often were turned against ruling classes and their agents. Dissenting literati (usually priests) led movements of this sort in every century in every part of the world. That the leadership of this uneven global movement – which has a thousand roots – was so often in the hands of literates may explain its irresistible urge to eradicate the forest of symbols, rituals and ceremonies which served to communicate the judgements of the rulers to the people. The great vernacularisation of the written word has everywhere been an iconclastic movement. It carried with it the delegitimisation of the oral and aural cultures which the bulk of the world's population had inhabited since the genesis of *homo sapiens*.

Because of its in-principle dependence on written texts, History is a discourse on hegemonies. 'Prehistory' refers to the period of human cultural evolution before the invention of writing. Historians have taken it as their brief to analyse and interpret past societies by means of written texts. Since these texts were usually prepared for the purposes of ruling regimes, they provide a partial view of the cultures of the working population. They embody the prescriptions of the ruling classes and imply a selective interpretation of the ruled classes in the light of usually unstated assumptions. The preliterate cultures of the localities where the work went on are submerged beneath the distorting prism of written texts. It can be argued that because the vernacular cultures of the past did not write down their own experiences for themselves, because they generated no authentic texts, they lie outside the brief of History. If this is so, History must interpret past societies through the eyes of the ruling classes. It also follows that much of what went on in sixteenth- and seventeenth-century England is 'prehistoric'.

In this case History cannot understand the most significant transitions of the past – the revolutionary conjunctures that have brought us, for good or bad, to where we are today. Privileged groups do not give up their privileges willingly. They may conspire in their downfall accidentally, by engaging in practices and policies which seem profitable in the short run, but turn out not to be so in the long term. The Henrician Reformation and the absolutism of Charles I were self-destructive 'conspiracies' of this sort. But the primary impetus comes from below. Historically, the groundswells that have transformed social organisation often began in the 'submerged' portion of the past, the part that inhabited the oral and aural cosmos. Oral communication leaves no trace. The origins of the vernacular revolution that made popular nationalism possible involved relations conducted in voices and gestures that are susceptible to historical analysis only to the extent that they left traces in written documents. The existence of such documents in itself implies systematic distancing from orality and aurality.

The scientific approach to life, in which the observer assumes distance and separation between self and subject, derives from the invention of writing. Preliterate cultures, writes Walter J. Ong, 'cannot develop a reflectively articulate account of . . . human action . . . other than in scattered aphorisms'.[18] He describes the consciousness of preliterate culture thus:

> Primary orality, the orality of a culture which has never known writing, is in some ways conspicuously integrative. The psyche in a culture innocent of writing knows by a kind of empathetic identification of knower and known, in which the object of knowledge and the total being of the knower enter into a kind of fusion, in a way which literate cultures would find unsatisfyingly vague and garbled and somehow too intense and participatory. Oral folk are not set off against their physical environment, given simply to soaking up existence, unresponsive to abstract demands such as a 'job' that entails commitment to routines organised in accordance with abstract clock time.[19]

'The technological inventions of writing, print and electronic verbalisation, in their historical effects,' however, 'have helped to bring about a certain kind of alienation within the human lifeworld':

> With writing, the earlier noetic state undergoes a kind of cleavage, separating the knower from the external universe and from himself.[20]

Writing makes this intellectual objectification of self and world possible, introducing the distancing that is inherent to the scientific approach to life.

Writing and print are ways of making knowledge, of *creating* information and of objectifying 'data'. Preliterate culture is 'more likely to be utterance collecting than information collecting'.[21] The aphoristic or proverbial character of the knowledge of oral cultures constantly interacts with the changing environment of succeeding generations. Literacy, on the other hand, led to a quest for 'closed system paradigms' which seek to capture the world in recorded discourse, *prescribing* it, as if it is not the unpredictable character of the universe that matters, not 'physics', but human discourse about it, 'metaphysics'.

Writing, then, creates opportunities for distancing. It is not a neutral medium, and cannot be, always implying interpretation, if only by selection. Early modern English cultures were situated at what Professor Goody has called 'the interface between the written and the oral'.[22] These chapters are fragments of a much larger story which saw the emergence into History of a new class and a new civilisation: respectively, the 'middle rank' and the 'bourgeois' civilisation of which it was the primary agent. Prior to the sixteenth century the habitat of this rank of English society was predominantly local and oral/aural. Between about 1450 and 1660 it was the agent of a fundamental transformation of English society through the media of manufacturing and trade, and travel, vernacular literacy and print.

The alienation introduced into discourse by writing (and science), in Paul Ricoeur's optimistic view, generates many interpretations and perspectives on phenomena. Reading texts quite literally takes the reader out of his or her own world and presents alternative possibilities. One interpretation can be measured against another. 'There are criteria of relative superiority', he writes, 'which may easily be derived from the logic of subjective probability.'[23] I am not sure I know what Ricoeur means by 'the logic of subjective probability', but the expression has the ring of a practical truth. These studies are attempts to derive 'ideal types' or 'structural models' from what I know of real historical situations. I think of them as emblematic studies. I hope they are food for thought. Agreement is another matter.

3

I show that the English and British nation-state was not constructed by narrowly political and constitutional activities, or by political elites alone. To understand the origins of nation-states we must deconstruct the perspectives that nationalism imposes on us. To understand the origins of modern society we need a new kind of history, one that begins in the localities but does not end there. These are local studies, but 'local' is relative: national histories are also local, as national myths are parochial, viewed comparatively and globally. Historically speaking the word 'country' is slippery, contentious and variable in meaning. Today it has two primary applications: (a) 'the territory or land of a nation'; and (b) 'the rural districts as distinct from the town or towns'. Both usages began to emerge between the fourteenth and eighteenth centuries, notably in the work of vernacular religious radicals. Wycliffe used meaning (a), and Tyndale meaning (b).[24] Both men travelled widely, thought deeply about common features of the English language as a unifying, popular-nationalist instrument, and were deeply preoccupied with creating a voice of the middle rank from which, like Chaucer and Langland, they sprang. The degree to which this was a conscious aim was variable and remains debatable. The practical effect was to overcome the divisive, variable and sometimes impenetrable mosaic of oral dialects and cultures that ensured the disunity of English people and kept them under the thumb of an alien caste descended from conquering continental warriors. This vernacular revolution, and the associated problem of the transition from a mainly oral and aural to a predominantly literate culture, is an essential part of the context of all the chapters of this book.

Wycliffe and Tyndale were visionaries, agents in the making of something that was not yet a tangible reality: a unified England in which the people was sovereign and independent; a nation-state. Before the nation could exist in our sense, there had to be constitutional acceptance of the proposition that *the people* (another word that is problematical and relative to context) was sovereign, not the king and/or the aristocratic descendants of eleventh-century conquerors. Before 'country' could be recognised as a synonym for 'rural parts', a significant part of English territory had to be visibly urban, which it was not until the nineteenth century. Before the word could acquire these meanings in the popular mind, the things to which it referred had to be constructed. These studies are about the making of 'country' in these senses, and it is therefore essential to begin with a general definition of what the word meant to most people when the process was in its early stages.

In the most general sense, a 'country' was 'a tract or expanse of land of undefined extent'. It was commonly used in the sixteenth and seventeenth centuries to mean 'a region, or district'. More specifically, a *countrey* (the usual contemporary spelling) was 'a tract or district having more or less definite limits in relation to human occupation, e.g. owned by the same lord or proprietor, or inhabited by people of the same race, dialect, occuption etc.'. As the *Oxford English Dictionary* states, 'with political changes, what were originally distinct countries have become provinces or districts of one country . . . the modern tendency being to identify the term with the existing political condition'. This was not the 'early modern' tendency, in which cultural characteristics and connotations were to the fore. The ubiquitous use of terms like 'stranger' and 'forraigner' to refer, in local records, to people whose dialect accent, gestures, dress and general demeanour identified them as not from that particular locality or district referred to a habit of mind that was embedded in the everyday lives of ordinary people.[25]

Between the fourteenth and nineteenth centuries, people whose routine operational contexts were highly localised, and who usually used 'country' to refer to their own local contexts – neighbourhoods, districts and regions – laid claim to and achieved, at least technically, sovereignty in the political nation. That, in a nutshell, is how 'country' in the district or regional sense came to mean 'country' in the national sense. Its use always carried affective connotations. It was difficult for people to see themselves as participants in a territorial unit, or state, the affairs of which were in no sense within their compass, but they could participate in the life of their *countreys*.

Strictly speaking, only one person in sixteenth-century England could use the possessive pronoun with reference to 'country' in the modern, national, sense: the monarch. The absolutist claims of the early Stuarts were a rearguard action to preserve a State imposed by Norman–Angevin conquerors and radically centralised by the last medieval dynasty, the Tudors. The term 'commonwealth' came into wide use to refer to a constitutional (and substantial) alternative to 'kingdom', and helped to make country in the national sense thinkable. These comments exaggerate, but only in order to illustrate substantial realities which it is the task of this book to probe more deeply.

The rise of the people as a sovereign entity was the rise of local people. This takes Local History beyond appeals to parochial sensibilities, questions of filling in gaps, or illustrating variables in some monolithic national history, however conceived.[26] Pride in and affection for specifically local cultures or 'countries' was a more powerful historical agency in early modern England than it is today. At certain key points – the Reformation era, 1642–3 – it was decisive. Interpretations that take nationalism and the nation-state for granted are quite simply anachronistic. The collective phenomena we mean when we use the terms were unfulfilled in sixteenth- and seventeenth-century England. They were 'under construction' as sociologists, semioticians and structuralists might put it. *Country Capitalism* contends that local history is central to a proper understanding of our past.

'Capitalism' is even more difficult to deal with, from an historical point of view, for two reasons: (a) its meaning is so controversial, and (b) the word did not exist before the nineteenth century and its use to refer to something that existed before then might be regarded as anachronistic. The primary reference here is to what Marx (and, more recently, Braudel) called *Manufacturing*, organised on a capitalist basis: i.e. the use of capital (funds, institutional power, religious authority, facilities, credit and equipment) by a few relatively rich people (nearly always men of low but by no means the lowest traditional status) to employ large numbers of relatively poor people to produce commodities for export. 'Export' here, for reasons outlined above, meant sale to people outside the district or region in which production went on. In the system of manufacturing, capitalists invariably owned the raw materials and controlled access to markets, and progressively tended also to own the tools of trade. Braudel suggests use of the term 'dispersed' rather than 'domestic' production for the system of manufacturing, because the latter might, mistakenly, be taken to mean that it was a democracy of industrious craftsmen. Landless craftsmen often saw it that way, but capitalist merchants organised production and controlled the key local institutions. They were often described in contemporary documents as 'yeomen'. They held freehold farms, often quite large ones. They admired the values of self-sufficiency, and were often capable of attaining it themselves. But they were first and foremost businessmen buying and selling on local, regional, national and, increasingly, international markets.[27]

The system of manufacturing differed from the factory system in that its workforce was dispersed. It had in common that production was organised by individual capitalists and not by the direct producers. It was the single most important agency of the restructuring of English society between the fourteenth and eighteenth centuries. The development of a significant manufacturing sector in England was foreshadowed (along with most of the religious and political themes touched on in this book) in other parts of the world. We should look for similar patterns in Bengal as well as Flanders and the northern Italian city-states.[28] The popular revolutions of the middle ages took place in the industrial regions of continental Europe.[29] The decisive difference was that, in England, industrial capitalism took root and developed in the 'country', i.e. parts distant from established towns. Hence *Country Capitalism*.

Part I
CRADLES OF CHANGE

1

CRADLES OF CHANGE
The manufacturing districts

'What is at issue here is the role of production as a cradle of change.'

Fernand Braudel

1

There is an extensive but fragmentary literature on the history of clothmaking in central Gloucestershire. A recent reference occurs in Eric R. Wolf's *Europe and the People Without History*, which names 'the Stroudwater Valley' as 'one of the first areas in which English weavers lost their autonomy and became hired factory hands'.[1] The district illustrates Wolf's theme of the 'global interconnectedness' of the processes by which industrial capitalism developed. In the eighteenth century Iroquois trappers 'demanded dyed scarlet and blue cloth made in the Stroudwater Valley(s) of Gloucestershire' in exchange for their furs.[2] This was the rich scarlet cloth worn by the soldiers sent to hold and expand the British presence in North America, their badge of warrior valour. The example is richer than Wolf realises. Gloucestershire cloth had been worn by settlers and visitors to the American colonies since the early seventeenth century.[3] In 1756 Colonel James Wolfe, shortly to die a national hero leading his troops in the taking of the Heights of Quebec, was sent to Stroud at the head of a company of soldiers to protect local clothiers from striking workers. In letters to his mother Wolfe described the district as 'up to the knees in mud', the striking weavers as 'starving', and observed that the only good thing that could possibly emerge from his visit was that it would allow him to obtain recruits from among the local unemployed. Some of them may have died with him in Canada.

'The cloathing trade is so eminent in this country,' wrote Sir Robert Atkyns in 1712, 'that no other manufacture deserves a mention.' Gloucestershire was a centre of industrial activities other than clothmaking. Across the Severn, the Forest of Dean was one of England's

21

major sources of iron, nails and edge-tools. Kingswood Chase, on the north-eastern edges of Bristol, was a major coal-getting district. Atkyns was not locating an industry isolated in an ocean of peasants. 'Reckoning the fine with the coarse, [he] computed that fifty thousand cloaths are made yearly,' worth £500,000 per year. At least fourteen different crafts were involved in processing from yarn to finished cloth. Every cloth was the work of a fourteen-person team. Assuming that each team produced ten cloths a year, about 5,000 'teams' were needed to produce Atkyns' total: 70,000 men, women and children, or about 60 per cent of a total population of 120,438. This is what Atkyns meant when he wrote that 'no other manufacture deserves a mention'.[4]

The muster-lists prepared by Smyth of Nibley 104 years earlier, in 1608, show that the industry was well established even then. Forty-three per cent (746) of the able-bodied men between 20 and 60 who attended the musters in the Stroudwater Valleys – the valleys of Saxton's *Stroude fluensis*, and the Wick, Slad and Nailsworth streams flowing into it from various watersheds on the central-eastern scarp of the Cotswolds, 'the Edge' – reported a clothworking occupation as their principal means of support.[5] A few miles south-west of Stroud in the Vale of Berkeley lay a branch centred on the market town of Dursley, spread through the villages of Woodmancote, Uley, Owlpen, Cam, Coaley, Stinchcombe and Slimbridge. Here 53 per cent (338 of 633) were clothworkers. The district around Wotton-under-Edge, another market town in the Vale of Berkeley, nestling under the towering Cotswold escarpment or 'Edge', was slightly more agricultural. In the lists for Wotton and its surrounding villages 39 per cent gave clothworking occupations.[6]

The figures for 1608 refer only to settled, fit, adult males between about 18 and 50. The cloth industry also provided work for unfit men, and women and children always provided at least half of the workforce. At least half of the people in central Gloucestershire depended on the cloth industry for their livelihood. Manufacturing on this scale was central to the social and economic life of the region: gentry, freehold and tenant farmers, graziers and shepherds, masons and carpenters, leatherworkers, tailors, butchers, bakers, shopkeepers and labourers, in short everyone mentioned or not mentioned in the muster-lists of 1608 was affected by it. Depression or boom in clothmaking meant depression or boom all round.

If the scale of the industry in the seventeenth century is not well understood today, it was proverbial at the time. The expression 'He'll prove a man of Dursley' was in use throughout England. It alluded to a particular kind of untrustworthiness, associated with trade and industry. Fuller mentions it in his *Worthies of England*. Smyth of Nibley cites it in his list of proverbs 'peculiar to the hundred of Berkeley' in

1639, explaining it thus. 'This (now dispersed over England) tooke roote from one Webb a great clothier dwelling in Durseley in the daies of Queen Mary, as also was his father in the time of kinge Henry the VIII.'

> Using to buy very great quantities of wooll out of most counties of England, at the waighing werof, both father and sonne (the better to drawe on theire ends) would ever promise out of that parcell a gowncloth peticote cloth apron or the like, to the good wife or her daughters, but never paid any thinge.

The people of Dursley (population about 2,000 in 1650) resented their notoriety. Smyth recollected hearing 'Edward Green vicar of Berkeley, in the first of kinge James, useing this proverb in his sermon there, wherat many of Dursley were present, had almost raised a tumult amongst his auditory, wherof my selfe [i.e. Smyth] was one'.[7]

Nearly a century earlier, in the reign of Queen Mary, an Act of Parliament aimed at suppressing rural industrial development was forced to bow to reality by exempting Stroudwater and the Vale of Berkeley from its proscription.[8] The cloth industry was too densely interwoven in the fabric of regional life for it to be thought practical to suppress it. Two centuries before Colonel Wolfe was sent there to suppress the rioting clothworkers, Camden saw Stroud as 'a mercat town sometimes better peopled with clothiers'. Alongside continuous references to the existence of large-scale manufacturing, we find a stream of (usually outside) observers who thought it was in decline. Stroud did not become the acknowledged centre of the Gloucestershire clothing industry until about half a century after Camden's visit. He was there during one of the routine but unpredictable recessions, one which affected Dursley, Wotton-under-Edge and the villages round about. At the time it was said that Dursley 'heretofore hath been famous in the said county for cloth', but was now famous only for the numbers of its poor. Leland rode through Dursley some time between 1520 and 1540 and found it 'a praty clothing towne'. The point that Camden missed was that clothing districts were always famous for the numbers of their poor, who were fully employed only when national and international markets were not disrupted by dearths, epidemics, diplomatic dislocations and wars.

Beyond the comparatively well-lit edge of the Reformation era, when much of the documentation on which social, economic and demographic historians today depend was first generated, we find ourselves in the twilight centuries on the edge of 'dark ages', with still no sign of a pristine agrarian culture before the coming of manufacturing. Fifty years ago Professor Carus-Wilson identified the period after about 1450 as the origins of a significant industrial concentration in the Stroudwater Valleys.[9] Complaints by the Bristol clothmaking guilds about unfair competititon from rural manufacturing date from the 1340s, just before the Black Death; they were frequent for the rest of the fourteenth century, and then die away: not because the competition had ceased, but because the cause was lost. Evidence relating to the barony of Berkeley supports the impression left by the complaints of Bristol's clothworking guilds. Professor Hilton's investigations of the Berkeley manors of Wotton-under-Edge and Cam in the 1320s led him to claim that it was 'an area on the way to industrialisation'. He deduces this partly from Carus-Wilson's research findings, partly from his own research on the social structure of the region as revealed in manorial sources. The 'division of the tenant population between the relatively few free and customary tenants of a yardland or more, the middle core of half-yardlanders and the mass of cottagers and other smallholders . . .', he writes, 'emerges clearly from every rental and survey which has survived'.[10]

These early fourteenth-century cottagers and smallholders, Hilton writes, 'could only live by being part-time wage-workers or craftsmen'. They were a third of the population in the century before the Black Death, so it is conceivable that rural clothmaking was of major importance in local life even then. A reference in Smyth's history of the lords Berkeley takes the issue beyond conjecture. On the basis of his study of the estate records of Thomas II, lord Berkeley (1281–1321), he observed that 'much of this Lord's wool [was] put out to spinning for making of cloth and clothing of the poor; in sortinge, pickinge, beatinge, oylinge, pullinge, cardinge, spinning, spooling, warping, quilling, weaving, tucking, shearing, dying, dressing, and the like'.[11] He doesn't say how many people were involved in cloth production on Berkeley manors in the late thirteenth and early fourteenth centuries (and says nothing of what was happening in neighbouring districts), but it is a clear reference to industry with an extensive division of labour, on the estates of one of the richest wool-producing magnates in England: a 'clustering' of specialist trades.[12]

Berkeley Castle figures most prominently in the national history as the place where Edward II was tortured and murdered. More consequential, but less dramatic, was the practical application on Berkeley manors of the maxim that raw materials should not be exported if they could provide work for local people who would otherwise be unemployed. This was probably as much proverbial economic doctrine in the early fourteenth century as it is today. Feudalism could be enterprising as well as brutally down-to-earth in its social disciplines.

Rural industry, centred on small market towns and dispersed through the surrounding villages and hamlets, enjoyed a number of advantages over its urban competitors. The country districts were not as badly hit by the Black Death as the major towns and cities. A very conservative reading of the evidence relating to Bristol concludes that at least a third of the city's inhabitants died in 1349–50.[13] Complaints by Bristol guilds against unfair competition from rural areas begin in the 1340s, are common for the remainder of the fourteenth century, and then die out.[14] The process suggests that the Bristol cloth industry never recovered from the Black Death because country clothmakers grasped the temporary advantage rural areas enjoyed during the catastrophic epidemics of the mid-century. They could do this because they already had advantages over their conservative urban competitors.

In the first place, labour was cheaper in the countryside. Food was cheaper and more readily available in dearths. Agricultural by-employments were available, and at least some of the households involved in clothmaking held or owned land. They were closer to natural resources: the Cotswolds and the Vale of Severn were internationally regarded wool-producing areas. Other raw materials like fuller's earth and woad were available in some localities. Above all, however, there were the fast-flowing springs, streams and small rivers flowing down from the Cotswold Hills. The power of the foot-fulling guilds had prevented the introduction of fulling mills in cities throughout Europe, but there were no guilds in the country areas.[15] There, mechanical fulling was introduced with little opposition. Production was cheaper in the country because the initial lack of labour organisations allowed the payment of lower piece-rates and the introduction of labour-saving technology.

Country production overhauled that of the old urban communes at Bristol and Gloucester some time in the fifteenth century. Very little cloth was being produced at Bristol or Gloucester in the sixteenth century, although they were still important organising and trading centres. Large-scale clothmaking, with an elaborate local division of labour, was evident in John Smyth's reference to make-work schemes on the Berkeley estates in the reign of Thomas, lord Berkeley, who held the barony from 1281 to 1321.[16] The wool-clip from Berkeley sheep sheared at Beverstone was processed into cloth by poor cottagers on Berkeley manors in the Vale, and fulled at Berkeley mills managed by local clothiers with contacts in Bristol, London and the Low Countries. Smyth, looking back from the late sixteenth century, when there was a 'rage' for parish- and manor-based 'projects' of this type, stresses that it came into existence to provide work 'for making of cloth and clothing of the poor'.[17] This was a significant enterprise, centrally managed by the Berkeley estate stewards. Cloth was being produced throughout Gloucestershire, to meet local needs. But the Berkeley initiative was large scale and corporate, and embraced an entire district. From the start it was probably geared to meeting overseas markets for undyed and unfinished 'white' cloth.

In the Stroudwater Valleys, development seems to have been less guided, more piecemeal, but it occurred over the same period. As Saxton's map of 1577 suggests, much of the district was rough wood and pasture where the limestone Cotswold escarpment was indented by rugged valleys. The French monastic lords who had been in possession of the valleys and tops since the Conquest, were dispossessed by the English Crown at the end of the Hundred Years War. On Bisley manor, which included the growing cloth town of Stroud, manorial supervision was non-existent for much of the fifteenth century.[18] Tax-collection in the district, however, kept pace with the increasing population of the valleys and the wealth it generated. The tax yielded to the Crown by Cirencester, the regional wool market and distribution centre, doubled between the early fourteenth and early sixteenth centuries. In the Stroud Valleys it increased thirteenfold.[19]

In the Vale of Berkeley industrial development began as a corporate enterprise. It involved some degree of centralised financing, organisation and decision-making, even though actual production was dispersed into households throughout the Berkeley estates in the Vale. The Berkeley cloth towns were strategically placed near to the main road from the North-West through the Vale of Severn to Bristol and Exeter: this road and the Severn were the Western region's main trade routes. By the sixteenth century clothmaking was concentrated in the towns and villages along this road, which detoured along the foot of the steep Cotswold escarpment, past the mills and streams, and through the market-squares of the twin cloth towns of Dursley and Wotton-under-Edge, before resuming its path towards Bristol. Circumstances natural and historical favoured the district, but the firm hand of the enterprising medieval Berkeleys, and their stewards, was almost certainly present at the birth of this particular industrial archipelago.

In the Stroudwater Valleys *weak* manorial administration and supervision eventually brought about a similar result. In the crucial early stages, the decisive circumstance was the opposite of that which prevailed in the Vale of Berkeley. Skilled clothworkers migrated into the district from the towns and the Low Countries, just as they did in the Vale of Berkeley, but here the process was organisationally diffuse, piecemeal, 'from below'.

These were the origins. By the sixteenth century clothmaking was increasingly centred within a triangle drawn on the map between Painswick in the north, Cirencester in the east and Wotton-under-Edge in the south. This was the centre of historical development in the region in the early modern period. New and potentially revolutionary ingredients are hinted at in the theology of William Tyndale, and these were complemented by the dissolution of the great regional ecclesiastical estates, and by the effects of ruinous disputes as to the legal title of the FitzHardings to the barony of Berkeley. In the century separating the Henrician Reformation and the Civil War the gentleman- and yeoman-clothiers of central Gloucestershire grew in power to a point where, in 1640, they were strong enough to resist and overcome the remnants of feudalism in the region.

The cloth industry is central to the history of Gloucestershire in the early modern period. Counting the labour of women and children, more hours were spent growing wool, preparing it, processing it into finished cloth, taking it to local, national and international markets, than were spent in any other activity, with the possible exception of sleeping. It filled more waking hours than anything else. Shepherds stood at one end of the chain, merchants, tailors and consumers at the other. In between were shearers, packers, loaders, carriers, unloaders, market officials, wool merchants, mill-owners and workers, clothiers, sea-captains and sailors, winders and spinners, cardmakers, carders, weavers, fullers, dyers and a wide variety of skilled finishers generally included in the generic term 'clothworker' to indicate someone who worked cloth into its finished state. Husbandry was oriented towards providing the manufacturing workforce with grains, vegetables, meat, cheese (an important commodity in the Vale of Berkeley), leather, wood, woad and a wide range of necessities and raw materials. Cloth brought more wealth into the region than anything else from 1300 to 1840. It explains an entire landscape, most especially its greatest stone monuments, churches, mansions, inns, tenements (in places like Winchcombe to the north, Tetbury to the east and Wotton-under-Edge to the south), farmhouses and cottages.

2

Acting as 'transformers', linking their local hinterlands into wider trade and communications circuits, Gloucestershire's thirty market towns had populations in 1550 which ranged from Micheldean's and Fairford's 434 to towns with 1,000–1,500 inhabitants like Newent, Tetbury, Berkeley and Thornbury. It is at this level of 'urban' development that the forces that reconstituted and reconstructed regional and national society between the sixteenth and nineteenth centuries start to come into focus. The traditional market towns, like the larger boroughs, stagnated or grew far more slowly than local centres of clothmaking like Painswick and Wotton-under-Edge (which quintupled in size between 1551 when the radical Protestant Bishop of Gloucester, John Hooper, conducted the first useful census of communicants in the parishes in his jurisdiction, and 1712), Bisley (a large parish with several hamlets, which quadrupled), and Stroud and Dursley (tripled). As in so many aspects of the region's history, the medieval field-of-force was receding. Manufacturing dominated the region's history in the early modern period.[20]

Table 1.1 ranks Gloucestershire towns according to the degree to which they specialised in manufacturing for markets beyond their own immediate hinterlands ('manufacturing' in Marx's sense). The figure determining a town's position in the list is given in column 3. It is

Table 1.1 Occupational specialisation and population growth in Gloucestershire market towns, 1551–1801

Town	Men in Occupations in 1608	Ratio in 1608	Population				
	1608	1608	1551	1603	1676	1712	1801
				(as a per cent of 1551)			
Stroud	300	25	12	967	155	170	310	560
Bisley	164	15	11	668	151	301	447	470
Painswick	161	17	9.5	600	151	302	500	525
Minchinhampton	169	18	9.4	835	120	146	216	409
Dymock	165	18	9.2	734	91	124	136	167
Newent	201	24	8.4	1,189	77	132	92	204
Wotton-under-Edge	257	33	7.8	668	304	431	523	730
Dursley	158	21	7.5	768	113	173	325	309
Wickwar	126	17	7.4	668	50	105	150	114
Tetbury	190	26	7.3	1,002	100	ND	120	249
Gloucester	490	72	6.8	4,000	ND	125	ND	193
Frampton on Severn	108	16	6.75	334	164	124	150	257
Cirencester	350	58	6	2,438	125	130	164	169
Tewkesbury	455	75	6	2,600	102	ND	96	161
Winchcombe	153	26	5.9	1,169	122	180	232	161
Marshfield	150	26	5.8	835	112	130	96	149
Leonard Stanley	67	12	5.6	439	95	78	91	134
Chipping Campden	159	30	5.3	810	144	163	333	210
Cheltenham	164	33	5	878	152	222	170	350
Micheldean	133	27	4.9	434	141	144	138	130
Berkeley	97	21	4.6	1,690	188	109	148	183
Moreton-in-the-Marsh	72	16	4.5	167	350	554	314	496
Chipping Sodbury	99	22	4.5	668	85	118	97	163
Coleford	71	16	4.4	200	142	ND	ND	ND
Northleach	105	24	4.4	668	110	128	135	122
Stow-on-the-Wold	74	20	3.7	584	114	89	222	252
Thornbury	109	30	3.6	1,169	243	119	94	73
Fairford	61	16	3.9	434	85	130	152	305
Newnham	93	27	3.4	247	202	184	162	332
Lechlade	62	20	3.1	334	120	130	150	275

produced by dividing the number of individuals mentioned in the muster-listing for that place in 1608 by the number of different specialist occupations mentioned in the listing. Thus manors associated with the town of Stroud, the top-ranking town, had 300 individuals spread across 25 different occupations, producing a ratio of 12. At the bottom of the list, Lechlade had 62 individuals in 20 occupations giving a low specialisation ratio of 3.1. In the absence of qualifying evidence, the higher a town's ratio, the more it tended to be a centre of manufacturing, as well as a provider of the usual specialist services to its immediate hinterlands. It was a small manufacturing centre as well as a market town. It produced some commodity, often woollen cloth, for extra-local markets. Qualifying evidence will be referred to as and when necessary.

Columns 4–8 provide a guide to a town's population history from 1551, where a base figure calculated from Bishop Hooper's census of communicants is given. The figures in columns 5–8 give the population in 1603, 1676, 1712 and 1801 as a percentage of the base figure, providing a guide to fluctuations in size.[21] The table provides a summary guide to long-term structural change. The apparent solidity of its statistics can be accepted only if all the other available evidence confirms it.

The top four towns, measured by their 'specialisation ratio', were Stroud, Bisley, Painswick and Minchinhampton, the centres of the Stroudwater Valley complex. Wotton-under-Edge, in seventh place, and Dursley, eighth, were the organisational centres of the Vale of Berkeley clothmaking district. Wickwar, ninth, was still an important clothing centre on the fringes of the Berkeley district in 1608, but clothmaking ebbed away thereafter, hence its anomalous population profile. The population columns show the impact of manufacturing on population size. The more it specialised, the more a town grew: on average the Gloucestershire cloth towns were five or six times bigger in 1801 than they had been in 1551. Places like Wickwar and Thornbury were clothmaking centres up to the late sixteenth century, but as the industry became increasingly focused on the towns of Wotton-under-Edge, Dursley and Stroud, the industry migrated north, migrants were attracted elsewhere, and their populations stagnated.

The population of the Stroudwater Valleys doubled between 1551 and 1676, and doubled again between 1676 and 1779 (see Table 1.2). In 1831 the district held six times as many people as it had 280 years earlier.

In other words, growth in this manufacturing district was twice that of the county as a whole. Within the district the pattern was more complex, but what stands out is growth in the parishes situating market towns – Stroud, Horsley, Minchinhampton, Bisley and Painswick.

Table 1.2 Population of Stroudwater parishes, 1551–1831

Parish	1551	1603	1676	1712	1779	1801	1831
Eastington	391	401	626	450	769	988	1,770
Stonehouse	468	474	641	500	759	1,412	2,469
Kings Stanley	234	728	1,085	1,100	1,257	1,434	2,438
Leonard Stanley	439	417	346	400	512	590	942
Woodchester	200	217	200	460	792	870	885
Frocester	200	351	326	250	262	362	414
Minchinhampton	835	1,002	1,219	1,806	4,000	3,419	5,114
Avening	434	400	584	600	856	1,507	2,396
Rodborough	401	259	267	750	1,481	1,658	2,141
Horsley	362	668	1,002	1,200	2,000	2,971	3,690
Cherington	117	167	219	120	158	181	251
Painswick	601	1,033	1,815	3,000	3,300	3,150	4,099
Bisley	668	1,503	2,014	3,200	4,905	4,227	5,896
Randwick	167	372	584	400	650	856	1,031
Standish	410	517	636	500	400	504	536
Pitchcombe	43	134	92	80	90	216	187
Sapperton	167	317	326	320	300	351	422
Stroud	969	1,508	1,671	3,000	4,000	5,422	8,607
Totals	7,106	10,468	13,653	18,136	26,491	30,118	43,288
As % of 1551	100	147	192	255	372	423	609

Table 1.3 Occupations in Stroudwater in 1608

Cloth worker	Other non-agricultural	Farmer	'Mr' or 'Gent'	Labourer	Other	Total
756	277	347	18	129	296	1,823
41.47%	15.19%	19.03%	0.98%	7.07%	16.24%	99.98%

Source: Men and Armour.

One of the reasons for this town-centred growth pattern is revealed by analysis of the muster-lists for these places in 1608, referred to above.[22] Closer analysis of the distribution of particular occupations shows that Stroud, as expected, was a major organising centre with a concentration of finishing and marketing trades – 16 clothiers, 3 dyers and 11 fullers. Painswick and Minchinhampton had 3 and 4 resident clothiers respectively. In the Vale of Berkeley the pattern was the same. The two leading towns, Wotton-under-Edge (19 clothiers, 2 dyers and 17 fullers) and Dursley (11, 5, 11) were the organisational focuses of their district. Other small towns like Tetbury (9 clothiers), Wickwar (8 clothiers), Chipping Sodbury (5), Marshfield and Mitcheldean (3 each) were part of a general pattern in which a handful of small towns provided 55 per cent of the regional clothiers, 61 per cent of the dyers and 50 per cent of the fullers, but only 36 per cent of the weavers and 26 per cent of the broadweavers, who were more likely to live in outlying villages. It is striking that, even on this 'cellular' scale, organisation was urban but production was rural. Raw materials were distributed through the districts via the market towns, and the cloth returned there for finishing at the mills and wider distribution. Development involved an intensifying 'clustering' of all the specialist trades, from spinners and weavers to fullers, dyers, shearmen and clothiers.

A similiar pattern of growth, centred on the twin towns of Dursley and Wotton-under-Edge, is evident in the Vale of Berkeley, though agriculture was marginally more important as an employer of labour in the Wotton district. Combining the two districts, we have a conurbation that never quite made it across the next threshold, marked by the exponential growth of places like Birmingham and Manchester in the nineteenth century. The Gloucestershire cloth industry collapsed in the 1820s, and the district gradually assumed the gentle rural appearance (and pace) it has today. But in the period that concerns us it was the dynamic (and problematical) heart of the region, affecting everything.

Towns which rank high in Table 1.1 had relatively large numbers of men working in specialist industries, indicating production for extralocal markets. The archetypal or 'traditional' market town, which provided specialist services only for its surrounding villages, would tend to have no more than one or two men per specialist occupation, but would have a relatively large number of specialist occupations.

These traditional market towns appear in the bottom half of the list. Of the top fourteen towns, no fewer than ten were specialist clothmaking centres. Dymock, a town in the north-west of the county, achieves its high ranking because of relatively large numbers of specialist agriculturalists. Its market probably served no more than these local consumers. Tewkesbury and Gloucester were regional entrepots supplying the smaller market centres with necessities and luxuries. Their importance is reflected not in large numbers of men per occupation, but in the number of specialist occupations – 72 and 75 respectively, as against an average of 20–30 occupations in the small market centres. As a rough guide, a score of 6 or less in column 3 indicates a market town of the traditional type, i.e. one that was little more than a supplier of the normal specialist goods and services to its hinterlands.

The little manufacturing towns experienced the most rapid and sustained growth. Stroud, Bisley, Painswick, Minchinhampton, Wotton, Dursley, Wickwar and Tetbury were all clothmaking centres in 1608. The exceptions prove the rule. Wickwar lost its role as a clothiers' town in the seventeenth century, and hardly grew at all in the next two centuries. Tetbury assumed other functions associated with its location as a road junction, while its clothiers and clothworkers became progressively less important to the town's fortunes. It grew much more slowly than the towns which maintained and expanded their clothmaking functions. Intensification began with the rise of 'industries in the countryside'.[23]

3

The system of domestic production which early modern cloth manufacturing typifies is often, misleadingly, thought of as a static, unchanging system. New technology, management and organisational improvements were introduced whenever they were profitable and did not arouse the irresistible opposition of the more numerous trades, particularly weavers.[24] The century after 1650, writes D. C. Coleman, 'was an age of investment and enterprise in English industry, not manifest in any spectacular changes as in the succeeding century, but vitally important in providing the stronger and more flexible bases from which that revolution could be launched'.[25] Gloucestershire clothiers responded to the 'cost–price squeeze' of the century 1650–1750 less by the introduction of new technology than by a process of organisational innovation. This involved the concentration or 'clustering' within a district of all the specialist trades involved in processing cloth to a finished state.

This was a step towards factory production in the sense that it involved localised clustering of all factors of production. Until the seventeenth century Gloucestershire mainly produced 'white' cloth which was exported to the Low Countries for finishing.[26] The clustering process was greatly facilitated by the confidence instilled in the clothiers of central Gloucestershire by the development of Protestant pastoral ideologies and social disciplines. This subject is explored in later chapters. First, however, let us consider the evidence of this clustering process at Dursley and Wotton-under-Edge, and its impact on social structure, during the seventeenth century.

Table 1.4 represents a very simple analysis of occupational data drawn from the 1608 muster-lists, and from 'censuses' compiled from the parish registers of Wotton-under-Edge and Dursley, the 'twin cloth-towns' of the Vale of Berkeley, of 1660–1700.[27] The table accurately represents the continuing dominance of clothmaking. Fifty per cent of Wotton's menfolk earned their living in it at the beginning and end of the century. At Dursley a fall is registered in its relative importance (from 69 per cent of men to 59 per cent), but, as the figures show, clothmaking was an even more important employer of labour there than at Wotton. The figures suggest a long-term tendency. The numbers of weavers, who worked in their own homes, remained static at Wotton, and rose at Dursley as a result of the introduction there of

Table 1.4 Occupations at Dursley and Wotton-under-Edge in 1608 and c. 1690

Occupation	Wotton-under-Edge		Dursley	
	1608	1689–1705	1608	1669–1690
Agriculture				
Yeoman	6	19	2	2
Husbandman	26	4	2	4
Shepherd	–	–	1	1
Gardener	–	1	–	–
Other	–	1	–	–
Total	32	25	5	7
% of all occs	12	6	4	2
Textiles				
Clothier	19	30	11	30
Weaver	72	77	51	48
Broadweaver	14	14	–	47
Fuller	17	3	11	1
Dyer	2	3	5	2
Tucker	2	–	10	1
Shearman	2	18	–	42
Scribbler	–	21	–	25
Clothworker	–	49	–	26
Cardmaker	–	5	–	5
Total	128	220	88	227
% of all occs	49	54	69	59
Market				
Merchant	–	2	–	–
Mercer	–	2	2	6
Chandler	1	3	–	–
Innkeeper	1	–	–	4
Victualler	1	–	–	3
Butcher	5	5	2	16
Baker	2	3	–	6
Maltster	–	4	–	2
Miller	3	3	4	11
Apothecary	1	3	–	1
Barber	1	–	–	1
Vintner	1	–	–	1
Attorney	–	3	–	1
Surgeon	–	2	–	–
Other	–	–	–	3
Total	16	30	8	55
% of all occs	6	7	6	15
Transport				
Carrier	5	5	–	5
Leatherwork				
Tanner	1	1	–	1

Table 1.4 (continued)

Currier	–	3	1	–
Shoemaker	21	27	8	15
Glover	2	1	1	1
Skinner	–	2	–	–
Total	24	34	10	17
% of all occs	9	8	8	4
Clothing				
Tailor	14	8	4	21
Hatter	–	2	–	3
Staymaker	1	1	–	3
Bodicemaker	–	1	–	–
Sergemaker	–	1	–	–
Feltmaker	–	2	–	–
Total	15	15	4	27
% of all occs	6	4	3	7
Building				
Mason	4	2	6	10
Tiler/Slatter	1	3	–	–
Thatcher	–	–	–	2
Plasterer	–	2	–	4
Glazier	1	1	–	2
Total	6	8	6	18
% of all occs	2	2	5	5
Woodwork				
Carpenter	4	7	1	8
Cooper	1	3	–	1
Other	1	–	1	–
Total	6	10	2	9
% of all occs	2	2	2	2
Metalwork				
Smith	6	5	3	3
Pewterer	1	1	1	1
Other	–	8	–	1
Total	7	14	4	5
% of all occs	3	3	3	1
Gentry	4	5	–	–
Labourer	16	37	–	9
% of all occs	6	9		2
Total occupations	33	46	21	42
Total individuals	259	403	127	379

broadcloth-making. The most obvious change relates to workers in the finishing-trades – shearmen, scribblers and clothworkers. None were recorded in 1608, when local cloth was still being finished elsewhere, often after export to the Low Countries.[28] By the end of the century workers in the finishing trades outnumbered weavers.

That this was also a trend towards proletarianisation is confirmed by cross-referencing men assigned occupations in the parish registers with the Hearth Tax listing of 1671 and the Poll Tax listing of 1689.[29] More than half Dursley's able-bodied men were employed in the cloth industry in 1608, when its population was about 1,000. Eleven clothiers provided work for 51 weavers, 11 fullers, 10 tuckers and 5 dyers. The relative importance of the industry was sustained during the seventeenth century. But organisation changed, and so did the social structure of the town. Of the clothing workers recorded in the registers in the late seventeenth century, 81 were weavers or broadweavers, but to them we must add 25 scribblers, 42 shearmen, 26 'clothworkers', 5 cardmakers, 2 dyers, 1 tucker and 1 fuller.

By cross-referencing the names and occupations in the parish registers with the Hearth Tax listing for Michaelmas 1671, we can get some idea of how occupations translate into social structure. The most remarkable fact that emerges from such a comparison is that the scribblers, shearmen and 'clothworkers' were *all* living in one-hearth households, exempted on grounds of poverty. The assessment lists 250 households; of these 137 (55 per cent) were exempt. The list shows that the town had no great manor-house. Only six persons were assessed at more than six hearths. All were clothiers: John Purnell (8), William Purnell (7), John Arundell (7), William Smith (6) and Henry Smith (6). Mary Woodward, probably the widow of Joseph Woodward, the Presbyterian minister of the town until his death (shortly before he could be ejected for nonconformity) in 1662, was also assessed on six hearths. Of the 15 people who paid the poll tax for servants in 1689, 12 were clothiers or their widows: it is clear that the clothiers formed an exclusive and narrow elite. They lived in the biggest houses, and had servants to do their menial work for them. Thomas Purnell, Francis Phillips and Sarah Hallowes, widow, even had menservants. They were from clothier families established at least since the early seventeenth century.

The middle-ground of three to five hearths, a substantial group of 53 households, was occupied by a range of occupations. Richard Cooper, a shoemaker, paid on five hearths; in 1689 he had five journeymen who, the tax-assessor recorded, 'will not make known their names'.[30] Perhaps Cooper expected them to pay the tax out of their wages. Equally, they could have been nervous about the risk of removal. Twenty-five years earlier, town officials were concerned about the number of 'strangers' and 'inmates', and five persons, at least two of whom were clothiers, were presented 'for taking in a stranger'. All were fined 6s 8d 'for every month' they were 'detayned'.[31]

George Spratt, apothecary, paid on three hearths, as did John Thurston (tailor), John Olliver (blacksmith), Isaac Hill (shoemaker), John Prince (blacksmith), Daniel Knight and John Purnell (clothiers), and John Williams ('farmer and renter'). The only other farmer, John Tilladam, was a substantial yeoman living in a five-hearth household. John Olliver (tanner) and two more clothiers, Arthur Crew and William Tippets, also paid on five hearths. William Martin (tailor) and two innkeepers, John Phillips and Thomas Everett, paid on four each.

This was the solid 'middle rank' or 'middling sort'. Of those engaged in the cloth industry, only clothiers occupied houses with more than two hearths: 36 households came in this category, and of them 9 were exempt. Each of the 9 was male, so it was not a question of two-hearth widows fallen on hard times. The very large list of exemptions included a bookseller, shoemakers, a thatcher, a pargetor (plasterer), masons, a carpenter, a millman and even two butchers. The rest were weavers, scribblers, shearmen and clothworkers.

Not one of the men involved in the finishing end of the trade, not a single scribbler, shearman or 'clothworker', appears on either list as substantial enough to pay the taxes.[32] This end of the trade moved earliest towards factory-type organisation. Cloth-finishers were employed in large groups at the local mills, or in workshops run by 'master-dressers'.[33] This tendency towards centralised control of production by the clothiers, which was a feature of the West of England clothmaking industry from its origins in the fourteenth century, also intensified in the seventeenth century.[34] Although the absolute number of clothiers increased between the beginning and end of the seventeenth century, the parish register evidence suggests that they were a smaller proportion of the total numbers employed in the industry in both towns, confirming Eric Kerridge's observation that technological and organisational change in the industry always tended to favour the larger clothiers at the expense of the small.[36]

A sharp increase in the total number of specialist occupations in both of these small clothing towns suggests that they progressively improved the services they could offer their local customers. The only attorney living in the Vale of Berkeley in 1608 was John Smyth, who lived in a manor-house at Nibley, which is situated mid-way between Wotton and Dursley. He was retained by lord George Berkeley, trying to sort out the mess inherited from his father, lord Henry. In 1700 Wotton had three resident attorneys to service the needs of the flourishing elite of yeomen, clothiers and local gentry, and another was located at Dursley. Anyone wanting a barber in 1608 went to Wotton; in 1700 they went to Dursley. One apothecary's shop at

Wotton in 1608 increased to three there in 1700 and another at Dursley. No surgeons are referred to in 1608; two are mentioned at Wotton in 1700, a town that was a national leader in the practice of inoculation against smallpox in the 1730s.[36] Bakers increased from two to nine over the period, when both towns acquired specialist maltsters to supply local brewers at the inns and alehouses. Dursley seems to have become a specialist grain-milling centre in the seventeenth century.

A pattern is evident. Bridbury's thoughtful study of medieval Salisbury shows that before the fifteenth century the larger boroughs were the organisational heart of English clothmaking.[37] Water-powered fulling tended to disperse the industry in organisational terms, favouring clothiers who lived close to fast, perennial streams like those which flowed from the Cotswold escarpment into the Vale of Severn. The sixteenth century saw further technological innovation involving watermills, this time concerned with the finishing process. Gradually smaller (single-parish) towns like Wotton and Dursley emerged as the organisational heart of the industry, dynamic centres of piecemeal experimentation in milling, finishing, management and labour discipline. Such parishes were to the early modern period what the factory was to the late eighteenth and nineteenth centuries: the routinisation of parochial disciplines, the strengthening of the roles of the larger clothier-families, and the concentration within districts and neighbourhoods of every stage of the manufacturing process, brought the factory forward as a practical possibility, something it had proven not to be in the earlier experiments of great country clothiers like William Stumpe in the 1540s.[38] Urban parishes like Wotton and Dursley were in the forefront of this movement.

4

These processes were related to the rise of Puritan pastoral disciplines. They were developments of the principle that the function of industry was to provide work for, and thus to provide a means of disciplining, the burgeoning class of landless people. It was as true of the so-called 'domestic mode of production', and of the towns and districts in which it operated, as it is of modern capitalist corporations that, without a restless and relentless search for labour-reducing technology and improved labour management techniques, they could not survive for long. The central Gloucestershire clothworking districts remained for so long leading centres of the industry because of the control exercised over the community by the clothiers (who were usually also yeoman-freeholders), and their consequent ability to move its economic life in directions which suited them, regardless of national events. The

Restoration, for example, does not seem to have held back the Presbyterian elders of Dursley and Wotton-under-Edge, who retained Presbyterian 'precisianism' and disciplines by their continuing influence in the vestry, while nominally conforming to prescribed religious practices.

The proposition that the parish was to early modern England what the factory was to the nineteenth century carries the implication that developments that are often categorised as religious must also be seen as social and economic. The very availability of data like those cited above implies the administrative revolution that took place in the seventeenth century in towns like Wotton and Dursley.[39] Even the handwriting of local officials changed, from the spidery eccentricities of seventeenth-century village hand, to the bold, forward-sloping copperplate that took over between 1660 and 1720. Experiments in bureaucratic routinisation are evident in the use of printed forms, indicating a routinisation of functions and attitudes that had emerged from the experiments of 1500–1660. In this aspect, Puritanism was an important moment in the genesis of modern management. At Dursley and Wotton-under-Edge the new system of monitoring parish business was finally set in place by the Presbyterian elders in the 1650s, under the leadership of Joseph Woodward, Minister of Dursley.

Woodward was the son of a tanner from Cam, who came down from Oxford in the 1640, was appointed Schoolmaster at Wotton Grammar School, and, according to a memoir written by his son in the 1670s, underwent a conversion experience as a result of being attacked by a pack of dogs in Wotton high street one night on his way home from the alehouse. He was appointed Minister of Dursley in 1645, when the Laudian incumbent, John Robinson, was apprehended by a crowd, roped facing backwards on a horse, and passed from parish to parish until he reached Gloucester, where he was thrown into a cell to await a decision on his future. He had favoured the 'Court party' in the years leading up to the civil wars; this may have helped to fuel rumours that he was of suspect morals.[40]

Woodward's successor was ejected for nonconformity in 1662, but not before the district had experienced a taste of rigorous Puritan discipline that was to survive the vagaries of religious history. His son wrote that 'Dursley was very much altered by his labours'.

It became one of the most wealthy and best trading towns in the neighbourhood. Some of the clothiers having told me, that they cleared a thousand pounds a year by the trade of clothing, in the time of his residence there. His presence in the streets [made] the guilty to hide themselves in corners . . . For his house being distant from the church, everyone got their families ready as he

came by, and stood in their doors, and so fell in with those that
followed.[41]

As well as normal services, Woodward taught the town's children to
read at a school in the church, and gave two special weekly lectures
every Tuesday and Thursday. It is also recorded that he was constantly
troubled by local 'sectaries', who rejected his Calvinist theology and
perhaps his social disciplines too.[42]

Woodward (d. 1662) organised the Presbyterian 'Ministers' Testimony' to Parliament, printed in London in 1648, and presided over
celebrations of the return of the monarchy in 1660, like Presbyterians
throughout England. But the disciplines he had helped to entrench,
and the orderly system of keeping a record of parish affairs, survived
him and were gradually streamlined between 1660 and 1690.[43] One
small consequence of this general movement was that the parish clerks
of both towns made fuller and more detailed entries in the parish
registers, recording the occupations of household heads. By comparing
the 'census' that emerges from analysis of these entries with the
occupational listings in *Men and Armour*, we have been able to obtain
a fairly precise outline of the changing local economy.

5

Stroudwater and the Vale of Berkeley were not the only industrial
districts in early modern Gloucestershire. Blast furnaces were introduced into the Forest of Dean in the 1580s and 1590s. They entailed
extensive workforces collecting wood and coal, and hundreds of
households in the Forest of Dean were involved in nailmaking and
other forms of metalwork. East of Bristol the woods of Kingswood
forest were being denuded steadily by the domestic and industrial
needs of Bristol. Coal was already being mined there in 1608, but the
strongest burst of growth did not occur until the second half of the
seventeenth century. It was to this district that Wesley came in 1739
to preach the first Methodist sermons. In his words, the colliers of
Kingswood were 'a people famous from the beginning . . . for neither
fearing God nor regarding man: so ignorant of the things of God, that
they seemed but one remove from the beasts'. He regarded them as
'Heathens'.[44]

But the cloth industry dwarfed all others, nationally and locally.[45]
The comparative data in Table 1.1 show how closely population history
was linked to economic function. Leaving Bristol aside (though its
history too conforms to the general pattern), the three regional boroughs, Gloucester, Cirencester and Tewkesbury, were clustered
towards the middle of the table, revealing them as only moderately

specialised centres. Gloucester ceased to be a manufacturing centre of note before 1550. With the growth of clothmaking in central Gloucestershire, the county town became a specialist in distribution. Distribution employs fewer hands than production. Gloucester barely doubled in size between the mid-sixteenth century, when it stood at about 4,000, and 1801.

Cirencester became a clothmaking centre, momentarily overshadowing Stroud and the other clothmaking towns, in the sixteenth century. Clothmaking, like the fierce independence of its citizens, seems to have died in 1643. In spite of a catastrophic wave of epidemics, caused by unemployment and poverty, which swept through Gloucestershire clothmaking districts in the 1570, finishing by wiping out a third of Cirencester's inhabitants in 1578–9, Cirencester managed a 25 per cent increase overall between 1551 and 1603. It continued to grow until the 1640s, and then fell away. Always susceptible to epidemics – unlike other, smaller, market towns, its market, and its main street, never closed – it had less and less to attract immigrant workers and new settlers and did little more than hold its own as the regional market town it remains to this day.

Country clothmaking first began to make inroads into the markets of its own urban counterparts, and those of Flemish and North Italian clothworkers, in the fourteenth century. The fifteenth century is obscure, but there seems to have been another cycle of growth between 1480 and maybe 1540. Unemployment seems to have been at the root of serious disturbances and catastrophic mortality crises in the 1570s, foreshadowing another period of growth which had ended by 1620, when thousands of clothmaking households were said to have been unemployed in Gloucestershire. The 1620s, 1630s and 1640s were decades of acute distress in the clothworking districts: blame gradually attached itself to the personal rule of Charles I, and clothworkers and clothiers were among the most radical opponents of the Crown.[46] The better-documented industrial disputes and riots of the eighteenth century were flash-points in a struggle which was as old as large-scale clothmaking in the English West Country.[47]

The struggle was ultimately about control of production. By the end of the seventeenth century the big clothiers were firmly in control of finishing processes. Two factors militated in favour of this. Firstly, mechanical fulling was a feature of rural production in the West Country from the outset: there were no established foot-fullers' guilds to oppose its introduction in the thirteenth and fourteenth centuries. At that time the great magnates jealously guarded their lucrative monopoly over fulling mills, but in the sixteenth century, and particularly with the fall of the great abbeys which dominated the region, this technology was firmly in the hands of a tightly knit *bons bourgeoisie* of new families of yeoman rank.[48]

Secondly, the expansion of English clothmaking depended on aggressive marketing in overseas markets, and a key feature of this was the ability to respond to and create fashions for new weights, textures and above all colours of cloth. In 1740 a weaver complained that clothiers travelled 'above a hundred miles' to sell their cloth while the weavers 'waited at home to hear news'. It was a naive comment, but it alluded to the resentment that the weavers continued to feel with respect to the power this gave the clothiers over the actual producers of cloth. If the weavers wanted to make a living, they had to produce the cloth the clothiers told them to produce. 'The introduction of new fabrics and techniques', writes Eric Kerridge, always 'enhanced the larger master's role.'[49] England's domination of international cloth markets depended on its ability to respond, firstly, to what Joan Thirsk has called 'the fantastical folly of fashion', and, secondly, to competitive pricing.[50] Both areas challenged the master-weaver's traditional belief that only he (or his organisations) should determine quality and value. Continued successful access to markets entailed constant erosion of the skilled clothworker's independence. Every phase of growth was an attack on his dignity, and the clothier was the man who had to deal with him at the coal-face of production.[51]

The trend towards proletarianisation accelerated in the seventeenth century.[52] Comparison of the muster-lists with later data shows that in the later decades of the seventeenth century the number of looms in Gloucestershire 'at least doubled and the number of clothiers increased by a hundred or more'. The illustrative cases of Dursley and Wotton-under-Edge tend to confirm Kerridge's assertion that the introduction of new fabrics and techniques increased the direct control of the big clothiers over all stages of the production process. Gloucester diocese probate inventories consolidate the impression of increasing polarisation between the merchants and clothiers and the rank and file workers (see Table 1.5), although the data tend to exaggerate the wealth of weavers and other clothworkers (because only a few of the more substantial production workers ever went through probate), and underestimate that of the richer clothiers. The wealthier men had their probate affairs handled by the Archdiocese of Canterbury.[53]

By the late seventeenth century Wiltshire and Gloucestershire concentrated on 'Spanish' cloth. Exports of 'Spanish cloth began to increase after 1703', writes Mann. 'By 1708 they had passed the level of 1663 and they rose steadily, with very few setbacks, to a peak of

Table 1.5 Gloucester diocese probate values in the cloth industry

Occupation	Sample	Period	Mean	Median	Highest	Lowest
Clothier	20	1666–85	296	228	1,307	4
Clothier	16	1725–38	97	28	655	5
B/weaver	14	1666–85	41	33	93	3
B/weaver	26	1725–38	40	18	234	5
Weaver	7	1666–85	44	48	120	4
Weaver	20	1725–38	28	18	115	12
Clothworker	8	1666–85	41	44	102	9
Clothworker	15	1725–38	26	16	109	4
Mercer	12	1666–85	395	275	1,129	46
Mercer	4	1725–38	72	–	193	9

over 25,000 pieces in 1717.' 'The first twenty years of the eighteenth century were, all in all, the most prosperous which the area had experienced since the beginning of the seventeenth century'; and, as we have seen, this 'prosperity' was at a much higher level of production, indicated by the increase in the number of clothiers and looms at work compared with the end of the earlier expansion, in the 1600s.[54] In the late 1720s, after probably fifty years of expansion, the region 'entered upon a long period of fluctuation'. Wage disputes in the Wiltshire branch in 1726 indicate that it suffered earlier than Gloucestershire, where there were no serious industrial troubles until the 1750s: markets for Stroudwater 'Scarlets' and 'Blues' held out longer against French competition.

Parish register data show remarkable population growth at Stroud, the main town in the Stroudwater complex, between about 1700 and 1750. In the 1690s baptisms at Stroud averaged 46 a year. From 1700 to 1709 the average rose to 70 a year, followed by a dramatic and unprecedented leap to 119 a year between 1710 and 1719. They remained above 110 a year until 1740 when they achieved the highest average for the eighteenth century, 130 a year. These figures give a slightly exaggerated sense of growth in that baptisms were unusually low in the 1690s, but there can be little doubt that Stroud's population doubled between 1700 and 1730, that is to say, when there was rapid growth in the export markets for Stroudwater (and Wiltshire) cloth.

Total population estimates for the whole Stroudwater complex, comprising eighteen clothworking parishes, show that the entire district underwent rapid growth betwen 1676, when the application of the customary multiplier (1.67) to figures for communicants gives a total population of 14,133, and the 1770s, when the reliable estimates of Samuel Rudder give a total of 26,491. This is an increase of 87 per cent. The baptism evidence just cited indicates that growth was concentrated into just two decades between 1700 and 1720, when markets were booming. Figures from the parish registers of other Stroudwater parishes suggest that Stroud was about a decade ahead, but the pattern of very rapid growth between 1700 and 1740 is confirmed.

Industrial rioting did not break out in Stroudwater until 1756. The parish register data show that Stroud's population peaked in the 1740s, fell back slightly in the 1750s, and then remained steady until the first decade of the nineteenth century. That is to say, the population data are remarkably consistent with what we know of the markets for Stroudwater cloth. When the markets collapsed, local populations were double what they had been fifty years earlier; and we may surmise that it was a younger population as a consequence of such rapid growth: James Wolfe's comment in a letter from Stroudwater in 1756, that he expected to leave with many recruits from the unemployed young of the district, complements this impression of an extraordinary spurt of growth, followed by depression, followed by riots, followed by a renewal of overseas war.

6

The rise of clothmaking in central Gloucestershire after 1300 impacted on the regional field-of-force like a high-energy vortex, altering the distribution of population, acting as an agency of population growth, facilitating the rise of the middle rank of yeoman-clothiers, institutionalising proletarianisation which became more pronounced as time went on, creating distance between the landed masters of local economies and the landless, establishing new problems of socialisation and generating new world-views and patterns of local administration in response. In short, rural clothmaking restructured the regional society and economy, making new *mentalités* and ideologies inevitable, and entrenching new types of social conflict. The central Gloucestershire clothing 'archipelago' is only one case of a phenomenon which was occurring in other parts of England and Europe at the time, producing similar effects – one of the many streams of 'country capitalism' which were to meet in the global explosion of industrial capitalism in the late eighteenth and nineteenth centuries.

The production side was a long process of piecemeal experimentation and innovation, characterised by many periods of set-back and delay. That clothmaking remained for five centuries (1300–1840) the chief producer of wealth and everyday maintenance in these districts gives it an appearance of inevitability, tempting the observer to take it for granted as an unchanging feature of local life, and thus to ignore its epochal structural implications. If the implications had been restricted to the districts in which such processes took place, there would be no grounds for claiming them as examples of the local

43

origins of the modern world. But the industries in the countryside were necessarily expansive, and sent their effects rippling out into the wider world, and into the future, in ways that will be explored in the following chapters.

2

TRAILS OF PROGRESS
The reorientation and intensification of traffic, 1600–1800

In the 1980s a new, conceptually confused, picture began to emerge of the historical development of English society in the sixteenth and seventeenth centuries. Historians focused with renewed intensity on local and regional cultures. The great national and state issues – the Reformation, the English Revolution – began to merge, at the local and regional level, with uniquely local and regional fields-of-force. Terms like 'Reformation' and 'English Revolution' came to mean different things in different places. As discourses of English History, it might be said, they are aggregates of all the local and regional communities shaping and being shaped by politics of state and underlying secular trends. It is now conceivable that English History will be rewritten from the local and regional bottom-up.

If this path is pursued, it will be necessary to guard against inflating the local into a research field that is sufficient unto itself, or treating it, on the one hand, as a bottomless well filled with richly textured special cases, or, on the other, as a source of footnotes to the history of the nation-state. Local archives are full of rich and idiosyncratic sources. If local and regional variety is undoubtedly one of the most evident characteristics of Tudor–Stuart England, so too is its intensifying interconnectedness. It was a society on the move. Its cells belonged to a pulsating organism; its communities melted in a myriad of ways into an increasingly dense *society*.

'Localism', it has been suggested, 'is a theory of *mentalite* . . . It defines the mental horizons that supposedly bounded the social and political world of most inhabitants of Tudor and early Stuart England.'[1] Yes, but 'localism' is not only 'a theory of *mentalite*', it must also be a history of the material contexts, circumstances and limitations which produced the 'mental horizons' in question. It is also misleading to suggest that theory has influenced the directions taken in recent years by the historiography of early modern England. Rather, the tendency for young scholars to begin their academic careers with highly focused studies of localities and regions has been a function of the opening up of local and county records by the energetic and imaginative efforts of two or three generations of county archivists. Even now, such studies tend to be conducted by means of quick 'raids' on county record offices, especially those located within easy reach of major university cities. The pre-eminence of East Anglian studies, for example, is a function of the region's proximity to Cambridge. Institutional circumstances, not theory and methodology (of which English historiography is profoundly suspicious), explain more than any other factor the directions which English historiography has taken. The results have been thoroughly enriching, but they have left a confused and incoherent map of a crucial period in the development of English society as a whole.

Localism was an important ingredient in the checkerboard milieu of sixteenth- and seventeenth-century England, but it is crucial to recognise that it was a circumstance inherited from the past, and that it was a function of the political, ecclesiastical and technological conditions of the past. These were changing remarkably quickly. The crises of the sixteenth and seventeenth centuries were engendered not so much by conflict between localities and the central state, as by the fact that the localities were becoming progressively more interconnected both with each other and, by means of the rise of London as an increasingly monopolistic centre of legal and commercial life, with the capital. In focusing on localism we focus on the residual cultures of the past, not on the forces which were changing them. What made England and its 'first empire' (Wales, Ireland and Scotland) the most powerful nation in the world in the nineteenth century was that it was the largest political–economic unit in the world, capable of coordinating and directing its resources (above all labour) with extraordinary but apparently effortless coherence. The role of the state was complementary, not central. The reason for this was that English *society* was unified – which is not to say there were no fundamental conflicts. This chapter examines the agency which above all others exemplifies the decline of localism and the unification of England: traffic.

More than any other factor, topography determined the local and regional basis of early modern cultures. Economic homogeneity along a north-west/south-west axis was mirrored in the road system inherited from medieval times. In his history of the road system of medieval England, Stenton observed that 'one of the best-recorded of medieval roads ran from Bristol through Gloucester, Tewkesbury, Worcester and Bridgenorth to Shrewsbury, and then, either by Ellesmere or Whitchurch, to Chester . . . England west of the Cotswolds and the hills descending from the Peak into the midlands enjoyed', by virtue of this road, 'something approaching self-sufficiency'.[2] Defoe's description in the early eighteenth century represented it extending south, via Bridgewater or Taunton to 'Excester', and north to Liverpool and Warrington, north-west to Manchester and 'other manufacturing towns in Lancashire'.[3] Landscape had tended to impose a north–south orientation on the West of England.

A glance at Saxton's map of Gloucestershire (1577) illustrates the way this traditional orientation shaped imaginative efforts to represent the landscape. Natural features dominate and, most significant of all, Saxton ignored roads. The perspective is mid-way between medieval attempts to represent the land in a vertical axis, as a traveller would see it, and the modern satellite-eye-view. The traveller Saxton had in mind was not the clothier or the carrier, but the armigerous gentleman whose walls the maps were designed to adorn.[4] They were emblems of gentry territory. Maps drawn for the more numerous but less prestigious middle ranks, the yeomen, farmers, traders and most substantial artisans, would embody different priorities.[5] Gentry and nobility still liked to imagine themselves riding across country without hindrance, accompanied by armed and uniformed retainers. Gentlemen 'in Sir Philip Sydney's time . . . were robust and hardy and fitt for service . . . They mett in the fields, well-appointed, with their hounds or their hawkes'. They 'kept good horses, and many horses for a man-at-armes . . . twas as much a disgrace for a cavalier to be seen . . . riding in a coach in the street as now 'twould be to be seen in a petticoate and wastecoat'.[6] Saxton took it for granted that his landscape was a theatre in which the aristocracy and gentry held centre-stage unchallenged.

The more profligate noble habits of medieval times were becoming less feasible with every decade, and had been since the late fifteenth century. Saxton did not consider the most powerful feudal household in the region worth marking with a specific symbol. Henry, seventeenth lord Berkeley, nearly bankrupted the dynastic estates trying to maintain an occasional retinue of little more than a hundred servants and soldiers in the 1550s.[7] He and his ancestors were never again to attempt a display of lordly circumstances on this scale. They couldn't afford it. Saxton does not mark Berkeley Castle, unquestionably the most powerful and impressive feudal bastion in the region.

Saxton's *Sabrina Fluensis* (the Severn) gives the cartographer's region a north–south orientation, the Cotswold Hills stretching from the north-west to the south-west strengthen the impression. Bristol, Cirencester/Ciceter (Saxton gives alternative names) and Tewkesbury are the chief urban outposts, protecting Gloucester, where William the Conqueror was crowned and Edward II was buried (having been painfully murdered down the road at Berkeley Castle), the county town and seat of the modern ecclesiastical diocese of Gloucester, formed at the time of the Reformation. The Forest of Dean protects

Gloucester from the South Welsh marcher heartlands. Gloucester protects the lowest land-bridge across the Severn, which broadens below Gloucester, exercises an impressive ox-bow meander past Newnham and the marshy Arlingham peninsular, the 'diggers' on the warth and waste of Slimbridge, Berkeley Castle, Chepstow and the mouth of the Wye, and out into the West of England's equivalent to the Thames/London nexus, the Bristol Channel, England's back door.

The greatest barrier to the passage of heavy or bulky goods (like cheese or cloth) from the productive Vale of Severn east to London, of course, was the Cotswold Edge. In 1779, by which time the region operated very much along an east–west axis, Samuel Rudder evoked the power that the Cotswold Edge still exercised in the imagination of contemporaries. 'There is no possibility,' he wrote, 'of passing directly from Oxfordshire, Berkshire or Wiltshire, to the Vale of Gloucestershire, without descending one of the hills in this great chain, which stands as a boundary between the Cotswold and the Vale, the latter being separated from the Forest by the interposition of the Great River Severn'.

> The turnpike from London to Worcester leads down Broadway-Hill. That from Stow to Tewkesbury, down Stanway-hill; from Cirencester to Cheltenham, down Windass-hill; from London, through Oxford to Gloucester, you descend Crickley-hill; but through Cirencester to Gloucester you descend Birdlip-hill: from the east part of the county, to either of the passages across the Severn at Framilode or Newnham, the road is down Rodborough-hill; from Bath to Gloucester down Frocester-hill; from Cirencester to Wotton, Dursley and Berkeley, down Wotton, Dursley and Stinchcombe-hills respectively; from Oxford to Bristol, down Sodbury-hill; but from Oxford to Bath, down Fryson-hill; and the great road from London to Bristol leads down Tog-hill.[8]

In Saxton's map the tentacular feeder streams of the Thames seem to reach like sinister fingers from the east, the fingertips of London, reaching to its sources in the Cotswold Hills. The proportion of Gloucestershire's produce travelling east across the hills to Cirencester, Lechlade and up the Thames Valley to London increased steadily in the sixteenth, seventeenth and eighteenth centuries. The effect was to shift the region from a north–south to a west–east axis. London and the rural manufacturing districts on which it depended grew at the expense of Bristol, and to a lesser extent the smaller regional boroughs, Gloucester, Tewkesbury and Cirencester.

Occupational data relating to Lechlade, 10 miles east of Cirencester at the westernmost navigable point of the Thames, provide a clue to the reorientation of the region. The cloth and cheese carriers from the

Vales of Berkeley and Gloucester avoided the steep haul up the Cots-wold Edge by gathering at convenient places along the tops.[9] Symond-shall was one of these spots, and Birdlip, a little further north, was another. Local producers carried their goods up the Edge on donkeys. The carriers then struck off across the Wolds through Tetbury or Cirencester, and on, via Lechlade, to Reading (a major cheese market for the bloated London market) and the capital.[10] Increasingly their commodities were off-loaded at Lechlade, which became a busy little inland port in the east–west carriage during the sevententh century.

Table 2.1   Lechlade's changing occupational structure, 1608–1706

Occupation	1608	1698–1706
Agriculture		
Yeoman	2	–
Husbandman	20	–
Farmer	–	9
Miller	2	1
Total	24	10
Crafts		
Weaver	6	–
Tailor	2	3
Glover	2	–
Shoemaker	4	3
Cordwinder	–	1
Smith	2	1
Carpenter	2	1
Mason	1	–
Slater	1	–
Glazier	–	1
Total	20	10
Market Town		
Butcher	3	2
Baker	1	–
Innkeeper	1	10
Victualler	1	1
Ostler	1	–
Mercer	1	4
Tallowchandler	–	5
Maltster	–	1
Shopkeeper	–	1
Fisherman	–	1
Total	8	25
Bargemaster	–	3
Labourer	8	69
Gent	1	2
Total occupations	19	19
Total individuals	61	119

According to the reminiscences of some of its oldest inhabitants in 1719, Lechlade's wharves and warehouses were built in the 1650s. The data in Table 2.1 present the occupational structure of the town as it appears in sources relating to the beginning and the end of the seventeenth century.[11] One innkeeper was recorded in 1608, whereas 10 are mentioned in the parish registers in the 1690s. During the seventeenth century labouring households increased from 8 to 69. Inns multiplied to service the influx of travellers and merchants, and a new hamlet called 'Little London' grew up west of the town to accommodate the families of the labourers who went from 13 per cent of able-bodied men in 1608 to 57.5 per cent of male heads of household in 1690–1706. They are not specifically referred to as dock-workers, but the building of Lechlade docks in the 1650s is the only available explanation for the increase. We do not know how regularly they were employed, or how many barges worked the river carrying cloth, cheese and other provisions produced in the hinterlands of the docks east to Oxford and London.

In 1608 Lechlade was a small-scale market town, barely clinging to survival as such against the competition of neighbouring Fairford and, above all, the major regional entrepot, Cirencester: the least specialised small town in Gloucestershire, as its position at the bottom of the ranking-list in Table 1.1 indicated. Its most valuable asset was St John's Bridge across the Thames, which a stream of wool-buyers and other travellers up the Thames Valley had crossed into Gloucestershire since time immemorial. River traffic and the navigability of the Thames had increased to such an extent by the 1650s that capital was raised to build new wharves and warehouses.[12] Deponents in a court case in 1719 estimated that 140–200 wagons of cheese were brought to the town for the cheese-fairs on St John's Bridge, besides that carried on horseback. There was also 'considerable traffic in stage-wagons . . . particularly carrying cloth from the Stroud region'. By 1739 commentators took for granted that 'the Gloucestershire men carry all by land-carriage to Lechlade and Crickley, and so carry it down to London'.[13]

Mary Prior's account of the fishermen, bargemen and canal boatmen of Fisher Row, a suburb of Oxford, confirms the impression given by the building of the docks at Lechlade in the 1650s, followed by a sudden influx of labouring households in the second half of the seventeenth century: west–east trade intensified during the seventeenth century.[14] The idea of improving the Thames navigation below Oxford seems first to have been canvassed in the 1580s. An Act for 'Clearing the Passage by Water from London and beyond the Citye of Oxford' was passed in Parliament in 1607; 'on 31 August 1635 the first barge reached Oxford from London'.[15] Many of the bargemen of Fisher Row had connections at Lechlade, which seems to have become an active inland port in the second half of the seventeenth century.[16] This process is too easily seen as an example of the city (London) colonising the country (in this case Gloucestershire). Lechlade's productive hinterlands to the south and west, notably the Wiltshire and Gloucestershire clothmaking districts, became more intensely connected with London because it served their interests. London wanted what Gloucestershire produced. The symbiosis explains why Gloucestershire, like London, was so firmly Parliamentarian in the 1640s. By 1600 most of the leading trading families in Gloucestershire had kinship connections in the London mercantile and legal communities.[17]

What these sources catch are one of the ripples flowing outwards from the development of commodity production in the Stroudwater Valleys and the Vale of Berkeley: 'waves' of intensification springing from the nodal industries in the countryside; waves of country capitalism. This axial reorientation was only one facet of a thoroughgoing transformation of the regional field-of-force. Basic trade orientations are one thing; the intensity of traffic is another which must also be considered in the search for the agencies responsible for the movement and change. Quantitative estimates of domestic trade are difficult for a period in which a large but indeterminate proportion of economic activity went unrecorded, but the leading authority on the subject, J. A. Chartres, estimates that 'the greater part . . . seems to have been generated internally, and the great bulk of domestic products was destined for the home market'.[18] The remainder of this chapter will attempt to trace the intensification of internal trade from the early seventeenth to the late eighteenth centuries.

The notion of 'internal' trade needs qualification, for most items destined for consumption overseas, especially cloth, had first to be transported across land and along English rivers. All trade was 'internal' at some point. It all generated increasing domestic traffic. As Chartres observes, the history of internal trade has to be traced in the (often vague and subjective) impressions of contemporaries, and in even less direct sources. Here I shall illustrate the intensification of domestic trade with reference to 'traffic', a common – and telling – contemporary synonym for trade.

Gloucestershire clothiers travelled widely in search of good-quality wool to be distributed to local households for working up into cloth, which they then took to London. Smyth of Nibley provides two telling images, one of clothier Webb, whose sharp dealing gave his home town of Dursley a reputation current from the Reformation era to that of the English Revolution. The other referred to the iconoclastic activities of an unnamed clothier from Cam who, 'in the raigne of kinge Edward sixt carried' a carved image which stood in the porch of his parish church 'to Colbrooke in a clothier's wain, 15 myles from

London, in his travell with his cloth thither towards Blackwells Hall'.[19] 'Symondshall Newes!' referred, in the Vale of Berkeley, to false or exaggerated stories circulated by the London carriers, who gathered on Symondshall Hill above the clothing towns, villages and hamlets of the Vale to await consignments of local produce dragged laboriously up the steep Edge for onward transmission to Cirencester, Tetbury, the Thames Valley and London. Three professional carriers attended the musters of 1608 from hamlets on the outskirts of Wotton-under-Edge, and more may have been on the road when the musters were held. Three carriers at Woodchester, and others at Stonehouse, Stroud itself and Kings Stanley, represented the transport fraternity that serviced the Stroudwater Valleys. Another six carriers lived on manors of Whitstone Hundred along the banks of Saxton's *Stroude fluensis* between Stroud and Framilode, on the Severn.[20]

Fifteen of the 49 professional carriers caught in John Smyth of Nibley's muster-lists (31 per cent) worked out of the clothmaking districts. The others were located in equally significant 'clusters'. On the North Wolds the traffic in raw materials – wool – was the determining factor, with carriers located at Sherborn, Bourton on the Water, Chipping Campden and Cirencester. Six carriers, three each in the neighbouring townships of Huntley and Longhope, provided carrying services for the commodity-producers in the Forest of Dean. The three boroughs, Gloucester (1), Tewkesbury (3 carriers and 4 'carmen') and Cirencester (3), and the industrial districts and suburbs on the fringes of Bristol complete the tally. According to this source, 78 per cent of professional carriers at the beginning of the seventeenth century were located to service the rural industrial districts, while the other 22 per cent were located in the larger towns. We should also note that 49 professional carriers is not many in a population of about 100,000. 'Market' in 1600 still meant, for the overwhelming majority of English people, a small town where the population of a district congregated for one day every week. Many farmers had their own carts for farm-work, and for carrying their own produce and that of their neighbours to the local markets, and to the strategically placed boroughs for transmission elsewhere. We can assume that most of the 927 yeomen and some of the 3,774 husbandmen recorded in 1608 provided themselves and their neighbours with local carrying services. The clothier's activities – there were 207 of them – have been mentioned.

Another category of professional trader mentioned in the 1608 muster-lists is that of the 'badger'.[21] Badgers were dealers in grain and other foodstuffs, supposed to be licensed by the county Bench, though in Gloucester this task seems to have been neglected before the weavers' riots of the 1750s. They also sometimes dealt in wool and yarn, though this was comparatively rare. The geographical distribution of references shows that, like carriers, badgers were clustered in strategic and significant locations in the early seventeenth century, servicing the populous manufacturing districts. No fewer than ten were concentrated in four neighbouring parishes on the west bank of the Severn between Tewkesbury and Gloucester, waylaying grain supplies from the north and re-routing them into the Forest of Dean to feed the colliers, coal-getters, leather-workers, metalworkers and even farmers of this pastoral, wooded, manufacturing district.[22] They purchased their supplies in the major market towns, or along important grain routes like the Severn, and were the early modern equivalent of mobile shopkeepers. They represent a kind of transitional zone of commoditisation, between the relative self-sufficiency of the medieval marketing district, and the modern network of permanent retail outlets (shops) which began to impose itself on the habits of Gloucestershire's manufacturing districts in the late seventeenth and eighteenth centuries.

The largest cluster of badgers, eight of them, occurs in the list for Birdlip, a hamlet at the top of the Cotswold Edge on the main London–St Davids highway mid-way beetween Gloucester and Cirencester. This spectacular location at the top of Birdlip and Crickley Hills was an ideal place from which to redirect supplies south along the Cotswold Edge to the markets of Bisley, Painswick and Stroud, where hundreds of clothworking households were dependent on their activities. Birdlip occupied a transitional zone between the 'private' and 'public' markets. The Birdlip badgers purchased their supplies at the four inns of Birdlip, which had no market charter, and had no need of one, situated as it was in a relatively thinly populated district just north of Stroudwater. They then carried it in their carts and set up shop in the open market-places of the Stroudwater region.

The demand generated by rising population in the clothworking districts is implied by a further six badgers located in manors of Whitstone Hundred, along the banks of *Stroude fluensis*, a district which also had six specialist carriers. These badgers picked up loads of grain and other supplies at Framilode, where the Stroud Stream entered the Severn, and carried it up the valley, stopping off to drop supplies at the populous clothworking villages along the way. In short, at least 14 of the 26 licensed badgers recorded in the musters of 1608 were supplying the Stroudwater Valleys: small beginnings, perhaps, but an unmistakable pattern. This evidence, undramatic though it is, underlines the importance of rural industrial development in the expansion of the private market, and the commoditisation of food production. Badgers were not the only people engaged in this trade. Millers were found throughout the county, mostly outside the market towns. But 70 per cent of the bakers recorded in *Men and Armour* were located in market towns, suggesting a tendency for trade households to cease baking their own bread. Bakers were as unpopular as badgers and millers in times of high prices and dearth. Malting was a speciality of only four towns – Gloucester, Tewkesbury, Cheltenham and Marshfield – which may mean that outside the boroughs home brewing was still a widespread practice in the seventeenth century.

The region was becoming Stroud-centred. Growth of population in central Gloucestershire, associated with the rise of clothmaking, was changing the patterns of life in the entire region. Other aspects of this theme will be taken up in later chapters, not least concerning resistance to the Crown from 1620 to 1649, which was very much the inclination of the clothworking districts. Associated with this intra-regional development, clothmaking was also the single most important branch of production, followed by large-scale cheesemaking in the Vale of Gloucester, leading to a global shift in the orientation of the entire region, from a north–south to an east–west axis.

In the 150 years after John Smyth conducted his muster-counts in 1608 this Stroud-centredness became more pronounced. Following serious industrial disputes in the clothworking districts during the 1750s, the county magistrates conducted their first serious effort to document and license food-dealers in the county. The lists they generated as a result of this once-off exercise are most instructive.[23] Technically all food-dealers had to be licensed by the county Bench, but the Gloucestershire magistrates seem to have been lax, or at least informal, in their approach to this problem perhaps because everyone knew that the industrial districts could not be supplied by any other means. Eighty-four (61 per cent) licences were issued to men from the Stroudwater or Upper Berkeley clothing districts. Seventeen (12 per cent) came from Gloucester, Cirencester, Tewkesbury or the suburbs of Bristol. Twelve (8 per cent) came from parishes bordering the Forest of Dean. Of the remaining 24, 9 were located at Lechlade, Fairford and Kempsford, whence grain entered the county up the Thames Valley from Berkshire.

The licences were recorded in the Petty Sessions Order Book in the form of a list. Each badger was required to deposit a £50 bond and to provide a guarantor who was to deposit half that amount. The names, occupations and parishes of legal settlement are given in all but a handful of cases for both the badger and his guarantor. Twenty-nine were described as shopkeepers, 14 as bakers and 25 as yeomen. All but four of the shopkeepers were from the clothmaking districts. In some cases the relationship between a badger and his guarantor appears to have been a relationship between wholesaler and retailer. Samuel Niblett, a grocer from the city of Gloucester, provided bonds for a chapman from Cirencester, shopkeepers from Leonard Stanley,

Kings Stanley (2) and Woodchester, a butcher from Kings Stanley, a blacksmith from Stroud and a yeoman from Cam: all clothworking centres. Giles Middlemore, a chandler based at Stonehouse near Stroud, guaranteed shopkeepers at Cam and Moreton Vallence, and also obtained a badger's licence in his own name.

By the mid-eighteenth century the central Gloucestershire clothworking districts were home to at least 40,000 people, slightly more than lived at the time in the districts which were later to merge into the conurbation of Birmingham. The Stroudwater Valleys in particular were unsuited to arable production, and the Vale of Berkeley increasingly specialised in cheese and livestock production. In effect, what we have is a conurbation forming within a 15-mile radius of Stroud. By the middle of the eighteenth century a battalion of middle-men was needed to keep these districts supplied with raw materials and necessities. By this time, Gloucestershire was for all practical purposes Stroud-centred.

Between 1600 and 1800 commodity production on a large scale led to the routine commercialisation of daily life. The general tax returns for the Vale of Berkeley in 1785 list 39 retail shops at Wotton-under-Edge and another 27 at Dursley, showing that the improvement in specialist facilities offered to their district continued in the eighteenth century: a smooth, gradual and progressive 'take-off into self-sustaining growth' is suggested by these two towns, their districts and their region.[24] They were becoming shopping centres in the modern sense. Seven of the smaller clothmaking villages had a man describing himself as a shopkeeper licensed as a badger in 1758–9. In his book on the economy of Gloucestershire, published in 1789, William Marshall described the result. 'The inhabitants of towns', he wrote, 'have no need of a weekly market. But the inhabitants of [agricultural] villages would find themselves awkwardly situated without one. They cannot, like the townspeople, go every morning to the shop. One day in the week is full as much as they can spare.'[25]

Every district involved in manufacturing and commodity production was a 'little London', transformed and transforming the habits and orientations of an entire region. The clothmaking districts of central Gloucestershire grew twice as fast and twice as much as the regional and national population. Centred on small market towns, the occupational structure of these local industries changed progressively as a result of technological and managerial innovations designed to reduce labour costs and improve labour discipline under the authority of clothiers who were also Puritans and parish elders. To dispose of their cloth, these districts looked less and less to the regional entrepots of the past – Bristol, Salisbury, Exeter and Southampton – more and more towards London. Without knowing it, the small manufacturing towns and the mushrooming capital were involved in a long-term conspiracy to eradicate the landscape of the medieval field-of-force: its abbeys went in 1540; the baronial bastions at Berkeley and Sudeley fell to Parliament after a final burst of resistance between 1643 and 1645; the medieval boroughs were in decline, relative to the rest of the region, throughout the period. The network that counted by 1640 was the one that connected the households and neighbourhoods of the manufacturing districts to the middling merchants and clothiers in the small manufacturing towns, and connected them with London, where merchant adventurers – by 1600 brothers and cousins and uncles of the clothiers in the provinces – carried their cloth to continental Europe, the Mediterranean and North America. Not the least important aspect of this intensifying network was that it was the arterial system of the Parliamentarian cause in the 1640s, an alternative communications system: the Royalists still liked to ride (or attack a town) across the fields.

In 1660 monarchy was restored but the traffic continued to intensify, heedless of ephemeral politics. Nonconformist priests were dismissed, but nonconformist networks continued to carry nonconformist gossip and literature, as they had since the Lollards and before. The drama of the bourgeois revolution was enacted in the households, neighbourhoods and towns, but the energy which drove it was generated by the movement along the lanes, tracks and highways. In the eighteenth century the tide of traffic became an irresistible flood. It no longer mattered if manufacturing industry survived in this or that particular district. Between 1500 and 1800 little capitalist industries created a national capitalist society. This, in the form of an illustrative region, was an essential part of the process underlying the rise of capitalism and the national market in England. In the eighteenth century, the era of turnpikes and 'flying wagons', the pace of change became visibly and, in some eyes, distressingly rapid and intense. Let us now turn to the intensification of 'traffic' in the modern sense.

Before the turnpike era, Gloucester and Cirencester were the county's two most important road junctions. At Cirencester three Roman roads – the Fosse Way, Ermine Street and Akeman Street – crossed. Ermine Street descended from the Cotswold plateau at Birdlip and continued across the Vale to Gloucester, across the bridge and into the Forest of Dean towards Monmouth and South Wales. The road from Reading along the Thames Valley by-passed Cirencester, joining Ermine Street at Perrot's Brook, where in 1690 the Jacobite county historian, Sir Robert Atkyns, nearly killed the whiggish Sir Christopher Guise in a duel occasioned by accusations of cheating at cards.[26] Akeman Street was no more than a straight rural track, and its fate was sealed in 1753 when the road a few miles north, from Oxford to

Cirencester and Bath, via Bibury, was turnpiked. The cut through to Perrot's Brook was similarly affected when in 1727 the road from Lechlade and Fairford to Cirencester was turnpiked. The major routes connecting Cirencester with Lechlade and the Thames, the Midlands, Oxford and Bath emerged from a complex network of local tracks as clear-cut, wide trunk roads in the time of the 'flying wagons', of which more in a moment.

At Gloucester the old road system from London to St Davids crossed the North–South route from Exeter and Bristol to Chester and the North-West. This too was a pattern laid down by the Romans. Stow on the Wold grew up as a road town in the north-west of the county. On the borders between the Gloucestershire and Wiltshire clothmaking districts, on the gentle eastern slopes of the Wolds, Tetbury became an important meeting-point for pedlars and chapmen from as far away as Scotland. Oxford–Bath coaches stopped at Tetbury for breakfast in the eighteenth century. Stroud, as we have seen, and, in the eighteength century, the royal spa-town of Cheltenham both generated and attracted an increasing proportion of the county's traffic.[27]

By the end of the sixteenth century the marketing structure of the region centred on thirty market towns, albeit many of them supplied in ways that I have described, through the 'private' market. Each of these market towns radiated its own network of tracks, etched into the landscape less boldly than the trunk routes. Local networks were turnpiked later than those associated with the main urban centres – Stroud, Cirencester, Gloucester, Bristol – which carried materials and people operating in regional and national commodity markets. Broadly speaking there seem to have been three phases of turnpiking activity. The first, beginning in 1693 with the turnpiking of Birdlip Hill, was barely under way when Defoe toured the county in the early 1700s.[28] It lasted until about 1740 and eventually affected most of the major trunk roads and the networks radiating from the main urban centres. The second phase covered the networks of towns like Stroud and Cheltenham. The through road from Cheltenham to Warwick via Winchcombe and Stratford-upon-Avon, for example, was not turnpiked until 1752. The minor roads of an out-of-the-way market town like Winchcombe, which had no significant industries, had to wait until the third phase, which began about 1790. Winchcombe's network was turnpiked in 1792. Similarly Coleford, not marked at all (like roads) on Saxton's map in 1577, was somewhat off the beaten track as far as major through routes were concerned. To cope with an increasing amount of traffic in the Forest of Dean, its minor roads were turnpiked in 1795. In the early eighteenth century Defoe thought Chipping Sodbury 'a place of note for nothing that I could see, but the greatest cheese market in all that part of England, except Atherton in Warwickshire'.[29] By 1750 cheese from the Vale of Berkeley was distributed by two factors living at Frocester, who sent it by packhorse and wagon to London, via Lechlade, and even to supply British armies fighting in the Low Countries. The two roads connecting Chipping Sodbury with the Vale of Berkeley were not turnpiked until 1799, a hint that its cheese market was in decline.

Travellers in the Australian outback will be more familiar with the problems of travelling on unsurfaced roads than English people. In the 'dry', stones, rocks and potholes are concealed by dust, in the 'wet' by mud. Many Australian outback roads are impassable in the wet, as were many English roads in the eighteenth century. When Arthur Young travelled along the Burford–Gloucester road, turnpiked in 1751, he described it as 'the worst I ever travelled on; so bad that it is a scandal to the county'.[30] Turnpiking was a technique which did no more than sustain, as against improve, the quality of road surfaces which, in the eighteenth century, were carrying an unprecedented burden of traffic. Young travelled across the Cotswold plateau 'with a very low opinion of all the places and counties it leads to, for if they were inhabited by people of fortune and spirit, . . . they would never suffer such a barbarous way of mending their capital road'.[31] Nor was he any better impressed with the stretch of road between Gloucester Bridge and Newnham, towards the Wye Bridge at Chepstow and on to Wales. Ruts were a problem, and Young made the somewhat irrelevant comment that Suffolk farm wagons would be too broad to travel in them. At Lydney Park, which straddled the road just south of Newnham, the Bathursts refused to allow commercial vehicles across their property, forcing them to make a detour along rough forest tracks. In 1756 they placed an advertisement in the *Gloucester Journal*, announcing that 'the road leading through the Forest of Dean to Lydney and from thence to Chepstow is now mended. Thomas Bathurst of Lydney Park gives permission to all gentlemen and ladies travelling in coaches and post-chaises to come through his grounds without charge'.[32] Commercial travellers had to pay, or make a lengthy detour.

The problems Young observed dated back to time immemorial. The *Journal* reported in 1740 that Newnham's market had been 'lost for many years past' due to 'the badness of the roads to the said town'. Notice was given to 'all farmers, bakers, badgers of corn and others, that the roads to and from the said town are now in good repair'. Newnham was intending to hold a weekly market 'for all sorts of grain, toll-free for the space of one year'.[33] The same year, however, the inhabitants of another market town, Newent, threatened to indict the commissioners of the Gloucester–Newent turnpike for their 'very great neglect and even perjury'. The road was 'so dangerous in many places that travellers can scarce pass them in safety . . . to the very great unease of those who pay so much to the turnpike'. There had been no maintenance 'for some years past'.[34]

After 1730 nearly every edition of the *Journal* carried advertisements and announcements about turnpiking somewhere in the county. In 1755, for example, major repairs were being conducted on Crickley and Birdlip Hills, and new Acts were under way for roads at Cirencester, between Burford and Stow, at Dursley, and, across the bridge at Gloucester, the 'Over Turnpike'.[35] They were part of a massive holding operation, an attempt to cope with a volume of traffic quite beyond the means of local parishes. In 1745 the City of Gloucester announced that it would prosecute 'all persons within the Liberties driving wagons with six or more horses'.[36]

On the trunk roads much damage was done by the 'flying wagons'. By 1760 there were at least eight major passenger routes through the county. By 1730 passengers could travel from Cirencester to London on Mondays, Wednesdays and Fridays, returning if they wished the following day. The coach from Gloucester to Bath via Bristol left every Wednesday and Friday in summer, Wednesdays only in winter. A return coach left Bath the same day. Passengers from Bath had to stay the night in Bristol in 1730, but by 1760 the journey was completed in a day. When the Gloucester coachmaster John Pitt died in 1726, his Gloucester–Oxford run was amalgamated with the Oxford–London run of William Haynes, making it possible to 'fly' from Gloucester to London with only an overnight stop. The same year Hereford was added to the route; Hereford to London was a three-day trip at first, but by 1766 it had been reduced to one and a half days. People were moving more and they were moving faster.[37]

From Gloucester to London via Cirencester took two days, perhaps because of the long haul up Birdlip Hill. In 1755, before the spa-boom transformed the town, a Cheltenham–London coach left on Monday mornings, passed through Northleach and Oxford, and arrived at London at noon every Wednesday. In 1759 a guinea paid for a ticket from Bristol to Birmingham, via Stow on the Wold. These were airline prices, accessible only to the middle and upper ranks. Half was demanded before leaving, the other half to be paid on safe arrival at the destination. Within seven years the journey had been reduced from two to one and a half days, and from a guinea to eighteen shillings a ticket. The same price would obtain a seat on the coach that flew along the highway between Oxford and Bath via Witney, Burford, Bibury, Cirencester and Tetbury. On the southward trip breakfast was served at the Bullfinch, Burford, and lunch was at the White Hart, Tetbury.

The colourful stage-coaches represent no more than the tip of an iceberg. 'Wainmen' and carriers moved more slowly, as did chains of pack-horses, but the sheer volume they represented must have played a significant part in pounding, rutting and cracking very variable road surfaces. The city of Gloucester had numerous professional carriers like Widow Arnold in the eighteenth century.[38] Micheldean coal carriers were in trouble with the inhabitants of Newent in 1755 because the latter thought they were being 'defrauded by the carriers' refusal to weigh' their coal using the traditional measures.[39] Sam Manning, operating out of Minchinhampton Common to the George Inn, Bristol, was only one of many carriers operating out of the clothing districts.[40] In 1755 John Leyes carried goods to and from the quay at Tewkesbury.[41] 'A machine for the carriage of salmon' caught in the Severn left Gloucester 'every Wednesday at 9 a.m. to arrive London Thursday night'.[42] Punctuality was becoming an issue. Ten years earlier 'the old Winchcombe and Cheltenham stage-wagon' began operating 'gentlemen's and Tradesmen's goods of all sorts' from the George Inn at Snowshill, to Tewkesbury, Stow 'and places ajascent'.[43]

In July 1745, John Restall, carrier of the Pack-Horse Inn, Tewkesbury, announced in the *Gloucester Journal* that he had 'fixed the stages for his packhorses'. Every Monday he set out from Tewkesbury, lunched at the White Hart at Gloucester, stayed that night at the Crown, Newport, and on Tuesday completed his journey to Bristol, where clients could contact him at the Horse Shoe Inn, Wine Street. He then travelled on to Bath, where he stayed at the Angel Arms. By Wednesday he was back at Newport, Thursday at Gloucester and Tewkesbury, and spent Friday night at the Bell and Unicorn Inn at Worcester. He 'likewise carr[ied] goods to Birmingham and Wolverhampton or any part of the North'.[44] Farmers from all over the county sent wagons to pick up coal from the markets at Gloucester, from Framilode, from the pits in the Forest of Dean, and from Coalpit Heath, depending on which was closest. Farmer George Andrews of Westonbirt, near Tetbury, used Coalpit Heath, which of course also supplied Bristol.[45] The coal carriers of Kingswood Chase destroyed turnpikes at Toghill in 1743 because they believed they should be exempt from charges. The commissioners disagreed.[46] Most parishes regularly sent wagons to collect coal for the use of the poor.

In the week commencing 2 June 1765, 259 coaches, 491 wagons, 722 carts, 206 drays, 11,759 horses and 675 asses passed through Lawfords Gate, Bristol.[47] The eighteenth century was no stranger to traffic jams. Bristol's roads were turnpiked between 1720 and 1750, but not without persistent resistance from the colliers, who thought they should not have to pay for the privilege of keeping Bristol's parlours warm and her industries going.

Initially the main roads bore the brunt of this intensifying traffic, and the lesser networks of the market towns were less badly affected. In time, however, expanding population in country districts and the appearance of village shops (implying large-scale, intensive marketing networks) drew local road systems into the orbit of the market economy. Towards the end of the eighteenth century they too were turnpiked.

Eighteenth-century tax assessments complement this picture of the traffic problem, and hint at the underlying pressures that it implied. In 1786 the tax returns for Dursley show that 49 people paid tax on 82 horses, 10 were taxed on 13 wagons, and 9 paid on 12 carts. Five Dursley clothiers maintained four-wheel carriages: Dursley was a town of only 2,000 inhabitants.[48] The weavers of Bisley (and other clothing villages) kept donkeys on the waste land for transporting their cloth to the local mills and finishing shops in the market towns. When attempts were made to enclose Bisley Commons in the early nineteenth century, the weavers marched through the district chanting 'Who stole the donkey's dinner!'. Horse stealing was the eighteenth-century equivalent of today's car stealing. Inns on Kingswood Chase and at Marshfield dealt in stolen horses in the 1730s, and there were no doubt others.[49]

On a rough estimate, using the Dursley figures as a base, there must have been at least 10,000 horses in Gloucestershire at any time in the eighteenth century. This means at least 40,000 acres of hay, or 4 per cent of the *total* (not agricultural) acreage.[50] The pressure on resources needed to feed a growing human population is obvious. In this sense the communications revolution of the late eighteenth and early nineteenth centuries – canals, synthetic road surfaces, railways – was a response to a growing ecological problem. Such evidence, though no more than a sample of what is available, testifies to the intensifying burden carried by Gloucestershire's roads in the seventeenth and eighteenth centuries. The circulation of goods and people it implies leaves little doubt that a long commercial revolution was taking place in this industrious and productive region. It is even possible that, in proportion to its population, the traffic on the roads was as heavy, or even heavier, than it is today.

It was the maintenance problem that attracted the attention of contemporaries. Thomas Rudge wrote in 1807 that 'few counties are more intersected by roads, but few have materials more variable in quality'. Cotswold limestone was 'generally dug by the roadside, to the annoyance and danger of the traveller'. It needed constant renewal because 'it decomposes by frost, and pulverises under the pressure of even small weights'. In the Vale good materials were hard to come by. They were 'so scarce' that maintenance became prohibitively expensive. Even where 'the stone of the county' could be obtained to provide adequate foundations, Rudge estimated that '120 tons of lime or Bristol stone' was needed 'to replenish the wear of a mile every year'. Considerations such as these must be set against the morose complaints of travellers like Arthur Young.[51]

Rudge mentions a number of experiments to solve the problem. In his view there had been some recent improvements, 'where but a few years since, the roads were all but impassable'. Until synthetic road surfacing became available, however, the maintenance problem would remain the despair of commissioners of turnpikes and travellers alike. Canals, as Rudge pointed out, were of limited use. They were practical only in certain areas. There was even talk in the late eighteenth century of a canal connecting the Severn and the North Avon to provide a link between Gloucester, Cheltenham, Winchcombe and Stratford-upon-Avon. Talk it remained, because the costs proved to be prohibitive in relation to the possible profits.[52]

Rudge sounded a prophetic note, however, when he wrote that 'the time is probably fast approaching when the iron railroad will supersede the further use of canals' like the Stroudwater and Thames and Severn. Systems in which 'one horse of moderate strength will draw many tons of compact heavy substances with ease' were already in use in the Forest of Dean and Kingswood Chase to carry coal from the pitheads to the Severn and South Avon Rivers respectively. But it was to be another forty years before the first steam-engine 'flew' along the route of that 'best known of all medieval roads' traversing the Vale of Severn from Bristol to points north.[53]

This process of intensification began in the early fourteenth century, and reached crisis-point in the period of classical industrialisation, roughly 1760–1830. It was a developmental 'cycle' having its roots in the flight of industries from the boroughs to rural districts, characterised by fast, perennial streams to power the fulling and finishing mills, and the subsequent development of large concentrations of proletarianised and semi-proletarianised workers. They were more mobile than land-based peasants, and came to be dependent on battalions of middle-men to supply them with raw materials and the necessities of life. It was a long revolution, a complete transformation of the English social landscape. It involved nothing less than the creation of new modes of wealth and power situated in new places, interconnected by new and increasingly dense and intricate networks: new organs and a new arterial system. The new system did not arise in conscious opposition to the old feudal network, and the values it embodied. It arose as a result of the very success of feudalism in imposing order in order to generate increasing wealth. In Gloucestershire, 'capitalism' (as good a term for this new system as any other) became the dominant mode of production between the late fifteenth and mid-seventeenth centuries.

It implied new ways of life. In the Stroudwater Valleys human beings replaced wild boars, squirrels and hunting lords as the dominant mode of life between the thirteenth and fifteenth centuries. In the Vale of Berkeley clothmaking worked its way into the pores of feudal agriculture which, to become more efficient and productive, favoured the rise, in every manor that has been studied intensively, of little elites of rich peasants and a proletariat of landless cottagers that constituted at least 30 per cent of the people mentioned in late thirteenth-century manor rolls – which leave out subtenants and temporary residents, always most common in manufacturing towns and villages. Medieval manorial rolls (like later records) generally give an accurate picture of the more substantial and permanent villagers; they are much less accurate where landlessness is concerned.

Extraordinarily powerful, revolutionary energies coursed out of the 'rural' industrial districts, along the new, 'alternative', arterial system. The sources of these energies illustrate the proposition that great changes may be facilitated by actions of the 'high' or 'top', the ruling classes and their subalterns, but the drift of elites is always, necessarily, conservative. The dynamism, the new ideas, the heresies, the drive, the enterprise, the conviction, passion and belief come from the geographical and social 'peripheries' or 'borders' – from 'below'. Not, as the history of the Tyndales and Trotmans will show, from the very 'bottom' of the social hierarchy, although its numbers and the squalid conditions in which its members spent their lives (and, very close to life in the early modern period, deaths) constituted the single most continuous and important problem for whoever or whatever class set down the administrative agenda.

More important than vertical class and status hierarchies, however, were the processes of 'horizontal' expansion described in this chapter. They changed the context in which class-formation and other kinds of social and political movements took place. They made the nation-state as we know it a possibility by creating an unusually large, unified market-place. To a great extent they escaped consciousness, driven by the piecemeal motives, decisions and journeys of people going about their business across several generations. The alternative structures they generated made the victory of Parliament over the King possible by creating substantial, much-travelled networks which gave the middle ranks a unity (sealed by the Press, which travelled the same highways) that built upon, but easily exceeded, the efficiency of the Norman–Angevin framework. They created a new world, new interpretations, new voices and a new language.

Part II

NEIGHBOURHOOD TO NATION

God does not inspire men for their own sakes, but for the sake of others; and another man's inspiration is nothing to me, unless he can satisfy me he is inspired.

John Tillotson, Archbiship of Canterbury (1630–1694)

For a dream cometh through the multitude of business.

Ecclesiastes

The advantage of the word *culture* is that it at least raises the possibility of a disjuncture between perception and reality.

Wiliam M. Reddy[1]

The distinctive quality of [humanity is] not that [we] must live in a material world, a circumstance we share with all organisms, but that [we] do so according to a meaningful scheme of [our] own devising.

Marshall Sahlins[2]

We are all prisoners of a rigid conception of what is important and what is not. We anxiously follow what we suppose to be important, while what we suppose to be unimportant wages war behind our backs, transforming the world without our knowledge and eventually mounting a surprise attack on us.

Milan Kundera[3]

Social system is . . . constructed out of passion, structure out of sentiment.

Marshall Sahlins[4]

3

PROVERBIAL CULTURE

The processes of intensification involved a long revolution in culture
and consciousness. In this chapter we explore the point of departure
of this cultural movement by means of a rare, perhaps unique source,
which provides an opportunity to explore a vernacular culture of the
period between the Reformation and the civil wars. In 1639 John
Smyth of Nibley wrote down a list of 'certain words proverbs and
phrases of speach, which wee hundreders [of Berkeley] conceive (as
we doe of certaine market moneys) to bee not only native but confined
to the soile bounds and territory thereof; which if found in the mou-
thes of any forraigner, wee deeme them as leapt over our wall, or as
strayed from their proper pasture and dwelling place'. The district to
which the words and phrases belonged was not large. A fit person
could stroll from Nibley to Stroud in a short morning. Wotton-under-
Edge lay 2 miles south of Smyth's manor-house, Dursley 2 miles north.
Smyth's list referred to only a part of this region: the Hundred of
Berkeley. It was part of *A Description of the Hundred of Berkeley in the
County of Gloucester and of its Inhabitants*, a collection of manuscripts
intended for his son, also John Smyth, his successor as Steward to
the Hundred and Barony of Berkeley.[5]

Smyth meant what he said when he described his list as of 'proverbs
peculiar to the hundred of Berkeley'. The 'pasture' and 'household'
metaphors were used with precision. They fed, imaginatively speaking, on a particular local-historical habitat, one that could be clearly
distinguished from district cultures elsewhere. The 'wall' which the
proverbs had to 'leap over' in order to gain currency in other parts of
England, was cultural, and culture was an incessant dialogue of language and landscape, mediated by the experiences, memories and
legends of generations.

Claude Levi-Strauss claimed, on the basis of a lifetime of anthropological reflection, that 'human societies exhibit a certain optimal diversity beyond which they cannot go, but below which they can no longer
descend without danger'.

We must recognise that, to a large extent, this diversity results from the desire of each culture to resist the cultures surrounding it, to distinguish itself from them – in short, to be itself. Cultures are not unaware of each other, they even borrow from one another on occasion; but, in order not to perish, they must, in other connections, remain somewhat impermeable toward one another.[6]

Language is the most fundamental source of this impermeability, the most important way cultures protect themselves from outsiders. The people of the Vale of Berkeley spoke the same language as other English people, but before the arrival of popular literacy and the Press – before the penetration of what Ivan Illich has called 'the alphabetisation of the popular mind' – dialect was a powerful force for cultural localism such as that described by Smyth. It was an agency which had to be overcome before nation-states could acquire anything like primacy in the identity of ordinary people, before nationalism could become the dominant ideology, not just in England, but throughout the world. Let us first consider the mortar in the bricks in the walls of early modern English country cultures: dialect.

'The dialect [of the Hundred]', wrote Smyth, 'seemes borne of our owne bodies and natural unto us from the breasts of our nurses.' 'A native hundreder, being asked where hee was borne, answereth, *"where shu'd y bee y bore, but at Berkeley hurns, and there, begis, each was y bore"* '. Or thus: *Each was geboren at Berkeley hurns.* Words ending and beginning with consonants were invariably connected with 'y', as in *come y hither, each ha kild a ferry fat y hogg, Watt y ge Tom y some nin y well y din'd,* and *hur is y gone.* 'V' was invariably pronounced as 'ff', as *fewed* for 'viewed' or *fenison* for 'venison'. Reversing this, words beginning with 'v' were pronounced 'f', thus 'fat venison' became *vat fenison.* 'G' and 'c' too were reversed, and 'cuckold' became *guckowe.* In the middle of words the 'u' was lengthened as in *doust* for 'dust' and *youse* for 'use'. *Thicke* and *thucke* meant 'this' and 'that'. Plurality was often indicated by the addition of 'n' instead of 's', as in *shoon* for 'shoes'. *Cham woodly aggriezed* meant 'I am wonderfully aggrieved'.

Some dialect words differed from those used elsewhere. *Pugg* referred to 'the refuse corn left at winnowing'. *Gait* meant 'all in haste'. A *goschicken* was a 'gosling', an *hoytrell* was 'a loose idle knave', *dunch* meant 'deaf', *hastis* meant 'angry', *hite* meant 'comely', *tyd* meant 'wanton', *blive* meant 'fast', *axen* meant 'ashes'. *dothered* meant 'amazed' or 'astonished', *attery* meant 'angry or cross-natured', a *shard* was a 'gap or broken place in a hedge', *loome* meant 'often' and to *loxe* was 'to convey away privately' thus 'to steal'. Butter and cheese were *the cowes white*, and to *be song'd to a childe* was to become its godparent. A change of vowel in the same word could change the meaning: *gaye!* 'is lett us goe, when myselfe goes as one of the company', but *goe!* 'is the sending of others when myselfe staies behind', as Smyth explained.

Smyth's dialect references remind us that before the coming of print, and the uniformity of 'standard English' that it was eventually to impose, localities were able to retain a certain opaqueness, and thus a certain particularism which was one of the defining characteristics of all human societies before the combined forces of the market economy, proletarianisation and labour mobility, and the coming of mass literacy and media diluted dialects into mere local accent. Smyth's use of the word *forraigner* to refer to people who came from outside the Hundred of Berkeley is telling, as is the universal use of the word *countrey* to refer to the kind of associational cultural unit that he had in mind. They are reminders that affective communities are historical constructs, functions, at least in part, of existing technology and the structural level that Braudel calls 'material life'. It is a universal human characteristic to seek identity in a community larger than the self, but the community (and identity) sought is always, in some sense, historically conditioned. Nation-states become 'imagined communities', as Benedict Anderson suggests, as a result of the agencies of print and routine schooling in monoglot literacy. The imagined communities of the pre-print era were communities of speech.

Only one of Smyth's proverbs referred directly to the cloth trade. 'He'll prove a man of Dursley' meant 'a man that will promise much but performe nothing'. 'This', explained Smyth, was 'dispersed over England.' Thomas Fuller confirms this by referring to it in his *Worthies of England*.[7] It 'tooke roote', according to Smyth, 'from one Webb a great clothier dwellinge in Durseley in the daies of Queen Mary, as also was his father in the time of kinge Henry the VIII'. The Webbes purchased 'very great quantities of wooll out of most counties of England'. When the wool was being weighed and negotiations over price were taking place, 'both father and sonne (the better to drawe on theire ends) would ever promise out of that parcell a gowncloth peticote cloth apron or the like, to the good wife or her daughters, but never paid anyething'.

The Webbs were a landowning business family of yeoman rank, a 'kin-coalition' with several branches in several manors and parishes in the Vale of Berkeley. As with other local families of their rank – Tyndale, Trotman, Harding, Nelme and about a dozen others – their epic began in the early sixteenth century, often with a clothier who had done well from investment in yeoman freeholds. The notorious Webb purchased wool in all parts of England and put it out for working up into cloth to the households of Dursley and its neighbouring villages. He was a descendent of Flemish immigrants of the early fourteenth century.[8] He collected the cloth, put it our for fulling, and sold it (not all of it unfinished and uncut, as the reference to the promised 'gowncloth peticote cloth apron' testifies, but much of it probably undyed, unfinished, and not of the very highest quality) to merchants in London or Bristol.

The people of Dursley didn't like the way the sharp-dealing clothiers had tainted their reputation. One Sunday in 'the first [year] of kinge James', Smyth was at Berkeley church when the Vicar of Berkeley, Edward Green, 'useing the proverb in his sermon there, wherat many of Dursley were present, had almost raised a tumult amongst his auditory, wherof myeselfe was one'. The Webbs' operation was on a large scale, though not perhaps as large as that of their contemporary, William Stumpe. Stumpe was the son of a North Nibley weaver who was rich enough in 1539 to purchase the buildings of the dissolved Abbey at Malmesbury, which he turned into a factory housing hundreds of weavers.

Dursley's clothiers were sufficiently well known throughout England to have become proverbial examples of routine duplicity. We must suspect that of all the proverbs peculiar to the hundred it was the one that was used most cautiously and sparingly at home. Cloth provided the capital but land was where the heart was. Too many people were embroiled in the cloth industry to be entirely comfortable with it. It was one of the only two proverbs that referred even obliquely to clothmaking, the other being the expression *I'll make abb or warp of it*, which meant 'if not one thinge then another'.

What gives the proverbs their local flavour is not so much the wisdom they embody, which was probably much the same among English 'aborigines' everywhere, but the social and geographical landscape from which the 'metaphorising' (Smyth's term) that they embody took as its point of departure. The *imagery* is local, 'peculiar to the hundred'.

Physical landmarks occur in several of the sayings. 'Simondshall newes' has been referred to.[9] The promontory of the Cotswolds above Wotton-under-Edge also provided the image for 'Simondshall sauce', which denoted 'a guest bringing an hungry appetite to our table: or, when a man eats little, to say he wants some of Simondshall sauce'. Smyth explained that the air atop the hill was 'the purest . . . of all the country', but that a family could only live there comfortably 'provided [they] hath a good woodpile for winter'. It was much colder and more windblown than down in the Vale under the shelter of the Edge – where Smyth himself had chosen to live. He had a substantial manor-house at North Nibley, 'adorned with gardens and a large park well-wooded'. He never went without wood, but one of his duties as a parish and estate official was to keep an eye out for wood-stealing.

After several decades of population growth, wood was becoming scarce.

Another local saying was 'Neighbour we're sure of faire weather, each ha' beheld this morne, Abergainy Hill.' This referred to the 'Sugar Loaf' at Abergavenny, which could be made out on the horizon on fine days from Stinchcombe, Nibley, or Simondshall Hills. This is one that Smyth said he 'often made use [of] in [his] husbandry'. At a time when printed almanacs and clocks were only just beginning to infiltrate popular habits of mind, the landscape was literally used to store information, like the 'memory palace' of the famous Jesuit missionary, Matteo Ricci, but less contrived.

'The real purpose of all these mental constructs', writes Ricci's modern biographer, 'was to provide storage spaces for the myriad concepts that make up the sum of our human knowledge.'[10]

> To everything that we wish to remember, wrote Ricci, we should give an image; and to every one of those images we should assign a position where it can repose peacefully until we are ready to reclaim it by an act of memory.

Scholars have assumed that this 'art of memory', which has classical origins and became popular with the literate intelligentsia during the Renaissance, was a discovery and instrument of the intellectual elite.[11] More likely, wherever and whenever it appeared, it was a natural adaptation of a universal characteristic of the 'aboriginal' oral cultures out of which, originally, the tools of literacy emerged. Literary versions of this 'art', like Ricci's, distanced their 'palaces' from any specific location. 'Since the entire memory system can work only if the images stay in the assigned positions if we can instantly remember where we stored them, obviously it would seem easiest to rely on real locations which we know so well that we cannot ever forget them.'[12]

> But that would be a mistake, thought Ricci. For it is by expanding the number of locations and the corresponding number of images that can be stored in them that we increase and strengthen our memory.

But there was another, simpler reason for this dis-location. Renaissance intellectuals aspired to universal knowledge. Proverbial cultures like that of the Vale of Berkeley were collective artefacts produced over generations for the use of cultures that were specific to a particular locality (or, in the case of nomadic peoples, particular routes). For such cultures, the idea of being distanced from the landscape was, literally, unthinkable. Literacy dis-located memory.

Seasonal habits of husbandry were triggered by sayings like 'When Westridge Wood is motley, then 'tis time to sow barley'. This meant start planting when the leaves in a local wood were turning colour, before they began to fall. 'When the crow begins to build, the sheep begin to yield' had application beyond this locality, but the principle was the same. Similarly, 'a misty moon in th'old o'th moon doth alwaies bring a faire post-noone', and 'my milke is in the cowes horne, now the zunne is 'ryved in Capricorne' pointed to routine conjunctures of seasonal signs and practices associated with careful husbandry. 'On St. Valentine's Day cast beanes in clay, but on St. Chad sow good and bad' referred to local festivals that were beginning to fall into disuse in Smyth's lifetime, but still survived in vestigial forms. 'When Wotton Hill doth wear a cap, Let Horton town beware of that' indicated that for dozens of generations local people had noticed that mist on the hills above Wotton often presaged rain or snow at Horton, a township a few miles south.

Sky, weather and landform provided basic elements in the mnemonics of a culture that was still – just – entrenched in a preliterate cosmos that stretched back to the beginnings of human society. The elaborate mnemonic systems that were practised by the intellectual elite of the time only became conscious artifices when print was beginning to erode older habits of mind and longer memories. They drew attention to natural processes. When, in March, after a cold, hard winter, the outlines of bones began to show on their cattle, men thought, or said, 'Lide pilles the hide', a phrase which sounds as if it has been honed by scores of generations. 'Lide' refers to 'the ides of March'. Put into unforgettable verbal form, a farmer learned to see into the future. 'When the days begin to lengthen, the cold begins to strengthen' warned that 'the coldest part of winter is after the winter solstice.' It alluded 'also to the rule of husbandry: that at Candlemass a provident husbandman should have halfe his fodder, and all his corne remaining'. Proverbs were the agricultural colleges of an oral culture that was clearly capable of expropriating images from alien cultures, as the proverbial reference to 'the ides of March' suggests, but which was overwhelmingly an ongoing 'reading' of the local habitat. Sprung from a culture that had no writing, it ensured that no useful observation was ever forgotten.

'When wheat lies long in bed, it riseth with an heavy head', 'Store is no sore', 'The owner's foot doth fatt the soil', 'Winter never dies in her dam's belly', 'Many seames, many beanes', and 'the owner's eye doth feed the horse' share the quality of all the proverbs in Smyth's list that refer to husbandry. They are not equally polished, but all use rhyme, rhythm and sound to memorable effect. Such sayings were tasted as well as heard, and were quickly implanted in people's minds. But it was more than cultural rote learning. Every proverb contained the prescription that life and work demanded of people that they be sharply attuned to their environments, and that they employ fore-thought and attentive intelligence in all their relationships, above all their relationships with the land.

Sky and landscape had for what remained of an ancient agrarian culture precisely the significance of landscape in the cultures of Australian Aboriginals. A sacred site was a particular formation of natural ingredients (a pile of great rocks, or 'Abergainy Hill' on a clear morning) which sparked in an observer a shower of meanings relative to the historical culture of the observer. The land was a memory palace, so that irrevocably to alter or destroy a landform (as in a mining operation, or in enclosures) was to erase a part of the collective memory.[13] We tend to think of the 'reform of popular culture' that was taking place in Smyth's lifetime as something that meant the proscription of rough and bawdy pagan festivals and customs. In fact this 'reform', of which literacy (an instrument of abstract representation) was the principal tool, marginalised local and regional cultures. Turning land into property could be done in one or both of two ways. First it could be done by turning its people off, as occurred in some sixteenth-century enclosures and in, say, the Highland Clearances of the eighteenth and nineteenth centuries. But it could be done just as effectively by changing the physical face of the land, eradicating (in one or two generations) many of the *signs* of the old culture, and making it difficult for people to imagine a time when the land was anything other than a commodity to be converted into cash. The massive manipulations and transformations of landscape that have resulted from the spread of capitalist values destroyed human memory. Landscapes are the 'scores' or 'Songlines' of preliterate cultures.[14]

Some learned their lessons well (Smyth seems to have savoured the sayings, and seen their applications work); no doubt others remained all their lives impervious to the meanings of folk wisdom. 'See the counsel better, be it worse' cautioned attentiveness and scepticism, and undoubtedly improved with age, as people accumulated mistakes to learn from. Smyth was fond of 'Poorly sitt, richly warm', explaining it like this:

> When on an high chaire wee sitt before the fire, the legs only are warmed: but sitting on the poor low stoole, then thighs belly breast and bosome face and head take benefitt and are warmed. Howbeit wee hundreders sometimes metaphorize this proverbe into a prudent counsell, directinge our worldly affairs.

This was elders' wisdom. Using the homeliest of metaphors – the hearth – it warns against assertive pride and pretentiousness. Unself-conscious humility will be rewarded by heightened perception and wiser judgement with respect to neighbourhood affairs. A grey-haired elder sits quietly over the fire, sometimes turns around to stretch and warm his back, reserving judgement on the subject under discussion until he is confident that everything has been said and only a final judgement required. When the judgement comes it seems so obvious that the neighbours wonder why they didn't think of it before. Now only action is called for. 'Warmth' is a metaphor for wisdom taken in through 'the empire of the senses', that is to say, through sense-organs not blunted by an incessant desire to project and impose the self upon the others. To possess authority, it suggests, was to be perceived by others as an indivisible and unintrusive particle of the group. But it is not a moral injunction as such. It is utilitarian: the wisdom of the group is enhanced. But within the new self-centred value system which Smyth, the literate, bourgeois lawyer, also embodied, the 'warmth' and 'wisdom' are capital accumulated through the senses.[15]

'A man may love his house well though hee ride not upon the ridge' made the same point more boldly. Without possession of a house, patriarchal headship of a household and the means and reputation to maintain them, status and position in the neighbourhood were unthinkable. But they could not guarantee the respect of the neighbours. The status of an elder could not be claimed, only recognised by others; property was necessary, but so too was unpretentious, unselfconscious humility. Pride precedes a fall.

The culture embodied in the proverbs was not unchanging. Some hint at relatively recent changes. Smyth's explanation of the saying 'Hee is an hughy proud man, hee thinkes himself as great as my lord Berkeley' hinted at underlying political–economic changes. 'Our simple ancient honesties', he wrote, 'knewe not a greater to make comparison by, when this proverb first arose.' The clue is in the tense. Smyth was a careful observer, and no man alive knew more about the history and business affairs of the Berkeleys than he did. Unreflective deference such as this was a thing of the past; it was *ancient* honest[y]'.

From the mid-twelfth to the fifteenth centuries the FitzHardings, lords Berkeley, had ruled virtually unchallenged in the Vale of Berkeley. They – and the people of the Vale – were victims of the Wars of the Roses, and litigation over some of its consequences was only finally ended by Smyth's efforts in the 1590s, by which time the estate's difficulties had been deepened by a few years of profligate feudal display on the part of Henry, the seventeenth lord, in the 1550s. Having spent a lifetime trying to guarantee modest survival for the lordship, Smyth knew better than anyone that feudal absolutism was a thing of the past. Collectively, the parish gentry, clothiers, rich tradesmen and yeomen of the district – Smyth's class – controlled more territory and their decisions affected more people than the Berkeleys could command. In the Vale of Berkeley the Norman yoke could only any longer bear light weights.

The fulcrum of power had shifted down the social hierarchy. It was said, for example, that the Berkeleys, who had always invested heavily in the abbeys and monasteries of the region, lost no fewer than eighty knights' fees as a result of the Dissolution. The stock of old families like the Poyntz's of Acton, and newcomers like the Throckmortons, rose to take up the space. Smyth explained the local meaning of 'Hee hath offered his candle to the divell' thus:

> Old Phillimore of Cam, going in anno 1584, to present Sir Thomas Throgmorton of Tortworth with a sugar lofe, met by the way with his neighbour: who demanded whither and upon what business hee was going, answered, *To offer my candle to the divell:* which coming to the eares of Sir Thomas: At the next muster hee sent two of Phillimore's sonnes soldiers into the Low Countries, where one was slayne and the other at a deere rate redeemed his returne.

Whether or not 'old Phillimore of Cam' was still alive when Smyth wrote this down, his descendents were. 'Offering a candle to the devil' is obviously not a phrase that was unique to the Vale of Berkeley, but its meanings were invested in a local character.

Another saying, to which Smyth thought it unnecessary to append a comment, put the matter succinctly: it went, 'Follow him that beares the purse'. The wisdom of elders and the prestige of rank commanded respect, but it was taken for granted that wealth was the basis of social power, and that the market-place was its only entrance. A cluster of proverbs bears witness to the fact that this culture was heavily market-oriented. 'Money is noe foole, if a wise man hath it in his keeping', 'hee hath sold a beane and bought a peaze', 'Hee hath sold a pound and bought a penny', 'Hee hath sold Bristol and brought Bedminster', 'The more beanes the fewer for a penny', 'Bones bring meat to towne', 'Barley makes the heape, but wheat the cheape', and 'A sowe doth sooner than a cowe, bring an oxe to the plough' are all the sayings of a market-oriented culture. 'Patch by patch is yeomanly; but patch upon patch is beggarly' refers to an aspect of the worldview of primitive capital accumulation. This need not mean the Vale of Berkeley was part of a commercial society in the modern sense. It could mean it was like the equally market-centred cultures of, say, nineteenth-century Bali. However, the dominance of mass-manufacturing, little noticed in the proverbs but observable in other records, makes it something else: a harbinger of the modern world.

As Joan Thirsk has shown, Smyth's lifetime was an age of entrepreneurial 'projects for gentlemen'. 'Dip not thy finger in the morter, nor seeke thy penny in the water' advised caution with respect to capital investment. 'Lord Coke, cheife Justice, in the yeare 1613', explained Smyth, 'brought this into the hundred at the maryage of the Lady Theophila Berkeley to Sir Robert his eldest sonne.' Since then it was 'growne frequent'. Smyth thought it 'a prudent dehortation from buildings and water-workes, for my follies in both, I may justly be indited'. By 'water-workes' he meant navigation improvements such as those projected by Sir William Sandys for the North Avon between Tewkesbury and Coventry. But Smyth also invested in colonial ventures to Virginia, which at this time were equally risky.

But these were not the projects that defined his self-consciousness and world-view; in this respect they were peripheral to him. Land came first. His was a yeoman sensibility, and in unguarded moments it was the habits of a yeoman that he emphasised. 'Fower and thirty years a professional ploughman,' he once wrote of himself, 'having all that time eaten much of my bread from the labours of mine own hands.'[16]

Much attention, we have seen, was given up to signs useful in husbandry. The agricultural proverbs probably represent the oldest in the group. But another group, equally large, related to capital accumulation by means of shrewd production for the market. Elsewhere Smyth expressed grave suspicions of this commercial 'sector'. Trade led people to 'seeke meanes and busy themselves how to deceive and beguile one another, as though it were the perfection of theire trading'.[17] He contrasted it with 'tillage of the ground' which he accounted 'the best and most harmless of bodily exercises, despised of none save fooles; ever by the wisest held the most noble, as sustayning the lyfe of men.'[18] 'Planteing tillage and manuring of the ground', he wrote, were 'the only vocation wherein innocence remaineth.'[19] There is already nostalgia for a lost way of life in these words.

It was lost because 60 per cent of the people living in the Vale of Berkeley were landless manufacturing workers. Agriculture was still the most desirable way of making a living, especially on a freehold farm, because the landless wage-worker's livelihood was so insecure, the market for his commodities so vulnerable to natural and man-made blockages in supply and demand. Occasionally a proverb hints at this world of the poor. 'Hee has met with an hard winter' alluded to 'one recovered from a pinchinge sickness: or to a beast cast down with hardness of fare'. 'Pinching sickness' referred to vulnerability to disease brought on by malnutrition. Not all its victims recovered. In the 1570s for example, unemployment in the clothmaking trades caused a series of increasingly devastating mortality crises to sweep through the band of settlements under the Cotswold Edge, up through the Stroudwater Valleys, finally resulting in 1578–9, in the death of a third of the inhabitants of the borough of Cirencester.[20] Conditions were nearly as bad again in the 1620s, and the civil wars of the 1640s were also profoundly disruptive. In 1648 the Rector of Slimbridge, John Halford, wrote to the county authorities seeking permission and financial assistance 'to place out many poore children that are nowe wandringe about our streetes and begging from door to door'.[21] Famine conditions were also experienced in the 1590s, and this leaves out isolated epidemics from time to time in individual parishes, the causes of which are obscure. The four horsemen of the Apocalypse still rode through the villages and towns of the Vale of Berkeley with monotonous regularity.

'Patch by patch is yeomanly, but patch upon patch is beggarly' hinted that class – based on landownership – was worn like a badge. 'Follow him that bears the purse' could also be a beggar's proverb, referring to trails of hungry children in the wake of the 'prime men' going about their business. 'The weakest goes to the wall' referred to the fact that men, women and children on parish relief or charity had to sit against the cold stone walls of the parish church, surrounding their more comfortably-off neighbours in the centre. Mathew Hale, who had strong kinship links with the Vale of Berkeley, wrote of the poor as 'the multitudes around us'. 'Multitudes' is abstract, like 'the many-headed monster' of Shakespeare's *Coriolanus*, but the imagery is strikingly physical, evoking a siege. Did these multitudes use these proverbs too? Smyth was as detached from their culture as Aubrey was from the culture of shrewd peasant farmers that Smyth identified with. 'Need and night make the lame to trot' could refer to many incidents of the power of the propertied over their poorer neighbours. 'A poare man's tale may now be told' meant that 'when none speakes the meanest may'. Otherwise, this seems to say, the poor man should be seen and not heard.

Twenty-eight of the proverbs in Smyth's collection draw directly on local landscape as the source of their 'metaphorizing'. Several prominent local landmarks are mentioned, and eight places – Bristol, Bedminster, Wotton-under-Edge, Dursley, Berkeley, Horton, Wanswell and Abergavenny – are referred to by name in one or more of the sayings. Eight were explained by Smyth by reference to a person who was either still alive or had died within living memory. Another large group of twenty-two drew on animal imagery. Domesticated and farm animals were easily the most often named: cats, with two mentions, were female, and dogs, also with two, occur in sayings which seem to have a predominantly masculine tone. Cattle headed the frequency list with five direct mentions, followed by horses and sheep with three each; pigs are mentioned twice, followed by chickens, geese, oxen, robins, crows, bees, hornets, herring, tench and salmon with one mention each. The predominance of domesticated species indicates that this had long been a peasant culture, having long eradicated the native wild creatures. Rabbits and deer are not mentioned, and were probably not mentioned much in everyday life. Poaching was probably a discourse of nods and winks.

Twenty-one sayings offered useful advice on agricultural production: eight of these relate to tillage, five to animal husbandry, three to arboriculture and seven were of broad application to all kinds of farming. Against this, there are only two oblique references to clothmaking. Judged by weight of references, collective consciousness was shaped by the local landscape, and by the predominant forms of *agricultural* production. If there were no other documentation for this culture, we would have to conclude that it was a culture of peasants. A group of twelve cautionary proverbs relating to the cash-nexus, explicitly referring to the importance of buying, selling, accumulating capital and investing it wisely, shows that they were (or tried to be) businesslike, even 'entrepreneurial', and several scattered references to the landlords and 'owners' (as in 'the owners foot doth fatt the soil' and 'the owners eye doth feed the horse') suggest that it was a culture of independent capitalist farmers.

This industrial and commercial milieu was no recent superimposition on a predominantly peasant culture. As Smyth knew, it could be traced back in the Berkeley muniments to the century before the Black Death. The collective consiousness of the classes to which these proverbs relate was that of a peasantry, but its political economy was that of agrarian capitalism and what Marx called 'manufacturing'.

Feudal hierarchy does not seem to have weighed heavily. Only two sayings – the ones referring to the Berkeleys and to Sir Thomas Throgmorton of Tortworth – allude to it, whereas six explicitly derive social authority and hierarchy from wealth. The practical (if not prescribed) implication is that wealth was three times more important than traditional status in justifying the authority and power according to which everyday life was ordered. There was still some way to travel to the right mix for England in the 1990s, but the direction is there.

The patriarchal basis of the culture is indicated by the fact that no fewer than thirty-three of Smyth's proverbs begin with 'hee', and only one begins 'she'. The six proverbs directly relating to sex also have a masculine orientation. 'Hee that's cooled with an apple and heated with an egg, Over mee shall never spread his leg' was described by Smyth as 'a widow's wanton proverb'. 'Begis, begis, 'tis but a man's fancy' was 'a frequent speech' which was first used, according to Smyth, by a local man who explained his marriage to 'a double whore' of 'William Bower of Hurst Farm', the son of 'William Bower the Elder, the old Bayle of this hundred'. Apparently this Bower 'had each second year one or more of his maidservants with child, whom, with such portions as he bestowed upon them, hee maryed [them] either to his menservants [perhaps also sharers with him], or to his neighbours of meaner ranke'. Asked 'why hee being of an estate in wealth well able to live, [he married] one of Bower's double whores', the originator of this saying replied 'Begis, begis, 'tis but a man's fancy'.

'All the maids in Wanswell may dance in an eggshell', for Smyth, was 'a lying proverb at this day' for 'it slandereth some of [his] kindred that dwell[ed] there'. It may have originated centuries earlier, when there was a notorious convent at Wanswell, and been maintained by the philandering of the Berkeleys' retainers. Wanswell was a suburb of Berkeley. 'An head that's white to mayds brings no delite' evoked regret: Smyth commented that it was the 'state [in which] my consitutcon now stands'. He was 72 when he wrote it down. 'The back of an herring, the poll of a tench, The side of a salmon, the belly of a wench' referred to 'our choicest morsells'.

Lusty appetite for food and drink was etched into the collective consciousness in eleven proverbs, which is perhaps not surprising in view of the fact that people who 'mett with a hard winter' were not uncommon. 'Two hungry meales [made] the third a glutton' and 'hungry dogs [would eat] durty puddings'. Cold weather, as mentioned, was 'Simondshall sauce'. 'Better a bit than noe bread' needs no comment. 'A good trencherman' was said to be 'very good at a white pott'. For 'westerne men' like Smyth and his neighbours, a 'white pott' meant 'a great custard or puddinge baked in a bagg, platter, kettle or pan'. 'Hee hath eaten his rost meate first', like several other proverbs, suggested that it might be a good idea sometimes to defer the greatest pleasures 'til last. 'I must play benall with you' alluded to household hospitality. It was 'a frequent speech when the guest, immediately after meat, without any stay departeth'. The decline of household hospitality was alluded to in 'A greate housekeeper is sure of nothing save a greate Tura at his gate'. Smyth wished 'this durty proverbe had never prevailed in this hundred, having from thence banished the greater halfe of our ancient hospitality'. Hospitality of the kind Smyth had in mind had been largely replaced, by this time, by formal welfare collections for the burgeoning landless classes – 'the multitudes around us'.

Landscape, agricultural production, marketing and consumption are well represented as prominent layers or levels of cultural consciousness. The six proverbs relating to sexual desire combine earthy awareness of its urgency with hints of the need for social controls. Household imagery is common in many of the proverbs, providing the framework for the fundamental unit of socially controlled reproduction, marriage, referred to in no fewer than twenty-one of Smyth's sayings. 'A faint heart never won a faire lady' meant the same as 'hee that feares every grasse must never pisse in a meadow'. Widows were assumed to be 'wanton', or potentially so. 'My catt is a good moushunt' was 'an usuall speech when wee husbands coment on the diligence of our wives, Wee hundreders maintaining as an orthodox position that hee that sometimes flattereth not his wife cannot alwaies please her'. Such 'flattery' was implied in 'As the good man saies, so it should bee, But as the good wife saies, so it must bee'.

'Gett him a wife! Get him a wife!' originated with 'William Quinton of hill' who had a 'pestilent angry unquiet wife, much more insulting over his milde nature than Zantippe over Socrates'. As a result he 'was oft enforced to shelter himself from those stormes, to keepe his chamber'. One day he 'peep[ed] out of his chamber window' on 'hearing his neighbours complayning loudly of the unruliness of theire towne bull, whom noe mounds would keepe out from spoiling of their corne fields, the bull then bellowing before them, and they then in chasing him towards the comon pound'. Seeing all this, Quinton leaned out of his chamber and 'cryed to them, "Neighbours! Neighbours! Get him a wife! Get him a wife!" ', astonishing them with the self-evident force of his logic.

Fear of dominant wives, and of the damage that an unhappy marriage could do to a man, is a recurring theme, but wives are always regarded as appendages to their men. 'If once againe I were Jack Thomson or John Tomson, I would never after bee good man Tomson while I lived', alluding to the accepted stages in a man's life, derived from another sad story which was explained to Smyth by his predecessor as Bailiff of the Hundred, William Bower of Hurst Farm. 'This Jacke Tomson soe called till sixteen, and after John Tomson till hee married at 24 . . .'

> was the only jovyall and frolicke younge man at mery meetings and Maypoles in all Beverstone, where hee dwelled: After his maryage (humours at home not well settling between him and his wife) hee lost his mirth and began to droope, which one of his neighbours often observing, demanded upon a fitt opportunity, the cause of his bad cheare and heavy lookes: wherto, hee sighing gave this answere: Ah neighbour, if once againe I were either Jacke Tomson or John Tomson, I would never bee goodman Tomson while I lived.

'Beware, clubs are trumps' was 'a caution for the maids to bee gone for theire mistresses anger hath armed her with a cudgell: or, to the silly husband to be packinge, for his wife draweth towards her altitude.' The sheer number of proverbs relating to dominant wives indicates that the tensions between the ideal of patriarchy and the realities of everyday living were a constant source of ironic comment. Hen-pecked husbands whispered to each other 'All is well, save the worst peece is in the midst' when 'the taylor first put on [their] wives new gownes'.

'The grey mare is the better horse' was said of marriages in which 'the most master goes breechless: when the silly husband must aske his wife, whether it shall be a bargain or not'. The official line was that business was men's business. 'If two ride upon an horse one must sitt behind' could be applied to marriage in general. It also referred to Smyth's assumption that hierarchy was inherent in all social relations. 'She is tainted with an evill guise, loth to bed and lother to rise' warned against another kind of bad wife, as did 'A style toward, and a wife forward, are uneasy companions'. A man who wished to rise in the world should make sure that he held the reins in his own household. One of the ways in which this could be done was suggested in 'A woman, spaniell and a walnut tree, The more they are beaten the better they bee'. The correct priorities were suggested in 'Ritch doth prove the man who hath the hand, To bury wives, and t'have his sheepe to stand'. A succession of well-endowed young wives would extend a man's property-holding and keep his morale high.

Horse and mare metaphors were common in a very unromantic and, in this list, exclusively male-orientated view of marriage. Perhaps women whispered a different set of proverbs to each other, out of the hearing of their wife-beating husbands. The ideal arrangement was stated in two pithy proverbs: 'Faire is the weather, where cup and cover do hold together' meant 'where husband and wife agree', and 'Things ne'ere go ill where Jacke and Gill pisse in one quill' put it crudely, precisely and expressively that unspoken unity of purpose between man and wife was the fundamental secret of success in this world.

This carries us into the heart of Smyth's culture, for the 'one quill' which in ideal circumstances gave precise focus to the consciousness of both Jack and Jill was the household. The household was the core institution, the locus of production and reproduction. Smyth's culture was household-centred. It was a culture of households in a landscape. It is of some interest that none of the proverbs in Smyth's list relate to the bringing up of children.

The beauty of the learning embodied in proverbs lay in their ability to spring from the historical landscape, be digested into language by the mind, slip or roll rhythmically from the tongue, be caught by the ear, sharpening the eye, shaping the tread of the foot on the ground and the ways the hands are used. It embodied a very down-to-earth – literally 'radical' – empiricism. Proverbs were collective artefacts which bore the mark and shape of the historical–geomorphological–linguistic materials from which they were wrought. Oral cultures invested the earth with language. The historical landscape was their memory.

But before we get too carried away with nostalgia for a lost *mentalité*, we should remind ourselves that the oral/aural cosmos was as capable an agency of collective amnesia and distortion as the print media which swept it into the background of collective consciousness. Although capable of assimilating new social realities, this example clearly demonstrates that it could also suppress uncomfortable, controversial and threatening ones. Statistically, manufacturing was the dominant mode of production in the Vale of Berkeley, and had been since the early fourteenth century. We would never guess that this was so if the proverbs were all we had to go on. The distortion in this case may originate in the personal affections of John Smyth of Nibley, for whom 'tillage of the ground' was as much a sacrament as it was for the Digger leader, Gerard Winstanley; and for whom local, rural life was infinitely more desirable then journeying along the trails of progress to the towns, where deception and bad faith, in his view, were a way of life. Smyth's world-view anticipated that of the romantic critics of industrialisation by two centuries, and it can hardly be doubted that it shaped his selection from what was probably a much richer, complex and conflict-laden proverbial milieu than his collection suggests. It is hard to believe that there were only two proverbs current in the Hundred of Berkeley in which the 'metaphorizing' arose from ways of life associated with the cloth industry.

In fact, Smyth's world-view demands qualification of an influential interpretation put forward recently by Martin J. Wiener. [22] The 'English disease,' he writes, 'suspicion of material and technological development and . . . symbolic exclusion of industrialism . . . appeared in the course of the industrial revolution'. This 'exclusion' is as old as manufacturing itself, and is almost certainly linked to the fact that for centuries manufacturing and industry were thought of as a branch of social welfare the only justification for which was that it provided work and subsistence for the landless. As such it was not thought of as in any way desirable, only, unfortunately, necessary. The only alternative was a redistribution of land, which would make it possible for all households to engage in the sacramental activity of tillage and thus maintain themselves independently. This option was inconceivable to men like Smyth who had dedicated their lives to engrossing as much land as they could. Smyth recorded the proverbial canon of the middle rank of the Hundred of Berkeley.

Still, I have thought it worth running the risk of reifying a partial and perhaps slightly nostalgic source in order to draw attention to some probably universal qualities of the *mentalité* of preliterate cultures. One in particular – the 'landscape as memory palace' theme – is of some relevance in a time of acute global concern about the environmental damage that industrial capitalism has facilitated everywhere in the world. Another – perceived dimly perhaps, in a hint here and there is the original insight which justified the culture of elders, reified after the Reformation into a culture of the propertied elite or 'elect'. This insight, embodied in the proverb 'poorly sit, richly warm', but implied in the entire collection, was that social authority should derive, not from any material possession, but from long, habitual association, observation and dialogue – from proven wisdom. No amount of information or evidence or wealth could serve if that was lacking.

4

TYNDALE AND ALL HIS SECT

I wold to god the plowman wold singe a texte of the scripture at
his plowbeme, and that the wever at his lowme with this wold
drive away the tediousness of tyme. . . . If God spare me life, ere
many yeares I will cause the boy that driveth the plow to know
more of Scriptures than you do.

William Tyndale (c. 1490–1536)

With Tyndale, we have to do not with upward mobility, in the
conventional sociological sense, but rather with a highly charged
geographical and ideological mobility, a passage from Catholic
priest to Protestant, from the Gloucestershire of his successful
yeoman farmer family to London and then to Continental exile,
from obscurity to the dangerous fame of a leading heretic.

Stephen Greenblatt[1]

The old heresy and the new begin to merge together from about
the time Tyndale's Testament came into English hands.

A. G. Dickens[2]

The exact place and date of birth of William Tyndale *alias* Hutchens
is not known, but scholars agree that he was born some time in the
late 1480s or in 1490, at Slimbridge, Stinchcombe or North Nibley, all
three clothworking villages in the Vale of Berkeley.[3] Tyndale stands
with men like Langland, Chaucer and Shakespeare as a maker of
modern English. Before the fifteenth century, vernacular literature was
not revolutionary in its implications, because it was not concerned
with the great founding or legitimising texts of the civilisation. John
Wycliffe lived a century before Tyndale was born. His advocacy of
vernacular scripture prepared the way for Tyndale, and he was a
more original philosopher and theologian.[4] Wycliffe was more of an
academic than Tyndale, although both men were contemptuous of
self-seeking conformism in the academic worlds of their day. Some
of Wycliffe's followers translated Christian scripture into English.[5]

Wycliffe's originality is generally acknowledged. Until recently Tyndale scholars have seen him, and the English Reformation generally, as entirely or predominantly derivative of Luther.[6] This assumption, first propagated by his arch-enemy Sir Thomas More, is unjustified. A recent study shows that Tyndale's theology is definitively Lollard (i.e. in the tradition founded by Wycliffe) rather than Lutheran. It is a moderate, careful and thorough work and will take some refuting.[7]

Its author is only superficially familiar with Tyndale's native Vale of Berkeley, but begins with sections on 'the specific shire' and 'the specific family' into which Tyndale was born.[8] The region 'had a long history of heterodoxy' back to the time of Wycliffe.[9] Tyndale's older brother, Edward, held important stewardships of Crown lands in the district in the period spanning the Reformation.[10] In 1530 the Bishop of London, John Stokesley, in a letter to Thomas Cromwell, alleged that Edward Tyndale 'daily doth promote his kinsfolk there [i.e. the Vale of Berkeley] by the king's farms'. Stokesley was trying to obtain the tenancy of a farm for his 'old servant', and feared that if his suit failed 'my friends there would think that Edward Tyndale might do more with [Cromwell] and was preferred in [Cromwell's] favour before me'. He underlined the subversive religious implications of Edward Tyndale's powerful position as 'under-receiver of the Lordship of Berkeley' by referring to him as *brother to Tyndall the arch-heretic*. Stokesley begged Cromwell to consider 'the common reproach and boast that Tyndall and others of his sect would make upon this triumph' if Cromwell favoured him over a bishop.[11] Stokesley implied that Edward Tyndall was a 'heretic' like his brother and that the spread of his 'sect' was related to his patronage in property dealings concerning the Berkeley estates, held by the Crown since William, Marquis Berkeley bartered them for titles in the 1490s.[12]

Edward Tyndale's predecessor as Crown Steward of the Berkeley estate was Sir John Walsh, William Tyndale's first patron, protector and employer. Previous authors have not noticed the precise interconnections involved in this conjuncture. The temporary demise of the most powerful secular magnates in the region, the Berkeleys, coincided exactly with William Tyndale's lifetime. Tyndale's thought, language and sensibilities articulated the mentality and ambition of the men who moved into the social, economic and political vacuum created by the removal of the Berkeleys.[13] Edward Tyndale was also warden of the Forest of Dean, and was appointed auditor and Steward of the Tewkesbury Abbey estate at the time of the Dissolution, another position previously held by Walsh.[14] Walsh's sympathy with religious reform, and his Lollard connections, have been recognised. Edward Tyndale's will contained 'bequests of prohibited books [which] reveal his sympathy with reform'.[15]

Scholars have long made passing reference to certain aspects of his native culture, but the details have never been coordinated into a hypothesis concerning its influence on his work. He illustrates Lucien Febvre's comment that 'the ultimate achievement of the Reformation was that it gave the men of the sixteenth century what they were looking for – some confusedly, others entirely lucidly – a religion more suited to their needs, more in agreement with the changed conditions of their social life'.[16] In the case of Tyndale, we should look at what the terms 'changed conditions' mean, first and foremost, in the specific *countrey* in which he grew up.

When William Tyndale was born around 1490 his family, which had several branches in the Vale of Berkeley, was of yeoman rank. We can assume that the family had a strong educational tradition. It is also possible, given their associations with the Lancastrian cause, that they were Lollards. But this is conjecture based on indirect circumstantial evidence.

The Tyndales were only one family or 'kin-coalition' of a substantial class of families like them in the Vale of Berkeley. There were families like them and the Trotmans in every English district in the fifteenth and sixteenth centuries. The yeomanry was not a revolutionary ingredient in itself. What made the yeomanry in the Vale of Berkeley a revolutionary class-fragment was the local cloth industry. Every family of yeoman rank in the Vale of Berkeley (there were perhaps thirty families or 'kin-coalitions' spread across perhaps 150 households) was involved in some way in the cloth industry. Senior branches were yeoman-clothiers and merchants (Tyndale's younger brother, John, was a cloth merchant); junior branches were master-craftsmen.[17] Their businesses centred on their households, which were also enclosed freehold or copyhold farms. Clothmaking and merchandising, and farming, were integrated dimensions of the activities of the yeoman households of the Vale of Berkeley, and in all probability they had been since the early fourteenth century.

The advantage of involvement in the cloth industry was that it generated a cash income. Most yeoman-farmers in the Vale had small sheep-flocks. Doubtless this provided the wool from which yarn was prepared in the household and woven into a cloth or two each year. Small-scale activity like this was a starting-point. The more successful men continued to live on their farms, but employed servants, apprentices, sons, daughters and other relatives to do the farm-work and perform the hands-on craftwork. The more successful they were, the more time they had to spend away from home buying wool for distribution to several, in some cases hundreds, of households and travelling to London to sell the finished cloth. Successful involvement in clothmaking had two important consequences. Firstly, it generated wealth that could be used to purchase more land, thus increasing the local power of the household. Secondly, it entailed travel, which broadens perspectives. For these two reasons, the yeomanry of the Vale of Berkeley was a 'rising' *and* 'expansive' class in the sixteenth century.

This social movement, premised on local clothmaking, did constitute a possible challenge to the social order. It meant that the local yeomanry accumulated estates that in the past would have been associated with men of esquire or even knightly status. And to compound this, involvement in the industry as a clothier or merchant involved the acquisition of regional and national horizons. Whilst the yeomanry was expected to govern in the localities, it had no constitutional authority beyond the locality. As freeholders yeomen could vote in parliamentary elections, but it was expected that they would invariably defer to their superiors, the lords. This ceased to be a reasonable expectation in the Vale of Berkeley in proportion to the declining prestige of the lords Berkeley. If they could not find it in themselves to defer to the Berkeleys, they were not going to defer to anyone else, short of the monarch.

Tyndale's lifetime coincided with a dramatic decline in the local influence of the Berkeleys, whose estate had been transferred to the Crown. The removal of the Berkeleys enhanced the status of local gentry families like the Throckmortons, Poyntz's and Walsh's and Tracys, with whom the Tyndales enjoyed good relations. Although the Berkeleys were not, on the whole, unpopular lords, their removal was bound to favour a more 'oligarchic' social structure in the district, involving networking of one kind or another between the rich yeoman-clothier families like the Tyndales and their minor-gentry neighbours. Edward Tyndale's Crown appointments gave him a good deal of patronage. His family encompassed several households in the Vale, and they were connected by frequent association and in some cases marriage to other kin-coalitions like the Trotmans, the subject of a later chapter. The middle rank of the Vale of Berkeley was a kin-coalition, densely interconnected as a result of having shared a particular habitat and status for several generations.

Scholars have often noted that clothmaking and heresy went together,[18] but the precise nature of the nexus remains largely unexplored and unexplained. In order to explore it more fully it will help to understand what clothmaking entailed, in practical terms, and then to consider how far Tyndale's 'heresy' gave it a coherent intellectual and spiritual framework. Let us first consider the background, career and thought of William Tyndale in a little more detail.

The Tyndale brothers were almost certainly educated at Wotton-under-Edge Grammar School, founded in 1384 by Lady Katherine

Berkeley.[19] There is a whiff of heresy about the Berkeley muniments at the time when Lady Katherine founded the school. Her chaplain at Berkeley Castle was John Trevisa, who transcribed his own translations from *Revelations* on to the ceiling of the castle chapel.[20] These translations were from Latin into Norman-French, a hint that this was still the vernacular of his masters, as distinct from that of the local population, which would have been a dialect of 'middle English' similar to that of Chaucer. However, Trevisa also wrote one of three surviving contemporary versions of *Piers Plowman*, which is set in the Vale of Berkeley and in the Malvern Hills, and 'celebrates the ordinary man, seeking goodness through humility, honest endeavour, and obedience to God'.[21]

'The history of Wycliffism in the area reaches back to Wycliffe himself when he met the parliament at Gloucester in 1378. The record indicates that he preached at Westbury and Bristol.'[22] Scholars have assumed that Lollardy was a strong undercurrent in the clothworking communities of central Gloucestershire throughout the fifteenth century, though the evidence is circumstantial.[23] The historian of the Reformation in Gloucestershire writes that 'the majority of those burned in Mary's reign were clothworkers and their ideas were thoroughly Wycliffite . . . The areas of dissent were the Cotswold textile area and the Forest of Dean.'[24] Smeeton's thesis is that Tyndale's theology and ideas were thoroughly Wycliffite.[25] The line clothmaking–Lollardy–Protestantism–Puritanism–Sectarianism–nonconformity is a clear theme in the history of the Vale of Berkeley.[26] 'Puritanism spread rapidly . . . among the shopkeepers, clothiers, tradesmen and craftsmen of the [clothmaking] districts.'[27]

Tyndale returned from Oxford in 1514 to take up a position as household chaplain to Sir John Walsh at Chipping Sodbury. Walsh had connections in the cloth trade.[28] Walsh and other local gentry like the Poyntz's protected Tyndale when John Bell, Vicar-General of the pre-Reformation diocese of Worcester began 'collecting evidence of heresy against him'.[29] *When I came before the Chancellor*, wrote Tyndale, *he reviled me, and rated me as though I had been a dog*.[30] As a result he left for London to seek the patronage of Bishop Tunstall. Tunstall showed no interest in becoming his patron, and instead Tyndale found refuge in the household of a Lollard cloth merchant whose name suggests that his family, like that of Tyndale, hailed from 'the borders of Wales': Humphrey Monmouth.[31]

Monmouth 'was a member of London's heretical underworld; he was known in Lollard circles, though his continental connections had brought him into contact with Lutheranism'.[32] In 1529 another man whose name suggests a Gloucestershire – and Tyndale – connection, John Tewkesbury, was arrested along with Tyndale's younger brother, both cloth merchants, for distributing Tyndale's translations. John Tyndale got off but Tewkesbury was burned, on Tunstall's authority, for 'heretical depravity'.[33] From start to finish, Tyndale's career was an epitome of the Vale of Berkeley/clothmaking/Lollardy/Protestantism nexus. Simon Fish of Bristol was the author of *The Supplication of Beggars*, a vitriolic polemic against clerisy and clerics which was coupled with Tyndale's *Parable of Wicked Mammon* as the most dangerous anticlerical work in England in the 1530s, when the writings of both men were prohibited by Tunstall.[34] When Fish died in 1530 his widow married James Baynham of Westbury on Severn, just across the Severn from Slimbridge. Baynham was burned by More for heterodoxy four years before Tyndale was strangled and burned at Vilvorden. Baynham died 'with Tyndale's New Testament in his hand in English, and *The Obedience of a Christian Man* in his bosom'.[35] It is difficult to believe that this regional nexus was just coincidence.

The expression 'Sure as God's in Gloucestershire' was proverbial throughout England from medieval times to the seventeenth century, when Fuller described it as 'no more fit to be used than a toad is wholesome to be eaten'. He explained it with reference to the fact that there were 'more and richer mitred abbeys [in Gloucestershire] than in any two shires in England'.[36] But proverbs change their meanings according to changed circumstances. In view of the litany of Gloucestershire interconnections in the Tyndale network (which linked the Vale of Berkeley with Bristol, London and Antwerp) this needs qualification. When the old religion was killed off in the sixteenth century, a new one rose to take its place. Tyndale was its prophet. His class and neighbours were its people.

Tyndale's native district was prematurely active on the reform front. Within a few months of the Reformation, in 1540, John Didson, Vicar of Coaley, a clothworking village near Slimbridge and an outlier of the Dursley–Cam cluster, was cited to appear at Worcester Diocesan Court for heretical preaching. 'He stated that the passion of Christ alone takes away our sins, past present and future; that faith alone was sufficient for salvation; and that penance is nothing else than sorrow for sins past and to amend the future life.' The reference is not clear enough to ascribe the theology with precision. It is compatible with Luther (who stressed redemption by faith alone) or Tyndale (who gave primacy to faith but, like the Lollards, stressed that in practice faith and works were inseparably related). Didson was also accused of owning and lending out books by Luther and Zwingli. It goes without saying that he would have known Tyndale's work. There would have been Tyndale's relatives in his congregation. Coverdale's adaptation of Tyndale's translations had been printed and distributed to every parish church in the kingdom four years earlier.[37]

At the same meeting of the Court, John Andrews, Vicar of Wotton-under-Edge, was accused of refusing 'to hear confessions and give absolution . . . he described the *autemps salve regum* and *et tuam sub protectionem* as idolatory and superstition, and . . . had admitted an unlicensed preacher'. Both he and Didson were suspended.[38] Dursley was an archetypal Tudor Puritan town.[39] Elite and populist streams flowed into the Reformation conjuncture in the Vale of Berkeley, but the popular stream was indigenous and by far the more radical. Cloth and heresy went together. The connections are exemplified by the network along which Tyndale's career ran. 'Protestantism' was indigenous to the Vale of Berkeley, its roots in the history and social structure of the *countrey* and the tentacles – the 'alternative social *bloc*' – which radiated out from it.

Tyndale's theology, embodied in his translation of certain key terms, was very much that of the yeoman households of the Vale of Berkeley. Quentin Skinner regards Tyndale's rendering of the scriptural Greek *ecclesia* (previously 'church') as 'congregation', and *presbyteros* ('priest') as at first 'Senyour' and then 'Elder', as events of signficance in the foundations of modern political thought.[40] Sir Thomas More recognised the socially explosive implications at the time. 'For *prestys* whersoever he speketh of the prestes of Crystes chyrche,' he wrote, Tyndale 'never calleth them prestys but always senyours . . . The chyrche he calleth alway the congregaycon and charitie he calleth alway love' – down-to-earth words that More saw, rightly, as radical subversions of the scriptural foundations of the Church as constituted since the fourth century. 'Nowe do these names in our englyshe tonge neyther express the thynges that be meant by them.' In fact they meant precisely what Tyndale intended them to mean, as More recognised: 'and also there appeareth (the circumstances well consydered) that he hath a mischievous mynde in the chaunge . . . For Tyndale is not angry wyth the worde but bycause of the mater.'[41] Tyndale seems to have read this carefully. Henceforth he changed *senyour* to *elder*.

These words, today, have strong religious connotations, largely because they were appropriated by the Presbyterians and Congregationalists later in the sixteenth century. Tyndale, however, took it as his brief to translate the scriptures into the everyday language of ordinary people of the middle rank. The words were secular words. While he wanted to dissolve the institutional framework of the Church as it existed in his own day, in no way did he wish to replace it with another kind of institution or organisation. He was against institutional religion. He wanted to bring religion into harmony with the secular culture, thus making it both meaningful to and an integral part of every detail of the everyday lives of ordinary people. If religion was meaningful, he thought, it was because it pervaded the quotidian.

When Tyndale wrote of rendering scripture into the language of 'plow-boys' and 'wevers', he literally pictured the ploughboys and weavers of his own Vale of Berkeley. And it was their language that he tried to make the medium of his vernacular translations.[42]

Tyndale wanted to sacralise secular culture by secularising religion. Much is often made of the passages of his book *The Obedience of a Christian Man* in which he addresses the fraught question of how a true Christian, in his sense, should behave with respect to the secular authorities (with regard to the clerical authorities he had nothing but contempt, dismissing their legitimacy out of hand, as More and Tunstall immediately and unavoidably recognised). In that book he writes, for example, that children are to be regarded as the 'goods and possessions' of their parents. Husbands are to command wives. Servants are to be with respect to their masters 'as his ox or his horse'. This was simply the conventional wisdom of the yeomanry of his native district.[43] His yeoman-clothier brothers and neighbours were the 'elders' who ruled the 'congregation' in the sense of the gathered people of the neighbourhood. This much was conventional. His next most powerful concern, after 'elders' and 'congregations', is the authority of the king. 'God hath made the king in every realm over all, and over him there is no judge.' His brother, the Steward of the Crown's estates in Gloucestershire, would have had no difficulty at all with this. Esquires, knights and barons, the intermediary ranks of the social order, are absorbed into the congregation of the people under the king. 'If a subject sins,' he continued, 'he must be reserved unto the judgement, wrath and vengeance of the king.'[44] The social hierarchy Tyndale had in mind was very simple: it consisted of congregations, elders and the physically distant authority of the king. It was a blue-print of the vision for which Gloucestershire's middle rank was prepared to take up arms to defend in 1643.[45] According to legend, Henry VIII admired Tyndale's book. Ann Boleyn gave him a copy to read, and he was impressed. 'This,' he said, 'is a book for me and all kings to read!'[46] It is superficially compatible with the Tudor emphasis on reducing the social authority of the intermediary ranks of the feudal hierarchy. But, as Tyndale well knew, the social authority of kings was a very distant thing in places like the Vale of Berkeley. In practice it came down to the authority of men like himself, his brothers and his neighbours: the 'elders' of the 'congregation'.

But questions of civil polity were secondary issues, tangential extrapolations from Tyndale's individual-centred theocracy. Readers of Tyndale's writing will agree with Stephen Greenblatt, who observes that his theology is not one of 'toleration and mildness' with regard to external authorities of any kind, even that of kings. He preached 'what one might call a violent obedience'. The yeomanry was not deferential.

91

At its heart, his theology is 'addressed to a soul conceived as the domain of power, the point at which all the lines of force in the universe converge'.[47] Like Luther, he taught that without faith there was no true religion. But unlike Luther, and like Wycliffe and the Lollards before him, he always stressed that in practice faith and works were inseparable. A person who believed that by his life and death Jesus had redeemed humanity would read scripture and from it learn how to live a properly Christian life. Possessing faith and the power to read, he would *inevitably* behave as a true Christian would. If he did not, he did not have faith.[48] So although he focused on the inner act of believing, he did not separate the inner act from the outward behaviour. This brought his theology (and that of the Lollards before him) into line with the conventional view of the English neighbourhood, that an 'elder' was a person who had earned the title by helping and advising his neighbours in thoroughly practical ways. He earned it by behaving and living like an elder.

This was a theology to appeal to men of the middle rank everywhere in England. It was revolutionary because it ignored the prescribed ecclesiastical *and secular* hierarchies inherited from the past, while providing theological legitimacy to a system based on elders, congregations and the king, who was a kind of super-elder. It was a class theology, and in practice it was meritocratic. It had built-in safeguards, since property was not the only requirement for an elder. Property was necessary but not sufficient. An elder had to be recognised as such by the neighbourhood. In a thinly populated kingdom and commonwealth, Tyndale's world was a federation of associational communities, slowly being 'networked' into a modern nation by extra-local connections like those which Tyndale's career explored. Property had to be used for the benefit of the neighbourhood as well as its owner, e.g. by providing work for less favoured neighbours. A clothier-elder would tramp off out into the wider world to buy wool which the local poor could convert into cloth; he would then tramp off up to London to sell it. Disputes could arise as to how much of the money all this yielded was kept by the elder, and how much was distributed to the poor. Tyndale wrote in the early days, and projected an ideal. In the three centuries after his death the populations of the towns and villages of his *countrey* burgeoned. The landless proportion increased most. The yeoman-clothiers he pictured in his mind when he wrote the words 'senyour' and 'elder' were to become increasingly detached in all but sentiment from the everyday lives of the bulk of the ordinary people of their *countrey*.

Most writers on the subject tend to assume an affinity between industry and religious radicalism. Of the Lollards, A. G. Dickens writes that 'all save a few belonged to the common people – weavers, wheelwrights, smiths, carpenters, shoemakers, tailors and other tradesmen'. 'Heretical ideas circulated freely about the countryside, in the cities and ports, in the little weaving towns.'[49] We should not assume, however, that 'common people' refers to a homogeneous mass. The terms 'weavers, wheelwrights, smiths, carpenters etc.' refer to men of variable rank, status and wealth. In the Vale of Berkeley, men who practised these trades were sometimes freeholding yeomen with quite considerable holdings. From the point of view of bishops and lords they were 'common', but from the point of view of their poorer neighbours, themselves very often plying the same trades, they were men of authority – 'elders', churchwardens, employers, clothiers, manorial officials. The view from above and afar compressed distinctions that were self-evident in the localities, and converted religious ideas that derived from practical *countrey* common sense' into mysterious and shocking heresies.

The question *why* clothworking and heresy tended to be associated is rarely addressed. Tyndale's origins and career suggest an explanation. Industry developed in *countreys* where a large proportion of the population was landless, and where the type of agriculture – wood–pasture – could not sustain large numbers of agricultural labourers. Industry began as 'make-work' schemes, and for centuries its primary justification was not that it produced wealth for individuals and the kingdom, but that it provided work for the landless poor. Once established, an industry like clothmaking institutionalised the landless component, which tended to grow fastest when general population growth was under way, as in the century after 1450. The socialisation of landless people entails very different problems from that of a peasantry. Dependent though they were on the capital of their wealthier neighbours for raw materials, market opportunities and even, increasingly as time went on, their tools of trade, artisan households necessarily operated according to internalised rather than external disciplines. Being landless meant also that they were masterless men and women. The invariable tendency of industrial towns and villages to grow in population itself generated a need for innovative socialisation procedures. Industry was itself such a procedure in its origins. Quantity aside, the population to be socialised was *qualitatively* different. The individual-centredness of Protestantism met this need. Possession of a pure conscience became more important than the possession of land.

Protestantism was not merely an inward-looking heresy. It was evangelical and it spread. Like the clothworkers, clothiers and cloth merchants, it travelled. Again we do not need to look far beyond the necessities of large-scale cloth production to explain why this was the case. Travel does broaden the mind, at least in the sense that it generates new and often unfamiliar information for the mind to process and come to terms with. The journeyman-clothworker, the cloth-ier and the carrier very often travelled alone, removed from the familiar companionship of their native districts. Dickens cites the illustrative case of 'William Bull, a young clothworker from Dewsbury, who went off to ply his craft in Suffolk, and returned in 1543 with violent, if now old fashioned views on holy water, extreme unction and the confessional'.[50] The lonely road generated the voice within.

Protestantism was a movement from below in the sense that it derived its energy from economic, social and demographic circum-stances that accompanied the rise of industry. The case of the Vale of Berkeley also illustrates the fact that for Protestantism to emerge as a genuine alternative world-view on the scale of entire regions and districts, the old regime had also to commit suicide. The ways in which this was done no doubt varied from district to district. The vagaries of the Berkeley family were peculiar to this particular district, but they anticipated the Henrician Dissolution, which was a national phenomenon, albeit one which stimulated different responses in differ-ent *countreys*. The presence of the cloth industry, and the degree to which commerce had impregnated the pores of Gloucestershire society generally, ensured that here, at least, there would be nothing resem-bling the Pilgrimage of Grace. Tyndale and all his sect saw to that.

Tyndale spoke with a plebeian, accented, vernacular voice, and he spoke for the localities of early sixteenth-century England where the work went on. More specifically, he wrote down, and caused to have printed and distributed, translations of scriptural Greek and Latin into English as spoken by his family and friends in the Vale of Berkeley, where he grew up. This was 'middle English' in many senses of the term. John Smyth of Nibley likened the spoken dialect of the Vale to the language of Chaucer and Langland.[51] These were the sources of vernacular literature. But to describe him as plebeian is not to say that he came from the lowest ranks. His class was where plebeian met, and negotiated with, genteel and aristocratic. It governed in the localit-ies, and it was well connected in the towns and cities, but it had no clearly constituted role beyond its local enclaves.

The revolution that took place in England between 1500 and 1800 was a revolution in the forms and figurations of civilisation in general. William Tyndale is a figure of national importance. English national historiography implies the historical construction of the modern nation-state, which is another theme here. It was premised on a degree of market unification, a tangible process that can be measured by the 'trails of progress' radiating out from the households of the middle rank of *countreys* like the Vale of Berkeley. Nationalism as a lucid focus of personal and group identity was a developing nexus of multivalent processes. Of all these processes the most important was the development of the *experience* of 'belonging' to a particular territory and sharing much in common with significant sections of its population. This experience entailed routine travel, such that *countrey*-consciousness was weakened at the expense of expanding geopolitical contexts. One's *countrey* was *seen* to be but one of many which together constituted not just an ideal condition or 'state', but a real, tangible country in the modern sense. The point is of more than antiquarian interest. By understanding how modern nation-states came to be incorporated in the collective mentality of their subjects, we can also begin to grasp how in the modern world, where the better-off classes, through travel and a certain familiarity with languages other than their own, are beginning to develop an international, or 'one world' mentality. From this emergent perspective, too, we can appreciate that regions, geopolitical conventions, are always cultural–historical constructs.

William Tyndale wrote in the language of his kin and friends in the Vale of Berkeley. Vernacularisation, for him, was a many-edged weapon in a struggle against institutionalised forms of religion. His anticlericalism was related to a broader nationalist vision. He blamed the Roman Church for the Norman Conquest, writing that 'neither should duke William have been able to conquer this land at that time, except the spirituality had wrought on his side'. In his lifetime it was becoming safer to criticise the Church than it had been since Wycliffe's days. Criticism of the state was another matter. There an author had to be especially careful, which was not always Tyndale's way. A reader who believed in the legend of the Norman yoke, and who believed, as many did, that for all their reforms and encouragement of new men the Tudors remained the direct heirs of the Norman–Angevin framework, would have been in no doubt what Tyndale's apparently bland condemnation of the Norman Conquest entailed: 'What blood did that conquest cost England,' he wrote, 'through which almost all the lords of the English blood were slain, and the Normans became rulers, and all the laws were changed into French!'[52]

Vernacularisation, for Tyndale, was an instrument by which the English would recover their indigenous roots and qualities, for so long suppressed by alien ruling castes and their institutions. It entailed recovery of terrain taken from his people by conquest. It would mean, in practice, a re-appropriation of territory. When he wrote, and for some time to come, genealogical connections with a Norman–Angevin line were still, in theory, the essence of membership of the ruling class. The legend of the Norman yoke had its counterpart in that of Norman superiority. No matter that everyone knew the lines were being transgressed all the time: the structure of the Old Regime rested on one final myth, and depended on its acceptance, more or less, by the population at large. In the century which began with Tyndale and ended with Shakespeare, English aboriginal elders overthrew the myth of the inherent superiority of the conquerors. It had taken them five centuries.[53]

William Tyndale's radicalism is hardly in doubt. He envisaged a radically simplified social polity based on the authority of local elders. It is true that he couched it in an exclusively religious framework, but only because everyday life, for him, was suffused with the benign influence of the deity, which only stubborn evil could deny and banish. In this he abandoned the dogma of the middle ages and sought to bring religion into life. He read the scriptures, not in the light of scholastic debates that had meaning only to scholars, but in the light of his own experience. The quality of his mind and faith took him away from his native Vale, to Oxford, to London, and then to a martyr's death at Vilvorden in modern Belgium. But his family and the culture of the Vale communities shaped him first, gave his thought its characteristic structures and expressions. They, before everything, were the people for whom he wrote.

5

NEIGHBOURHOOD TO NATION
The Trotmans: A middle-rank
kin-coalition, 1512–1712

For the State and eminency of the yeomanry, this hundred is allowed the preheminence before any of the other thirty hundreds of the county . . .

John Smyth[1]

It is only in the context of the house or the household that the family may be placed within the scope of a quantitatively defined social group. The network of family connections differs for each person concerned and cannot be statistically defined.

Michael Mitterauer and Reinhard Sieder[2]

Kin relations . . . are the product of social synchronization achieved in the course of socialization. The private relation of trust may thus be translated into co-operation in the public realm.

Eric R. Wolf[3]

Not many years after Tyndale's death, a Cam clothier set off for London with an unusual and subversive cargo. The story is told in Smyth's description of the tenurial history of the village. 'The ancient dedication of this Church of Cam', he wrote:

> was to St. George, accompted the tutelary Saint thereof, whose great picture artificially cut in wood and standing at the porch of the Church was from thence in the raigne of kinge Edward the sixt[h], caryed to Colbrooke in a Clothier's waine 15 myles from London, in his travell with his cloth thither towords Blackwell Hall; whose settlement begate the great Comon Inne called the George in Coldbrook to this day, 1639.[4]

A local clothier expropriates a sacred medieval icon ('tutelary Saint'), throws it into his wain, and sees that it is converted into the most profane of signs outside a 'Comon Inne' on the road from Gloucestershire to London. The episode is a symbol for the entire conjuncture that nurtured Protestantism in the Vale of Berkeley: the clothier, his travels, his Protestant iconoclasm, his routine connections with London, and, not least, his determined confidence, grim sense of irony and firmness of purpose. It is hard to imagine a more matter-of-fact rejection of the old order.

One of the candidates for this theatrical piece of iconoclasm – Smyth does not give his name – is Thomas Trotman, clothier or 'cloathman' of Cam.[5] A prosperous clothier living at Cam in the 1540s and 1550s, his family had connections with the Tyndales. In 1543 he and his son, 'John the Elder', witnessed the will of Alice Tyndale of Melksham Court, Stinchcombe.[6] Melksham Court was 'a big manor house'.[7] It had been associated with the Tyndale family since the late fourteenth century, when it was called 'Milkeshames'. William Tyndale inherited a half-share in it on the death of his father in 1506.[8] Stinchcombe was a chapelry of the parish of Cam, and it is possible, given his witnessing of Alice Tyndale's will, that Thomas Trotman was churchwarden of the parish at the time. The relevant parish records have not survived for the sixteenth century, but in the earliest surviving records, dating from 1600, Trotmans appear as churchwardens of this Puritan parish in 1600, 1604, 1610, 1612, 1613, 1618, 1621, 1622, 1623, 1625, 1635 and 1639.[9] They were the kind of men Tyndale had in mind when he used the term 'Elder': 'The churchwardens', he wrote in *The Practice of Prelates*, 'ought to take the benefices into their hands in the name of the parishens, and to deliver the preachers of God's word their dwelling and present a sufficient living, and divide the rest among the poor people.'[10]

Thomas Trotman was an exact contemporary of William Tyndale and his brothers. He was from a yeoman family like the Tyndales and may also have gone to Wotton-under-Edge Grammar School. His son, 'Richard the Elder', married Edward Tyndale's daughter, Katherine, and through her the Tyndale estates in the Vale of Berkeley eventually passed to the Trotmans.[11] The population of the Hundred of Berkeley in 1551, shortly after Edward Tyndale's death, and seven years before Thomas Trotman and his wife, Agnes (daughter of another Cam clothier, William Harding), died in the influenza epidemic of 1557–8, was a little over 7,000 souls, fewer than 2,000 households situated in thirteen parishes. Yeomen married their sons and daughters to the daughters and sons of other men of the middle rank. They comprised about 20 per cent of local households in the sixteenth century.[12] The Trotmans and Tyndales were leading yeoman families in a *countrey*-based kin-coalition consisting of perhaps 200 households. Marriage between the daughter of the Steward of the Crown estates and the son of a wealthy clothier was not in the least surprising. It joined two of the most powerful middle-rank families in the Vale.

The Trotman take-off began in the early sixteenth century. Thomas

Trotman was active in the cloth trade from the later years of Henry VIII until just before Elizabeth came to the throne. His father, Henry Trotman, was a clothier from a family settled in the Vale of Berkeley since the thirteenth century, perhaps much earlier. John Smyth of Nibley traced the family to 'the time of Edward II', when a Richard Troteman was named in the Berkeley estate records as a tenant of Maurice, lord Berkeley. This was the period which saw the rise of a local cloth industry with an elaborate division of labour. Sixty years later a John Troteman held land at Stancombe in the parish of Stinch-combe. Stancombe is a 15-minute walk across Stinchcombe Hill from the 'praty clothing town' of Dursley, as Leland described it in the 1520s. The reference means little in itself. He could have been a substantial peasant with small blocks of land and pasture in other manors. It is also possible, given the Germanic name, that the Trot-mans were Flemish or German clothiers encouraged to settle in the Vale to help organise the infant cloth industry there, the incentive being an offer of land. Another of the great Vale clothing families of the sixteenth century, the Webbs, definitely came over as immigrants in the early fourteenth century. In 1386 a 'Henry Trouthyman' was arrested for being in possession of grain stolen from a Severn barge. In this time of social crisis, he could have been a fourteenth-century moral economist, or a receiver of stolen goods. There are many possibi-lites, and not much can be said except that the Trotmans had lived in the Vale for two centuries before, according to legend, the Tyndales came there during the Wars of the Roses.[13]

When Henry Tudor defeated Richard III at Bosworth Field, around the time when Tyndale was born, one Elias Trotman was feoffee of the Church House at Dursley, a vestryman and, in all probability, a clothier. Elias's son or nephew, Henry, purchased the watermill and lands in the parish of Cam from a man named Mabson, in 1512.[14] Henry is not specifically described as a clothier, but his son Thomas was his sole heir and inherited the mill and his lands, and he was described in his will (dated 1558) as 'clothyer'. The mill remained in the family for over a century, and is usually called a fulling mill in later references.[15]

Henry Trotman arranged for his son, Thomas, to marry the daughter of another leading clothier family of Cam, the Hardings, and the estate Thomas accumulated from his earnings in the trade formed the basis from which the branches descended from two of his sons became gentry. Thomas Trotman was an associate of the Tyndale family and his second son, Richard, married Katherine, the daughter of Edward Tyndale. Katherine was co-heiress with her brother, Thomas Tyndale, to Eastwood Park, a property acquired by their father at Moreton, near Thornbury. Thomas Tyndale 'of Eastwood, gentilman . . . died at Master Pennes house in London, 28 April 1571' and his brother-in-law Richard Trotman was one of his executors.[16] Richard's eldest son, Edward, was then 26, and about to marry Anne Watts, the daughter of a Puritan clothier from Stroud. Eastwood Park became his inheritance, although it was not formally passed to him until his mother's death in 1602.[17] A passing reference in the *Berkeley Manuscripts*, almost certainly relating to the 1590s suggests that Edward Trotman was now one of the 'prime men' in the Vale ('with whom', the proverb stated, 'all will agree'): 'Mr [John] Smyth, Mr Chester and Mr Edward Trotman dined together with Mr Trotman, and walked out after dinner in Eastwood Park.'[18]

The three generations following Henry's purchase of the fulling mill in 1512, then, made good progress. Thomas inherited 'all his [father's] mesys, lands, tenements, mylls, rents &c', and when he died in 1558 the patrimony was bequeathed intact to his eldest son 'John the Elder', whose will describes him as a 'cloathman'. This term signified that he was a merchant, like William Tyndale's younger brother. John the Elder was the eldest of three sons. The second-eldest, 'Richard the Elder', inherited 'two messuages with their appurtenances called Long-fords' in the parish of Cam, 'and one other messuage and halfe a yardland in Whetenhurst', a neighbouring parish: 180 acres of prime pasture and arable land, more a parish gentleman's inheritance than that of a yeoman. Richard the Elder was already in possession of a house called Pull Court and 'some lands in Bushley, Worcestershire,' acquired on his marriage to Edward Tyndale's daughter, Katherine.[19]

The Pull Court estate was leased to Edward Tyndale in 1531 by the Abbot of Tewkesbury, and when he became auditor and Steward of the Abbey estates after its dissolution he must have taken steps to obtain a more secure tenure to it.[20] Some strands of the Tyndale–Trotman connection are obscure. The Trotman family has been well researched, the Tyndales less so. Smyth of Nibley mentions that in 1635 the Tyndale family records were kept in a chest in the steeple of Stinchcombe chapel, and that 'he could never obtain [permission] to see them'.[21] Smyth was a determined and single-minded man. His silence suggests that there may be something in the allegation by John Stokesley, Bishop of London, that 'Edward Tyndale, brother to Tynd-ale the arch-heretic and under-receiver of the lordship of Berkeley . . . may and doth daily promote his kinsfolk there to the king's farms'.[22] Stokesley knew the Tyndales – and the Vale of Berkeley – well, though not as well as the Tyndales and Trotmans knew each other and their *countrey*. He was Rector of Slimbridge, the living of which was in the hands of Magdelen College, Oxford, from 1506 until his elevation to the bishopric in 1530.[23]

Thomas Trotman's third son, also called John, was left in possession of a substantial clothing business.[24] All three of Thomas Trotman's sons were described in their wills as 'the Elder of Cam'.

John the Elder's clothing business flourished, and out of the profits he purchased yeoman freeholds at Slimbridge, Thornbury, Bradstone and Berkeley, and several fields spread across these and his own parish of Cam. Like his father, he increased his estate by purchasing land from gentry landowners like the Berkeleys (lord Henry was chronically short of money to finance his high living and gambling), Lord Wentworth, Sir Thomas Throgmorton and Sir John Thinne.[25] His brothers Richard and John witnessed his will, dated 24 July 1577, but were not beneficiaries. They were substantial householders in their own right, and would in their turn see to their own branches of the family. John the Elder left several cash bequests, including one of £200 to his clothier son, William, who also inherited 'certain implements that [his father] left with son Nicholas at Bredstone', some 'cups that Youghan Skill gave [him]' and 'two dozen of silver spoons'. Thirty years later William Trotman was one of the richest clothiers in the region. He attended the musters of 1608 at Rodborough, in the Stroudwater Valleys, accompanied by six young servants.[26] All four of John the Clothier's sons received this gift of silver spoons, proverbial reminders of the starting-point of their good fortune.

Bequests of 20 shillings each to the poor of Cam and Slimbridge, and 40 shillings each to be distributed at the market towns of Dursley and Berkeley, suggest that these were the places where he 'set the poor on work' by providing them with wool to work up into cloth. The business of setting the poor on work was a religious duty in the Vale of Berkeley, thought to be a more certain means of redemption than giving alms without conditions. The piety of the local clothiers was legendary, although not perhaps as legendary as their bargaining, not considered entirely honourable.[27] He had an interest in the local road network, and left 5 marks 'to the mending of the Heiway between Lydegreen and Lawrinch Bridge'. This too would give work to poor labourers and enable their labour to be of service to the community.

His brother Richard was born about 1520, when his grandfather Henry, was still alive. When Thomas Trotman and his wife died within a month of each other in 1557, Richard inherited 'Longford's', purchased from another Cam clothier, Richard Brayne, in 1539. It was a substantial yeoman estate consisting of three houses and associated farm buildings, the nuclei of 180 acres of prime meadow and pasture at Cam and the neighbouring parish of Wheatenhurst. Richard immediately 'built a faire house' on the land, consolidating the three farms into one. But it turned out that Richard Brayne had not paid the previous owners the full amount owing on it when he, in turn, sold it to Richard's father. A legal wrangle between Richard and the previous owners was not finally settled until 1579, when he paid them off and established the estate 'to the use of Richard Trotman and his heires'.[28] Richard died 'sick[l]y in body' at Cam in 1592, having lived the life of a prosperous yeoman farmer all his life.

Richard Trotman the Elder, Yeoman of Cam (the full title, one senses, was carried proudly), inherited a very substantial yeoman estate, purchased out of the profits of his father's clothing business, and by judicious marriage and industriousness was able to leave a *countrey* gentleman's. His will has fewer touches of conspicuous consumption than that of his older brother, John the 'cloathman'. He left fewer and smaller cash bequests than either of his clothier brothers. Richard and Katherine Trotman ran a very substantial mixed-farming enterprise. His one charitable bequest, of 20 shillings, was to the poor of his home parish. He kept a plough-team of four oxen, bred beef and dairy cattle and had his own bull – most of the farmers in the Vale depended on a collectively owned beast called the 'town bull'. He kept 'store pigs' and left 'half the bacon in [his] house' to his son Griffith, to whom he had already passed a yeoman farm at Breadstone, another addition to the corporate patrimony. 'Patch by patch is yeomanly' catches the mood of Richard's will. There were few indications of luxury: half a dozen silver spoons to a granddaughter, a silver cup 'called the Turne' was obviously a treasured heirloom, and two stone jugs 'covered with silver and gilt', one called 'the worst', the other 'the best', were passed to his daughter-in-law, Griffith's wife, and his daughter Edith, now married to Thomas Warne, a Stroud clothier. Pot-hangings, brass and pewter pots, three wainscot chairs and three three-legged stools with 'arras quishons' [cushions], pot hooks, a flock bed, two blankets and a bolster, hempen sheets, a brass candlestick 'with flower broken off', a bed and 'one chest standing at the high chamber door' went to son Griffith along with forty sheep 'and half my corne'. He knew what his possessions amounted to down to the brass candlestick with the flower broken off. The absence of cash bequests suggests that he did not keep cash hanging about, quickly converting it into something of substance, something useful, paying off mortgages on purchased lands and keeping the household comfortable but with few touches of conspicuous consumption. The remainder of his estate, Longfords and Eastwood Park, he left to his son Edward (born 1645), who henceforth was to be known as 'of Cam', even though he lived at Eastwood.[29]

Richard Trotman avoided involvement in the cloth industry. There is no hint of it in his will. His brothers both added to their own inheritances, and left considerably more cash bequests in their wills than did the old yeoman. Yet it was Richard's son, Edward, who received a grant of arms in 1616. Edward also avoided involvement in the cloth industry. 'Certain Markes on Shields comonly called Armes have been and are the onely signes and demonstracons eyther of prowess and valour atcheyved in tymes of warre or of good lyfe and civill conversaycon in tymes of peace.'[30] Since Edward Trotman was never a soldier, the award in his case must have been for his 'good lyfe and civill conversaycon'.[31] It was difficult for clothiers and cloth merchants to avoid the taint of secretive and misleading dealings, and thus to acquire the kind of reputation required for formal awards of arms.

Local or informal awards were a different matter. By the early seventeenth century at least two branches or households of the Trotman family were regarded by their contemporaries, or at least by John Smyth of Nibley, as gentry. Smyth of Nibley described Edward Trotman of Eastwood Park and John Trotman of the Knapp, Cam, the heirs respectively, of the branches descended from John the Elder of Cam, clothier, and Richard the Elder of Cam, yeoman, as 'Gent.' in the muster-lists of Cam and Moreton.[32] While the occupation of clothier was compatible with the status of yeoman, it was not yet compatible with that of Gentleman, who had to be distanced from industry and commerce, though not necessarily from trafficking in, and accumulating, land. Smyth's explanation of the saying 'He'll prove a man of Dursley', referring to proverbial prejudices about the double-dealing of clothiers, may help to explain the difficulties clothiers had in obtaining formal grants of arms. While Edward Trotman's inheritance derived ultimately from wealth accumulated in clothmaking and dealing, by the time the award was made he was two generations removed from the industry. Thus the branch which made it into the county gentry had first to distance itself from the industry on which the family fortune rested.

At least thirty-three Trotman men and one Trotman woman were recorded in Smyth's 1608 muster-rolls. Richard Trotman the Younger of Slimbridge, Richard the Elder's grandson, was a tall young man of some substance, since he contributed to the subsidy earlier in the year, and was not assigned an occupation. He inherited yeoman rank, and a yeoman estate, when his father died ten years later in 1618. He was a great-grandson of John the Cloathman.[33] Edward Trotman of Eastwood Park did not attend personally but was represented by four servants and a man described as 'Mr Trotman's shepherd'. The remaining thirty-one were assigned occupations, so it is possible to do something of a breakdown of the kin-coalition in the Vale. Two Trotmans were described as Gentlemen, another (Edward Trotman, the eldest son of Edward of Eastwood) was working as an Utter Barrister at Micheldean in the Forest of Dean, and was accompanied to the muster there by five servants. William Trotman was a mercer at Dursley, three were yeoman (indicating occupation as a farmer rather than rank, since all of the men described as clothiers were also of yeoman status) and one was a husbandman. The rest – twelve clothiers, seven weavers or broadweavers and four fullers and tuckers – were engaged in the cloth industry. The Trotman clothiers constituted 37.5 per cent of all references, and men engaged in clothmaking generally were 75 per cent of the total. Although what was by now the major branch of the family – the heirs of old Richard the Elder – was distanced from industry, clothmaking remained easily the most important basis of the clan's substance and two of Edward of Eastwood's sons became cloth merchants in the City of London, one of whom (Throgmorton) had interests in Hamburg and Virginia.

A stranger arriving in the Vale of Berkeley with a message for Edward Trotman would have had a hard time of it in the early 1600s. There were five candidates: Mr Edward Trotman of Eastwood, Mr Edward of the Court of Cam, Mr Edward the Barrister, living at Micheldean in 1608 and accompanied to the muster there by five servants, Mr Edward of the Court's son Edward (but he was in London), Edward Trotman the Clothier at Mabson's Mill, Cam, and Edward Trotman who farmed a freehold estate near Tetbury.[34] There were at least five John Trotmans: three John the Weavers from Tytherington, Stinchcombe and Synwell near Wotton-under-Edge; a John the Clothier from Stinchcombe, probably John the Weaver of Stinchcombe's father; and a Mr John of Upthorpe, Cam, grandson of John Trotman the 'cloathman'. Williams were just as common. Edward Trotman the Clothier of Cam's son, William, was working at his father's mill, Mabsons, as a fuller. William of Rodborough was a man in the prime of life; one of the most successful clothiers in Gloucestershire like his father and grandfather before him, he wore his own armour and brought his own weapons to the muster at Rodborough, and was accompanied by a servant his own age and five strapping young men in the youngest and tallest category. They could probably take care of themselves 'in the case of a rout or so'.[35] William Trotman of Black Burton farmed a yeoman freehold near Stinchcombe purchased from Sir Anthony Hungerford some years earlier; he also held a part share in Stinchcombe manor, purchased from Lord Wentworth in 1560.[36]

All were living and working signs of the weakening of the fabric of feudalism, now thoroughly threadbare in the Vale. Henry lord Berkeley's bravado of the 1550s had lasted only a few years. As soon as the yeomen, esquires and knights who formed his retinue in the years under Mary Tudor discovered he couldn't pay them, the maintenance of a retinue such as even his most powerful ancestors would have had difficulty financing for more than a month or so without resorting to plunder became impractical. John Smyth of Nibley was employed to fix up and run what was left of the estate, and the middle rank continued to run things more or less as they had already been doing for two or three generations, since the heady days of the Tyndales.

William Trotman the Husbandman from Cam was a short man; most Trotmans were of middle-to-tall stature.[37] There were five Richards, a Thomas the Clothier of Cam, Robert the Tucker of Tytherington, a notable centre of Dissent throughout the seventeenth century.[38] Christopher Trotman, Yeoman of Wickwar, carried his own musket and was a member of the trained bands. Francis the Tucker lived at Tortworth, a few miles south of Cam. Alexander Trotman, tucker, was a tall young caliverman from Woodmancote. Mary Trotman sent her 'aged servant, Hugh Asgrave', a tiny old man, with instructions to inform whoever was in charge of collecting names and information for Mr Smyth that he was there to represent her and that he was to be sure her name was written down.[39] Mr Smyth was a stickler for detail. In total, he caught at least thirty-three Trotman men and one Trotman woman in his operation, which demonstrated beyond any doubt that if the middle rank of that region was required to organise a large-scale operation, it would be organised properly, down to the last detail.

Technically no Trotman had the right to call himself, or be called by his neighbours, 'Mr' or 'Gent'. The formal grant of arms was not made until 1616, to Edward of Eastwood (and/or Cam) 'and his heirs'. The family genealogist finds this qualification interesting.[40] Did it mean that Mr Edward could create gentlemen in the family just by leaving them something in his will: 'heirs' is plural in the grant, unqualified. The impression gained from the history of the family in the seventeenth century is that any descendent of Edward Trotman who could inherit, acquire and maintain an estate and lifestyle observably that of a gentleman could and did, if he wished, describe himself, and be accepted as, a gentleman. Here, at any rate, was room for a lawyer to move in. Three of Edward's six sons were lawyers. A century of accumulating wealth and properties, transferring and financing them, making everything clear in wills, arranging marriages and settling dowries, in short, dealing with lawyers, underlined the need for a legal branch connection. Richard the Elder's son Edward became 'the Elder', but only on his tombstone.[41]

Consolidating the impression of yeoman substance, six of the Trotman clothiers, William the Mercer of Dursley, and two of the yeomen were paid-up Subsidymen.[42] Samuel of Stinchcombe, Clothier, Edward the Clothier of Mabson's Mill, Cam, Thomas the Clothier of Stinchcombe and William the Mercer of Dursley were members of the trained bands; and six more Trotmans wore their own armour and carried their own weapons to the musters.

Had they chosen to do so, it is clear that the Trotmans could have exercised great power and authority in the Vale of Berkeley. In terms of freehold possessions, they were qualified to sit, vote and serve as churchwardens in the vestries of Cam (which they dominated), Dursley, Stinchcombe, Slimbridge, Wotton-under-Edge, Berkeley, Moreton and Thornbury, Rodborough, Wickwar and possibly Tetbury, Tortworth and Micheldean. They owned land throughout the chequerwork of manors that criss-crossed the old Berkeley estates, all but disintegrated into a sea of yeoman freeholds, the network of administration in feudal times. Since the early sixteenth century the Trotmans had quite literally filled the abstract space defined in the theology of William Tyndale. They were 'elders' in every parish in the Vale, and as yeoman-freeholders and clothiers (usually both at the same time), they were very considerable employers of local labour; overwhelmingly, the Trotmans were of the employer class. Edward Tyndale, through his patron Thomas Cromwell, was the first 'godfather' of the middle rank of the Vale of Berkeley. The Trotmans were well connected there. When they were granted arms their shield was quartered with the shield of Edward Tyndale and his heirs. Edward Trotman the Elder of Cam, Gent, had carved on his tombstone that his father was of Pull Court to underline this connection. Pull (or Poole) Court was once in the gift of Edward Tyndale, like Eastwood Park, where John Smyth of Nibley dined with Edward Trotman in the 1590s. The Trotmans absorbed the Tyndales. In the long run, their corporate network was more solid, better grounded, denser, and in the early seventeenth century it was still growing fast.

The tap-root was Cam, the other roots firmly implanted throughout the Vale. Interconnections between the various branches were numerous. Thirteen marriages involving a daughter of one of the branches of the family living at Cam took place between 1575 and 1611. Four were to cousin Trotmans. Such marriages ensured that the family patrimony remained under the Trotman trademark. One gets the impression of the sixteenth-century Trotmans that, although they were very successful accumulators, they were very reluctant to give anything away. Well-endowed daughters stayed in the family, unless they could improve the corporate stock by forming the medium for an alliance with another branch of the *countrey* bourgeoisie like the Selwyns, Hardings, Plomers, Haines's or Hutchens (Tyndales) or, even better, effect an alliance with a gentry family in need of capital to finance a 'project for gentlemen'. Old Thomas Trotman the Clothier arranged a marriage for his son with a daughter of Giles Carter of Swell. By the time they got there, the Trotman bid for a formal acknowledgment of their gentility had been active for three generations.

Each generation had to know what it was about, and what its part was. How the rules were transmitted from generation to generation, and what the rules were, has gone the way of all oral traditions, merged immediately in what happens next, distorted, occasionally refurbished, perhaps lost forever, in child-rearing practices, proverbs and a family milieu that is by definition secret to all but those who belong to it. The rules, we may surmise, were written on the walls of old Richard the Yeoman's farmhouse at Cam, spoken casually in proverbial forms in the household, observed in the precise and careful behaviour of the adults.[43] Many were 'traditional', like some of the proverbs. The continuing success of the Trotmans – their rise *and* their territorial expansion – suggests the rules were applied rigorously and systematically. Some of them were too obvious to need emphasis: get money, get land, get more money, get more land, have many sons and bequeath each of them a yeoman estate or the means to acquire one, marry them to yeomen and minor gentry, if not to a cousin, train them in law or apprentice them to a Gloucestershire merchant in London (preferably a cousin or uncle), keep production going in the Vale of Berkeley, strengthen the linkages between the Vale and London, bid for arms, marry heiresses or daughters of influential men, keep the money rolling in, keep it in the family, purchase estates acquire 'county' status, be elected as knight for the shire . . .

By the early seventeenth century the Trotmans had gone about as far as they could go in the Vale of Berkeley. What lay ahead was either stagnation or expansion. Through the sons of Edward of Eastwood they took the expansionist path. Three were lawyers. His eldest son, also Edward, born at Eastwood Park some time in the late 1570s, was a Bencher of the Middle Temple, something of an academic lawyer with a flair for the practical; his life-work was an abridgment of Coke's *Institutes*. Lord Chief Justice Coke traced 'the grounds of the Common Laws . . . beyond the memory or register of any beginning, and the same which the Norman conqueror found within the Realm of England'. On another occasion he dated them 'from Anglo-Saxon times'.[44] He was a leading proponent of Ancient Constitution ideology, and we may reasonably assume that his abridger, Edward Trotman, was too. So was William Tyndale.[45] Coke's son, Sir Robert Co(o)ke, held and lived on an estate in the suburbs of Gloucester, was married to a daughter of Henry, lord Berkeley, led 'the pretended holy side' in the elections for the Short Parliament, and fought for Parliament in the civil wars.

Edward Trotman's youngest son Samuel was 'about to start for London' when his mother died in 1635. He was a Barrister at Law of the Inner Temple, and did well in the Civil War/Commonwealth period. His line will be examined later. Richard Trotman of Cliffords Inn and the Middle Temple was an Attorney at Law in London until his death in 1635. Each made successful marriages into minor gentry families like their own. The second oldest son, Thomas, was a merchant in the City and married the daughter of another merchant, one Coleman of Foster Lane. But the most interesting of Edward the Elder's sons was Throgmorton Trotman, merchant of Moorfields.

Throgmorton Trotman was born at Cam on 21 July 1594.[46] His grandmother, Katherine, left £10 in her will in 1602 to be conveyed to him when he was of age.[47] Like his brother Thomas, Throgmorton became a merchant in London, though never a member of a registered company. He was invited to join the Company of Haberdashers, but never took up the offer. It is likely that he first came to London when he was in his twenties, when his brothers were already establishing themselves in the law. Edward, his father, invested his capital, not in land, as his father and uncles and their fathers and uncles before them had done, but in providing his sons with bases in the law and commerce in London. The venture stretched the family resources in the Vale. Longfords, Richard the Elder's yeoman freehold at Cam, inherited by Edward the Elder and then, in turn, by his eldest son (Throgmorton's brother) Edward was mortgaged several times in the 1620s and early 1630s, and was finally sold to a local clothier, Francis Webb, in 1635.[48] Two or three generations earlier such a loss would have been disastrous; Richard the Elder had concentrated all his resources into paying off the mortgages that he had inherited on the farm, and had built a fine house on it. Edward the Younger's legal scholarship gave the family prestige in national legal circles and beyond, but it was an expensive business. One of the mortgages – there were six more – was held, when the estate was finally sold in 1635, by Throgmorton Trotman, who by this time was establishing himself as an international cloth merchant. The loss of Longfords was more than compensated by the gain in national influence represented by Edward's legal and mercantile sons.

In terms of historiographical conventions, with the generation of the children of Edward Trotman of Eastwood Park we pass from the conjuncture of the Reformation to that of the English Revolution. The Reformation as conceived by William Tyndale involved a process in which 'elders' like himself, his brothers and his neighbours and kinsfolk the Trotmans undertook the spiritual as well as the material leadership of the network of congregations which made up the working world of the early sixteenth century. In essence, it was a reification of practical working conditions and authority structures in the parish. In the generation of Edward Trotman's sons, this vision was projected on to a national stage, a projection which took place because so many of the descendants of William Tyndale and his class contemporaries had achieved what could be achieved in the localities, and had been successful enough, and shrewd enough, to recognise that no further progress was possible without expansion. We need not assume that they made the transition from neighbourhood to nation with anything resembling conscious revolutionary intent. What is important is that they made it with strongly grounded confidence and, above all, detailed knowledge of how the country worked, how its people made their livings, and how complex the networks which held them together were. The subtlety with which social, geographical, political, economic and religious aspects of the new nation were integrated into an expanded version of Tyndale's world of elders and congregations can be observed in the vision of Throgmorton Trotman.

Throgmorton died, a wealthy man, in 1663. His will provides fascinating insight into the national vision of a Puritan merchant of the Commonwealth era.[49] He began by stating that he was 'of perfect memorie and understanding' and by bequeathing 'my soule into the hands of my merciful Saviour and Redeemer trustinge for Salvacon by His merrits and satisfaction'. He wished 'to bee interred without vaine ostentation'. Then came a list of twenty-five bequests of between £10 and £200 to named individuals, adding up to a total of over £2,000. First came his 'cozens': Trotmans, Pages, Popes, Selwyns, Hills, Haynes's, Tyndales, all from families in the Vale of Berkeley, intermarried with the Trotmans over several generations, now living at Bristol and London as well as places like Stinchcombe and Cam in the Vale. 'Cozen Edward his daughter in Vergena [Virginia]' was left £50, and 'Mr James Baker my Factor in Hamburgh' was left £150. Throgmorton Trotman was a man with national and international connections.

The Company of Merchant Adventurers in London was given £600 to be used as venture capital, 'to be lent free of interest for three years to two young men free of that company; then to two young men successively for ever'. This was enough capital and enough time to equip and stock a return voyage lasting three years, perhaps two or three such voyages across the Atlantic. Someone, almost certainly his father, had performed such a service for Throgmorton at the beginning of his career. Throgmorton never married and had no sons to leave his capital to; so he helped his country by leaving money to foster colonial trade. The international dimension of his world-view is confirmed in a bequest of 'two books called Mercator Atlas' to 'Mr Joh: Dogget, Merchant of Bush Lane'. Throgmorton was a man of strategic global vision. In his mind was a map as wide as the known world, as drawn by the great cartographer from the Low Countries, Gerard Mercator, who gave us the word 'Atlas'. His work was first published in English in 1635; Throgmorton's version could have been any one of several published in quick succession in the late 1630s and 1640s.[50]

He was also a man of strategic religious vision. He left £2,000 to the London Company of Haberdashers 'to purchase lands of the annual value of 100 pounds for ever': £20 was to be spent 'to maintain a lecture to be preached every lord's day forever at 6 a.m. in the parish church of St. Giles Cripplegate'; £20 was to maintain 'a weekday lecture in the same church on Thursday afternoon'; £2 each went to supplement the pay of a parish clerk and a sexton to dig graves and look after the church grounds. Knowing the uncertainty of the times – the Restoration settlement was still unsettled – he added that 'if the lectures are not permitted at St. Giles then they can be given in some other parish church determined by the Company. And in the case that those lectures will nowhere in the citie or countrie be permitted' the money was to be spent in maintaining the poor of St. Giles. Of the remaining £56, £30 was to be spent towards building almshouses at Cam, 'where I was born', or, at the discretion of the Company, 'towards a stock to set the poor [of Cam] on work'.

Another bequest of £2,000 was to finance 'a lecture on market days or some other day in Dursley, Gloucestershire', or, 'if there is a lecture already . . . to be given the lecturers for their incourajment'. Under the leadership of their Puritan minister, Joseph Woodward, the clothiers of Dursley had done very well in the 1650s.[51] Woodward's successor, Henry Stubbes, had been ejected in 1662 for nonconformity. Throgmorton Trotman was an elder of the Congregationalist England that came close to imposing itself in the 1650s, but was moderated with popular acclaim on the restoration of monarchy in 1660. His was an integrated vision, a social blue-print that laid great weight on the activity of evangelical ministers and sound parochial discipline. He left a final bequest of £500 to be distributed to 'ministers put by their employments' by the Act of Uniformity in 1662. He appointed nine men to administer this bequest. To 'these forenamed mynisters (or lately were so)' he left 'the inheritance of the house I now dwell in', ten houses 'ioining to my house', and 'the rest in Butlers Alley for the educateing of poore scollers at the Universities to fit them for the Ministrie for Convertion of Soules'. It was to go 'onelie to such as are poore whose parents cannot bee at that charge with them'. Once they qualified, 'if they [could not] be imployed in England' they were to be sent 'to preach beyonde seas'.

Two of the ejected ministers he appointed as trustees to administer this programme were Anthony Palmer and Carnsew Helme. Bernard Capp names them as members of 'an influx of new leaders' associated with the millenarian London underground of the 1660s.[52] After the defeat of the Royalist party in Gloucestershire in 1645, the two men were sent into the North Cotswold/Vale of Tewkesbury district to replace disaffected clergy in the one part of Gloucestershire that was a centre of indigenous Royalist resistance. In 1653 they and several other leaders of what they called the 'independent congregations' were challenged to debate their theology and ecclesiology with the dispossessed Rector of Sudeley, Clement Barkesdale. Helme, Palmer and others accused Barkesdale of being 'an opposer of Reformation', alleging that he 'administered holy things to Prophane Wretches, the haters of Godliness'. Barkesdale, it appears, privately administered the sacraments, and offered comfort to people who would not accept the new religious disciplines. In a letter to Barkesdale, Palmer accused him of 'Praelatical, formal, superstitious usages'. Barkesdale felt that the new men were too hard on the locals. Only those who demonstrated their faith by adherence to the strict, disciplined life advocated by the new preachers were to be accounted members of the congregation of believers.

Barkesdale's position was that 'God . . . will accept us [in Christ] not weighing *our merrits, but pardoning our offences'*. His reply to Palmer stated that he would 'countenance none in their corrupt, loose ways, but on the contrary, shew the danger of such looseness'. But he would not withhold the sacraments from those who seemed to him 'to thirst after it, and receive it with feare and reverence, after profession of Faith and Obedience'. Palmer informed Barkesdale that he 'had no call' to minister to the population, and should submit to the authority of Carnsew Helme, who had been appointed Minister of Winchcombe and nearby Naunton. Barkesdale replied that 'if Mr H[elme] hath as lawfull a Call as I, I will seek communion with him the next day I know it'. He referred to the new preachers as 'out-comers' (people from outside the district), and was bold enough to point out that the 'conditions of the new Covenant' from which they took their authority were 'not right in the eyes of very knowing, orderly, and well-disposed People'. His 'opposition to [their] wayes proceede[d] meerly of duty'.[53]

Barkesdale represented a more patient, tolerant and paternalist pastoral ideal. He left it to God to judge 'black sheep' and would not deny them the sacraments, as was the policy of the missionaries. On 9 November 1653, 'betweene nine and tenne in the morning', he debated his theology with 'Mr Helme Minister at Winchcombe, . . . Col[onel] Ailworth Justice of the Peace, Mr Tray Minister at Oddington, Mr Welles Minister of Tewkesbury, Mr Chaffy Minister at Naunton and some other[s]'. From the point of view of the Puritans, the Winchcombe district was a dark and superstitious corner of the land, where there was no manufacturing, no substantial middle rank to speak of and thus no natural indigenous constituency from which preachers and ministers could be drawn; the clothworking districts could provide their own ministers. The principal occupation of the labouring poor in the Winchcombe district was working on the great gentry-financed tobacco plantations, not an economy that nurtured strict household disciplines because few of the local people worked in their own households.[54] It had therefore been necessary, once the Royalist gentry who had dominated the district since the dissolution of the abbeys of Hailes and Winchcombe had been put in their place, along with their leader, George Brydges, lord Chandos of Sudeley, to send in missionaries.[55]

Seven years after the 'disputation' at Winchcombe, Clement Barkesdale published another, this time triumphant, pamphlet titled *The King's Return: A Sermon*, on the text of Samuel II, xv. 25: 'If I shall find favour in the Eyes of the Lord, he will bring me again.' In 1662 Helme, Palmer and their associates refused to conform to the requirements of the Act of Uniformity, and retreated to London, where Throgmorton Trotman, who came from a district or *countrey* where the middle rank had been imbued with independent Congregationalist ideas and ways of life for over a century, provided them with accommodation and encouragement in the continuation of their mission.

What does this association between Throgmorton Trotman, merchant of Moorfields, and these Fifth Monarchist preachers imply? In asking them to distribute £500 to other members of the 'influx of millenarian leaders' who came to London after the ejections of 1662, we must assume that he knew and trusted them to place the money as he would have approved. Trotman's will shows him to have been very attentive to detail and broad in his grasp of strategic considerations. He could think like one of Christopher Saxton's county maps, but he could also connect those maps into a world as wide and detailed as Mercator's *Atlas*. His will also shows that he was acutely conscious of the precariousness of the Congregationalist vision. He suspected that several of his bequests to fund lectureships and finance Congregationalist appointments and schools would be impossible to execute, although he was hopeful enough to think it worth trying. The wind had changed many times in the past two decades, and it might change again. If so, £500 distributed among carefully chosen leaders might keep the movement alive for a few more years. Throgmorton Trotman's will extrapolated the theocratic vision embodied, 150 years earlier, in the language and ideas of William Tyndale on to a field of operation made available to him by the success of his ancestors, the elders of the Vale of Berkeley. His mind had expanded to take in the new vistas made possible by the trails that led out from the developmental hot-spots of early modern England. He formulated his practical vision in what were perhaps the last months of its existence as a conceivable alternative to the Restoration compromise. Henceforth it was to be enshrined in the unwritten English constitution that capitalists could not be saints, and the once-mighty dissenters were to become enterprising nonconformists.

In family terms, Throgmorton was a dead-end in the map of the Trotman kin-coalition. The visionary austerity of the old bachelor's nationalism and internationalism was indeed a lucid extrapolation of characteristics bred into the kin-culture by generations of elders. In this sense, there is little in this 'Calvinist' vision that is not reducible to indigenous circumstances. The elders of the Vale of Berkeley had little to learn from Luther, Zwingli and Calvin. They were pious, practical and down to earth, and the solidarity from which they sprang was the solidarity of kin-coalitions that had been generations in the making.

Throgmorton Trotman had no children. His younger brother, Samuel, a lawyer, had eight. He was to lead the corporation to new heights during the Commonwealth period and, equally successfully, through the Restoration compromise. His descendants illustrate further developments in the expansion of the family's field of operation. Samuel Trotman was born at Cam in 1599 when his father, Edward of Eastwood, was 54 and still had seventeen years to wait before the formal grant of arms. His mother's will, dated 1635, catches him 'about to start for London'. Presumably he had already qualified as a lawyer at the Inner Temple, and knew his way around the city. He died on his estate at Bucknells, Oxfordshire, in 1684, and his body was carried back to Cam to be buried in the parish churchyard, alongside his father and grandfather, Richard the Elder.

His first marriage took place in 1638, but was short-lived, producing only one child. His second, politically more important, was to Mary Warcup of Bucknells, a niece of Mr Speaker Lenthall. It took place in 1647, when Lenthall was Speaker of the Long Parliament. This connection may mean that Samuel Trotman was a 'trimmer', less committed than his older brother Throgmorton to the full revolutionary vision, but nonetheless solidly grounded in the cause of Parliament, as long as it did not become too extreme. As a Barrister at Law, Samuel would have been familiar with the technique of articulating lucid arguments in which it was not necessary, personally, to believe with all one's heart. His wife inherited the Bucknells estate, and in 1651, as a result of his knowledge of movements in the property market arising from Royalist sequestrations, he purchased Siston Court, near Bristol.

In 1677 he settled the manor of Siston in tail upon his eldest son, also Samuel, along with two other manors he had purchased at Skelswell and Newton Purcell.[56] The manor of Bucknells, and some other property, were left to his second son Lenthall, named after his mother's uncle. Samuel Trotman Jr continued in the family tradition of increasing the range of the family influence by sitting in Parliament for the seats of Bath and Sutton. His first wife, like his mother, died young, after giving birth to a daughter, Dorothea. His second wife, the second daughter and co-heiress of Lord Chief Baron Montague of the Exchequer, and widow of Sir William Drake,[57] had illustrious connections, but failed to produce any more children. By an oversight, old Samuel Trotman made 'a great mistake' in the settlement of his major estates of Siston, Skelswell and Newton Purcell in 1677 'by the omission of the word "male" in the limitation to son Samuel'.[58] For his part, son Samuel failed to produce any sons, thus making it possible that, for the first time in seven generations, the prime estates of the corporation might pass into the hands of a man whose name was not Trotman.

By 1710, when Lenthall Trotman of Bucknells died and left his estate to his son, another Samuel Trotman, it was clear that there would be no sons to inherit the Siston Court line. The solution was to revert to a practice that had been used very effectively many times by earlier generations: a Trotman heiress would be married to a Trotman cousin. Accordingly, a marriage was arranged between the two grandchildren of Samuel Trotman Sr, Dorothea and Samuel. The date and venue were fixed – 16 October 1712 at Siston – and Trotmans everywhere were informed that the merger was imminent.

Among them were two of old Samuel's granddaughters, Susannah, now 62 and the wife of Sir Richard Holford, Master in Chancery and lord of the manors of Avebury in Wiltshire and Westonbirt in Gloucestershire, and Sarah, her younger sister, 45, wife of 'the learned George Hickes D.D., Dean of Worcester 1683–91'.[59] Both were invited to the wedding, as were all the known Trotmans. Sarah's manservant, John Sanders, wrote an account entitled 'John Sanders, his Book, 1712: the Account of my Travils with my Mistress'.[60] It provides a vivid and guileless portrait of the world of the leading branches of the Trotman clan in the early eighteenth century, to contrast with that of their ancestor, old Richard the Elder, yeoman of Cam, and of his older contemporary, William Tyndale.

The first stage of Sarah's journey from Aylesbury, where she was living with her husband, to Siston, involved taking the coach to London, where she was met by one of Sir Richard Holford's servants and delivered to his mansion at Lincoln's Inn. There Sarah and her manservant found Lady Holford 'in aweful condition', which meant a delay in leaving for the west. Ten days later, on 11 August, Lady Holford was fit enough to travel. Susannah was Sir Richard Holford's third wife. His first and second marriages had brought him mortgaged estates in Wiltshire and Gloucestershire, which he paid out in cash. Every year, Sir Richard would leave Lincoln's Inn for what he called his 'annual ramble in the country'.[61] In 1712 Sir Richard would remain at Avebury seeing to estate business while his wife and sister-in-law continued to 'ramble' to Siston for the marriage of their great-niece and great-nephew.

Sir Richard's coach, with Sanders 'on ye outside' braving the elements, took two days to reach Avebury. On the first night they dined and slept at 'Spinumlands in Nubery parish', where Sanders was enthusiastic about talk of a 'great fight in the sivill wars, four noble Dukes [were] thare killed and carried into that very house whare [they] dined'. He was even more taken by the 'antiquities' at Avebury. 'It is a noble larg antient seat, built with larg stons,' he wrote of the Holford country residence. 'It did belong to the late noble lord Stoil who was born thare and our Queen Anne dined thare.' Some of the 'larg stons' in the district had proved too large and hard to be of use to local builders, and many superstitions attached to the ones that still stood as originally placed. Sanders wrote that 'Avebury is compassed about with a walled ditch which was thrown up in wars they say 1000 years before Christ'. In terms of contemporary biblical scholarship, this was shortly after the Garden of Eden. 'Thare is two larg stons as you enter the town, which they call gates. Thare is many larg stons standing up as big as those at Ston Edge,' he wrote, meaning Stonehenge.

Sarah and Susannah remained together at Avebury until 22 August, by which time Sir Richard was embroiled in the subtleties of manorial administration at Westonbirt, where there were loud whisperings that the man to whom he leased the manor farm was a 'buggerer'. Holford considered this an outrageous slight on his honour as a lord, not the first he had received from the stolid natives of Westonbirt, but for the moment he put the rumours down to the stupid and perhaps mischievous willingness of the neighbourhood to believe every nasty story it heard. A coach was being sent from Siston to pick up Lady Holford, always in fragile health (Holford called her his 'ffrog'), while the more intrepid Sarah and her manservant went off on horseback, with her 'portmantow' on the 'back of Sir Richard's punch-nag'. Sanders 'had a verry daingerous fall' when, coming across 'a great deep myer accross the land . . . [his] Mrs's portmantow broke' and dumped him in the bog. But 'god preserv'd [him]' and they arrived safely at the mansion of Robert Wadman Esq. of Imber, Wilts, Tinhead Court. This was another Trotman connection. Wadman's first wife was Hannah, the oldest daughter of Samuel Trotman Sr, Sarah and Susannah's sister. At Tinhead Court they found that the second Mrs Wadman had only that day arisen 'from a long confinement with the gout'. Nevertheless, they were made 'hartily welcom'. Next day the little party went out to pay their respects at the graveside of the first Mrs

Wadman, who 'had the misfortuen to break one of the panbones of her knees, and to dislocate the other, which caused her to undergo much pain and misery', from which, after a long confinement, she died. Sanders was impressed with the appropriateness of the inscription on the tombstone: 'Thou shalt make me hear joy and gladness, that the bones which thou hast broken may rejoice' (Psalms 41, 51:8). Scriptural providentialism still ran strong in the family.

They remained a month at Sarah's brother-in-law's house, and on 26 September 'went from Tinhead by the Salysbury coach to Bath, whare Esquier Trotman's horses and men met [them] and brought [them] the same night to Siston Court, at 9 o'clock'. Sanders was very impressed with 'Squire Trotman's house'. It was 'a very larg hansom stateley great seat, fitt for a nable man to reside in'. His mistress's brother was very grand. One of the servants at Siston Court told Sanders that James I's wife had once slept in a room upstairs called 'the Queen's Chamber'. The Trotmans were now unquestionably 'county gentry'. Samuel Trotman had recently taken out a contract with a Dutch draftsman to have his mansion engraved for inclusion in Sir Robert Atkyns' compendious *Ancient and Present State of Gloucestershire*, published at Gloucester that very year.

Esquire Trotman was no squire in the Macauley or Squire Western mould. The accoutrements of his seat were distinctly patrician, though not as grand as Sir William Blaythwayt's recent construction at nearby Dyrham, or Badminton.[62] Outside the house there was 'a verry larg bowling green, pleasant walls and a butiful garden', wrote Sanders. The interior was 'well furnished and adorned with a bundance pictures, sum of them very valuable'. But what impressed him above all was 'the noble housekeeping. We ware so lucky . . . to come in the nick, as half a dozen gentilmen ware carying supper into the parlar', into which he and his 'Mrs' were 'ushered', there to be met by 'a grate deal of good company and many frends and relacons'. There was 'ye honoured Lady Drake', stepmother of the bride, and 'ye honoured and very rich Lady Reade', the widow of Sir James Read, Baronet, of Brocket Hall, Hertfordshire. Lady Read's daughters, to Sanders, were 'vast fortunes and heiresses'. One of them, he was informed, was betrothed to 'the worshipful Mr Dashwood', heir to the 'vast estate' of Sir Robert Dashwood of Norbrook. Sanders was taken with the 'nability' of the company, but it never for a moment occurred to him that it came down to anything but 'vast estate'. *Follow him that bears the purse.*

Esquire Sam Trotman made his aunt Sarah and her manservant 'extraordinary welcom'. The wedding festivities were already under way. Forty people sat down that night with the groom, Samuel Trotman Esq. of Bucknells, at the head of the table looking down the tunnel of faces through the sparkle and haze of gilt dishes, candelabra and crystal. Sanders 'suped' with 'about 40 of us [servants]' in the servants' hall, where their 'tables were plentifully cover'd, and all the servants ware very kind, and took a greate deale of care of [him]'. Every day he was at Siston everyone was 'plentifully covered'. 'Every day thare was a nable larg ox killed, beside muton and lamb and piggs, and of all sorts of fouls both tame and wild, with these the slaughterhouse and wet larder were plentifully furnished, besides read dear [red deer] and fat dow [doe] and a bundance of sort of fish from the sea and freshwater.'[63] It was a more abundant feast than anything that might have been envisaged by old Richard the Elder 150 years earlier, but he would have understood the principles involved perfectly. The next day, Sunday, 'thare went six coachfulls of gentry' to Siston parish church, followed by '30 or more sarvents on foot'.

The wedding itself was strictly family only. 'Thare ware 8 coach fulls of near relations went out of this famely to church at the wedding,' Sanders confided. The solemnity at church being over, all returned in the same manner as they went. Back at Siston Court they were welcomed by 'a set of mussissiners' who had been hired to accompany the wedding celebrations, looking down on the assembled Trotmans from 'a galerie over the grate stares'. Sanders counted twenty-four different dishes on the table. 'Pastry venison and roast beef on the side, besides the changes of fish in the place of crawfish soup, and read dear in the place of rich soup at the lower end.' For dessert there were 'three larg perimids of the finest and best sweatmeats and besides them 16 large chainy [china] dishes of wet sweatmeats and gelly and frutes and other things which made the desart as nable as the dinner'. After the feast there was dancing and 'several sets of card players all made up out of our own famely no naighbors being thare that day, it being called a priviate wedding'. It was private corporate business, and only members of the corporation were required to witness it. The elders of Cam were there in spirit.

After the diversions came supper, capped by a 'rich bride cake garnished on the top with fine dried sweatmeats stuck very thick on it'. The next morning 'every chamber window ware surrounded with music to call us all up'. The 'priviate' part of proceedings now being over, 'friends' began to arrive 'to join us in joy and feasting and card-playing, ringing of bells and drinking health and joy'. One hundred and fifteen people sat down to dinner that night. In the servants' hall 'the poor labourers feasted that day with us, which made our number at dinner of 115, besides 50 poor sarved at the door'. In 1712 two disastrous harvest years had only recently been alleviated by a moderately good grain harvest. The year before, the entire region had been devastated by a particularly virulent smallpox epidemic. At Tetbury, a market town 20 miles north-east of Siston, on the other side of the Cotswolds near Sir Richard Holford's manor of Westonbirt, 800 of 1300 inhabitants were afflicted by it.[64] The pattern was repeated in other Gloucestershire parishes, particularly in the populous clothworking districts. Of the 800 victims at Tetbury only 80 died, a recovery rate of 90 per cent. But for a few months it had seemed as though the harvest might fail, not because there was no grain, but because there were too few healthy people to get it in. The poor at the back door of Siston Court could have been from collier families working on Kingswood Chase, which adjoined Siston parish in the south. These were the 'heathens' John Wesley came to preach to thirty years later.

On Saturday the music and feasting, card-playing and dancing were repeated, and that night a weary Sanders wrote 'quite tired we all went to bed, all being surfitted with the noys of music night and day'. Everyone had had enough by then, so 'the mussissiners ware discharg'd'. Squire Trotman had hired a 'forayn man cook . . . to assist Lady Drake's cook the three grand festival days', and he too was sent on his way. As the tradespeople left on Sunday morning, six coachfuls of friends and six coachfuls of Trotmans were carted off bleary-eyed to church, where the parson preached them a light-hearted and risqué sermon on the text of Proverbs 18–19: 'let thy fountain be blessed: and rejoice with the wife of thy youth. Let her be as the loving hind and pleasant roe: let her breasts satisfy thee at all times: and be thou ravaged always with her love.' The perspective was a little patriarchal. No doubt a few middle-aged male and female Trotman eyes glazed over a little at all this, mentally observing that biblical erotica might serve corporate purposes by inducing fertility, the lack of which had given rise to all these festivities in the first place. In 150 years and five generations, the Trotmans had come a long way. The stern god of the elders now wore a softer expression.

Later the bridegroom became known as 'the mad Trotman', rather for eccentricity than for anything resembling dangerous insanity. He sat for Woodstock in Parliament in Walpole's time. He and Dorothea failed to produce heirs. Signs of weakness began to appear in the chain connecting the Trotmans with their ancestors, the clothiers and elders of the Vale of Berkeley: too much society and politics and not enough commerce, perhaps. When Samuel died, the estate, somewhat contracted by his expenses, passed to Fiennes Trotman of Skelswell, Oxfordshire, the son of Samuel's uncle Lenthall. Fiennes died a bachelor and the estate passed to another Fiennes Trotman, a 'riband weaver' of Northampton who had married Lenthall Trotman's niece and heir. This reinfusion of commercial blood revived the family. Building on his good fortune, Fiennes served as MP for Northampton, Sheriff of Gloucestershire (where the weavers were very turbulent at this time) and, Whig to the last, finally refused an offer from Pitt the Elder of the vacant viscountcy of Saye and Sele.

The Trotmans, like the Tyndales, began by filling the social and economic space created in the Vale by the abdication of the lords Berkeley. They did so by assiduously converting money made in the cloth industry into yeoman estates. Their 'take-off' began with the acquisition of a fulling mill in 1512. By the third generation – that of Richard the Elder of Cam – the largest estates in the family were those of parish gentry rather than the yeomen they began as. By the end of the sixteenth century their neighbour John Smyth of Nibley regarded several descendants of Henry the Clothier as gentry, even though the title had not been formalised with a grant of arms. That came in 1616. By then the family had legal and mercantile branches in London.

Throgmorton Trotman's will provided an epitome of the social and geographical space conquered by families who owed their rise to the expanding English cloth industry. His world stretched from Cam to Moorfields, and from Antwerp to Virginia. His younger brother, Samuel, followed his father in the legal profession, married into the family of the Speaker of the Long Parliament, and was well placed to pick up some choice Royalist estates. His children and grandchildren settled into the landed gentry. By this time the social, economic and political networks which earlier generations had etched into the landscape by their activities and vision were in place.

The degree to which the Trotmans can be regarded as a *class*-fragment, and the 'kin-coalition' seen as an agency in the long rise of a distinctive English bourgeoisie, remains conjectural. How many such 'coalitions' existed, in the sixteenth century, in other parts of England? How many expanded out, to colonise and interconnect in a genuinely national class in London in the decades before the civil wars? With regard to these substantive questions, this chapter does no more than put forward a hypothesis that needs further exploration.

It does, however, clarify an area of conceptual confusion. It is usual to think of class-structuring in terms of hierarchies, as in the 'rise' of the gentry or yeomanry, or in 'high', 'middle' and 'low' classes. It is easy to forget that this is no more than a metaphor. The 'rise' of new groups and classes usually involves the expansion of networks in social and territorial space: a form of colonisation. This, I have suggested, was a key feature in the career and thought of William Tyndale. It was also an important dimension in the 'rise' of the English middle rank in the sixteenth and seventeenth centuries. The rise of the English 'bourgeoisie' was a cumulative process of territorial expansion, a conquest of space.

Part III

TWO REVOLUTIONARIES

6

'SMALL THINGES AND GRANDE DESIGNES'

A revolutionary's history of the English Revolution

'Generall histories doe seldome approach the fountaine of action . . . Whereas there appeare in particular branches those lively sparklings and more secret motions of life and heate . . . Not only the remarkable changes of the universe, the grand periods of kingdoms and common-wealths, the chief and turning points of state affaires, but particular platforms, lives, examples, and emergent occasions also, are to be observed and laid up for posterity. . . .

And this is the life of history, that ought to declare the delinquency of state as well as its accomplishment and perfection.'

John Corbet[1]

1

A PURITAN REVOLUTIONARY

The English Revolution is 'inherently controversial . . . Civil wars and revolutions are by their nature divisive'.[2] Few accounts take us closer to the heart of the debates than John Corbet's *Historicall Relation of the Military Government of Gloucester from the Beginning of Civill Warre Betweene King and Parliament*, published in 1645.[3] For R. C. Richardson, Corbet was an ancestor of the 'local and regional studies of seventeenth-century England that have become one of the most thriving branches of the recent historiography'. He was 'an acute observer of the local scene' and 'his comments on the social composition of the Parliamentarian side in the Civil War put future historians in his debt'.[4] Richardson was probably thinking of the 'debts' of Christopher Hill and, in particular, Brian Manning, who put Corbet to good, if controversial, use.[5] They cite Corbet to support the view that the English Revolution was a 'people's revolution', driven on by popular pressure. 'Acute' observer he undoubtedly was; his arguments on this point are plausible, but a doubt remains over the accuracy of key statements in

123

his account – and these are the statements Hill and Manning cite to support their arguments.

A nineteenth-century nonconformist writer rightly described Corbet as 'sternly and avowedly puritanical'.[6] Corbet stressed the revolutionary leadership of what he called 'a practicall ministry'. As chaplain to the Parliamentarian governor of Gloucester, Colonel Edward Massey, he was a revolutionary Puritan minister himself, and provides useful references for historians favouring a 'Puritan Revolution' interpretation. This may be the context for John Morrill's belief that Corbet was a 'bigot'.[7]

Corbet was fiercely critical of the nature and role of the gentry, and might also be thought bigoted on that count. He thought gentlemen and nobles who fought for the king did so not out of any love for monarchical government, but out of an inbred desire to reduce their 'neighbours' to 'vassals'. They were inherently parasitical because, as rentiers, they 'lived in the breath of other men'. In the event of war, they confirmed his prejudice by 'dis[con]certing their country either by open enmity or detestable neutrality'. Here he was probably right. He respected the martial valour of some knights, but assumed that men of that rank lined up with the king as a matter of course. The Royalist governor of Sudeley Castle, Sir William Morton, was 'high spirit[ed] and bold . . . a knowing man, able in the profession of law, and versed in the wayes and actions of men'. But he was bound by rank to be an enemy to Corbet's side. 'He was . . . more strongly linked into [the king's] cause by the late honour of knighthood, which by the state is held no better than a note of infamy, to stigmatise those persons that have been eminent in the disservice of the commonwealth.'[8] The son of a Gloucester shoemaker, Corbet had an invariable prejudice against feudal titles of any sort. Throughout his book he referred to Parliament as 'the state', and thought of the 'commonwealth' as the aggregate of property-holders, irrespective of what he regarded as anachronistic and intrinsically inappropriate titles. In this he obeyed the biblical injunction not to respect rank, but to judge people by their piety and activity for the commonwealth.

He confirms John Morrill's review of 'a good deal of recent work [that] has shown a growing self-confidence and independence in the attitude and behaviour of substantial yeoman-farmers, craftsmen and so on'. This work, Morrill writes, 'call[s] into question the assumption that it is the gentry alone who determined the political alignment of a county in the civil war'.[9] Corbet was always uncompromising, but never more than on this point. 'The yeomen, farmers, cloathiers, and the whole middle ranke of the people', he wrote, 'were *the only active men.*' If Corbet's social analysis of the war can be relied on, he takes the debate back to where Christopher Hill stands, on the ground occupied by the English Bourgeois Revolution.[10]

English historians tend to be impatient with the long-term determinants, or 'deep structures' that condition events, ruling out all save a few options. 'The kind of society that England was determined the kind of civil war that was possible' in 1642, writes G. E. Aylmer in a recent general account of England's revolutionary decades. 'The whole previous geography and history of the country helped to determine this, but did not actually cause the war which broke out as and when it did.'[11] Aylmer then spends a page listing the relatively fixed (Braudel would say 'slow-moving') conditions on which the great French structuralist would have spent a thousand pages, and then apologise for 300 or so pages on 'ephemera', passing episodes, the surface spume blown up by subterranean currents and unpredictable winds whose scales are global and whose historical depths induce vertigo. Corbet's analysis, taken in conjunction with other contemporary sources, reveals the epistemological fallacy in Aylmer's (and, from the other side, Braudel's) distinction between 'deep structures' and 'events'.

Corbet was something of a 'conjunctural' historian as the term is used by Pierre Vilar. 'Broadly speaking,' writes Vilar, 'the conjuncture means "the totality of all the conditions in which a problem or an event is located".'

> The historian, like the man of action, must constantly define this 'general conjuncture', since even the apparently most remote facts may influence the understanding of a given moment.[12]

Corbet was scholarly, but he was not interested in analysis of events and structures for their own sake. He had to get his facts right in order to make things happen in ways that were compatible with the cause for which he was fighting. The distinction between scholar and man of action is as meaningless in Corbet's case as it would be in the cases of Lenin, Mao or Trotsky's *History of the Russian Revolution*. Corbet was a historian *because* he was a revolutionary. It was necessary to try to understand 'the grand periods of kingdomes and commonwealths, the chief and turning-points of state affairs', but this had to be done through examination of 'those particularities, and minute passages . . . that come home to men's businesse'. He was conscious of a reverberating dialectic between 'particulars', 'small thinges' and the 'grand designe'. On the 'small thinges' he is reliable; his 'grand designe' is more questionable.

Like many modern historians, Corbet was interested in 'agency', how to make things happen. Like our 'bottom-up' historians, he looked for 'the fountain of action', historical causation and agency, in the 'low bottome and meane beginning [from which] great things [are]

125

raised'. He rejected the perspective of 'all . . . who respect only great, and excelse objects, which peradventure may flourish with ostentation and pomp'. He urged consideration of what he termed the 'moral influence' of 'particulars' which, 'if applyed unto the life of man bring forth an effect like the birth of mountains'. History, for him, had an exemplary critical purpose, for 'only by examples of all sorts must we learn to except and distinguish, and by consequence to use or abate the rigour of politicall maximes'.

As an eye-witness to many of the events he described, and as a participant, he was particularly conscious of one of the basic truths of revolutionary moments: decisions are made by people who by custom and law have previously been regarded as subjects of the state. Revolutions can never make complete sense when viewed from the perspective of states and ruling classes and groups; by definition much of the action is generated at the grass roots.[13] Whatever their outcome, this is their nature. Whether we regard them with romantic admiration or appalled horror, they happen. Every so often societies rise up and overthrow states that are proving inadequate in their institutional and ideological assumptions. Corbet put forward an argument about the grass-roots sources of the English Revolution (or in his metaphor, the turning of the 'wheels of Providence'). We shall consider how well – how accurately – he did it.

Born in 1620, Corbet was an exact contemporary of George Brydges, Gloucestershire's leading Royalist. The son of a Gloucester shoemaker, he was educated at Gloucester Grammar School and Magdalen College Oxford, where he was admitted bachelor of arts at the age of 19, in 1639.[14] On completion of his degree he took holy orders, and returned to his native city to conduct pastoral duties in the parish of St Mary de Crypt, to preach, lecture and teach under one of the most radical thinkers in England, the Socinian divine, John Biddle, at the Grammar School. Gloucester was a little bastion of the English bourgeoisie, one of the most radical towns in England; Puritanism, or, as its enemies called it, 'the pretended holy side', predominated in all of the most populous parts of Gloucestershire: at Cirencester and (to a lesser extent) Tewkesbury, in the little cloth towns and villages along the steep Cotswold escarpment (Painswick, Stroud, Dursley, Wotton-under-Edge), even in the households of Cotswold yeomen in the combs of the hills which stretched south from Shakespeare's country to the spa town of Bath, not then the fashionable resort it was to become in the eighteenth century. Wherever manufacturing and commerce flourished, and in few parts of England did they flourish as in Gloucestershire, the middle rank predominated, and where the middle rank flourished there was Puritanism.

The name is subject to controversy. I have never encountered the word 'Puritan' in contemporary documents relevant to the region and the period.[15] Hostile sources refer to 'men with close-cropp'd hair' and 'the pretended holy side'. John Corbet described the social movement we mean when we say 'Puritan' and 'Puritanism' in some detail, subjecting it to what we would call 'sociological' and 'political-economic' analysis and classification. His perspective had a practical edge, History with a purpose.

When Gloucestershire was invaded by the king's men in 1643 Corbet was appointed domestic chaplain to the Parliamentarian governor of Gloucester, Edward Massey. On these grounds we must be aware of an element of propaganda in his intentions. He believed intensely in the justice – indeed, the holiness – of the struggle. But he meant what he said about historians recording the 'delinquency of states', and throughout his book he used the term 'state' to refer to his own, the Parliamentarian, cause. He was frequently critical of his own side. He wanted an efficient revolution.

Corbet's *Historicall Relation* is an important source-document of the English Revolution for a number of reasons. The events with which he dealt were intrinsically important: arguably, the defence of Gloucester in 1643 against the full force of Royalist siege was a turning-point in the first civil war, sustaining the morale of Parliamentarians in London and other parts of England at a time when it looked as if the cause might have been lost.[16] But it is also important for its intellectual qualities. Corbet was a self-conscious historian and social analyst, and opened his account with a discussion of historical method and theory (How should the past be analysed? Once analysed, how do we assign it meaning? In what general context should contingent, short-term events be placed?). His approach has affinities with twentieth-century Marxists and *annalistes*, yet also radical empiricists – although of course the modes of thought implied in these terms had not yet divided from the mainstream of European post-Renaissance rationalism. Events, for him, were 'conjunctures' of more momentous, long-term historical movements. The terminology he used was not that of the twentieth century, of course, but there are affinities with late twentieth-century historiography. Allowing for his obvious prejudices, he was a reflective and critical historian of events in which he had played a significant role.

Secondly, Corbet set his events in a context that will be familiar to modern social historians and historical materialists. Having discussed method and theory, he gives a carefully formulated account of the social–structural context of the struggle in Gloucestershire. His account of social structure is interwoven with a political–economic explanation; that is to say, he explains the outbreak of civil war in terms of systematic – 'structural' – relativities of wealth and power. He assumed that loyalties (a central aspect of consciousness) were determined by material circumstances. Unlike Marx, though perhaps like his contemporary at Gloucester, John Biddle, 'the father of English Unitarianism',[17] he saw 'Divine Providence' behind these structural circumstances. Like eighteenth-century Deists and the 'imperial sensationalists' of colonial Princeton, he analysed reality as if consciousness was explained by material circumstances which, in turn, were ground out by 'the wheeles of Providence'.[18] In this sense he was a proto-Enlightenment historian, and an American founding grandfather. These features of his writing make him an interesting, indeed inspirational, writer; they do not make him right.

Corbet's *Historicall Relation* is intellectually exciting as well as methodical in its approach to factual detail. He tells the story of an heroic passage in the early years of the conflict, by and large, without exaggeration. To set against the prejudices which obviously mark the work of a man who never doubted whose side he was on, his work has the authenticity of a man who was actively engaged in a localised but nationally crucial struggle which, at any point between February 1643 and July 1644, could have gone either way. I focus in particular on passages dealing with the political–economic and social–structural foundations of the revolution in Gloucestershire: these have remained the most controversial part of his interpretation. I 'unpack' what Corbet had to say on this subject, and examine its validity in the light of other contemporary or near-contemporary evidence, much of it susceptible to quantitative reconstitution and analysis. I consider his theory of the conjuncture, and his promise to subject affairs of state, the actions of his own side in the struggle, to rigorous, moralistic criticism. I shall explore the reliability of Corbet's testimony on the events in Gloucestershire, and assess how far those events were revolutionary. Was Corbet right, and if he was, was he a participant–observer in the 'bourgeois revolution' in the Marxian sense?

2

'SMALL THINGES AND GRAND DESIGNES': CORBET'S PRACTICAL HISTORIOGRAPHY

Corbet set out to make the events in Gloucestershire 'knowne unto more than them that acted, or beheld [them] at a nearer distance'. He aimed to inform readers who were not present, and those who had been so embroiled as actors that it became difficult to see beyond the chaos of events: he was after a kind of middle ground. He was conscious that the events were only a part, though not 'the meanest part of the present warfare, the event whereof all Christendome may expect with admiration and horrour'. He was writing 'but one branch of the history of these times' – but what times they were, in his view! 'The action . . . transcends the barons' warres, and those tedious discordes betweene the Houses of Yorke and Lancaster, inasmuch as it is undertaken upon higher principles, and carried on to a nobler end, and effects more universall.'[19] What made the civil wars of the 1640s different from all the others before them was that they were led by men inspired by conscious 'principle'. They were not trying to substitute one set of lords for another, but were fighting to create a new world. They had in mind 'universall effects', a thorough social revolution.

He was aware that perspective necessarily shapes any account of wars in which 'three kingdomes are engaged, and no part of them stand free as spectators only'. To combat bias, he advocated close attention to detail. Many of his generalisations would appeal to radical –empirical revisionists. At times his approach uses the conceptual tools lately expropriated by 'postmodernists', referring to History as a 'multiplicity of interwoven discourses', which can only 'be viewed in severall parcells'. Methodological individualists would part company with Corbet at his belief that the 'interwoven discourses' comprised a totality, even if the totality was unclear to merely human eyes. Corbet was convinced that 'small thinges' were 'turned upon the Wheeles of Providence; too high for the imitation of men'. This is a reference, quite literally, to 'revolution', and a reminder that conscious revolution in the modern sense begins with Corbet's generation of English people. Corbet believed men had set the wheel of Providence turning, as secondary agencies of divine Providence. Revolution, to him, meant breaking out of the vicious *cycle* premised on Original Sin. He was groping towards a millenarian, linear time-conception, a Progress determined by bringing human behaviour into line with the will of Providence by means of Godly discipline and valour.

While he was aware of the momentous significance of the events in which he participated, it was a matter of principle for Corbet to concentrate on details. This was the human role in the divine plan. He warned against over-ambitious generalisation. 'They that gather up so many divided plots [as now acted] into one modell,' he wrote, 'are wont to endeavour after a smoother path, a greater harmony, and more exact symmetry of parts; whereas the face of things is conscious of more disproportion, sometimes a confusion of businesse.' 'In the midst of action . . . the reasons of the same counsells is one in the Senate; another in the field. . . .' 'The piercing subtilties of wit are broken and shattered by the course of things more knotty, rude and violent.' He is at pains to stress contradictions between formal policy-making and the contingencies of practical actions.[20]

Corbet's history turns constantly to analogies between scholarship and practical action.[21] Neither, he suggests, can be premised on grasp of the totality. Indeed, at one point he seems to suggest the Weberian conclusion that 'Providence' is necessary as a convenient fiction because of this inevitable limitation on human knowledge: 'but things more grand and lofty *seeme* to be turned upon the wheeles of Providence; too high for the imitation of men'.[22]

He reminds us that, while History is written in studies and libraries, it is not made there:

> The worke of a politick or martiall man is to fixe his design, and then to expect the accomplishment, not by one sudden or great atchievement, but by a series of many particles, and through an infinite variety of emergent occasions . . . Besides, the chiefe skill is not the generall knowledge of the maine undertaking, but a certaine dexterity in meeting every point, in working through many mazings and windings, since sundry passages of small purport intervene to disturb or promove it. Experience tells, that many universall scholars are the most uncouth persons to civill employments, which so happens, because they study bookes more than the course of business, in which they gaze upon high objects, and binde themselves to the rigid observance of received canons . . . [23]

'From a low bottom and meane beginning are great things raised,' he concluded. This implied his act of faith: that the actions of humanity add up to more than the sum of their parts. The 'high' emerges from the 'low' through the agency of the universal 'grande designer'.

Corbet's history is 'academic' in the sense that it is the work of an academy-trained scholar, but not in the sometimes pejorative sense that it is sufficient unto itself, or relevant only to closed professional discourse. His constant references to actions, agencies and practicalities are meant to stress that, at its best, scholarly history is (or should be) an urgent, practical activity. Whether or not circumstances and nature made it possible for him to do this, he took pains to get his facts right, and to select and represent them as judiciously as he could, in order to provide posterity with a text from which it could learn, in the quiet aftermath of great events, in order to improve upon the past by learning its lessons and acting upon them. He put the past at the service of the present, in order to build a better future, yet with constant reminders of the limitations of human understanding and ability to grasp and control the whole. His act of faith was that it *mattered*, and that somehow, if people set out to make the 'small thinges' work well, the 'grand design' would follow. He was a revolutionary before he was a historian.

He expected his book to be published and read by influential men and he was aware that he 'hazarded the censure of these knowing times'. He was a committed anti-monarchist, and had no fears of the old regime, which lay in ruins as he wrote, as a result, in small part, of his own struggle and that of his party. The exact composition of his 'party' is where controversy lies. His statements of historical philosophy were intended to give legitimacy to his criticisms of his own party. His scholarship had to be good because he was a revolutionary criticising the revolution.

3

'THE ONLY ACTIVE MEN': CORBET'S SOCIAL ANALYSIS

Corbet's account of the social dynamics of 'the beginning of action' was no gestural preface to his account of events. His intention was 'to declare the grounds of that affection which the country did express, and were common unto them with many parts of the kingdom, that were devoted to the same cause'. He meant his social analysis to *explain* why the war occurred, to describe the conditions without which it would not, and could not, have taken place. He also thought that conditions in Gloucestershire prevailed throughout England – but with less intensity: he thought the circumstances which explained armed resistance to the king 'might appear in a greater degree, and have a clearer evidence in the present example'.[24]

In Corbet's account, a class of middle-rank countrymen comprising roughly 25 per cent of all householders, imbued with belief in 'a well-bounded freedom, and regular priviledges', organised by 'a practicall ministry', resisted and overcame an armigerous elite comprised of 'powerfull' magnate Royalists and evasive but nonetheless 'tyrannical' gentry. For him it was a war between the middle rank and the magnates, rooted in different circumstances of life, different ideologies and different conceptions of religion. The majority of the population below the middle rank – Corbet calls them 'common people', 'the multitude', 'the ignoble multitude', and (implying the key distinction, a reference to relative material circumstances) 'the needy' – was not 'at the will of the gentry, but observed those men by whom those manufactures were maintained that kept them alive'. His prejudices with regard to the 'needy . . . multitude' were platitudes of the day, shared by Royalist lords and Parliamentarian clothiers alike. The 'common people', they all assumed, was economically dependent and politically deferential, an essentially passive, if unpredictable and mercurial, constitutional force. This will require qualification. Evidence suggests that Corbet's 'needy . . . multitudes' gave the events of the early 1640s their dynamism, their driving force.

131

The function of the middle rank in providing employment, and thus sustaining the lives of the poor, was a cornerstone of their claim to social and political legitimacy. The principle is expressed on a contemporary memorial tablet to Hodgkinson Paine on the walls of Cirencester Church. Paine, a clothier, was slain still grasping the Parliamentarian Colours by the Royalists in the market-square during the siege of Cirencester. It reads:

> The Poore's Supplie his life and calling grac'd
> 'Till Warres made rent and Paine from Poore's displac'd
> But what made poore unfortunate Paine blest
> By warre they lost their PAINE, yet found noe rest.[25]

This strand in the ideology of the manufacturing middle rank mirrored the conventional wisdom of the Cavaliers, that clothiers and other organisers of large-scale industry were exploiters and expropriators of the poor.

'Neither they of the middle rank, nor the needy', wrote Corbet, 'were devoted to the examples of the gentlemen who turned back, betrayed their trust . . . but had learned to reverence their liberties, and to acknowledge their native happiness.'[26] This was the cornerstone of Corbet's interpretation: an alliance of the middle rank and the common people fought in the name of liberty and independence against the tyranny of the traditional ruling class. He saw the common people as assistants but not active agents in a struggle that they did not understand.

Corbet had a coherent view of the structure of his society, which he used to explain events. For him, the events of the early 1640s brought to a head a momentous struggle between the 'middle ranke' and an anachronistic, disdainful, bastard-feudal elite. Those who displayed 'open enmity' were motivated by 'a desire for vast dominion, dignity, revenge, or rapine', and wished 'to rule over their neighbours like vassals'. The antagonists were marked by opposed sensibilities, intentions and everyday practices. Both sides knew what they were fighting for and against. Muddling and short-sighted policies may have brought events to this impasse, but when the time came the business of taking sides was predictable because rooted in social circumstances which everyone understood.

For Corbet, then, the war was essentially a conflict between the scions of the armigerous old regime and the 'middle ranke'. Other contemporary sources support his view without confirming it. They confirm that the old elite constituted no more than 2–3 per cent of the total number of households in Gloucestershire, ruling over the least heavily populated districts. His middle rank constituted about 25 per cent, and in normal times they controlled the most heavily populated

districts. Corbet's point that 'there was no excessive number of powerful gentry' in the county makes a comparative point that would require
analysis comparing Gloucestershire with other parts of England.[27] The
Revolution was a split within the ruling class only in the sense that
hitherto the middle class and the magnates had constituted a kind of
ruling-class 'bloc', with the armigerous elite governing at county and
national levels and the middle rank handling affairs in the localities.
Corbet's point that the 'needy multitudes' blindly and inevitably supported whoever happened to dominate the particular districts they
happened to live and work in will require qualification.

Let me recapitulate the 'particulars' of Corbet's account. First there
is his proposition that the middle rank were 'the only active men'.
Second, that they were organised and led by 'a practicall ministry'.
Third, that the gentry and aristocracy were either Royalist or 'detestably neutral'. Fourth, that the middle rank had a coherent revolutionary ideology, grounded in material circumstances. Fifth, that the
common people followed the middle rank and not the gentry. Sixth
and finally, that Gloucestershire was an exemplary case of the circumstances that led to resistance, war and revolution – and if so, why?

When Gloucestershire was threatened with invasion by the king's
forces stationed at Oxford, between August 1642 and February 1643
(when invasion in fact took place), 'the business [of organising the
resistance] chiefly rested', in Corbet's words, 'on Sir Robert Cooke, Sir
John Seamore, Master Nathaniel Stephens, Master Edward Stephens,
Master Thomas Hodges, with the rest of the deputy lieutenants':

> And setting aside these men with some gleanings of the gentry,
> the yeomen, farmers, cloathiers, and the whole middle ranke of
> the people were the only active men.

'The gentlemen in generall denyed their concurrence,' he stressed,
'dis[con]certing their country either by open enmity or detestable neutrality.'[28] Modern scholarship, based on a wide range of evidence not
available to Corbet at the time, confirms his account. Gentry who were
active in the cause of liberty were few enough to name.

Other sources make it possible to quantify these social groupings.
The musters of 1608 generated occupational listings of able-bodied
men in every manor and borough in Gloucestershire, and have been
carefully studied.[29] The musters were conducted twelve years before
Corbet was born, and thirty-five years before the outbreak of civil war
in the region, so they can be used only as a rough guide to the
proportions constituted by the occupational and status groups mentioned in his account. Hearth Tax listings for 1664 and 1671 provide
useful, if not definitive, information on social structure.[30] The sources

are not exactly contemporary; short-term fluctuations occurred. Nevertheless, it will be of some value to use them to make quantitative sense of Corbet's categories.

The Tawneys counted 430 'knights, esquires and gentlemen' in the 1608 muster-lists, which compares favourably with a more recent estimate, derived from a variety of other contemporary sources, that 'noble and gentry families probably contained no more than 2,600 individuals, or about 3–4 per cent of 131,000 according to the 1664 Hearth Tax assessments'.[31] This is roughly what Corbet meant by 'powerfull gentry': an interconnected elite of families, most of whom claimed Norman–Angevin knightly and esquire estate, and many of whom had been resident in the county for centuries.

The 'middle rank' was more numerous, and more problematical. Corbet gives two general descriptions.[32] The first lists 'yeomen, farmers, petty-freeholders, and such as use manufactures that enrich the country'; the second, 'yeomen, farmers, cloathiers, and the whole middle ranke'. The Tawneys counted 927 yeomen and 207 clothiers in 1608, which leaves doubt over which classifications in 1608 should be accounted equivalent to Corbet's 'farmers', 'petty-freeholders' and 'such as use manufactures'. 'Cloathier' needs much qualification, later.

In 1608 only one farmer and one grazier were listed in the entire county: the terms were not then in general use. In addition there was the wide-ranging term 'husbandman', used to describe 3,774 of the men listed in 1608. Assuming a strict distinction between freeholding yeomen and copyholding husbandmen, which cannot be taken for granted, we then have to decide what proportion of husbandmen to include in the 'middle ranke'. This comes down to a relatively arbitrary calculation as to what percentage of husbandmen were large tenant farmers, as against the majority, who were smallholders who had to supplement their income with labouring work or a trade. Let us make an informed guess that the average manor, in addition to men designated as freeholding yeomen, had at least two substantial tenant-farmers who lived comfortably (i.e. were unlikely to be described at any time in their active life as 'needy'), but worked rented land. The musters relate to 444 manors, which yields a guess of 888 'farmers' yeomen, clothiers and 'farmers' together adding up to 2,022 able-bodied men out of a total of 19,402: 10 per cent, not including the final category 'such as use manufactures'.

Early modern status categories (lord, knight, esquire, gent, 'Mr') are fairly predictable in their use, but occupational categories are always problematical: what is important is that all the evidence, such as it is, should point in the same general direction. With 'such as use manufactures that enrich the country and passe through the hands of the multitude', we encounter difficulties that can be only partially resolved by closer investigation of Corbet's text, and other sources. Thus far, we are probably not straying too far from Corbet's intentions and assumptions if we say that at most 40–50 gentry households lined up in the Royalist camp, actively opposed by 10 per cent of the local population, to which, in due course, we shall have to add an indeterminate number intended by the phrase 'such as use manufactures'. This does no more than translate Corbet's phrases into rough quantities. Quantification and classification of this sort, however accurate, can only yield an abstract class, or grouping, of people. Such a class cannot be regarded as an actual historical agency, only as a more or less useful way of grouping and counting data. What Corbet had in mind was something much stronger (or more 'empirical'): not a 'class' or 'rank' *in* itself, but one that was united in consciousness, mentality, ideology and loyalty – a 'class' or 'rank' that was united *for* itself. Organisation, therefore, must be regarded as a crucial variable determining the character of the 'middle ranke'.

The unifying force, in Corbet's view, was religion. 'A knowledge of things pertaining to divine worship, according to the maine principles of the Christian profession,' he wrote, had produced a strong independent-mindedness in the members of Gloucestershire's middle rank. 'The more knowing are apt to contradict and question,' he wrote, 'and will not easily be brought to the bent':

> For this cause the ambition of the times hath endeavoured the undermining of true religion, to promote a blind and slavish generation of men, which kind of bondage the meanest person that performes a reasonable service cannot but resent and fear.[33]

Knowledge of these 'maine principles' had been propagated and encouraged in his region 'by meanes of a practicall ministry . . . and in this kind of knowledge,' he wrote, 'this city [Gloucester] and county was more happy than many other parts of the kingdom'. It had given rise to 'no ignorant and slavish generation', like the 'common people addicted to the king's service [that] have come out of blinde Wales, and other dark corners of the land'.[34] For Corbet the wars – 'a fire kindled and fomented by Jesuited Papists and their adherents' – came down to a struggle between two pastoral ideals, one authoritarian, the other independent.[35] These statements were designed to appeal to the prejudices of Corbet's constituents, the middle rank. And it is not surprising that a university-trained cleric would see events through clerical spectacles, assigning a crucial role to ministers of religion and viewing mentality as pervaded with theological and pastoral (as against utilitarian and political) assumptions. But Corbet's loyalties were not, first and foremost, to the ministerial profession, but to his own 'middle rank' (he was the son of a shoemaker). What is implied, in the light of his social–structural and political–economic analysis, is that men of a certain class or rank tended towards a particular pastoral ideal, i.e. their consciousness was determined, or at least profoundly shaped, by their social circumstances. Corbet suggests that clerics did not create the ideological propensities of the middle rank; they just gave coherent voice to them.

Corbet's stress on the crucial role played by a 'practicall' and separatist ministry compares favourably with an account, put forward five years earlier, in March 1640, by one of his professional colleagues at Gloucester, John Allibond, an Arminian canon at the Cathedral. Allibond wrote a letter to a colleague in London, Peter Heylyn (later editor of the Royalist newspaper, *Mercurius Aulicus*, and another cleric with Arminian convictions), describing and explaining the circumstances of the Gloucestershire elections for Knights of the Shire to what was to become the 'Short Parliament'. In this letter he explained that the divisive candidature and campaign of Nathaniel Stephens (whom Corbet later named as one of the leaders of the Parliamentarian party), had been organised by Puritan ministers in different parts of the county, whom he listed by name. In his view they were the ones who had 'rolled this stone' in order to put 'the king's nose to the grindstone'.[36] Allibond's letter also contains invaluable information – this time from a hostile source – on the organisation and social dynamics of Corbet's revolutionary party, and is worth exploring in detail.

4

WEAVERS AND SHEPHERDS: THE ELECTIONS OF MARCH 1640 AS SOCIAL DRAMA

The elections of March 1640 were precipitated, after eleven years of government without Parliament, by the king's need for money to raise an army against the Scottish Presbyterians, currently in occupation of the North of England. The elections in Gloucestshire were the occasion of a revolutionary 'social drama' in the sense outlined by Victor Turner. 'Whether it is a large affair, like the Dreyfus Case or Watergate,' he writes, 'or a struggle for village headmanship, a social drama first manifests itself as the breach of a norm, the infraction of a rule of morality, custom or etiquette in some public arena.'[37]

This breach may be deliberately, even calculatedly, contrived by a person or party disposed to demonstrate or challenge entrenched authority – for example, the Boston Tea Party – or it may emerge from a scene of heated feelings. Once visible, it can hardly be revoked. Whatever the case, a mounting crisis follows, a momentous juncture or turning-point in the relations between components of a social field – at which seeming peace becomes overt conflict and covert antagonisms become visible. Sides are taken, factions are formed, and unless the conflict can be sealed off quickly within a limited area of social interaction, there is a tendency for the breach to widen and spread until it coincides with some dominant cleavage in the widest set of relevant social relations to which the parties in the conflict belong.

Turner's point is that all human situations contain latent conflicts, but as long as they remain unexpressed, as it were 'repressed' or 'contained' by the tacit understanding that to express them is dangerous, they can be controlled and the semblance of social harmony can be maintained. An example in English culture is what amounts to a taboo on free discussion of class. Class distinction is one of the most obvious features of English culture, at least to outside observers. But in England it tends to be a suppressed subject, not suitable for polite conversation. This is probably because it is the most socially explosive ingredient of the social and cultural field.

Let us first consider some of the conflicts that were part of the understood background *milieu* of the elections of 1640. In 1635 and again in 1639, the people of Gloucestershire had been among the most intractable tax rebels in the kingdom. Twenty years earlier William Laud, whose efforts to impose Arminian church government on the Scots had led to the present crisis, had been a functionary in the Gloucester diocesan bureaucracy headed by Bishop Godfrey Goodman. Goodman was a suspected Catholic, accused by Bastwick, Burton and Prynne in 1628 'with having introduced altar-clothes . . . with crucifixes embroidered on them . . . and with having suspended' the minister of Little Dean 'on the ground that he had preached that an obstinate papist, dying a papist, could not be saved, and if we be saved, the papists were not.'[38] Sentiments like these went back, in Gloucestershire, to at least the time of William Tyndale.[39] Royal taxation and religious government were divisive issues in Gloucestershire long before the Scottish problem forced the king to call a Parliament. But the elections of 1640 became a watershed, a significant parting of the ways, a 'social drama' through which people became conscious that conflict with the king was also a divisive *social* conflict.

The tone and sympathies of John Allibond's letter to Peter Heylyn, who was Prebendary of Westminster and Chaplain in Ordinary to the king, were Royalist and Arminian. Early modern parliamentary elections have sometimes been seen as formalities, a popular rubber-stamp on decisions really made by the county gentry behind closed doors. This, with certain qualifications, is how Shakespeare saw populist politics in his play *Coriolanus* (1609), and Shakespeare knew this region very well: the Cotswold Hills were Stratford's back garden.[40] Allibond expected 'the gentry [to] sway the plebeians'.[41] Whatever was the case usually, the expectation was not met in March 1640. This was one of the 'infractions of a rule of . . . custom' that occurred during the elections for the Short Parliament. Another was that candidates should be nominated by a committee of the county gentry, as appointed by the king to the county Bench.

The 'general accord' of the Gloucestershire gentry, who met early in March to 'pitch upon' candidates, was for two knights, Sir Robert Tracy and Sir Robert Cooke, 'the one a Cotswold gentleman, and the other of Highnam, near Gloucester'. This was more than an innocent remark identifying the addresses of the two men. It referred to a 'covert antagonism' in the 'public arena'. The Tracys were kin to the Brydges, lords Chandos of Sudeley. Sir Robert Tracy's great-grand-mother was a daughter of Sir John Brydges, first Lord Chandos. His grandfather, John Tracy, was knighted by Queen Elizabeth when she was at Sudeley Castle in 1574.[42] The reference was to two different worlds, two distinct 'parties'. That different parties existed was acknowledged. Cooke wore his hair 'close-cropped', and was identified with an extensive party of men with short hair. Allibond took it for granted that Heylyn would know what and who this meant, but he went into detail later in his letter. Tracy belonged to the 'powerful gentry'. Besides his connections with the 'kings of the Cotswolds', he descended from an illustrious and ancient knightly family, with an ancestor who murdered Thomas a Becket in Canterbury Cathedral in the reign of Henry II, and another whose anticlericalism was such that Henry VIII ordered his body exhumed and spread across the land-scape. The Tracys were no subservient monarchists, and their tra-ditions were firmly Protestant (i.e. anti-papist, nationalist). What mat-tered was that they were Norman in descent, *powerfull* gentry, men with ruling in the blood. That is all they had in common with Charles I, whose Scottish ancestry would not have impressed the Tracys, who had been fighting against the Scots since Domesday.

The coupling of the rich merchant (Cooke) and the stately Tracy was a compromise made by the gentry in order to satisfy both popular and elite feeling without the people being seen to determine the out-come. The inheritors of Norman–Angevin feudalism, for whom the Protestant Reformation had been no more than a final victory over long-detested Abbots, and an acquisition of much of their best land (as indeed it had been for the middle rank too), would be satisfied, in difficult circumstances, with this gesture of generosity towards lesser men and businessmen. The lesser men and businessmen did not see it this way.

In a sense, Cooke and Tracy represented the oldest parties of all, the country and the city, trade and agriculture. Cooke's manorial interests lay in the suburbs of Gloucester. The borough proper had increased in population from 4,000 in the 1530s to 'just over 5,000' in c.1640, of which 'the major share came from immigration'.[43] Cooke's acceptability lay in the fact that, in spite of his associations with the radical city of Gloucester, he was a knight himself, and the son of a knight. In 1608 his father, Sir William Cooke, had attended the musters at the head of a personal retinue consisting of 13 household servants, 8 yeoman, 2 husbandmen and a clothier (the 'middle ranke'?), who were also described, in feudal style, as 'servants to Sir William Cooke'. Behind them came 53 more tenants who included 15 miscellaneous tradesmen, a clothier and 4 weavers, and just 4 labourers, who would have found plenty of work on the market gardens of the neighbourhood, which produced grain, vegetables and dairy produce for the Gloucester markets. Although Sir Robert Cooke fought actively for Parliament, and was Parliamentarian governor of Tewkesbury, his son was a Royalist.[44] Gloucester was a highly literate borough, a 'puritan county town' with a 'growing commitment to radical politics before and after 1640'.[45] Cooke was definitely identified with the Puritan side because at one point during the first day's polling, 'Tracy's side challenged Cooke of infidelity', and Tracy's election organiser, 'Mr Dutton', swore 'that for his sake he would never more trust any man that wore his hair shorter than his ears'. Here were signs that the elections became 'a scene of heated feelings', one of the conditions which Turner argues is necessary before repressed knowledge becomes articulate.

The candidates 'pitched on' by the gentry, then, were a moderate puritan knight with trade, legal and urban connections, and a moderate loyalist knight from the hills. Both would be expected to show firmness with respect to the king (one of Tracy's supporters, John Dutton, had been imprisoned for his opposition to Ship Money); both were knights, and might be expected to hold no sympathy with populist, levelling tendencies. The expectation was that Tracy would instruct his supporters to vote for Cooke, and vice-versa, thus avoiding the risk of stirring up too much popular activity in troubled times. Cooke wrote to John Smyth of Nibley, probably in February 1642, that 'our competition for K[nigh]ts of the Shire did seeme to be thoroughly settled at the last Sessions by the connection of Sir Robert Tracye and myselfe, made by my cosin [Sir Maurice] Berklye and Mr [John] Dutton'. It is clear, however, that rumours and tensions were building up in the weeks prior to polling, for Cooke added that 'the confidence of it hath bin much interrupted by jealousies and unexpected canvassings'. Cooke told Smyth that he was 'going to Cisseter to meet with the same gentlemen . . . with an expectation that things may be quieted for the ease of our countrye'. It was nevertheless possible, in Cooke's opinion, that tensions were already boiling over, and sides had already been taken, for he added that

> if it falles out otherwise I must reforme to such strength as the love and fidelity of my friends affords, and amongst whom I shall much entreate the constancy of your [Smyth's] helpe and favour . . . [46]

The 'unexpected canvassings' to which Cooke referred were in favour of a radical Puritan candidate, Nathaniel Stephens Esq. of Eastington, a clothworking village on the banks of the Stroud River, 10 miles south of Gloucester.

On the first day of polling Tracy was sick, and 'made bold to favour himself and kept at home', leaving affairs in the hands of John Dutton, at the head of a party of 'divers gentlemen . . . with their tenants and retinue'. But at the last moment 'suddenly there was set up, and forcedly, as he pretends, Mr Stephens of Eastington, for opposing of the Ship Money, in which cause he had suffered, having been put out of the Commission of the Peace, and with an opinion of much zeal towards the zealous'. Cooke's letter to Smyth suggests that Stephens' candidacy was not quite as 'sudden' as Allibond thought. John Dutton, Tracy's principal agent in the elections, saw Stephens as 'over-reached by weavers', suggesting that his opponents saw him as a distinctively *popular* candidate from the manufacturing districts, as against the 'official' candidates, who had been 'pitched upon' by the county Bench.

At first Tracy's men ignored Stephens' party, casting their votes as arranged in the expectation that Cooke's supporters would honour the agreement made by the gentlemen of the Bench (from which Stephens had been excluded on account of years of opposition to and intransigent obstruction of Crown policies with regard to the cloth industry and Ship Money). But Cooke 'had either charmed his party so coldly . . . that he had left them indifferent to any but himself, or else, which was vilely suspected, had given some underhand invitations for his partisans otherwise to dispose of themselves'. Allibond believed the latter, as he had 'heard some of Cooke's tenants busily stickling for Stephens'. His view was that Cooke was 'double in his dealing', and he added a contemptuous '*Hem fidem puritanicam!*'. Such is the good faith of Puritans! The allegations of double-dealing against Cooke were unfair, even though he unquestionably belonged to Stephens' faction. It seems that he had been unable to persuade 'the gentlemen' (almost certainly Tracy and Dutton) whom he met at Cirencester before the polling, and was forced by their intractability to 'reforme to such strength as the love and fidelity of [his] friends affords'. Cooke was still hoping that a compromise could be reached in October, for in the lead-up to the elections for the Long Parliament he was enquiring of Smyth of Nibley 'whether you hold it sensible that the countrye may be persuaded to cast theire vote upon Sir Maurice Berkeleye . . . if so I shall endeavour with you that way: if not whom you incline to name joyned with Mr Stephens'. He thought 'these parts as yet capable of a suspension . . . but doubt how long it will be maintained'.[47] Like his father Sir Robert Cooke was a committed anti-Absolutist; and he was by reputation a Puritan. But, given these commitments, he does seem to have tried to keep a very unstable brew from boiling over. The pressure was coming from below.

'Tracy brought at the first day's polling 800 voices to Sir Robert Cooke, and received not 20 back!', Allibond reported. Men like this could not be trusted; they had no honour.[48] Another 'rule of morality, custom [and] etiquette' had been 'breached'. The next day Tracy rose from his sick-bed and rode to Gloucester, where he was met by Dutton and his retainers and supporters. Stephens' men streamed in from Eastington and other parts of the manufacturing districts in the Forest of Dean, the Stroudwater Valleys and the Vale of Berkeley, and there was a sharp exchange which, though brief, gave articulate form, perhaps for the first time, to the sociological, religious, economic, geographical and above all political and cultural circumstances which had transformed the region. 'Structures' were imposing an inexorable logic on 'events', and events were loosening structures.

The protagonists confronted each other, the main parties on restless horses, backing into crowds of supporters on foot, confined by the narrow streets with their overhanging tenements. Shopkeepers would have moved to their doorways with their customers to watch the interchange, knowing full well what was afoot. Many of them, aldermen and freemen of Gloucester, would have been supporters of Stephens. Dutton could not contain himself. He 'challenge[d] Cooke of infidelity'. Allibond tried to make Cooke seem shifty, reporting him as replying 'that he had dealt with them as far as they would be dealt withal'. Edward Stephens of Sodbury (Nathaniel's older brother) 'not long since high Sheriffe, & one of no meane power & truly fayre esteem', according to Allibond, was 'likewise charg'd by Mr Dutton of ungentleman-like dealing in violating his promise and deserting the compact [of the county Bench]'. The gentlemen were questioning each other's honour. Feelings were becoming heated. Dutton questioned Cooke's fidelity by referring to a letter he had written to Sir Maurice Berkeley informing him that he need not put himself to the trouble of attending the elections 'with a Band of 500 men' because 'there was not like to be any opposition'. The implication was that Cooke had known of Stephens' intentions, and had lied when he informed Berkeley that the elections were a mere formality, and there would not be 'any neede of [his] service'. *Hem fidem puritanicam!*, Allibond repeated.

Tracy then spoke, throwing caution to the wind by expressing in a few words the disdain of men of his caste for new-rich upstarts like Stephens, and alluding in his words to the sources of Stephens' 'estate'. He *'profess'd his scorn to be webb'd and loom'd in respect to Stephens his pedigree; fetch'd not many generations off from clothiers'*. Dutton immediately took up the theme: *'never was any man as Stephens so overreached by Weavers,'* he said. Stephens' reply was calculated to further infuriate Tracy's knightly sensibilities. *'Weavers might well enough rank with Shepherds,'* he said. The irresponsibility lay with Tracy and his party. It was they, not he, who by their remarks had *'divided the country into Cotteswold Shepherds and Vale Weavers . . . like faccons of the Guelphs and Ghibbelines'*. The underlying issues could hardly have been expressed more vividly and economically. The structural circumstances underlying the crisis in this part of England were out in the open.

The symbolism of 'Cotteswold Shepherds' and 'Vale Weavers' is simple and straightforward, as is that of 'Guelphs' and 'Ghibbelines'. Contemporaries would have understood them instantaneouesly. The episode was one of those 'small thinges' which referred directly to and made articulate an aspect of the 'grand design' which Corbet took for granted in his references to the importance, in the making of the English Revolution, of 'manufactures'. The heated exchange between the Puritan gentleman-clothier from Stroudwater and his Cotswold-based antagonists, whose wealth derived from the sheep's back, expressed long-standing distinctions between different *countreys* or districts within the region. It acknowledged that geographical and economic divisions were now explicitly political divisions. Cooke represented the legal/mercantile/urban, and Tracy the pastoral/fedual 'parties'. These were acceptable, traditional features of the field-of-force throughout medieval times. Stephens' candidature introduced a new and more radical voice into the political field-of-force: the manufacturing interest.

This was a crucial development, of momentous significance for the future. Tracy's party (and everyone else) assumed that Stephens represented the clothworking districts, which provided employment for half the households of Gloucestershire east of the Severn.[49] Large-scale clothmaking for national and international markets was practised in the most densely populated districts of the county, centred on a string of small towns – Painswick, Stroud, Minchinhampton, Nailsworth, Rodborough, Horsley, Woodchester, Dursley and Wotton-under-Edge – along the Cotswold Edge south-east of Gloucester, and along the river Stroud from Chalford (via Eastington, Stephens' seat) to Frampton-on-Severn. Tracy represented the 'shepherds', symbols of pastoral interests which stretched back to the time of the great Cotswold abbeys of the middle ages; Cooke represented 'trade' in the old urban, mercantile, sense. Stephens represented 'industries in the countryside', 'trade' with overwhelming connotations of densely populated industrial districts, manufacturing, production. It was the most dynamic and potentially dangerous element in the constitutional equation.

Five years later Corbet would take it for granted by assuming that the 'middle ranke' included not only yeomen, farmers and petty-freeholders, but also clothiers and 'such as use manufactures that enrich the country'. Corbet worked in the old mercantile centre of Gloucester, where his father was a shoemaker; his colleague at the Crypt School, Biddle, was from Wotton-under-Edge. They would have known without having to think about it what the expression 'weavers and shepherds' signified. If ever an episode or 'social drama' deserved treatment as a momentous conjuncture, it is this brief verbal exchange between the political representatives of 'Cotteswold Shepherds' and 'Vale Weavers' during the Gloucestershire parliamentary elections of March 1640.[50]

Stephens was the most influential representative of a grouping that eighteenth-century English people would call the 'gentleman clothier', in practice the most successful elite of a social bloc which stretched down through 'yeoman-clothiers', 'husbandman-clothiers', 'yeoman-weavers', 'master-craftsmen', journeymen (clothworkers who had not yet been able to establish themselves as independent householders), apprentices and a range of other clothworking occupations from shearers to spinners who depended entirely on the work put out to them by the clothiers. He was the lord of the manor of Eastington, and owned a fulling mill worth £350 per annum in 1661.[51] What emerged into the light of constitutional affairs with his intervention in 1640 was not a new personality – he had represented the county in Parliament already, in 1628 – or a new class, although he was only an esquire. The novel element was a 'bloc', the manufacturing interest. It is hard to imagine Stephens being 'over-reached by weavers' like many of his tenants at Eastington, from whom he would have expected deference and respect in measure equal to that which Tracy would have expected from his shepherds.[52] Rather, Stephens' mentality and ideology were framed by technical and ideological problems of social control in densely populated industrial districts which were intensely affected by the ups and downs of national and international demand. The problems faced by Tracy in his native district in the north-east of Gloucestershire had to do with social control, but of a different kind of population.[53]

The symbolism of 'shepherds' was also richly allusive. Over 90 men from North Cotswold parishes gave this occupation in 1608. John Dutton's manor of Sherborne (then in the hands of his father, William Dutton) returned no fewer than 9 men of that occupation, easily the largest single concentration anywhere in the country. Before the Dissolution, Sherborne had been a manor of Winchcombe Abbey, and every year its extensive flocks were all sent there to be sheared.[54] The form of William Dutton's return had feudal pretensions: 1 gentlemen, 13 yeomen, 9 husbandmen and 2 shepherds were collectively described as 'servants to the said William Dutton Esq.'; only 4 other returns out of 444 (including Cooke's father) used this form to indicate an explicitly servile relationship to the lord of a manor. Whoever wrote the return for Sherborne saw these men as Dutton's retainers.[55]

The distinction between 'shepherds' and 'weavers' was a distinction between the producers, on one hand, and on the other the processors and merchandisers of wool. Conflict between these two 'sectors' went back at least to the 1560s, when the Wiltshire and Gloucestershire clothiers explained the difficulties of the cloth manufacturing industry by alleging that large-scale wool producers were cornering the markets and demanding exorbitant prices for their commodity. Of all the producers in Gloucestershire, the Duttons were best placed to exercise such practises.

'Shepherds' had romantic, mystical connotations for the great magnates. When Queen Elizabeth visited Gyles Brydges at Sudeley Castle, during a 'progress' in the 1590s (when there was plague in London), she was welcomed to the castle with the performance of a pageant and masque, introduced by an actor performing the part of an old shepherd. 'Vouchsafe to hear a simple shepherd,' he announced, 'shepherds and simplicity cannot part':

> Your highness is come into Cotswold, an uneven country, but a people that carry their thoughts level with their fortunes: low spirits, but true hearts; using plain dealings, once counted a jewel, now beggary. These hills afford nothing but cottages, and nothing can we present to your Highness but shepherds. The country healthy but harmless; a fresh air, where there are no damps, and where a black sheep is a perilous beast; no monsters; we carry our hearts at our tongues' ends, being as far from dissembling as our sheep from fierceness . . . This lock of wool, Cotswold's best fruit, and my poor gift, I offer to your Highness; in which nothing is to be esteemed but the whiteness, Virginity's colour: nor to be expected but duty, shepherds' religion.[55]

Shepherds were the proverbial symbols for straight-dealing, uprightness, 'whiteness', health, duty, as clothiers exemplified double-dealing, dissembling, and Puritans represented hypocrisy. Shepherds exercised absolute authority over their 'flock', an authority earned by absolute concern for the well-being of their charges; they knew their place and they knew their responsibilities. They were hardy, inured to the crisp, cold, clean air of the open hills. Weavers and clothiers inhabited the proverbially unhealthy, dirty, overcrowded, damp little villages and townships in the Vale. They were the 'black sheep' in the great patriarchy of England, as it was conceived by men like Tracy.[57]

The symbolism of 'weavers' and 'shepherds' referred to genuine geographical and political–economic differences. Contemporaries would know without pausing for thought that the terms referred to the home districts, respectively, of Tracy and Nathaniel Stephens. The district that stretched along the north-western edge of the Cotswolds between Cheltenham and Chipping Campden and the clothmaking districts across the Cotswold plateau were to be Royalist and Parliamentarian, respectively, when war came. Everyone knew they were different. The archival record allows us to document the differences with precision. At another level, what was implied was a difference of *habitus*, 'schemes of thought and expression . . . that are the basis for the . . . invention of regulated improvisation',[57] or culture, in the sense of the symbolic meanings assigned to actual differences – and these, as Sahlins observes, 'are never the only ones possible'.[59] The exchange reified a clash between two cultures, and the reference to 'Guelphs and Ghibbelines', the proverbial parties of populist politics in early Renaissance Florence, itself the proverbial case of endemic political conflict and violence, was intended to signify that the implied geographic, political–economic, social and cultural distinction was now political. The reference to medieval Florentine politics, with hints of uprisings of the *populi*, of Savonarola and of Machiavelli, had a sinister edge. At each stage it need not have been so: Stephens' remark signified that the magnates had made it so by insisting on excluding the groups he represented. Matters were not quite that simple, but there was a great deal in what he meant.

The exchange of March 1640 was not yet finished. Edward Stephens of Sodbury, like Nathaniel Stephens and Sir Robert Cooke 'a favourer of the pretending holy side', defended his brother's candidature against these opposition taunts, on the grounds that John Dutton, Tracy's proxy, was himself guilty of 'ungentlemanlike dealing'. Why, he asked, had Dutton's powerful kinsman, Sir Ralph Dutton, not 'shown himself in the business'? Sir Ralph was the ambitious head of a cadet branch of the Dutton family who had spent a small fortune and nearly bankrupted his estate trying to maintain strong links to Charles's court.[60] Why was Tracy not at the election on the first day? Did this imply contempt for popular feeling on the range of issues that had been raised by eleven years of rule without Parliament? Did

Tracy's party in fact support the elections at all, or were they simply going through the motions? Stephens suggested that he was wavering in his own view of widespread rumours to this effect, but the failure of Tracy and Sir Ralph Dutton to appear on the first day's polling settled him on the issue. He cast his vote for his brother. Allibond expressed his opinion with another *Hem fidem puritanicam!*

Allibond was convinced that Stephens' candidature was the visible product of a conspiratorial popular movement organised by Puritan ministers, a view shared by the Puritan Corbet, who took for granted that the 'middle ranke' was organised by 'a practical ministry'. 'I hold it worthy of your notice', he told Heylyn (who, no doubt, would in turn have informed the king), 'that those who first rolled this unwilling stone were principally men of our own coat, a pack of deprived, silenced and puritannically affected [clergy]men'. He then named thirteen of 'the most earnest sticklers in so holy a cause'.[61] All thirteen held office in districts associated with trade and manufacturing. 'If their hearts be known,' wrote Allibond, their intention was to 'effect nothing more than to hold the king's nose to the grindstone, and ruin the Church.' Corbet's name did not appear on the list. He had only just come down from Oxford, and although Allibond would probably have met the new Usher at the Crypt School, assistant to the scholarly Biddle, he was of the younger generation who did not come to the fore until the wars.

The elections occasioned a parting of the ways, but the significant movement was not in creating a wave of opposition to the king and his ministers. A few months earlier it would have been difficult to find anyone in the county prepared to defend the king's policies and practices. Congregationalist Protestantism was indigenous to the manufacturing districts, richly documented back to the time of Tyndale. Since then it had ebbed and flowed, but mainly the latter as a result of the accident that, except for brief periods (like the martyred Bishop Hooper's brief time at the Cathedral in the 1550s), the diocese had been governed by bishops and bureaucracies which were openly corrupt, incompetent, insensitive, arrogant or all four together.[62] The mainstream English Protestantism outlined by Professor Collinson, grounded in assiduous and conscientious pastoral effectiveness, was never really given a chance to succeed in Gloucestershire, and this long-term factor helps to explain the continuing strength of various forms of independency and 'neo-separatism', i.e. of radical Puritanism, in the county.[63] It is not the whole explanation: the importance of manufacturing industry in creating social problematics that necessitated new approaches to socialisation and new world-views must also be stressed.

We are now in a position to understand more clearly what happened in the early 1640s to make a constitutional conflict into a social conflict. Clearly the king and his 'evil advisers' were catalysts; but a chemical solution had to be present to be catalysed. Charles's need to call a Parliament to vote him supply was a decisive factor, and behind that lay his refusal to call one for over a decade, and every other blunder and insensitivity on his part in the intervening years. But the election itself summoned long-standing and deeply rooted social divisions: on one side a class of magnates with neo-feudal (or 'Absolutist') pretensions; on the other the heterogeneous ranks and classes of people associated with the mercantile and manufacturing districts. Neither Charles I nor his advisers had any part in creating this structural division, only in making it possible for it to erupt into violence.

Material circumstances had to be present for the cultural interchanges to have meaningful references. Differences of culture were rooted in genuine geographical and socio-economic differences. The extent to which it was inevitable that when the time came the magnate class, virtually to a man (or, more accurately, to a 'household' or 'estate'), *insisted* on a particular interpretation of the meaning of those differences, i.e. that they were an inherently superior *caste*, is another matter. They did so because their values were embedded, by long practice and by the continuous re-invention of traditions, in the feudal past. Tracy's candidature represented a coterie of magnate households, mostly situated in the 'underdeveloped' (pastoral- and plantation-based) north-west of Gloucestershire and focused on the household of the Brydges, lords Chandos of Sudeley, self-styled 'kings of the Cotswolds'. Since the Reformation these households had tried to re-impose the field-of-force that had been broken, in 1540, by the dissolution of the great monastic houses that had dominated the region since the twelfth century. The legal and mercantile elite, represented by Sir Robert Cooke, they could just tolerate: for merchants and mercantile towns were as old as feudal lords. The seething manufacturing districts, proverbially slandered for their poverty, disorder, drunkenness, licentiousness, insubordination and – worst of all – self-righteous, puritanical neighbourhood elites, Corbet's 'middle ranke', they could not.

For more than ten years these same magnates had more or less stood firm with the rest of the population against the religious and economic outrages committed by the regime of Charles I. John Dutton, like Nathaniel Stephens, had been imprisoned for his stand against Ship Money. Dutton, the wealthiest man in the county, was a particularly shrewd reader of what was happening, socially, and of how the regime's insensitivity threatened to crystallise very real social divisions and potential conflicts of interest. What they wanted to prevent, above all, was occasion for the predominantly Puritan, or neo-Puritan middle rank to take the initiative themselves, for this would challenge the social system of which they, the regional magnates, were the principal beneficiaries. Classes in the Marxist sense already existed. What they wanted to prevent, and sought to prevent by prominent opposition to the king's policies, was an outbreak of violent class struggle in which the middle rank took the initiative. For if that happened there might be no turning back.

The outburst of heated feelings during the elections for the Short Parliament resulted from antagonistic perceptions, in Turner's words, of a breach of norms and an infraction of morality, custom and etiquette. This breach both demonstrated and challenged entrenched authority. 'Once visible,' as it was made visible during the exchange in the streets of Gloucester, 'it [could] hardly be revoked.' A mounting crisis followed, aptly described as 'a momentous juncture or turning-point in the relations between components of a social field'. Sides were taken, factions formed, and it was not possible to 'seal off' the regional 'field' from the 'dominant cleavage in the widest set of relevant social relations', namely the relations between Crown and Parliament.

In the light of recent historiographical interest in local and regional studies, it is important to stress that we cannot separate the local, regional and national contexts, all of which were intimate aspects of the conjuncture. Nor can we separate long-term structures from short-term events. Without the manufacturing districts of Gloucestershire there would have been no irresistible opposition worth speaking of. The towns would have been isolated in a stolid, apathetic countryside peopled by autarkic peasants. The problems which gave rise to Puritanism as a widespread movement would also not have existed.

Manufacturing, as Marx claimed, was the dynamic element in the field-of-force. It alone made the kind of civil war which took place in the 1640s possible. In this sense long-term developments were decisive. But as the social drama explained above showed, 'events' played their part by providing occasion for the long-term structures to find political expression.

5

THE ONLY ACTIVE MEN (CONTD): MANUFACTURES AND THE MULTITUDE

Corbet saw the matter in this way. The 'middle ranke', 'the state's [i.e. Parliament's] adhearants', embodied 'an inbred propensity to freedom . . . by which this country did seeme well disposed to comply with the parliament's grande designe'. Against this, the small 'contrary faction' was motivated by 'a desire of vast dominion, dignity, revenge, or rapine'. Before accusing Corbet of exaggeration, we must acknowledge that, between the events of 1640 and the time when he wrote, the county had been invaded by a Royalist army which did indeed exhibit precisely these qualities. For Corbet, the qualities of both sides were, as he put it, *inbred*. What did he mean by this?

The 'powerfull gentry', he wrote, 'care not to render themselves the slaves of princes', in spite of their willingness to fight alongside them. Rather, their real motive, as he thought, was 'to rule over their neighbours like vassals'. Their instincts were feudal, inclining towards 'vast dominion' and 'dignity', habits of 'rapine' motivated by 'revenge', and wishing to reduce their 'neighbours' to 'vassals'. He refers to their 'superstitious adoring of their old way' which 'imbittered their spirits against reformed religion, which seemed to them a peevish affectation of novelty'. They had a 'hatred and feare of ecclesiasticall discipline', besides 'an hatred of the commons and a strong disposition to the ends of tyranny'.[64]

On the other side were the 'well affected', the 'middle ranke', whose 'propensities' for 'freedom' and 'liberty' were 'inbred'. They had opposed and 'continually thwart[ed] the intentions of tyrannie unto which they only are moulded, who, detesting a close, hardy, and industrious way of living, doe eate their bread in the sweat of other men, and, neglecting a secure estate, rejoyce rather in the height of fortune though inconstant and dangerous': this was a reference to the quality Jones calls 'honour', and which Shakespeare exemplified in the eponymous 'hero' of his play *Coriolanus*.[65] It was 'the predominant humour of gentlemen in a corrupted age'.[66] Although 'the whole body of the commons' was 'very weake one by one, yet brought together they ballance each other, and when no man hath power to impropriate much, each man expects only a proportionable share in the publicke interest'.[67]

What made Gloucestershire a potential force for Parliament was that there was no 'excessive number of powerfull gentry': had there been, he implied, the region would have been for the king. 'If not made fit for the yoke by dependence on the gentry,' he wrote, people were able to 'discover the fraud that lyes under the fairest pretext'.[68] But the middle rank had to he distinguished from 'the needy multitude', which, 'besides their naturall hatred of good order', was politically passive, its loyalties determined by 'an usuall restraint and subjection', imposed by 'the guidance of superiour agents'.[69] This is the key to Corbet's explanation of the events of the early 1640s. 'The multitude' followed its resident 'superiours'. Where these were 'powerfull gentry' the 'rabble' was active for the king. At Bristol 'the king's cause and party were favoured by two extreames, . . . the one the wealthy and

powerfull men, the other of the basest and lowest sort'. That engagement, early in 1643, 'disgusted the middle ranke, the truest and best
citizens, . . . [and] taught men to distinguish between the true commons of the realm and the dreggs of the people'. Discussions at
Gloucester as to the reasons for the surrender of Bristol seem to have
led Corbet to his view of constitutional affairs, in which the middle
rank were 'the most vehement asserters of publicke libertie', and the
'needy multitude' was 'the first rise of tyrannical government, and the
foote-stoole upon which princes tread when they ascend the height
of monarchy'.[70]

The key variable determining the affections of the 'multitude' was
the composition of local government. Where it 'consisted chiefly of
yeomen, farmers, petty-freeholders, and such as use manufactures that
enrich the country, and passe through the hands of the multitude', the
people below the middle rank tended to act for Parliament.[71] The
reference to 'manufactures' that 'passe through the hands of the multitude' is an allusion to the fact which Corbet and his contemporaries
knew without having to think about it: that the 'rabble', 'multitude',
'needy', etc. in Gloucestershire meant manufacturing workers.

Their masters, the middle rank, were 'a generation of men truely
laborious, jealous of their properties, whose principall aime is liberty
and plenty, and whilst in an equal rank with their neighbours they
desire only not to be oppressed, and count themselves extreamly
bound to the world, if they may keepe their owne'.[72] Corbet's 'countryman' (this is another of the generic terms he uses to describe the
'middle ranke') was a self-consciously independent property-holding
householder, often with some involvement in 'manufactures'.

The two issues that now concern us are, firstly, to conclude the
calculations as to the proportion of the total population of Gloucestershire that should be included in the middle rank; and, secondly, to
examine the composition of 'the ignoble multitude', and the nature of
its relationship with the middle rank. In this way we shall attempt to
draw some general conclusions about the social dynamics of the events
of the early 1640s.

With respect to the first question, we have already established that
'yeomen, petty-freeholders, farmers' covered roughly 10 per cent of all
households. With respect to Corbet's phrase 'such as use manufactures
that . . . passe through the hands of the multitude', there is ambiguity
as to whether this means producers, consumers or both. I shall assume
the latter. We cannot simply count the number of craftsmen listed in
the 1608 musters and add the total to the previous 10 per cent, for
we have no way of knowing how many of the tradesmen would have
qualified as *independent* members of the middle rank as Corbet conceived it. The term 'weaver', for example, could refer to a substantial

yeoman farmer who was primarily engaged in weaving cloth, assisted by sons, apprentices and perhaps a journeyman or two, in the year the musters were held, but might not be so employed when markets were down and such activities were less profitable. In such times he would lay off journeymen and labourers and resume working his farm personally. A weaver could also be someone with a part-share (i.e. with a brother) in a freehold farm, a copyholding husbandman who rented property and combined it with clothmaking, a master-craftsman with no land at all but employing servants, journeymen and apprentices, and occasionally acting as a clothier; he could be a married journeyman with several children living permanently on the borders of necessity and poverty, an unmarried journeyman with expectations of a freehold or copyhold inheritance from his father, or a journeyman with no expectations at all. Similar observations could be made of all craft occupations, and we haven't even begun yet to explore the decisive element of a man's personality and habitual demeanour, which could also be a decisive factor in the way he was regarded by his neighbours. A craftsman could be an elder of the neighbourhood, a 'licentious' tavern-haunter, or somewhere in-between. John Corbet's father was a 'shoemaker'. What did this mean? Probably an independent householder and citizen of Gloucester running a substantial enterprise with the assistance of waged servants and journeymen, given that he could afford to send his son to Oxford. Some craftsmen could afford to send their sons to grammar school and university, while others sometimes couldn't afford to send them down the lane to the alehouse for a jug of ale. Early modern occupational listings conceal an enormous range of potential variables.

In the Tawneys' aggregate figures for the county, 5,723 of the 19,402 men assigned occupations in the musters of 1608 clearly fit the 'manufacturer' classification, that is to say 29 per cent. We need some way to distinguish more carefully, and I shall do this by using Hearth Tax records and later lists of freeholders. In 1712, after a half-century in which freeholders are thought to have declined as a result of the consolidation of estates, my calculations for the whole county show a ratio of 4.7 unenfranchised, non-freeholding households for every one freeholding voter.[73] This can probably be taken as a minimum proportion qualified to vote in 1640: i.e. approximately a fifth of the households in the county, whom Corbet identified as those with influence over the 'multitude'. On this basis, Corbet's 'countrymen' of the 'middle ranke' constituted 20–25 per cent of the total number of households.

Nobles and gentry were about 3 per cent; except for 'some gleanings' they were mainly Royalist or 'detestably neutral'. The middle rank of independent households was at most 25 per cent. The 'multitude', then, must have been the remaining 72 per cent. Hearth Tax listings for 1671 give additional plausibility to these estimates: aggregating all the settlements which included what looks like a full list of exemptions yields a mean for all Gloucestershire tithings, parishes and town wards of 58 per cent of households with only one hearth, 19 per cent with two, and 22 per cent in the 'middle rank' with 3–9 hearths.[74]

All this provides us with are some very rough quantitative dimensions for the social structure John Corbet had in mind when he wrote his account of the events of the early 1640s. Of greater importance are the criteria he employed in making his distinction. The gentry, in his view, were defined by the fact that they 'lived in the breath of other men'; it was important to him, and, by implication, to the men of the middle rank with whom he identified, that they did no work and lived off their rentals. The middle rank, by contrast, 'lived of their owne'. In his mind this probably meant that they lived off what they produced, not that they were subsistence operators (although this was almost certainly a factor). At one point he seems to imply that the rest (72 per cent!) were 'needy'. What did this mean?

Corbet judged the world from his own class perspective, which was roughly as follows. The ideal condition of a man of the middle rank was ownership of a freehold farm which was operated by himself and his family, assisted perhaps by one or two indentured servants in husbandry, and casual labourers at certain times of the year. He did not rent land to or from others, and he had no pretensions to gentility. He was pious towards God, dutiful towards his family and respectful towards his neighbours. He sold produce not needed to sustain the members of his household in the local markets. He was a member of his parish vestry, and expected to be listened to when he offered his opinion on neighbourhood affairs. He was willing to contribute funds to support the poor, but preferred that these funds be used to 'set the poor on work'. He judged others (e.g. the local minister of religion) not by pious words but by neighbourly actions and demeanour. He was willing to attend church, but his most important religious observances centred on his own household, and he reserved judgement as a matter, finally, for his own conscience, informed by reading of scripture, daily prayer and experience. He deferred to no *independent* man, and expected no such man to defer to him: 'the needy', women and children were another matter; they *were* expected to defer to his judgement, though, as a reasonable man, he would consult them and take their interests into consideration.

When Corbet described him as a 'countryman' his principal intention was to describe the primary source of his affective loyalty: 'country' in this context meant something like what we would mean by the term 'district'. His universe was a series of contexts radiating out from the individual self or soul, through family, kin, neighbourhood, 'country' or district, county and finally the nation. He had no aspirations to national prominence, but God help anyone who came into his country and tried to tell him how things should be done, especially if the person so doing entertained extravagant notions of his own importance. He was literate and kept himself informed on what was happening in the wider world. An independent voice in elections to Parliament went with his property. He would listen to advice as to how this vote should be cast, and if a powerful gentleman like (e.g.) Sir Maurice Berkeley, who came from an old Gloucestershire family, made suggestions respectfully, in circumstances which were not suspicious or suggestive of ulterior motives, he was quite willing to follow his lead. He was literate and believed in education. If he sent his son to university, he expected his son to bring his education and knowledge home and to use it for the benefit of the neighbourhood and 'country'. If he apprenticed a son to a merchant in London or Bristol he likewise regarded it as an investment to yield capital in the form of benefit, first and foremost, to kin, neighbourhood and country. He was parochial and practical, but he was also interested in 'universal principles'. The best way to describe his mentality is to say that it was autarchic and empirical. It was essentially an extrapolation of the world-view of the rich peasant of medieval times, informed by Protestantism, the extension and deepening of the cash-nexus, literacy and the print revolution of the sixteenth and early seventeenth centuries.

The ideal had been considerably adapted by and to the rise of large-scale manufacturing. All of the Gloucestershire clothing families that I have studied in any depth were originally of yeoman stock, although in some cases it is difficult to disentangle the yeoman from the clothier. It seems likely that clothier families like the Webbs of Dursley and the Clutterbucks of Eastington and Frampton, who were originally from the Low Countries, were tempted to settle in the Vale of Berkeley by the opportunity of a freehold farm. The importance of this basic requirement for 'independency' had to do with the unpredictable ups and downs relating to the production and markets for food and the national and international markets for cloth. In times of dearth even comparatively wealthy clothiers might experience difficulty in obtaining necessities in the market-place. They wouldn't starve, but they might experience an uncomfortable week, month or year from time to time. For this reason every clothworker would aspire to the possession or tenancy of a subsistence farm: this was an essential part of 'living of one's own'. Similarly, a yeoman farmer or copyholder who lived in clothier country (say, the Stroudwater region, or the Vale of Berkeley) would tend to at least dabble in the production of cloth from time to time. In the first place it removed the necessity to pay cash for clothes for the family; but, most importantly, it brought in a cash income which would go towards the paying of statutory dues of one kind or another, and in some cases created an accumulating kitty which might be lent out to neighbours at interest, thus increasing one's influence in the neighbourhood, and eventually might be used to purchase more land.

His attitude tended to be that clothworking was first and foremost an activity for the needy, i.e. his landless neighbours. But this priority could also be applied to his own sons and daughters, whose contributions to the household would be considerably enhanced by the acquisition of a trade like spinning or weaving. After all, they too were landless until he died, or until they earned enough money to set themselves up in an independent (i.e. landed) household. So it was a matter of common sense to combine farming with clothworking (which was manufacturing for the market *par excellence*), even though clothworking would always be a low-status activity compared with freehold farming, which alone could provide *independency*.

'Independency', then, had little or nothing to do with the sectarian tendency that became associated with Oliver Cromwell, at least in the early stages of the conflict. It was first and foremost a set of ideas and ideal circumstances with which everyone could identify: a sufficiency of (preferably freehold) land combined with a trade by means of which to bring in hard cash, marriage, family, and respectable place in neighbourhood life – all sealed into a coherent self- (i.e. conscience-) centred universe grounded in the indigenous 'elder'- and 'congregation'-centred Protestantism embodied in William Tyndale's translations of scripture.[75] It was from this 'small bottome' that 'greate things' were raised. Since 1625, Court interference in the cloth industry, Arminian reforms of church ceremonial and theology, royal enclosures in the Forest of Dean, and finally Ship Money accumulated into a convincing (if ultimately spurious) argument that the King's Party were responsible for preventing a majority of men from attaining independency. The exclusion of Nathaniel Stephens from the Bench, and thus from candidature for Parliament, seemed to confirm that there was a conspiracy on the part of the 'powerfull gentry' to suppress the active voice of the middle rank, which had been convinced that theirs was a *holy* cause by a 'practicall ministry' comprised largely of sons of the middle rank. The revolution that the Protestant Reformation as envisaged by William Tyndale had always implied was imminent.

'AN UNDESCERNED GUIDANCE OF SUPERIOUR MEN': CORBET AND THE IGNOBLE MULTITUDE

Corbet admitted that the struggle was initiated by 'the ignoble multitude', and could not have been maintained without its support. Control of its irrational and unpredictable excesses was another matter. He was convinced that the normal expectations of the 'multitude' with respect to leadership determined whether a country was Royalist or Parliamentarian, and provided the final test of all government. The key question was who controlled the multitude, who, in a routine sense, was responsible for keeping it in 'an usuall restraint and subjection'. Where the agent of control was the 'powerfull gentry' (as in the tobacco-growing and pastoral country around Cheltenham and Winchcombe, Tracy's district), the 'rabble', he alleged, was active for the 'king's party'; where it 'consisted chiefly of yeomen, farmers, petty-freeholders, and such as use manufactures that . . . pass through the hands of the multitude', the multitude tended to act for Parliament.[76]

Corbet's fullest treatment of the role of the multitude in carrying the conflict to a new stage of intensity, as it were Gloucestershire's equivalent to the fall of the Bastille, occurs in his discussion of the attempt by George Brydges, lord Chandos of Sudeley, to present the king's Commission of Array at Cirencester, in August 1642. Cirencester was 'universally esteemed the key to Gloucestershire'.[77] Chandos's attempt, backed, in Corbet's words, by 'some other disaffected gentlemen', 'was stifled in the birth, and crusht by the rude hand of the multitude'.[78]

> The chief abetter thereof [i.e. Chandos] was like to suffer violence by the meanest of the people, whose fury constrained him to promise, and give under his hand, that he would never more deale in this business.

Corbet uses the occasion to make some important and interesting points about general social structure and dynamics. He refers to 'the fury that took hold on the ignoble multitude, in whom not alwaies the deep sense of their owne interests doth provoke this extasie of passion' – an allusion to the irrationality of mobs in general, and 'the common people', it appears, at all times. He is keen to show that they always needed to be led. 'They glory to vent their humours,' he wrote, 'by reason of an usuall restraint and subjection.'[79] Normative discipline occasionally produced explosions of licence. 'Nevertheless,' he continues, 'they have produced good effects, *and oft times a more undescerned guidance of superiour agents turnes them to the terrour of the enemy.*'

'Prudent men promote and maintaine . . . unexplicable selfe-ingage-ment upon the common people,' he wrote, 'yet no further than them-selves can maintaine and moderate.'[80] In this respect – its relations with the 'multitudes' – Corbet's middle rank was on common ground with its opponents, the 'powerfull gentry'. They differed only on how social discipline should be fostered, and who should be in charge of the exercise. In this sense, the main issue of the English Revolution was who should control the landless labouring classes, and to what ends.

Corbet's general view was that 'most men . . . did undoubtedly foresee greater hopes of liberty from the parliament than the king's party': there was a just alliance of 'Prudent men' of the 'middle ranke' and the more irrational representatives of 'the common people'. It is an important contemporary statement about the social structure and dynamics of the events of the early 1640s, and worth considering in a little more depth.

A letter written 'to a worthy member of parliament' the day after Chandos's abortive attempt to present the king's Commission, gives a significantly different version of the events of August 1642 at Cirenc-ester, and leaves some doubt as to the precise character, and the role in proceedings, of 'the ignoble multitude'.[81]

The witness states that Chandos wrote 'severall letters to divers of the principall of the Gentlemen of our County' a week before his proposed visit, warning them of his intentions. As a result, 'country-men and the volunteers got notice of it . . . [and] there came at least a thousand armed men to assist the townsmen'. Meeting with the gentlemen on a hill beyond the town, Chandos was warned there would be trouble if he pursued his intentions. He was allowed to enter the town only after disarming his men, and went to the house of a local magistrate for discussions with 'the Justices of the Peace'. While they were inside 'the *souldiers and armed men* came and beset the house' and demanded to know his intentions. The letter states only that the initiative was taken by 'the souldiers and armed men'. Chandos came out and told them that he came 'only to confer with the Gentlemen of the Peace of the County'.

This was not satisfactory, and the besiegers 'required him to deliver up his Commission of Array unto them or otherwise they would bring him to the Parliament'. Chandos had to sign a document promising to abide by their wishes and he was allowed to return into the house. Later that evening Chandos was 'conveyed away very privately by Sir William Masters and other gentlemen' through the grounds of the house, leaving his coach behind to cover his escape. The next morning the 'souldiers coming to look for him . . . and finding him gone were extremely enraged and had like to pull down the house, took his coach and drew it themselves into the market place, cutt it and tore it in pieces'.[82]

This writer described himself as 'an eye and ear witness' of the proceedings. Corbet, who probably was not there, described the agents of the outrage as 'the multitude', 'the meanest of the people', 'the ignoble multitude', and 'the common people'.[83] The eye-witness account is different, referring to 'our countrymen and the volunteers', and 'the souldiers and armed men'.

Corbet stressed the role of the middle rank and its organisers, the 'practicall ministry'. The latter crystallised already existing social formations into a coherent and self-conscious ideology which drew together long-standing strands of popular mentality and gave them a revolutionary edge. Was his interpretation influenced by political considerations? How important was any need, in 1645, to consolidate the support of the middle rank by appealing to its prejudices and flattering its sensibilities; or perhaps by expressing a degree of wishful thinking with respect to the popular character of the first civil war? Did he play down the influence of the working people, the 'multitude', and understate the potency of resistance from below the middle? The convergence of interest and action between the puritanically affected middle rank and the multitude was highly exceptional. Frequent dearths and near-famine conditions in the manufacturing districts generated bad feelings about freeholding farmers, the suppliers of local markets, and against middle-men and clothiers. The alliance Corbet described was unusual – perhaps unique – and it probably explains the tenacity of the region's resistance: it was, and remained with regard to the Royalists, enemy country. The issues could not be resolved by military occupation. Because it had no lasting voice, the motivation of the multitude is something we can only speculate about. By his own testimony, Corbet's middle rank wavered in the tenacity of its adherence to the Parliament, at least in the dark months of occupation. It may be that years of depression in the clothworking districts were blamed on Crown and Court, and not on the direct bearers of bad news, the local clothiers. Rampaging cavaliers would have done nothing to ameliorate the collective conviction that Charles I and all those who chose to identify with his cause were completely out of touch with what life was like, or worse still, knew and did not care. At least the local elites, when they proclaimed the cause of the poor, knew what they were talking about. More commonly, before the 1640s and afterwards, the craft-workers would riot against clothiers, engrossing farmers and 'hucksters' suspected of cornering the market in foodstuffs, and they would tend to be supported by the landed gentry, who also had no love for the middle rank, which at times appeared to be challenging their divine right to rule. Historically speaking, the factor which stands out in the early 1640s is this unholy alliance between the capitalist middle rank and its natural enemy, Corbet's 'ignoble multitude'. Corbet touches here, albeit unknowingly or ingenuously, on the key to the victory of Parliament over Crown. Court policy on enclosures, the cloth industry and taxation had made possible an otherwise unlikely alliance between the middle ranks and the 'vulgar multitudes'. This alliance began to fall apart immediately victory looked assured.[84]

7

LEADERSHIP: NATIONALIST MISSIONARIES?

Corbet's account, as historians supporting a Marxist interpretation of the events of the 1640s have noticed, is more than merely compatible with a class-based explanation of what happened and why it happened. Terminology aside, Corbet offers a class analysis and explanation that Marx himself would have been happy to own. The powerful, neo-feudal gentry, and the rich merchants of cities like Bristol, supported the king and the status quo. The lesser gentry, caught between two equally undesirable extremes, were 'detestably neutral'. What made resistance and revolution possible, Corbet believed, was the existence of a substantial and progressively independent-minded middle rank of freeholding property-holders: not only its existence, but its active engagement in the events themselves.

In most districts of Gloucestershire men of the middle rank organised production, and grounded the legitimacy of their authority, and their cause, in their functions as suppliers of work and subsistence to the needy multitudes. An affinity for broadly congregationalist – local, vaguely 'separatist' – Protestantism and the possession of land and capital formed the basis of their sense of autonomy, and the employment and organisation of labour at the grass roots was the source of their sense of constitutional legitimacy. The language Corbet used to describe the labouring poor combined contempt and paternalism in equal measure. Shakespeare's 'many-headed monster' was an irrational mass, a 'naturall enemie to good order' as a result of its 'usuall subjection'. But if organised properly, subjected to 'ecclesiasticall discipline' organised by the middle-ranking elders of its neighbourhoods, propagated by 'a practicall ministry', it could be put to good effect and made 'a terrour to its enemies'. Corbet made no bones about the proposition that the 'needy multitude' was there to be *used*. He took it for granted. In peace it was to be organised to labour, in war to serve as cannon-fodder in a struggle it could by no stretch of the imagination understand. Corbet describes a struggle for control of the social relations of production, and there is no reason to doubt that his propositions would have appealed to the sensibilities of his chosen constituency.

Corbet's was the unqualified voice of the English bourgeoisie. What needs stressing about his account, however, is that his was the voice of a man who had been active in the struggle from the outset. In his treatment of the *military* struggle, he does not hesitate to emphasise the decisive influence of the energy, patience and tact of Colonel Massey and his officers. In July 1643 'the enemy breathed out threaten-ings, many false friends sought cunningly to make us afraid'. When the county was occupied by a Royalist army, 'the country-men in generall were taken off, especially when Cirencester was taken, in which they did repose so much trust'.[85] During the siege of Gloucester, he wrote, 'the well-affected would not declare themselves, because a running army could be no lasting support'.[86] The cause faltered. 'The greatest mischief of all' was that 'many were not wanting to debate upon the main cause of the kingdom: malignant spirits took the advan-tage of our misery, and unstable minds . . . became crest-fallen . . . The whole countrey forsook us.'

When Corbet used the phrase 'the whole countrey' he meant the people who governed its everyday activities. 'They were at their wits end,' he wrote, 'and stood like men amazed, feare bereft them of understanding and memory, begat confusion in the minde within, and the thronging thoughts did oppresse and stop the course of action.'[87] The middle rank faltered, but not, it seems, the 'vulgar multitude'. 'The whole countrey was quickly full of this disaster', he wrote of the impact of the taking of Cirencester. At that point 'thousands of men armed and unarmed flocked together, and resolved to undertake the enemy under the conduct of a grave and well-minded patriot . . .'.[88] The 'desired leader' (Corbet does not name him), however, 'was con-scious of the peoples' madnesse, and knew well that they made a loude crye afarre off, but if once brought up to the face of the army they would never abide the fury of the first onset'. When this hap-pened 'the people bitterly railed against him, and curst him as a traitor to his countrey; neither could the experience of these times disposesse them of that absurd conceit'.[89]

The middle rank faltered, but 'the people' did not. Corbet's preju-dices are evident here. We are not told where the thousands of people 'flocked together', but the most likely candidates are the clothworkers of the Stroudwater Valleys. They had their own organisations and a reputation for collective action. Cirencester was 'their' town: in 1608 it had the largest concentration of clothworkers in the county; it was situated close to the head of the Stroudwater Valley, a few miles east of Sapperton, which may well be where the gathering took place, in the fields on the slope below the church. Corbet supported the 'well-minded patriot' (Nathaniel Stephens?) in his view that the crowd would have quickly scattered, or been slaughtered, or both, when faced with the well-disciplined Royalist cavalry. No doubt this was an accurate prediction, an example of 'the undescerned guidance of superiour men'. The important point is that the 'guidance' was not in whipping up opposition to the Cavaliers, but in *moderating* it. Corbet had a vested interest, in 1645, in promoting the middle rank as 'the only active men'. At a time when debate was beginning on the question of how, now that the king was in retreat, English government was to be reconstituted, politically speaking, it was important to stress the role of the respectable, Puritan, ministry-led middle rank as the single, solid agents of a great victory over tyranny. This was Corbet's class and constituency. At the same time he was too honest to deny the crucial agency, often in the darkest of times, when men of his own class had faltered, or at best pleaded cautious prudence, of the 'common people', 'the vulgar multitudes'. Imprudent, it probably was. But Corbet's account leaves little doubt that the prudent middle rank was under pressure from 'below'.

When the morale of the middle rank collapsed, temporarily as it turned out, the army took over. 'The officers [gave] in full resolve, that no place be left for an after dispute', and 'the governour appeared in publicke, rode from place to place with a cheerfull aspect, and bearing before him no change in the sudden alteration of fortune'.[90] There is no reason to doubt Corbet's assertion that in Gloucestershire the middle rank, and especially the clothiers, were quite vehemently Parliamentarian. Looked at more closely, his account of the darkest years of the war in this part of the country shows that the key functionaries were the military officers, and in particular Edward Massey. They, rather than the middle-ranking clothiers and farmers, provided the 'guidance' and encouragement to the 'needy . . . rabble'. They were the most passionately committed of the 'middle rank', the 'revolutionary vanguard' as it were. This qualifies our understanding of the unwavering solidarity of 'the *whole* middle rank': not that it was not, by and large, the natural constituency of Parliament, but that it was vehement and unwavering in its commitment to military struggle. Here we must stress the role of a minority of passionately committed men like Corbet and Massey.

Gloucester held, the Royalist army of occupation was called away, piecemeal, to engagements in other parts of England, and Massey began to lead expeditions beyond the walls to recover the country. It is with these expeditions, covering the months from September 1643 to May and June 1644, that the bulk of Corbet's book is concerned. Massey's tactics then confirm Corbet's social, economic and political overview. He set out to attack the Royalist garrisons at Sudeley, Beverstone, Berkeley Castle and Lydney, the fortified houses and castles respectively of the county's 'powerfull gentry': lord Chandos, Sir Maurice Berkeley, lord George Berkeley and Sir William Winter, 'the scourge of the Forest'.[91] In each case the aim was to relieve 'the well-affected people' of adjoining industrial districts like 'Stroude, a place most exposed to spoyle', and the district around Berkeley Castle, 'the richest part of the county'.[92] In this sense, the shape of the war in Gloucestershire was determined not by strategic military exigencies, but by the degree to which a neighbourhood or district was likely to be inclined to be 'well-affected' towards king or Parliament, and this was determined by its economic structure, that is to say by centuries of historical development.

Corbet engaged in a rare but significant moment of exaggeration when he wrote that 'the whole middle ranke were the only active men'. In 1645 Parliament needed to consolidate its support in the electorate and, as Corbet suggests, that support undoubtedly wavered in the dark years of the war. It would be astonishing, given the circumstances, if it had not. The decisive factor in the achievement of military victory was not that the middle rank had remained unwavering in its support, but lay in a conjuncture of two decisive circumstances. One was the extraordinarily energetic leadership of Edward Massey and his officers and soldiers, and the sustained commitment of Puritan ministers like Corbet himself. The other was the 'force from below', that obscure but insistent agency in explanations of the civil wars: at whatever social level our research is pitched, if we concentrate hard we hear another level 'lower down', or 'out of range', but definitely there. Gentry studies hear the clamour of the middle ranks; the testimony of John Corbet, albeit reluctantly, draws attention to the passions and activities of the landless labouring poor.

The main difference between the leaders and the rank and file of the middle rank was in the intensity of their commitment, their implacability. Corbet also alludes to an important difference of emphasis in the loyalties of the leadership and those of the 'country people'. 'It was the usual mistake of particular associations to confine every enterprise to their own counties, and divide the commonwealth into so many petty kingdoms', he wrote in his summing-up.[93] At times the war threatened to degenerate into 'light skirmishes, and surprizals betweene petty parties on both sides'.[94] Leaders with a *national* vision were a prerequisite for victory. Corbet summed up the position with reference to Massey's dealings with 'great multitudes of the countrey people [in Herefordshire] appearing in armes, but standing on theire owne . . . and declaring themselves for neither side'.[95] 'A third party cannot be in England,' he wrote; nor, by implication, a fourth, fifth or hundredth, as the fragmentation of the resistance into counties, 'countreys' and even neighbourhoods sometimes threatened to bring about, and probably would have brought about had it not been for the *nationalist* leadership.[96] Massey and Corbet had thought this through, and gave it patient and practical application, often in very difficult circumstances. At no time 'did [Massey] suffer his souldiers to ransacke any place that he took by storm, giving this reason, *that he could judge no part of England an enemie's countrey, nor an English town capable of devastation by English souldiers'*.[97] Professor Aylmer describes Massey's 'role in Gloucestershire and the southern marches of Wales [as] almost exclusively military, not political'.[98] Corbet's account shows that the military, the political, the social and the economic represent different dimensions of the same mercurial events and circumstances.

Popular mentality in the mid-seventeenth century was still overwhelmingly *countrey*-centred. In this sense the proposition that local leaders of the Parliamentarian cause turned *countrey*-based resistance, made necessary in the first place by the intransigence of the Crown, into a *nationalist* war of liberation merits further investigation. This shift, the underlying 'structural' grounds for which have been discussed in earlier chapters, may be the key change that took place in the first civil war. Class antagonisms played a part in fostering the resentments that made so many members of the middle rank 'well-affected' towards Parliament. By their words and examples, men like Massey and Corbet sustained local resistance by constantly reminding parochial elites that theirs was a national struggle. They were nationalist 'missionaries' on ground prepared for them by underlying structural changes that had been centuries in the making.[99]

Corbet's explanation of the English Revolution in Gloucestershire is altogether more complex and accurate than historians arguing from all sides of debate have allowed. The account of the social, geographical and political–economic structure of the region that is implicit in his statements is confirmed by a wide range of contemporary and near-contemporary sources. His contention that the middle ranks were the only active men requires qualification. They were active for Parliament, but they were not the *only* active men, and at certain times, by his own account, they were not very active at all. Indeed, it is possible, by means of a close reading of his discussion of the role of the 'rabble', to perceive a desperate implacability in the struggle of the people below the middle, who perhaps had least to lose because, in many cases, they had nothing to lose.

Above all, however, a reading of Corbet's account that makes allowance for his propagandist instincts leaves an indelible impression of the extraordinary complexity of energies that were released in the 1640s, and of the extraordinary conceptual powers that were required to make sense of them and mould them into a politically and socially meaningful struggle. This, in the final analysis, is what revolutions are about. The structural forces must be present, but they must be articulated in a form that is comprehensible to all sorts of people. The great irony of John Corbet's *Historicall Relation* is that he gave the English middle ranks a revolution they did not fully deserve, and that they have spent the past 350 years trying to deny. But that, as Marx and Engels repeatedly pointed out, is in the very nature of bourgeois revolutions.

7

CUNNING MAN AND QUAKER
John Roberts of Siddington St Mary

'Tis no more than their own Reason might have directed them to, had they properly considered the case.

John Roberts[1]

O king, . . . we will not serve thy Gods . . .

Daniel, 3:18

And in all matters of wisdom and understanding, that the king enquired of them, he found them ten times better than all the magicians and astrologers that were in all his realm.

Daniel, 1:20

1

John Roberts, *alias* Hayward, was 'the ringleader of the Quakers in this country', and a magistrate said of him in 1660 that 'if [he was] not suppress'd all [i.e. the Restoration] will signify nothing'.[2] He was born about 1620, the son of a yeoman-freeholder, fought under Cromwell in the 1640s, married c. 1649, fathered six children 'in the time of Oliver' (of whom three survived to maturity), and died in 1683.[3]

He is first mentioned in the Quaker records of persecution as one of nine men 'committed to Prison at Gloucester . . . for Meeting together to worship God' at Cirencester and Tetbury' on 'the 1st of the 4th Month [July] 1660'.[4] Later the same year he was one of five Quaker leaders arrested at a Meeting at Cirencester, 'to which came the Deputy Lieutenant of the County with a party of Horse and Foot, who entered the Meeting with Swords and Pistols in Hand, and commanded five persons to go with them to the King's Commissioners. They were tendred . . . the Oath of Allegiance and for refusal to take it sent them to Prison'. These raids began a systematic sweep of Gloucestershire's major centres of Quakerism: Aylburton was raided a week later, Gloucester and Cirencester (again) the week after that, yielding 8 and 13 arrests respectively, Tetbury three days later, Nailsworth the day after the Tetbury raid, and, finally, Broad Campden Meeting was raided on 20 November.[5] Military resistance began at Cirencester in February 1643, and the authorities thought resistance to the Restoration was likely to begin there in 1660. Roberts was active in 1643, and he had not mellowed in the intervening years.

Prosecution of Quakers began five years before the Restoration campaign. Roberts is not mentioned in earlier records, although he had been a member of the Society of Friends since 1655. He was one of twenty-eight men arrested on 9 September 1662 at Cirencester for refusing the Oath of Uniformity, following a raid by 'soldiers' on a 'Mute Meeting' there three days earlier.[6] There is a gap until 'the tenth of the Month called *July* [1670]' when 'Thomas Master, a Justice' broke into a Meeting at Cirencester with some of his servants. One of these, 'one John Cooke, a wicked fellow . . . and Jenkins, said to be an Hangman . . . threw the Friends down Stairs', injuring 'an ancient Widow, named Hewlings' so 'lamentably [that] she soon died'. The 'hangman' was apprehended, 'but the Justice having an influence over the Jury, who were most of 'em his tenants . . . gave in their verdict *that she died of God's Visitation*. Thus the Murderer escaped . . .'. Roberts and the magistrate, Thomas Master, had known each other since childhood. They were students at Cirencester Grammer School in the 1630s. Master took it for granted that Roberts was the leader of the Cirencester Quakers, and it was to him that he addressed his questions at the outset of the raid.[7]

In 1681 'Cattle, Malt, Goods and Money [were] taken from him for Tithes, at Severall Times, to the value of 76 pounds'. The same year he 'was committed to Cirencester gaol, at the Suit of George Bull Priest; but the Lady Dunck . . . paid the Priest about 4 pounds and also the Gaoler's fees, and so set him at Liberty, saying, *that she could not be at Peace 'til she had done it . . .*'.[8] This is the last time Roberts is mentioned in the *Sufferings*, but his surviving sons, Anthony, Daniel and Nathaniel, each receive several mentions between 1682 and 1690.[9] They too were Quakers.

Shortly after Roberts died his son Daniel 'commit[ted] to Writing some memorable Passages [of his father's life], the Chief of which were transacted in [his] time'. He thought it 'a great Pity those singular Providences of the Almighty should not be recorded for the benefit of posterity'. The manuscript was 'for [his] own Perusal and that of [his] family, and some few Particular Friends'. Among other incidents of Roberts' life, it describes 'several Conferences [his] father had with the Bishop of Gloucester, and others'. Daniel was 'careful to pen them down in the same words they were then expres'd in, as near as I could recollect, or at least to retain the genuine Sense and Purport of them'.[10] This is not an automatic guarantee of the accuracy of his version of his father, but wherever cross-referencing with other records is possible it stands up. Like the founder of Christianity, John Roberts 'did not write any books; or if he did, which seems highly unlikely, they have not survived'. We have to rely 'on what he is reported to have said and done'.[11]

Quakers gave close attention to the historical dimension of Christianity. 'Our religion,' Roberts told Bishop Nicholson of Gloucester, 'as thou mays't read in the Scripture (John, iv) was set up by Christ himself, between sixteen and seventeen hundred years ago':

> And he had full Power to establish the true Religion in his Church, when he told the Women of Samaria, that neither at the Mountain nor yet at Jerusalem, was the place of true Worship. They worshipped they knew not what. For, said he, God is a Spirit, and they that worship him must worship in Spirit and in Truth. This is our religion, and hath ever been the religion of all those who have worshipp'd God acceptably thro' the severall ages since down to this time; and will be the Religion of true spiritual worshippers of God to the World's End; a religion perform'd by the Assistance of the Spirit of God, because God is a Spirit; a religion establish'd by Christ himself before the Mass-Book, Service-Book, or Directory, or any of those Inventions and Traditions of Men, which in the night of Apostasy were set up.[12]

This rejection of the 'inventions and traditions of men' in favour of inner enlightenment was the basis of Roberts' radicalism.

Other passages in the *Memoir* suggest an anxiety to be historically accurate; although Daniel is reporting his father's words, the fact of doing so suggests he thought about their implications. With one exception – the *Memoir* dates his 'conversion' to Quakerism in 1665, ten years later than it actually took place, as we shall see – Daniel Roberts' account checks well against other contemporary sources. It is of course written from a Quaker point of view.

2

Social–structural studies of Quakerism show that it drew its adherents predominantly from groups whose experience necessarily took them beyond the neighbourhood, physically and intellectually, as a matter of routine.[13] Richard Vann states 'that Quakerism at the beginning drew adherents from all classes of society except the very highest and the very lowest, ranging from the lesser gentry down to a few totally unskilled labourers'.[14] A list of Quakers imprisoned at Gloucestershire County Gaol between 1677 and 1697 which gives the occupations of

99 local members of the movement supports the assessment. Of the 99, 20 were husbandmen, 18 yeomen (including 1 'farmer'), 7 mercers and 2 chandlers, 5 maltsters and 2 tanners, followed by an assortment of tradesmen including shoemakers (4), tailors (3), blacksmiths (4), woolcombers (2), joiner/carpenters (3) and weavers (2). The lower end of the social scale was represented by six labourers.[15] For the most part it was a movement of respectably independent middling people. They were not, on the whole, those whom contemporaries described as 'dependents', the 'labouring poor'. Being independent – and of course independence is always qualified, and one of the characteristics of the Quakers was that they believed in unrestricted independence – in the material sense made it easier to be independent in the intellectual and spiritual sense.

The Gloucestershire Quakers were overwhelmingly from Corbet's 'middle ranke'. The social composition of Gloucestershire Quakerism substantiates Alan Cole's view that 'the movement made more headway among the peasantry than the Levellers had done', but only if we add the qualification that few of the yeomen and husbandmen imprisoned in Gloucestershire would fit the classification 'peasant'. Vann uses three censuses of ocupations, dated 1608, 1662 and the 1690s, to reach a similar conclusion; his interpretation fits the case in Gloucestershire.[16] Quakerism was primarily a religion of Corbet's 'middle ranke'. John Roberts was a yeoman, a rank then as now regarded as the very backbone of the middle class of sixteenth- and seventeeth-century England.

The weakness of Vann's analysis is that its samples are too static. Terms like 'yeoman', 'clothier', 'gentleman' and 'labourer' each, in their own way, underwent transition during the seventeenth century. 'Yeoman' continued to mean either a freehold farmer or a tenant farmer with substantial capital in the form of livestock and equipment, but the actual lives of yeomen in fact changed quite considerably during a period in which commerce began to impregnate the smallest pores of English society.

The three generations of the Roberts family that are touched on in the *Memoir* illustrate the point. Daniel Roberts and his brothers grew up on their father's freehold farm at Siddington St Mary, but they became shopkeepers and petty merchants. John Roberts travelled around the market towns and fairs of his district as a routine part of his farming activities. Less is known of his father, who is only briefly mentioned in the *Memoir* to illustrate the long-standing nature of the family's radical Protestantism, but he was roughly the same age as John Smyth of Nibley and lived through a time of transition from highly localised marketing activities and 'living of one's own', to a time when it was necessary to be embroiled, economically and politically, in the affairs of one's 'country' (a term which was enduring rapid change as a result of the practical changes to which I refer), simply to survive.

The Civil War experience was crucial. In the early 1640s many men of Roberts' rank left home to fight for a conception of 'country' in the modern, national, sense in order, they believed, to preserve the independence and integrity of self, family, household, neighbourhood and 'country' in the district sense. Such men were not, like many others of their class, merely resisters of Royalist invasion. In 1642 Roberts 'and his next neighbour . . . went into the army under Oliver Cromwell'. This was probably in August and definitely in 1642, before his own 'country' (the Cirencester district) was directly threatened. There they 'continu'd 'till they heard Cirencester was taken by the King's party; when they thought it proper to return home, to see how it fared with their Parents and Relations', who were active in Parliament's cause too, but in a more defensive mode.[17]

To what extent can Roberts' actions then and later, his affinity for a certain type of religious profession, indeed a certain type of epistemology, be explained as a function of his position in society? Roberts was not exclusively religious in his preoccupations, and he was no 'quietist'. He did not stand 'entirely aloof from war and politics'; far from it.[18] His life and beliefs cannot be understood in isolation from the particular configurations of social power and popular belief at the time. This chapter necessarily abstracts Roberts from his society, highlights him, brings him to the forefront − but partly in order to shed light on his society, a society at a particular level of social organisation and complexity.

I proceed as follows. Following the order of Daniel Roberts' *Memoir*, I begin with an account of Roberts' family, his 'kin-coalition'. I then explore his first experience of the 'inner light': February 1643, the aftermath of the siege of Cirencester. This touches upon the *revolutionary* significance of those events, at least in the life of my subject here. This section is followed by an account of his 'conversion' (or, more accurately, 'discovery') by Richard Farnsworth in 1655, and a discussion of the nature of the early Quaker movement. We then explore his first 'testimony of truth' in the 'steeple-house' at Cirencester, and touch upon his relations with George Bull, Rector of Siddington St Mary, conservative theologian, and later Bishop of St Davids.

George Bull shared the view of the neighbourhood that Roberts was a 'cunning man' or 'wizard'. Unlike the neighbours, who often found Roberts' skills useful, Bull wanted him to be prosecuted and convicted of witchcraft. The reasons why he was unable to do this are of some interest, and touch upon the historical and anthropological character of the wisdom of wizards, and its relationship to the Quaker inner light. I suggest that the Society of Friends was a movement of the cunning people or 'wizards', those who, in earlier times, would have been more likely, and more able, to carry out their activities quietly and routinely in the proverbial cultures of agrarian England. Such people, more than any others, were the victims of the rise of the specialised professionalism which is one of the defining characteristics of the modern state. It is testimony to their 'cunning' (a word which originally meant, quite simply, 'knowledge' and 'knowing', as 'wizard' meant something very similar to the term 'elder' – a 'wise one') that, when persecuted locally, they were able to adapt to the new circumstances and transform themselves into a *movement*, an alternative *society*. They were persecuted by the Puritans and then by the restored Arminians, who shared the characteristic that they derived their legitimacy from the state, only differing over the kind of State in question.

This touches upon the fundamental ambiguity of Roberts' epistemology. He was an empirico-rationalist, a man of the Enlightenment *and* a 'white witch', a man who, like all Quakers, drew upon supposed supernaturalist inspiration to solve difficult cases. On balance I stress the rationalist rather than supernaturalist impulses in the wizard–Quaker conjuncture. I also suggest that men like Roberts filled a role similar to that of the ancient Hebrew *Nabi'im*.[19]

3

Daniel Roberts' *Memoir* begins with a 'short account of his family', which testifies to the Roberts' solidly respectable Protestant connections. Daniel's grandfather 'lived reputably on a little estate of his own, which he occupied'. He lived 'of his own', a phrase which was redolent of 'Independency', and had political overtones. John Roberts' father was a yeoman, but one with gentry connections. 'He married Mary Solliss, sister to Andrew Solliss Esq., who was in the Commission of the Peace.' Roberts fled to his uncle's house after he was wounded in the aftermath of the siege of Cirencester in 1643, although, at the time, Andrew Solliss cannot have been at home, since he was among the prisoners taken by the King's Party to Oxford. Daniel only hints at Uncle Andrew's role in the Parliamentarian cause by stating that he 'sustained great spoil in the Time of the Civil War', but it is certain that he was one of the main figures in the defence of Cirencester.[20] John Roberts' mother, Daniel Roberts' grandmother, was of solid gentry stock.

Daniel tells the story of how his father, still suffering from the wounds he had sustained a few weeks earlier at the siege of Cirencester, was called from his refuge at the Solliss house to witness his father's death. 'They greeted each other with many tears, and a great Intermixture of Joy and Sorrow', for it was clear that the old man was very ill. 'After some Time, my father perceived him to tremble to such a degree, that the bed shook under him. Upon which [John Roberts] asked him how it was with him?':

> He reply'd, 'I am well: I feel no pain. 'Tis the mighty Power of God that shakes me.' After lying still some Time, he broke out in a sweet Melody of Spirit, saying, 'In the Lord only have I Righteousness and Strength! In God have I Salvation!'

The 'spirit' was 'within' him, revealed by the 'trembling' (or 'quaking') induced by its imminent departure from the body under the 'Power of God', in whom alone the old yeoman saw his salvation.

If his father's Protestantism was stolid, that of his mother's line was positively illustrious. After returning from service with Cromwell some time in the late 1640s, John Roberts 'took to wife *Lydia Tyndal*, daughter of Thomas Tyndal of Slincombe' (Stinchcombe, near Dursley in the Vale of Berkeley, a chapelry of Cam parish, the home of the Trotman family, and a mile or two from John Smyth of Nibley's house). Somewhat understating the matter, Daniel described the Tyndales as 'a religious family, and one of those under the denomination of *Puritans*'. She was a descendent of Edward, William Tyndale's brother. 'Matthew Hale [afterwards Lord Chief Justice of England] was [his mother's] Kinsman,' wrote Daniel, 'and drew her Marriage-Settlement.' The Roberts' were linked into the most illustrious kin-coalition of the region. They were elite members of Corbet's 'middle ranke', bordering gentility.[21]

The gentry connection (something, no doubt, that showed in his manner and appearance) helps to explain his authority in certain situations. As a Quaker, Roberts put himself outside or 'beyond' the social order, but as an hereditary yeoman with gentry connections he was solidly respectable. He always addressed his contemporaries as equals from conviction, but bishops and magistrates would have found it easier to accept his 'quiet' authority and directness of address because in terms of prescribed order he was, more or less, their equal. His authority also drew on his reputation as 'cunning man' derived from these qualities. But whether he liked it or not, inherited and marriage-related status would undoubtedly have made the authorities of Cromwellian and Restoration Gloucestershire more willing to 'negotiate' and converse with him than they would had he been a labourer, a weaver, or even a rich clothier.

Roberts' predisposition to Quakerism cannot be reduced to his rank and class. A majority of the pro-Parliamentarian middle rank in his region stopped short of radical independency, formed the nuclei of the 'Puritan' settlement between 1645 and 1660, and made their compromises with the Restoration establishment fairly comfortably.

Very few became Quakers, although his class definitely formed the backbone of Quakerism in the region, and, according to most authorities, everywhere. This is only to be expected. It was to such people that the 'discoverers' who arrived in the county in significant numbers in 1654-5 inevitably looked for hospitality and a degree of protection. Such men had claims to 'eldership', and they had houses large enough to offer lodgings to itinerant Quakers from the North. Whatever their religious convictions and behaviour, they were listened to and respected in their neighbourhoods. They were in a position to win converts from their own subordinates and workers, i.e. those of their neighbourhoods who did not qualify as 'independent', i.e. who could not 'live of their own' like Roberts, and who were thus technically defined, by such as the more conservative John Smyth of Nibley (or even, from a different perspective, Throgmorton Trotman), as 'dependent'. Class made a difference, even, in spite of themselves, to Quakers.

People like Roberts followed the logic of Independency to its philosophical and theological conclusions: radical individualism, the ascendancy and sanctification of personal experience, intuition and judgement, over and above duty to family. They embodied the fact that, throughout the most populous and industrious districts of England, older types of religious belief, based on passing realities of kin-based neighbourhood life, no longer described, explained or made coherent sense of prevailing circumstances of life. They articulated this at a time (1654–1690) when it was generally unacceptable to do so, at a time when people were hoping that the social dysfunctions and dislocations embodied most clearly in the civil wars would go away. England was traumatised in the 1640s, and the country was in a state of collective shock for decades to come. Given this pathology, it is not surprising that Quakers, in bearing witness to what had, in fact, taken place, touched raw nerves, drew attention to the bad faith of others, and met with violence that was quite out of proportion to its occasions. Sometimes, too, the violence had a class basis, the Quakerism of 'respectable' men like Roberts providing an opportunity to vent normally suppressed class resentments.

4

The 'transcendence' of kinship-loyalty is illustrated by an episode which occurred shortly after Roberts joined the Society of Friends in 1655. It illustrates one aspect of the revolutionary radicalism of the Quakers – their explicit and fundamental rejection of the family as an absolute reference-point. Roberts was imprisoned by a magistrate, John Stephens of Lypiatt (older brother of Nathaniel Stephens), for holding illegal Meetings at his house.[22] His uncle Solliss came to the prison and arranged for him to be released. At home in bed that night Roberts was visited by the Spirit of Truth, causing him to tremble violently. The Spirit told him to confront Stephens, who was as yet unaware of his release. He got up the next morning, told his wife what he had to do, and set off across country for Stephens' house near Stroud.

On the way 'he let in the Reasoner, who reasoned him out of all his courage'. The voice of 'Reason' told him, quite sensibly, 'that his uncle Solliss and his neighbours would say, he had no regard for his Wife and Family, thus to push himself into the Hands of his greatest Enemy'.[23] Spiritual Truth was all very well, his uncle and his neighbours would say, if he was the only one to suffer for it. Hadn't Roberts caused enough suffering to his wife and children already? Which had precedence, the voice of God expressed through conscience, or the voice of secular morality?

'The Reasoner' so troubled Roberts 'that he alighted off his horse, and sat down on the Ground, to spread his Cause to the Lord'.

> After he had waited some time in Silence, the LORD appeared and dissipated the Cloud, and his Word was to him *Go, and I will go with thee, and will give thee a threshing Instrument, and thou shalt thresh the Mountains.*

Roberts had consulted his wife. 'The Lord requires hard things of me,' he told her. 'If thou art fully persuaded the Lord requires it of thee', she replied, 'I would not have thee disobey him.' After he left she was troubled by the probable outcome of his determination – further imprisonment, leaving her to cope with three young sons not yet able to run the farm. She travelled to Tetbury, where the Quaker organiser William Dewsbury was staying. She arrived and a Meeting was called. At the Meeting 'Dewsberry walk'd to and fro in a long Passage, groaning in Spirit'. 'By and by [he] came up to [Lydia Roberts], . . . laid his Hand upon her Head, and said, "Woman thy sorrow is great: I sorrow with thee".' He walked up and down a little longer, again 'groaning in Spirit', and then said, 'Now the time is come that those who Marry must be as tho' they had none; for the LORD calls for all to be offered up'.

'Hard things' were demanded of all Quakers. Sooner or later all would have to confront a choice between loyalty and duty to family and loyalty and duty to the 'inner light'. It was also a fragment of a more general historical conjuncture, marking a conscious transition from domus-centredness to individual-centredness, one of those 'migrations of the holy' which took place as a result of the Protestant Reformation.[24] Tyndale withdrew legitimacy from the Church of medieval Christendom and invested it in the elders of associational 'congregations'. In Smyth of Nibley (1567–1643) it migrated from the parish church to the household. In John Roberts it migrated from the household and family to the individual.

The changing nature of society militated in favour of individualism. But it became necessary to reject loyalty to family as an irreducible axiom of social life only when it had first been decided to take a stance of radical opposition to the state and its functionaries. For, if the choice was not made and justified, consciously and explicitly, rebels would never be able to resist the obvious, conventional retort and accusation that to act in a certain way, according to the dictates of the inner light, would be to the detriment of those closest to them. This did not at all mean that family life was not of fundamental importance to the Quaker. Far from it. If the inner light did not cause one to act lovingly, honourably and conscientiously with respect to those with whom one shared one's life, it became indefensible.[25]

5

'The steps of a good man are ordered by the Lord; and he delighteth in his way. He is his strength in the Time of Trouble' (Psalms 37:23, 39): this epigram appears on the title page of the *Memoir*. It was taken literally. Consider, first, Daniel's account of his father's escape from Cirencester during the town's greatest 'time of trouble', the Royalist siege of 1643 and its aftermath. John Roberts, like many of 'the early Quaker leaders . . . had been in arms for Parliament'.[26] Roberts and the 'near neighbour' with whom he rode back when they heard Cirencester was threatened were active in its defence, members of the handful of cavalry left in the town after its main strength rode across the North Wolds to take and occupy Sudeley Castle. As soon as it was evident that the Royalists had broken the back of the defence, Roberts and his friend tried to get out of the town on horseback. They were pursued and 'quitted their horses', probably in an attempt to get out through narrow passages and houses where they knew horses could not follow. Once out in the open fields, they 'took to their heels' towards marshy scrub where, once again, they would have the advantage over their mounted pursuers. But 'by reason of their Accoutrements [they] could make little speed', and were again spotted.

The two cavaliers (probably members of Sir John Byron's troop) 'came upon my father first', wrote Daniel, and 'laid upon him with their Swords, cutting and slashing his Head and Arms, which he held up to save his Head'. As this was happening, 'it pleased the Almighty to put it into his Mind to fall down upon his face; which he did'. This put the cavaliers in two minds. Should they dismount and finish him off, instead of 'continuing to strike and prick him about the jaws', rather ineffectually, from the saddle? *'Alight! and cut his throat!'*, yelled one of the cavaliers. At that moment they noticed Roberts' companion across the field, running for his life, 'whom they presently overtook and killed'. This gave Roberts his chance. After a moment's indecision 'it was said in his Heart *Rise and flee for thy Life!'*. Once again he obeyed the voice 'within', that definitive 'Strength in Time of Trouble', and his life was saved.[27]

The episode leads into the description of the death of his father, which took place a few weeks later, when Roberts was fit enough to make the journey from his uncle Solliss's to witness his father's last words.[28] The Quakers were always to stress 1643, and the 1640s generally, as the time of 'enlightenment' or 'awakening'. For them this awakening was a positive experience, in stark contrast to the symbolic significance of the 1640s in official testimony and, through it, the collective consciousness of the English people generally, where it has assumed a negative significance – as 'the Great Rebellion', for example, a transparently misleading characterisation of what happened (who were the rebels – the King's Party or the Parliamentarians? The middle rank in Gloucestershire, whichever side they finally took, were never in any doubt that it was the former, as I have shown). One of the most important subtexts in Quaker witnessing was that they remained witnesses to events which, even as early as the 1650s, most English people wanted to forget, erase from the collective memory.

Here we encounter the most controversial issue in English historiography. Was 1642–3 a 'turning-point' in English history (as well as in the spiritual biographies of people like John Roberts), and therefore a revolution? The consensus of post-Christopher Hill historiography, of 'revisionism', is that, in the end, the civil wars changed very little in English history. This is even true of social historians like Keith Wrightson, who rightly point out that the fundamental structural changes were already in place before the 'revolution'. I have no difficulty with this line of reasoning, as long as it is not used to argue that it implies that the events of the 1640s were not revolutionary. The rise of capitalism in England was indeed a 'long revolution', as I have suggested. But the 'structuralist' approach, based today on techniques derived from historical demography and 'community reconstitution', and most evident in the work of historians like Wrightson and David Levine, ignores or plays down the effect of the events of the 1640s on individual and collective *conciousness*.

It is not just a question of counting and cataloguing the things that did change as a direct result of the 1640s, and those that did not, and balancing one against the other. The Court of Wards was abolished but the House of Lords came back. The Presbyterian oligarchs remained in control at Dursley and Wotton-under-Edge, but after 1660 they conformed, at least nominally. The cloth industry continued to dominate certain districts before, during and after the 1640s . . . and so on. Even in Gloucestershire the impact of the 1640s was uneven. Gloucester and Cirencester, bastions of bourgeois resistance in 1643, never recovered their centrality in regional life after 1660. Surely, it might be argued, this testifies to the *failure* of the bourgeois revolution in Gloucestershire (and England).

The revolutionary significance of the civil wars lies in the fact that they led to a heightened consciousness, an articulation, of the massive structural changes that had taken place, establishing once and for all that the kind of social reforms advocated, primarily, by 'Puritans', rooted as they were in social–structural changes, had to be accepted. Institutional changes that were primarily concerned with disciplining and controlling the labouring poor, the direct producers, which had been introduced piecemeal in the century before the wars, were introduced systematically after the Restoration. The Settlement Laws were the most important of these: they were much more important than the reactionary measures directed against nonconformist divines in the same year (1662), for they quietly recognised that household disciplines could no longer be relied on to serve as the basis of social control. The 'dependency system' as favoured by John Smyth of Nibley, for example, had become impractical, because the balance of landed households to landless households was such that the former simply could not assimilate the latter as 'retainers' or 'servants'.

The civil wars articulated these structural changes in a very simple way. They literally uprooted men like John Roberts. The mobility of English society had already been intensified by print, production and commerce. The civil wars suddenly, and as it were 'accidentally', heightened this experience a hundredfold. The experience had to be assimilated. The Quakers often did this by *continuing* to travel extensively, albeit for their own reasons, to 'discover' others who thought like they did. Family, household, neighbourhood, 'country' solidarities could no longer serve to protect people. In the fields outside Cirencester, fields in which Roberts had played as a child and which he worked as a man, the only thing that saved him was his 'inner light'. Social forms which had served to order the everyday life of English people ever since the coming of agriculture, were, finally in the 1640s, 'by the sword divided'. Henceforth the nation-state, the playground of Parliament as well as the Caroline Establishment, was to become the fundamental unit of organisation and affective loyalty. The Quakers rejected it, preferring the concrete associations of 'friendship'. For them the fundamental 'bad faith' of the English Revolution was that it replaced one kind of absolutism, one kind of abstract loyalty, with another. They came to rest in the only loyalty that remained: the individual 'self' or 'conscience'.

As a result of this shift towards the 'inner light', *all* symbolic representations of prescribed, conventional order became problematical. Truth was no longer external, but internal. Meaning could not be determined *a priori*, particularly the meaning of 'consecrated houses . . . Bells . . . , names of Saints, . . . Surplices, Gowns, Cassocks, . . . [religious] Ornaments, . . . Holy Ground . . .', and of course 'Priests'.[29] One aspect of the Quakers was that they took the 'cutting down' of the 'forest of symbols' that had accumulated during the 'night of Apostasy' as far as it could be taken, insisting on the right of the 'inner light' alone, the 'light' of personal observation and experience, to ascribe meaning.

A secular rationalist would explain the 'voice' that came into John Roberts' mind, and saved his life by overcoming his shock-induced panic, in terms of survival instinct derived to some extent from his experience as a soldier under Cromwell in the early months of the war, before he returned to help in the defence of his native country. However we explain it, we cannot reduce and dissolve it. For ten years, thousands of English men experienced moments like these. *Sudden* death became an everyday threat for them, and, as an indirect consequence of the wars, death by famine and disease which were induced and intensified as a consequence of war. Consider, for example, the women and children and old people left behind in villages like Slimbridge after the men had all gone off to fight. Who worked John Roberts' yeoman-freehold after his father died, and he had returned to fight, "til near the Conclusion of that Dreadful Eruption, when he returned to his sorrowful Family at Siddington'?[30] Only collective psychoanalysis – history? – could understand the neuroses that such cataclysmic events introduced into the collective consciousness of English culture. 'Rebellion' is too innocuous a term for all this. And the Quakers are still with us, quietly working on in the belief that the phenomenal world can be 'perfected' through the operation of the 'inner light'.[31]

The presentation of the *Memoir* stresses continuity between the explicitly radicalising experience of 1642–3 and formal membership of the Society of Friends some thirteen years later. The intervening years, during which we are told that Roberts continued in the army under Cromwell "till near the end', are somewhat obscure: Daniel simply records his father's marriage, and he was not born until 1650, and so can have known of the 1640s only from what his father told him (and, no doubt, from curiosity with respect to the scars his father carried as testimony to the trauma of February 1643). The continuity of connections between the military and 'political' struggles of the 1640s and

176

the 'religious' radicalism of the Quakers is therefore somewhat obscure in Roberts' case. Nevertheless, Daniel unhesitatingly assumed that it existed, and there seems no good reason to doubt it.[32]

6

Travelling members of the 'Valiant Sixty', 'witnesses to Truth' from the North-West of England, first came into Gloucestershire in 1654 in search of 'such as fear God' in several townships: Cirencester, Gloucester, Tewkesbury, Frenchay, Painswick, Nailsworth, Tetbury, Minchinhampton all date the foundations of their Meetings to 1654–5.[33] John Audlam, John Cam, Humphrey Smith, Thomas Goodyeare, Christopher Holder and a local man, John Thurston of Thornbury, are named as the principals of the movement in Gloucestershire, but there were others. Daniel Roberts records that 'in the year 16[55], it pleased the Lord to send two women friends, out of the North, to Cirencester, who, enquiring after such as feared God, were directed to [John Roberts] as the likeliest person to entertain 'em'.[34] This establishes that Roberts was already identified by his neighbours as a 'sectary', or as a Seeker (the terms are not necessarily the same).

The two women called at Roberts' farm 'and desired a Meeting'. Roberts 'granted it, and invited several of his Acquaintance to sit with 'em'.

> After some Time of Silence, the *Friends* spake a few Words, which had a good effect. After the Meeting, my Father endeavour'd to engage 'em in Discourse: But they said little, only recommended him to *Richard Farnsworth*, then prisoner for Testimony of Truth in *Banbury* gaol, to whom they were going . . .

Shortly after the women left, Roberts rode to Banbury and 'mett with the Two Women', who were part of a crowd being denied entrance to the gaol by the 'Turnkey', who had been instructed 'not to let any of those *giddy-headed people* in'. If they did enter, he told them, 'he would keep 'em there'. Roberts spoke to him, with some authority it seems, for as a result 'they were conducted through severall rooms to a Dungeon where *Richard Farnsworth* was preaching, thro' a Grate, to the People in the Street'.[35]

Richard Farnsworth or Farnworth (there are a number of alternative spellings) was one of the founders of the Quaker movement. Like Roberts, he was of yeoman rank, having grown up on his father's estate in Yorkshire. He was with George Fox when Fox was inspired to climb Pendle Hill, leaving Farnsworth, 'physically a cripple',[36] to wait for him on the road along which they had been walking. 'Atop the hill [Fox] . . . was moved to Sound the Day of the LORD: and the

LORD did let [him] see atop the Hill in which Places He had a great People to be gathered.'[37] Farnsworth was with Fox and Naylor at Swarthmore Hall in Westmoreland, where the strategy of the movement was conceived. Sixty like-minded people were 'discovered' in the district in the later months of 1652, a number of whom had fought, like Naylor and John Roberts, with Cromwell. Such men were already an historical elite, original companions of the man who now ruled England.

Among them were many women, a fact which testifies to the movement's spiritual egalitarianism.[38] Most of the well-known leaders were male, but their reputations were acquired by achievement and energy, which may have been something to do with the fact that it was easier for them to travel without being harassed than it was for women. Roberts' reception of the 'two women from the North' indicates that, like other men who joined the Quakers, he was as willing to 'receive Truth' from women as from men.

Farnsworth was something of a 'wise one' or 'wizard'. We learn a little of the impression he made on contemporaries from an account written by a man whom Farnsworth discovered and co-opted into the movement in Worcestershire in 1654, shortly before he went into Oxfordshire and ended up in Banbury gaol, where Roberts met him. 'In our discourse together on the Rode before parting,' wrote the Worcestershire man, 'Hee speak of the Glory of the first body, & of the Egyptian Learning, & of the Language of the Birds, & of wt was wonnderfull to mee to heare, so that I believed he was of Deep and wonnderfull understanding in naturall, but especially in sp[iri]tuall things . . . I loved his Company, & to bee with him & to heare him, and his memoriall is blessed to many.'[39] This evokes a man of keen observation with a profound and gentle affinity with 'naturall things', and a keen interest in making rational and spiritual sense of his 'empirical data' ('the Language of the Birds'). He probably struck many contemporaries as the very epitome of a wizard.

People wanted to hear what he had to say. One day, perhaps, someone will write a universal history of such people. The popular legitimacy of the learning they embodied is paralleled by the ancient Hebrew *Nabi'im*, an analogy which is, of course, of some significance in the consideration of what, after all, was a self-consciously Judaeo-Christian sect.[40] The term *Nabi'im* means 'literally, mouthpieces of God'.[41] They were not priests but, as long as they could 'overcome the inevitable problem . . . of convincing others that [they were] what [they] claimed to be', they enjoyed enormous popular prestige. Wilson suggests that one of the ways they did this was by working 'miracles' and 'tricks', like Moses striking the rock and making water gush out.

This meant causing an event that in the eyes of their observers appeared to have no natural cause: conjuring, using 'magic'.[42]

The supernaturalist overtones of wizardry are usually stressed at the expense of more mundane, but no less surprising, aspects of their legitimacy, such as a long and hard-won reputation for (a) acting eccentrically or unconventionally, as in a cripple taking up a travelling life, and (b) simply getting things right, by being very observant and making logical deductions from one's observed experience.[43] One of the things that supporters of empiricism often miss, in assuming that it is somehow 'common sense' to operate in this way, is how extraordinarily unusual it is for people to live according to its principles.

Nabi'im, writes Wilson, 'tended towards an ascetic, "back to nature" outlook' and 'could be anyone, a courtier like Isaiah, priests such as Jeremiah and Ezekial, even a woman, such as Deborah, but quite often an uncouth countryman' like Jesus of Nazareth, Richard Farnsworth and John Roberts. Such people – whose authority derived from popular reputation which was not necessarily sanctioned by the ruling powers – are bound to arise in any Judaeo-Christian society, except that there are also non-Judaeo-Christian examples like the Bakhti saints of Hindu tradition (the guise of which Gandhi adopted) and Chinese figures like Lao T'su.

'Soon after [Roberts] and his companions' entered his cell, and 'after a little Time of Silence' for Farnsworth to gather himself, 'turning to them, he spake to this Purpose':

> That *Zaccheus*, being a man of low stature, and having a Mind to see CHRIST, ran before, and climbed up into a Sycamore Tree: and our Saviour, knowing his good Desires, called to him *Zaccheus, come down! This day is Salvation come to thy House.* Thus Zaccheus was like some in our Day, who, are climbing up into the Tree of *Knowledge*, thinking to find CHRIST there. But the Word now is, *Zaccheus come down! come down! for that which is to be known of GOD is manifested WITHIN.*[44]

Roberts later told his son that Farnsworth 'had spoke to his Condition as if he had known him from his Youth'.[45] Roberts had been like Zaccheus, a seeker after truth in the 'tree of Knowledge' (*Cabbala*). Farnsworth taught him that truth resided in 'that which is to be known of God . . . manifested within'. The practical effect is the same if the words 'to be known of God' are omitted from this sentence. But in either case the message is to trust personal experience absolutely.

The Quakers cut down the 'tree of Knowledge', the accumulated symbols of the 'night of Apostasy', replacing it with what they regarded as the more 'down to earth' wisdom that derived from the 'inner light'. They erased all conventional meaning in order to begin again, insisting, for practical purposes, on their own personal right to determine what was true and what was not according to 'enlightenment', observation and reason endowed with certainty through the legitimising agency of the 'inner light'.

Like many of his contemporaries, Roberts, a devout man from a pious family with Puritan connections, had been unsettled by the profusion of religious professions in the years following 1642–3, and also by his years as a 'russet-coated captain' in Cromwell's cavalry. He acquired the reputation of a Seeker, that is to say, a person who visited *all* the churches in his district, including that of the temporarily dominant Baptists,[46] in order to make a rational choice, using comparative methods, as to his religious affiliation. Unable to choose between them, but rather finding that they all had tenets and practices with which he could agree but others with which he could not, he acquired the reputation of a man who was unusually devout and pious, but who asked troublesome questions in and of the various congregations that he visited.

He was a solid, respectable Seeker.[47] Farnsworth taught him that he had been looking for truth in the wrong places. *All* churches were suspect. Religion was personal, not institutional. This confirmed Roberts' suspicions, and enabled him to trust his own judgement and intuition in a way that had not been possible before he was 'confirmed' by the wise one at Banbury gaol. This was his enlightenment. It also allowed people to protest actively against the religious foundations of the secular state without necessarily committing treason and incurring the ultimate punishment of the law – though Roberts was also explicitly critical of that too. His conversion was a 'particle' in the history of the Enlightenment – except that, unlike the Deists, God was not dispatched to the abstract edges of the universe but incorporated into the self. And knowledge was not rendered as part of an abstract system, but invested in the phenomenal world.

The early Quakers, beginning with Fox, Farnsworth, Naylor and the Valiant Sixty, were not so much 'preachers' as seekers in the land, travelling to enjoy the companionship of others whose spiritual pilgrimages through everyday life had led them to the same conclusions. All over England there were people like Roberts with the experience, observational and reasoning ability, and imagination to have 'exhausted the resources of the old religion[s]'.[48] Seekers were people who, while remaining within the gathered people of the neighbourhood, the 'congregation' as Tyndale understood the term, could never quite satisfy themselves with any of the institutional expressions that were available to them. As Puritans, they had rejected the infrastructures of Anglicanism in all its Tudor and Stuart forms, but they also became disillusioned with the congregations that took institutional form in their neighbourhoods and districts after the political and military foundations of Caroline Arminianism had been crushed in the mid–1640s. They found all these expressions, from the Baptists to the Presbyterians, too exclusive, too restrictive and therefore too authoritarian to contain their experience and their ideals. If the Quakers had come to Gloucestershire before 1654–5 they would probably have been too early. Too few people would have been *thoroughly* disillusioned by the compromises, incoherencies and corruptions of the various new professions that sprang up 'under Oliver', as Roberts always described the 1650s. They would not have had time to consider the old associations.

The Quakers created a new kind of associational community. Peter Laslett observes in *The World We Have Lost* that seventeenth-century England was a 'one-class society', that class being the gentry with its near-universal literacy and its constitutional opportunities for regular association. Harold Perkin has something similar in mind when he calls 'preindustrial' England 'a federation of country houses'. The Quakers were also a 'one-class society': plebeian and associational, local and national.[49] Conversion to Quakerism involved taking the step of leaving the 'congregation' in Tyndale's sense of 'the gathered people of the neighbourhood'. In the case of travellers like Fox and Farnsworth it literally meant that: physically pulling up one's roots, leaving one's 'parish of settlement' as the law was to define the proper operational context of all ranks below that of yeoman, in 1662. They abandoned the symbolic communities of the past: family, household, neighbourhood and 'country'. Allowing for exceptional gentry Quakers, the movement was literally a one-class 'society', in this case an overwhelmingly plebeian one, set in opposition to the established ruling class, at least in its religious dimension.[50]

The Quakers stepped out of the neighbourhood-centred 'congregations' of the past, into the infinite (open) space of yet-to-be-defined new forms of community.[51] They created a social *tabula rasa*, and then began to fill it by 'discovering' others who believed as they did: a new society. It in no way denigrates the courage involved in this step to say that they embodied the fundamentals of bourgeois-capitalist ideology: empiricism, Reason, globalism, individualism. But there was more. The Quakers differ from the bourgeois civilisation of which they were early symptoms in that they also stepped easily across what later became quite rigid racial and national boundaries. They left the parish and entered the modern world, but they also 'deconstructed' the 'power discourses' of the modern world. That is why their message, their 'key', remains, today, as radical as it was in the seventeenth century.

181

John Roberts' spiritual life began in 1643, but not until his conversation with Richard Farnsworth at Banbury in 1655 was he able to 'patiently [bear] the cross'.[52] His first act as a Quaker occurred shortly after his final conversion. 'A necessity was laid upon him [by God], one first-day morning,' wrote Daniel, 'to go to the Public Worship-house in Cirencester in the Time of Worship, not knowing what might be required of him there.' Arriving at Church, in the midst of a congregation of at least 500, the spirit instructed him to remain standing and to keep his hat on. Seeing him, 'the Priest was silent for some time . . . Ask'd why he did not go on? he answer'd, he could not, while that Man stood with his Hat on'.[53] Upon this, several men 'took him by the arm, and led him into the Street, staying at the door to keep him out'.

The Quakers called this activity 'declaring truth in Steeplehouses', and hundreds were fined, arrested and beaten up for doing it. Roberts was probably the first to do it at Cirencester. It was not his home parish. The population of the borough in 1650 was over 3,000, although how many of these were in church when he made his first 'public declaration' is impossible to know: 500 seems a conservative estimate. It is not difficult to imagine the drama of the event: a man standing resolute and defiant, in spite of whatever equanimity he was granted by his submission to the 'inner light', the voice of conscience or intuition derived from memory and experience, no doubt glancing from time to time at neighbours and acquaintances in the congregation, many of whom, like him, had fought to defend the town against the Royalists thirteen years earlier, but for the most part levelling his gaze at the minister trying to conduct his service in front of the kneeling congregation, laying down the correct procedures in ritual and everyday behaviour. Mute it may have been, but 'declaration' of some kind it most certainly was. What, precisely and practically, was the 'truth' to which he was bearing witness?

The answer is given in the Memoir in three dialogues between Roberts and the Bishop of Gloucester. The first took place when Roberts was cited to appear at the Bishop's Court at Gloucester, accused of holding Meetings at his house.[54] On that occasion he was interrogated personally by Bishop Nicholson about his religious beliefs. He was allowed to return home under threat of visitation by the Bishop's bailiffs. That night, Daniel reports, 'he desir'd [his sons] not to let the bailiffs in upon him . . . that he might have counsel with his pillow'. Dreams – or 'visions' – were of some importance to him, and, like the biblical Daniel (whom he often cites, and after whom the author of the Memoir, his eldest son, was almost certainly named), he put great faith in his interpretations of what they were telling him to do. 'In the morning,' wrote Daniel, 'he told my Mother what he had seen that Night in a Vision':

> I tho't, said he, I was walking in a fine, pleasant, green Way; but it was narrow and had a Wall on each Side of it. In my Way lay something like a Bear, but more dreadful. The sight of it put me to a Stand. A Man, seeing me surpris'd, came to me with a smiling Countenance, and said, *Why art afraid Friend? It is chained, and can't hurt thee.* I thought I made Answer, *The Way is so narrow, I can't pass by but it may reach me. Don't be afraid*, says the Man, *it can't hurt thee.* I saw he spake in great Goodwill, and thought his Face shone like the Face of an Angel. Upon which I took Courage, and, stepping forward, laid my Hand upon his Head.

'The Construction he made of this to my Mother', wrote Daniel, 'was: *Truth is a Narrow Way; and this Bishop lies in my Way: I must go to him whatever I suffer.*[55]

It is tempting to put another construction on this dream. The 'narrow . . . fine, pleasant, green way' represents the linear time of progress and 'development'. Unlike their Puritan antecedents, the Quakers remained true to the conviction that the great symbols of the 'Night of Apostasy', the Bishops, stood in the way of progress. Reason and experience convinced people of this, but courage was required to follow it through. The inner light of faith provided them with the courage by convincing them that they would win through. And so it was to prove, up to a point, with the Bishop of Restoration Gloucester.

Roberts rode to the Bishop's palace at Cleeve, near Cheltenham, where the second dialogue took place. The third and final dialogue occurred when the Bishop, by now clearly fascinated by Roberts, and, as the vision had predicted, inclined to be friendly towards him if Roberts would let him, stopped at the Roberts farm with his visitation entourage to ask for refreshment. This time Nicholson asked Roberts to explain his reputation as a cunning man. Roberts was able to satisfy the Bishop that accusations by the Minister of Siddington St Mary, George Bull, that he employed illegal witchcraft practices would be difficult to sustain in court.

During these discussions Roberts made a number of unambiguous statements explaining his position with regard to Church and state. These were positive (what he stood for) and negative (what he was against). They make it clear that, although religion was Roberts' primary concern, he was also critical of the state, and thus hovered perilously close to the borders of sedition. He operated very skilfully in what, in the decades after the Restoration, was obscure and ambiguous conceptual and legal territory concerned with the precise nature of the grounds of legitimacy of the post-Restoration English state. During his second discussion with the Bishop, occasioned by his dream, he was informed that it was 'The King's Laws you have broken: and to the King you shall answer'.

Nicholson invited Roberts to state his view of established law. 'Suppose a Man steal an Ox, and be taken and hang'd for the Fact,' he asked him, 'what restitution is that to the Owner?.' 'None at all,' replied Roberts. 'But tho' it is no restitution to the Owner, yet the Law is fully satisfied.' Roberts criticised 'the Corruptness of such Laws, which put the Life of a Man upon a Level with the Life of a Beast'.

'What,' exclaimed the Bishop, 'Do such Men as you find fault with the Laws?' 'Yes,' replied Roberts, 'and I'll tell thee plainly, 'tis high time Wiser Men were chosen, to make better Laws. For if this thief was taken and sold, for a proper Term according to the Law of Moses, and the Owner had Four Oxen for his Ox, and four Sheep for his Sheep, he would be satisfied, and the Man's life preserv'd, that he might repent, and amend his Ways.'[56]

Roberts did not avoid questions about the legitimacy of the secular state,[57] although, for the most part, his talk is about religion, a marginally safer subject. His critique is first and foremost a critique of the religious foundations of secular society, but when occasion demanded he went further : ''tis high time Wiser Men were chosen'. These were bold words in Restoration England.

During their third dialogue, he was concerned to refute the Bishop's allegation that 'those Meetings . . . which you keep at your house [are] the terror of the Country'. 'If any Plotters or ill-minded Persons come to my House, to plot or conspire against the king or government,' Roberts replied, 'if I know it, I'll be the first Informer against them myself, tho' I have not a Penny for my Labour.'[58] But 'if honest and sober People come to my House, to wait upon and worship the GOD of Heaven, in Spirit and in Truth, such shall be welcome to me as long as I have a House'.[59] This was ambiguous, to say the least, for the state still grounded its legitimacy in official religious profession, orthodoxy.

The Bishop stood in Roberts' 'Way'. The Bishop pointed out that in the end Roberts had to obey the king and his laws. Roberts did not evade the issue. He stated unequivocally that he 'ventured his throat for *Religion* in Oliver's days'.[60] He had not changed his position, for he immediately added, 'as I do now'. The Stuart position on matters like these is well known: no bishops, no king. And, it follows, no priests, no bishops. Roberts seems to have been aware that 'the history of religion is the history of the state', as Marx put it two centuries later. When he bore mute witness to Truth in Cirencester 'Steeple-House' (and later in his own parish church, after the arrival in 1658 of a worthwhile adversary, George Bull), he was saying that he, at least, remained uncompromsingly loyal to the beliefs that had motivated him in 1642–3, even if his neighbours and others did not: 'There were two or three Priests who stood honestly by their Principles, and suffered pretty much . . . in Oliver's days';

> But a far greater number turn'd with the Tide: And we have reason to believe, that if *Oliver* would have put Mass into their Mouths, they would have conform'd even to that for their Bellies.[61]

Increasingly during the 1650s, and emphatically after the Restoration, there was intensifying concern among the authorities as to whether the state and civil society could hang together without the legitimising agency of religious uniformity. George Bull, who was sent to serve the cure at Siddington St Mary, put the position clearly in a defence of the Common Prayer Book, which Roberts, of course, regarded as just one more product of 'the night of Apostasy', an efflorescence of *'the Beast [with] many Heads, and Many Horns, which push against each other'*: one 'tree' in the 'forest of symbols' which the Quakers wished to cut down.[62] 'How proper such applications were then to the People', wrote Bull,

> we may recollect from the posture of affairs in which we then were; for the swarms of sectaries which over-ran the nation in the time of the Great Rebellion had carried their hypocrisy so high, that upon the Restoration, some men thought they could not recede too far from the behaviour and practice of those persons who had made religion a cloak for so many villainies.[63]

Radical religion like that of John Roberts, in Bull's view, was merely 'a cloak' for other 'villainies'. Bull thought Quakers were secular revolutionaries in religious disguise. Others thought so too. 'Haywood, you're afraid of nothing,' one of the Bishop's officials said to Roberts on one occasion. 'I never met with such a Man in my Life. I'm afraid of my Life, lest such Fanaticks as you should cut my Throat as I sleep.'[64]

In Roberts' eyes, George Bull was a 'proud, ambitious, ungodly Man':

> He hath often sued me at Law, and brought his servants to swear against me wrongfully. His servants themselves have confess'd to my servants, that I might have their Ears; for their Master made 'em drunk, and then told 'em they were set down in the List as Witnesses against me, and they must swear to it: And so they did, and brought treble damages. They likewise own'd they took Tythes from my Servant, thresh'd 'em out, and sold 'em for their Master. They have also several Times took my Cattle out of my

grounds, drove 'em to Fairs and Markets and sold 'em without giving me any Account.[65]

Roberts was concerned not with what Bull stood for, only with what he did. Bull was a great believer in catechism over preaching, as 'the instructions from the pulpit very often miscarry for want of laying a good foundation in the first principles of religion . . . It is a vain attempt to reform the world, without seasoning the minds of youth with that necessary knowledge of the Christian mysteries upon which all religious practice must be built'.[66] His eighteenth-century biographer wrote that Bull 'reconciled the minds of his parishioners to the Common Prayer Book, before the use of it was publically restored'.[67]

One of his parishioners, at least, was never reconciled. 'You are men who pretend to know more of Light, Life and Salvation, and Things pertaining to the Kingdom of Heaven, than we do,' he said to the Bishop:

> I would ask in how long a Time you would undertake to teach us as much as you know, and what shall we give you, that we may be once free from our Masters? But here you keep us always learning that we may be always paying you. Plainly 'tis a very Cheat. What! Always learning and never able to come to the Knowledge of GOD! Miserable Sinners you found us, and miserable sinners you leave us!

Roberts' conception of religion was precisely that of William Tyndale five generations earlier, at the beginning of the Protestant Reformation in his country. 'I call the People of God the Church of God,' Roberts said, 'wheresoever they are met to worship him in Spirit and in Truth.' The Bishop pointed out to him that 'of all others, Quakers struck at the very Root and Basis of our Religion'. 'I am glad of that,' Roberts replied:

> For the Root is the Rottenness, and Truth strikes at the very Foundation thereof. That little stone which *Daniel* saw cut out of the Mountain without Hands will overturn all in GOD's due Time, when you have done all you can to support it. But as to those other religions thou mention'st, there is so little Difference between you, that Wise Men wonder why you differ at all; only we read, *The beast had many Heads, and many Horns, which push against each other.*

Roberts was a millenarian, but not a 'quietist' or 'introversionist'. Although the final destruction of Daniel's 'beast with many heads' (Nebuchadnezzar's Babylon, or Restoration England) would come 'in *God's* due Time', he, Roberts, clearly regarded himself as an instrument

186

of His purpose, and acted in accordance. His religion, the legitimacy that lay behind and within his actions, was 'neither on the mountain, nor yet at Jerusalem'. It was a revolutionary spirit.

That was what worried his contemporaries and neighbours. After being ejected from Cirencester parish church after his first testimony to Truth, the men who had removed him remained 'at the door to keep him out'. He stood 'a little in stillness' until, finding 'himself clear', he began to walk away across the marketplace. 'As he passed the market-place the Tie of his Shoe slackened; and, while he stooped down to fasten it, a man came behind him, and struck him on the back a hard blow with a stone, saying, *There, take that for JESUS CHRIST'S sake!'* Roberts quietly stood up and walked off, saying *So I do*. That was not quite the end of the incident. 'A few days after the man who threw the stone came and ask'd forgiveness' for 'he could have no Rest since he had done it'. Was this conscience, or was it fear of Roberts' reputation as a wizard? We shall now consider this aspect of his reputation.

8

'I have heard Mr Bull say strange things of you,' the Bishop told Roberts at one of their meetings; 'that you can tell where to find any thing that's lost as well as any Cunning Man'.[68] We shall now consider Roberts' reputation as a cunning man or 'wizard' (the former is used by a contemporary to describe some of his activities, the latter is not, although in Roberts' time they probably meant much the same thing, as Keith Thomas assumes[69]) and its relationship to his Quakerism. I shall tell five stories that relate to these activities, as they are told in his son's memoir. They illustrate the breadth of the cunning people's field of operation, a field which is now occupied by a range of professional specialists who acquire their legitimacy from state-confirmed qualifications. Thaumaturgical techniques are explicitly referred to in three of these cases, though the precise nature of the thaumaturgy remains to be analysed. The others are basically applications of empirical reasoning, as Roberts himself realised. But they were probably seen by his neighbours as evidence of his close contact with supernatural forces of some kind, which he used to assist him in solving difficult cases. 'White' magic involved the application of thaumaturgical techniques to do good, i.e. to help others. 'Black' magic was using the same techniques to do harm. Roberts did good, so, apart from his eccentric religious behaviour, there was probably not much doubt in his neighbours' minds that Roberts was a 'white witch', a particularly highly endowed 'wise one' or 'cunning man'. They may well have

187

assumed that his religious eccentricities were a necessary part of the spiritual reputation of one such as he.

Cunning people were ubiquitous in early modern England. Like *Nabi'im*, they could be men or women although, as the principal victims of witchcraft persecutions and convictions, female cunning people probably became less common as the seventeenth century wore on, their talents being rationalised into specialist functions like midwifery. Quaker women were in particular demand in this role.[70] Thomas is guarded in his calculations as to the precise numbers of cunning people, 'for if he [sic] were lucky the cunning man left no records behind him'.[71] There were reasons other than luck, however: cunning people almost certainly used straightforward empirical–rational techniques as often as they used techniques with explicit or implicit magical content, and it was difficult (and/or embarrassing) to prosecute someone in such cases. Thomas reports that 'at the turn of the sixteenth century well-informed contemporaries . . . thought the wizards roughly comparable in numbers to the parochial clergy'.[72] That is to say, every neighbourhood was likely to have a resident 'wizard' who could cure the ailments of man and beast, locate lost and stolen goods, and generally offer effective advice to their neighbours, sometimes for money, sometimes for nothing. Roberts did it for nothing, thus proving himself more 'neighbourly' than most of those who grounded their faith in neighbourliness.

Tension, then, might easily arise between the wizard, who derived his or her authority from local reputation, and the priest, whose authority originally derived from the state authorities – although there was nothing to prevent a priest also acquiring the reputation of a 'wise one', given the right skills and practices. But for this to happen the priest had to *earn* his reputation. George Bull was an authoritarian priest, who placed himself unequivocally on the side of higher authority. Thus it is not surprising that, quite apart from fundamental religious differences, Bull was envious of Roberts' local reputation as a cunning man.[73]

Roberts was a seventeenth-century country wizard. What we know of him and his theology may help us to de-mystify the institution, to understand it better. The *Memoir* gives episodes which are relevant. Here is the first.

The wizard and the lady

Roberts was invited to dine with Lady Dunch of Ampney St Mary, a neighbouring village. Unknown to him, she also invited the Minister of Cirencester, a colleague of George Bull's named William Careless. Her plan was to engage the two men in disputation, for her afternoon's entertainment. As he rode along the track to her house, Roberts met the priest going in the same direction, they conferred, and concluded that 'the Lady had projected to bring them together'.[74] Arriving at the house they were informed that Lady Dunch was 'very ill in a Fitt of the Stone'. She sent instructions that Roberts was to be brought 'up the back stairs' to see her alone, as she wished to consult him with regard to her disposition. She chose the wizard over the priest.

'I have heard you have done good in many Distempers', she said, hoping that Roberts could help her with hers. 'I confess I have,' he replied, 'but to this stone I am a stranger.' But he could offer a general remedy:

> I once knew a man (he proceeded), who lived at Ease and fared delicately, as thou may'st do, and whilst he continu'd in that Practice he was much afflicted with that Distemper. But it pleased the Lord to visit him with the knowledge of His blessed Truth, which brought him to a more regular and temperate life, and this preserv'd him free from it.[75]

'I know what you aim at,' she exclaimed. 'You want to have me a Quaker!' In fact Roberts seems to have been saying that in order to cure her ailment she had to live more plainly: more exercise and a good plain diet seem to be the gist of it. In order to acquire the motivation and discipline to change his life, the man in his 'parable' needed more than just the rational knowledge that it would cure him: he had to be 'visited' by 'his blessed Truth' before he could *act* according to the dictates of Reason. Plain human reason was enough to decide what needed to be done, but 'inner light' was needed as the motivating power. Reason was the instrument, but not the agency.

We should also note the 'oracular' nature of the advice. Roberts was careful not to imply that he, personally, had supernatural power, or that supernatural power operated through him. If she could be cured, it would be because the supernatural power ('his blessed Truth') was 'invited in' by Lady Dunch. Nor does he advise her to do this. He only tells the story of another man who acted like that and was cured. One aspect of the 'cunning' of the most successful cunning people, one suspects, was, as Keith Thomas notes, their ability never to appear in the official records as such, i.e. as subjects of prosecution. This was quite important at a time when unlicensed thaumaturgy was still a capital offence, which, of course, was why George Bull wanted to see Roberts convicted of it.

The servant was sent downstairs to bring William Careless up to join them. 'Being persons of different persuasions', she invited them to 'soberly ask and answer each other a few Questions, so that [she] should be less sensible of the Pains [she lay] under'. Careless launched the debate, at her instigation, by accusing Roberts of belief in 'that Damnable Doctrine, and dangerous tenet, of Perfectibility in this Life'. This, he said, was 'Papist' doctrine, and so Papists and Quakers were the same. Roberts turned the argument around, 'proving' that Careless was 'like a Papist in so many Things, he had need be a Wise Man to decide betwixt them', admitting along the way that he did indeed believe in 'Perfectibility'. 'Pray tell this poor Woman whom thou hast been preaching to for thy Belly', said Roberts, 'whether ever, or never, she must expect to be freed from her Sins, and made fit for the Kingdom of Heaven?' Could it be 'an hour or two' before death? Careless agreed that it could. A day or two? Another reluctant nod. 'And my father brought it to a month or two,' Daniel wrote, 'and so gradually 'til he brought it to seven years, the Priest confessing he believed the same.'[76] At that point the priest decided to leave, and Lady Dunch informed Roberts 'that she should not have believed Mr Careless could have been so foil'd in Discourse by any Man'. She asked him 'to let her know when [he would next hold] a Meeting at his House' and said she would attend.[77]

No doubt a version of this clash written from Careless's point of view would read somewhat differently, but it would still signify a clash between two cultures, one prescribed, the other empirical–rational, 'Enlightened' in the epochal sense. Roberts' view of the Church would be hard to distinguish from Voltaire's. We know what George Bull would say: inner light and perfectibility sound very fine, but in the real world external disciplines were necessary, 'seasoning' with 'catechism' or systematic schooling of one kind or another. But, as we saw in an earlier chapter, Church disciplines were by no means the only ones available in early modern England; there was also a proverbial grass-roots culture which literally ignored the Church.

The cunning people grew out of this culture, they were 'organic intellectuals'. 'Cunning' had three sets of meanings prior to the seventeenth century. It meant 'possessing knowledge or learning', 'possessing practical knowledge or skill', and, lastly, 'possessing magical knowledge or skill'. The last was an alternative possibility, it was not necessary. Only in the seventeenth century does 'cunning' begin to acquire its slightly pejorative modern connotation of 'craftiness'.

Cunning people were persons skilled in knowledge of people, usually particular people, their neighbours. This was not all they knew: they had to be observant and experienced in the application of a wide range of empiricals. Their knowledge was 'substantive' and 'empirical' as opposed to 'theoretical', and they did not need the licence of the state to endow them with legitimacy. Their reputations for 'cunning' ('knowing', being 'wise') came from the fact that their empirics worked.

John Roberts lived at a time when the secular trend towards special-ised professionalism was in its early stages. Professionalisation was associated with an educational revolution which, as an accidental by-product, was a practical challenge to grass-roots cultural wisdom, which did not derive from professional qualification, the blessing of the modern state.[78] One aspect of this educational revolution was over-production of graduates, who, in the late sixteenth and early seventeenth centuries, began to encroach into areas once monopolised by the cunning people. Now the over-production of graduates has been seen as an important element in the rise of anti-episcopalian Puritanism.[79] Qualified divines, unable to get jobs, became resentful, and began to preach against the state which, it seemed, was denying them jobs. In doing this they were also forced to reform popular or proverbial culture, which also offered an alternative source of wisdom, alternative 'qualifications'. The rebellion of Puritanism against the state has always received much greater attention from scholars because it was one of the key factors generating the 'Great Rebellions', and, of course, being a war between two *literate* parties, it also generated written accounts by both sides of the conflict.

The proverbial culture was less well placed to leave records of its side of the argument: it was an oral culture. The cunning people, the organic intellectuals of the proverbial culture, were not professional, literate intellectuals, although they were very frequently literate. And they were disliked and actively opposed by reformers on both the Puritan and Arminian sides of the elite, well-documented, struggle. Quakerism welled up from the proverbial culture. It is an overstate-ment to say that it was a movement of the cunning people to assert, bear witness to, their continuing presence by marching out onto the territory of the Arminians and the Puritans without adopting their authoritarianism. The Society of Friends was an alternative to the absolutist state, a collectivity which did not rest its authority on hier-archical principles. And it used literacy, the speciality of the Puritans, as the 1640s had taught them that it could be used.[80] Quakerism was predominantly a movement of the cunning people, an attempt to carry traditional, agrarian notions of associational *communitas*, the ideal state of the old world, into the more abstract space of the modern world.

This helps to explain some of the paradoxes of the movement: eminently rational and empirical, yet resting on the intuitive faith of the inner life, the feeling that rationalism left too much out. It was eminently literate, more so than any other counter-cultural movement that had ever existed, yet also intensely suspicious of the spoken and written word, embodying the intuitive awareness of the cunning people that so much of what we know to be true gets left out in the spaces between the words – something that Wittgenstein has tried to 'say' in the twentieth century: the emphasis on silence, on listening, on leaving space for intuition. It is a profound injustice to the Quakers that this aspect of their faith has been called 'introversionist', as if only what is spoken and written, explicitly articulated, is active, as if all that can be known must be stated, can be stated. As if only that which is articulated can be 'rational'.

What were Roberts' qualifications as an intellectual, a man capable of using his mind? His 'empiricals' worked.

The wizard and the poor neighbour

'John,' said the Bishop, 'I have heard Mr Bull say strange Things of you: that you can tell where to find any Thing that's lost as well as any Cunning Man.' Roberts told the Bishop that he was not 'bred up at *Oxford* and *Cambridge*'. He was 'a Layman, and bred up at Plow-Tail', but yet understood 'the singular and plural Numbers'.[81] The Bishop asked him to explain three examples of his 'magic' that Bull had mentioned. The first of these involved a 'poor Neighbour' with a wife and six children, who had lost 'six or seven cows' which he was 'permitted to keep on the Waste'.[82] Distraught with fear that this loss would mean that he and his wife 'must go a-begging in [their] old age', the neighbour's wife turned to Roberts for assistance. He told her 'to be still and quiet in [her] mind; perhaps [her] husband or sons may hear of 'em tomorrow'. If this did not happen she was to 'let [her] Husband get a Horse, and come to [him] Tomorrow morning as soon as he will; and [Roberts thought], if it pleases GOD, [he would] go with him to seek 'em'. Such was Roberts' reputation that 'the Woman seem'd transported with Joy, crying, *Then we shall have our Cows back'*. Roberts' faith was in God, but the poor neighbour's faith was in Roberts.

On this occasion Roberts openly admitted to the Bishop that he had to seek thaumaturgical assistance. 'Her faith being so strong,' he said, it 'brought greater exercise upon me with strong Cries to the lord, that [God] would be pleased to make me instrumental in His Hand, for the Help of the poor Family.' The cattle failed to turn up, and the next morning the old man appeared at Roberts' farm as instructed. 'In the name of God, says he, which Way shall we go to seek 'em?' Still unsure and 'being deeply concerned in [his] mind', Roberts listened to the old man repeating the question three times before the light came to him and he could break his silence. The cattle would be found at Malmsbury horse fair, he said, and that turned out to be the case. Transported with joy at finding the cattle, the old neighbour threatened to make a great fuss. Roberts said 'he was ashamed of [his neighbour's] behaviour', and 'begged of the Poor Man to be quiet and take his cows home, and be thankful, as indeed [Roberts] was, being reverendly bowed in [his] Spirit before the Lord, in that He was pleased to put the Words of Truth into [his] Mouth'.

The wizard and the hare

One day George Bull's steward came to Roberts in desperation because he had lost some of the Rector's sheep, and knew he would be extremely angry about it. He knew Roberts 'went pretty much abroad . . . in his travels', and would he keep his eyes open for them. 'The next day, as [Roberts] was riding towards [his] own Field, [his] dogs being with him, put up a Hare, and, seeing they were likely to kill her, [he] rode up to take them off, that she might escape, and by meer Accident, [he] espied the Sheep' in a gorse thicket. In gratitude, Roberts told the Bishop, 'George Bull hath endeavour'd to improve [the incident] to [his] disadvantage'.[83]

The wizard and the missing horse

'One Edward Symons came from London, to see his parents at Siddington.' On arrival, he put his horse to pasture in an enclosure close to the house. The horse went missing, and Roberts was asked to put his skills to use to locate it. His knowledge of horses told him that the animal, being from London, 'might endeavour to bend homeward'.[84] His knowledge of the neighbourhood reminded him that east of the field (i.e. towards London) were several acres of waste, called 'furzen leazes . . . which [were] so overgrown with Furze bushes, that a Horse may lye concealed there a long time'. Roberts 'advised [his neighbour] to get a great deal of company, and search the places diligently, as if they were beating for a Hare'. Sure enough, the horse turned up in the thickets. 'Where's the cunning of all this?' Roberts asked the Bishop. ''Tis no more than their own Reason might have directed 'em to, had they properly considered the case.'

The wizard as veterinary

The steward of James George, a member of one of Cirencester's leading families, a Member of Parliament and a magistrate who was vigorously threatening to distrain Roberts' goods in lieu of tithes due to George Bull at the time when this incident occurred, told his master that his cattle were mortally sick of the murrain. The steward told George 'he must send for John Roberts, or he would lose all his cattle'.[85] George refused this advice on the grounds that he had 'warrants out against Roberts and his sons', and told his servant to 'send for anyone else'.

No one else could do any good, and so finally Roberts was sent for. He came immediately 'to drench and bleed' the cattle. After it was done, George offered to pay Roberts for his services. Roberts 'would have none of [his] Money', for, he said, 'what purpose is it for me to take a little of thy Money by Retail, if thou come and take my Goods by Wholesale?' 'Don't think your coming to drench and bleed my cattle shall deter me from executing the King's Laws,' replied the Magistrate. 'I seek no favour at thy Hands,' said Roberts. 'When thou has done me all the Displeasure thou art permitted to do, I will notwithstanding serve thee or thine to the utmost of my power.'

What made Roberts so difficult an adversary was his simple refusal to be directed by others. In matters of judgement – that is to say, in all matters he was *independent*. He was a 'loner'. But, self-evidently, he used his independent judgement to help others. Equally self-evidently, if everyone behaved in as neighbourly a fashion as John Roberts, priests, magistrates and all the paraphernalia of the state would be redundant. His life was a *demonstration* of this fact.

10

However else it can be explained, Roberts ascribed his power to 'the key of David, which opens and none can shut, and if thou shutt'st, none can open':

> And that is no other but the Spirit of our LORD JESUS CHRIST. It was the same Spiritual Key that open'd the Heart of *Moses*, the first Penman of Scripture, and gave him a Sight of Things from the beginning. It was the same Spiritual Key that open'd the Hearts of all the Holy Patriarchs, Prophets, and Apostles in Ages Past, who left their Experience of Things GOD upon Record: which if they had not done, you Bishops and Priests would not have any Thing to make a Trade of; for it is by telling the Experience of these Holy Men, that you get your great Bishopricks and Parsonages; and of the same Spiritual Key hath, blessed be to GOD, open'd the Hearts of Thousands in this Age; and the same . . . hath, in a measure, open'd my Heart, and given me to distinguish Things that differ.[86]

What did Roberts mean by 'the Spirit of Lord Jesus Christ'? He meant 'God', and stated that 'God is a Spirit'. To this Spirit, God, he ascribed all his power. It was what enabled him to act as he did, and it informed all others who had acted as he did, and would always act as he did. Thus he was saying that God is an active principal in History, 'through all the various Ages'. He knew this from his reading of scriptural texts, and from his observation in his own life. 'Spirit' has manifold meanings, all of which can probably be reduced to 'vital principal'. The term 'God', as the authors of the *Oxford English Dictionary* observe, is of disputed meaning and etymology.[87] But it probably traces to an Indo -European root, *gheu*, and through it into Sanskrit and the Teutonic form *gott*. These have two meanings: 'to invoke' and 'to pour, or offer sacrifice'. These semantic definitions do not help us to find the referential, that which is invoked or sacrificed to, but we can easily see their application in Roberts case. In justifying his position he refused to invoke any authority or to sacrifice himself to any authority other than God. This invocation and sacrifice enabled him to 'distinguish Things that differ'.

Now the man described in Daniel Roberts' *Memoir* was what we would call a rational man. On some of the occasions related in the *Memoir* he clearly states that a perfectly satisfactory result could be achieved by the simple exercise of observation, memory and logical deduction, as when he was able to predict where his neighbour's missing horse was to be found. He arrived at his conclusion by means of conscious cerebration. But in the incident involving his confrontation with John Stephens of Lypiatt, following his uncle's influence in having him released from prison, Roberts clearly states that 'the Reasoner', conscious cerebration based on experience and deduction, was an inadequate agency because it implied scepticism, doubt. It could enable a person to distinguish but not to choose. On its own, Reason paralyses. Which of many possible options revealed by Reason to take, Reason cannot determine. This is what Dostoevsky and Nietzsche meant when they pointed out that 'if God is dead, everything is permitted'. Many courses of action are possible, and it is possible to predict fairly accurately by means of empirical-deductive reasoning what the consequences of each course of action will be. This is also what Marx had in mind when he wrote that 'hitherto the philosophers have only interpreted the world. The point is to change it'. This does not mention a fact of which Marx was also aware, that as a matter of fact particular interpretations have changed the world by inducing (or coercing in their name) people to act in certain ways. It states only that interpretations change the world only when they become actions, i.e. are stated, written down, translated into laws backed up by a variety of coercive forces which derive their legitimacy from elsewhere.

Beyond Reason, people need to feel that the ways they act are somehow necessary. Why, they ask, *must* I behave like this and not some other way? Otherwise every choice is ultimately an arbitrary one. Reason can easily justify murder and genocide, for example. There is nothing intrinsically irrational about murder. Human beings have found reasons to commit it throughout history. Even the celebrated injunction to love one's neighbour as oneself collapses if one hates oneself. If we accept that children embody fundamental evil, as in the various doctrines of Original Sin, then a good case can be made, not only for beating them mercilessly, but for killing them. If, on the other hand, we accept that all human beings, however wicked they may seem, are perfectible, then it must be wicked to cut their lives short. Either way, an act of faith is involved, choice of an axiom.

William Tyndale, to whom Roberts was distantly related by marriage, observed that scripture 'hath but one, simple, literal sense, whose light the owls cannot abide'. 'As a result,' writes Mervyn James, 'scripture was transformed, no longer exhibiting the many-layered Joycean complexity (as difficult and fascinating as *Finnegan's Wake*) in which the medieval culture had wrapped it. Instead it acquired the linear clarity of a realist novel or of a historical narrative.'[88] But this 'simple, literal sense' is a variable. It implied particular – cultural – readings. It implied what readers who were already committed to certain cultural ideals brought to their reading. When they came to scripture they came seeking truth, that is to say, they came in a certain spirit of humility. They came looking for last words on disputed subjects, i.e. for confirmation of the things which they already believed or knew were the deeper truths of their own culture. These had to do with loving families, neighbourliness and, ultimately, universal equality, the condition which, as I argue in a later chapter, was invoked by carnivalesque calendrical occasions, which, by reversing the prescribed social order, revealed its ultimately arbitrary character, its status as a *construction*. This, as Victor Turner has observed, meant the invocation of *communitas* by the removal, if only temporarily, of *structure*.

The Quakers, then, were profoundly traditional. As Hobsbawm and others have shown, traditions must be constantly renewed and revised, their relevance revealed.[90] Otherwise they die. Carnivalesque invocations revealed only that *communitas*, absence of inequality, contest, competition and strife, was the condition of first and last things. In between come the constructions, the imperfect and variable cultures and societies of men. In 1642–3 men went off to fight – to overturn the established order, to throw off imposed hierarchical structure. Some were inspired by a belief that the world could be perfected. Most took the outcome in the 1650s as evidence that this was an unrealistic expectation, a 'god that failed'. Quakers like John Roberts, spiritual egalitarians, retained their conviction that perfection was possible and continued to work for it by other means. At their best they were not so much 'witnesses to truth' as veritable embodiments of it.

Part IV

THE MULTITUDES
AROUND US

COMMUNITY AT THE BORDERS
Mockery and misrule in an eighteenth-century industrial village

The struggle between rich and poor is a contentious effort to give partisan meaning to local history . . . The details of this struggle are not pretty, as they entail backbiting, gossip, character assassination, rude nicknames, gestures, and silences of contempt which, for the most part, are confined to the backstage of village life.

James C. Scott[1]

Only in the *local* network of labour and recreation can one grasp how, within a grid of socio-economic constraints, these pursuits unfailingly establish relational tactics (a struggle for life), and autonomous initiatives (an ethic).

Michel de Certeau[2]

Comedy may be considered to deal with man in his human state, restrained and often made ridiculous by his limitations, his faults, his bodily functions, and his animal nature . . . Comedy has always viewed man more realistically than tragedy, and drawn its laughter or its satire from the spectacle of human weakness or failure. Hence its tendency to juxtapose appearance and reality, to deflate pretence, and to mock excess.

C. Hugh Holman et al.[3]

1

This a study of a neighbourhood in 'one of the first areas in which English weavers lost their autonomy and became hired factory hands'. It focuses on the village of Randwick during 'the onset of the industrial revolution in the valley of the Stroud', in Gloucestershire.[4] 'Randwick' means 'farm on the border', a name which has been traced to its origins, in the twelfth and thirteenth centuries, as a colony of a neighbouring manor, where it retained arable strips and commons up to the early nineteenth century.[5] It is on a geographical border, sited on the Cotswold escarpment 600 feet above the Vale of Severn. Its character as a border settlement goes back at least as far as the time when it was a frontier fort of the Belgic Dobunni, who had a settlement of some kind here in pre-Roman times.[6]

Eighteenth-century Randwick straddled a number of cultural frontiers. The Cotswolds, traditionally, were viewed as a land of shepherds, the Vale and valleys as lands of weavers. The inhabitants of Randwick lived in the hills and worked in the valleys. They were 'woolly-backs' without land, entirely plebeian. Randwick was a living symbol of the depths of unrespectability. It confronted pretension and challenged prejudice. It looked at the respectable folk and found them wanting, and had an ingrained scepticism as to the legitimacy of cherished social conventions. It nurtured tricks and stratagems for bringing the mighty and would-be mighty down to earth. It is the culture of the football crowd rather than the dinner party, seminar room or soirée. It included (and gave birth to) the radical side of contemporary popular culture, voiced most commonly as a humorous scepticism towards all pretensions based on prescribed hierarchy, genealogy and tradition or wealth gained through trading goods made by other people in places like Randwick. It belongs to a universal type, authentic (as against appropriated and contrived) carnivalesque humour, and merges effortlessly with bawdiness. It turned the world upside down to demonstrate that the order it assumed was arbitrary. According to John Corbet, it hacked lord Chandos' coach to pieces in the market-place at Cirencester, in 1642. It was more likely to be Antinomian than Puritan, Methodist than Anglican, and as likely as both to be blasphemous and irreligious. These were not alternatives, they lived next door to each other.

If it saw through the absurdity of conventional social arrangements, it did not necessarily draw the practical conclusion that they should be thrown down in a revolutionary manner and replaced. The threat was there, substantiated by historical experience and living memory. Clothworkers were prominent in anti-cavalier demonstrations and riots in 1642–3, and it was uniformly assumed that *weavers* were vehemently pro-Parliament, the clothworking districts responsible for the defence of Gloucestershire against invasion by the king's armies in January and February 1643. Such tales grew in the telling, but they were not without foundation. Respectable society was conscious of the muffled but ominous threat of the multitudes. In the 1690s, Sir Matthew Hale warned his contemporaries of the collective threat posed by the poor of industrial districts like his native Vale of Berkeley. The smouldering threat of clothworking communities to public order had been taken for granted by succeeding authorities since the early sixteenth century and beyond, to a time when it was taken for granted that Lollardy and weaving went together. The radical independency which clothworking households and neighbourhoods managed to sustain through centuries which saw their material independence progressively eroded to a point where they were to all intents and purposes modern proletarians with nothing to sell but their hands, and nothing to live by but their wits, was finally crushed in the 1830s and 1840s, when dispersed production ('protoindustry') ended in central Gloucestershire.

Population and occupational data suggest that Randwick became an industrial village in the second half of the sixteenth century, when its population doubled, from 167 in 1551 to 372 in 1603. Growth continued to 584 in 1676, 650 in 1779, 856 in 1801 and (its peak, just prior to the near-collapse of the woollen clothing industry) 1,031 in 1831.[7] 'The lack of agricultural land in the parish and the large population suggests that most of the inhabitants of Randwick were engaged in the cloth industry from the seventeenth century or earlier.'[8] Weavers, fullers and a dyer from Randwick attended a military muster in 1608.[9] There was a mill in the village in the thirteen century and it was used for fulling at the latest by 1574.[10]

Its religious history is quite typical of late English upland/woodland settlements.[11] It was a chapelry with a history of neglect back to 1551. In 1650, after a century of industrial development, a government survey recommended that it be made an independent parish, but nothing was done.[12] Eleven nonconformists were recorded in 1676.[13] Methodism came early: Whitefield preached there twice in July 1739, Wesley paid visits in 1739 and 1742, and there was a Wesleyan Sunday School in operation by 1804.[14]

There was probably conflict between sceptical traditionalists, 'old Dissenters' and the Methodists, as there undoubtedly was elsewhere in the Stroudwater Valleys. In 1743 a Methodist lay-preacher was dragged down the stairs of his house at Minchinhampton, across the valley from Randwick, and ducked several times in 'a sink-pit full of noisome things and stagnant water'.[15] In the early eighteenth century there was also an indeterminate but probably high number of absentees from all forms of worship.

Trade unionism is documented in the Stroud district in 1756–7, and may go back much further.[16] Eric Wolf's interconnection between Stroudwater and the North American colonies echoes in letters written by his namesake Colonel James Wolfe, who was sent to Stroudwater to protect clothiers and strike-breakers from angry clothworkers in 1756.[17]

Well-documented industrial disputes and moral economy riots occurred in the West of England clothing region in 1726–7, 1738–9, 1755–7, 1766, 1783, 1792 and 1825.[18] These eruptions of the labouring poor are often regarded as 'exceptional', reflecting 'abnormal' circumstances, not in any way suggestive of the everyday consciousness and behaviour of the 'bottom forty per cent' of regional society which was sustained by the cloth industry.[19] The logic goes something like this: riots got into the newspapers (or were noticed by the central government), their newsworthiness testified to their exceptionality, thus riots did not signify any permanent threat to good order. Now if they had gone on all the time . . .

It is more realistic to think of riots as eruptions of routine resentments and life-conditions. They were exceptional only in scale and intensity. The carnivalesque ('bring 'em down') side of popular culture was a continuum linking gossip, scandal, political satire, jokes, 'rough music', moral economy riots, industrial disputes, certain calendrical festivals (the 'carnivalesque'), insurrections, rebellions, millenarian upheavals, and finally even revolutions. These can be classified within a continuous field premised on two necessary and sufficient conditions: a systematically inegalitarian or class-structured society, and what Ernst Bloch called 'the principle of Hope', the belief that people can live in harmony, but only if what they produce is rigorously and observably shared out on an equal basis. It is not necessary to take this very seriously for it to survive, and its survival means that sooner or later someone will take it seriously. Respectable people would like to stamp it out, but fear that over-zealous repression will only intensify conviction in it. And so it continues.

Conservative accounts emphasise the exceptionality of riots, insurrections, rebellions and revolutions. There is some truth in this view. Large-scale eruptions to which we attach these labels are far from routine in the worst of times. But there are also substantive and theoretical continuities linking them with the everyday experience and consciousness of the subordinate classes, 'the bottom forty per cent'. Riots (or in twentieth-century terms, 'football hooliganism') are messages advising that all is not well with the socialisation of the vulgar multitudes; life is getting a bit rough down below. The rougher things are, the more frequent riots and football hooliganism. At times – in the circumstances surrounding the Gloucestershire riots of the 1580s and 1590s, 1620s, 1640s and 1680s, 1709–13, 1726–29, 1738–41, 1755–8, 1766, 1780–1840 (when local populations grew very rapidly) – they are rougher than others.

Insurrections, rebellions and revolutions are connected to 'quotidian struggles' like those which I shall describe here. The incidents that got into the newspapers and left mounds of official testimony for historians to examine were exceptional only in scale and intensity. The events described in this chapter relate to a general field of class struggle encompassing all systematically class-structured societies. Accounts which 'seal off' individual episodes necessarily fail to understand their significance.

I shall proceed as follows. In the next section I show that Randwick was generally regarded as the poorest village in Gloucestershire, and that this perception was accurate. Section 3, 'The case of the indiscreet landlord', uses depositions associated with a bawdy-court case in 1713 to explore and evoke the quality of social relations in this notoriously poverty-stricken clothworking village; it is the only clue to the kind of social irregularities associated with Randwick's poverty that I have been able to find in the archives, but one confirmed as representative by similar cases in other Stroudwater parishes in the same period.

Section 4, 'The Lord Mayors of Randwick', examines a curious calendrical festival, or 'revel' that took place at Randwick every year in the second week after Easter – very much a 'traditional' carnivalesque occasion that had to do with what is usually seen as 'reversal' of class and gender relations. I suggest, in the light of the material in the case of the indiscreet landlord, that what went on was probably more in the line of a celebration of the sorts of things that went on at Randwick all the time. It 'turned the world upside down' in the sense that the celebration was insistent and public, claimed as a rightful custom against the desire of the magistrates, who tried to suppress it. But in truth it advertised only what was *normal*.

Section 5 analyses 'The Lord Mayor of Randwick's Song', which, according to a detailed account of the revels published in 1784, was used every year to usher in a week of 'misrule'. I show that this song unmistakably embodied an historico-mythical explanation of Randwick's poverty, and expressed an ideal of egalitarian *communitas* – the *reason* for misrule – and this provides us with insight into the collective political consciousness of a community that lay on the border between what Marx called 'the epoch of Manufacturing' and that of industrial capitalism. It was a moment in the history of the democratic movement that lay on the border between older, preliterate, locality- and district-specific labour traditions and the directions taken by these traditions in the new conditions of the nineteenth and twentieth centuries.

2

The chasm between people who know hunger and people who don't was another border that Randwick straddled. Poverty was ubiquitous in eighteenth-century England. Life was a more or less continuous struggle to maintain a decent living for about 40 per cent of the population. Randwick was the poorest village in its region. In 1671–2 exemptions from the Hearth Tax averaged 40 per cent in the Stroudwater Valleys. At Randwick, with a population of about 450, the figure was nearer 70 per cent.[20] 'In 1677 the parish was said to be unable to maintain its poor and a rate was ordered to be levied on other parishes in the Hundred' to which it was attached.[21] In 1712, Sir Robert Atkyns wrote that Randwick was 'the highest charged to the Poor Rate, of any parish in the country [he meant Gloucestershire], and some years pays above five shillings in the pound'.[22] He also noted that more people were buried there each year than were baptised.

Two years before a gentleman stumbled across and recorded its curious 'revel' in 1784, a workhouse was taking in the paupers of the neighbourhood, and in 1811 a salaried official was appointed to convert it into a branch of the pin-making industry at Gloucester.[23] Adam Smith used this industry as the exemplary case of the advantages of the division of labour in manufacturing, so once again this obscure and impoverished village is situated on a much-investigated border region. 'I have seen a small manufactory of this kind', wrote Smith, 'where ten men only were employed . . . But though they were very poor, and therefore very indifferently accommodated with the necessary machinery, they could, when they exerted themselves . . . make upwards of forty-eight thousand pins in a day.'[24]

Time and again we see in the history of English neighbourhoods, districts and regions affected by industrial development, right back to the early fourteenth century, that the 'prime mover' in processes we identify today as factors in 'growth' and 'development' was large numbers of poor, landless people.[25] It was always assumed that the basic justification for the cloth industry lay in its 'employing and rendering useful many thousand hands who otherwise would be a heavy burden on the Publicke', as a Gloucestershire clothiers' petition put it in 1774.[26] Industry, then and now, was 'to set the poor on work', to make them 'profitable to the commonwealth', as John Smyth of Nibley put it in 1639, speaking of the nearby Severnside squatter community at Slimbridge.[27] By the second half of the eighteenth century Slimbridge had been tamed by the virtual eradication of manufacturing. Traditions of independency were still celebrated annually at Randwick.

The struggle to maintain them was a losing one, and for most of the inhabitants of Randwick since the sixteenth century it had always been borderline. Independency was an ideal in many more households and minds than ever achieved its necessary condition – a trade and a self-sufficient yeoman-freehold. Even more desperate times lay ahead, in 1784, five years before the first British convicts were herded ashore at Sydney Cove. The 'take-off into self-sustaining economic growth', in Stroudwater translates into 4,000 of the district's 10,000 families dependent on weekly parish relief. At Randwick the figure was 110 (55 per cent) of 206 families.[28] The Minister of Randwick reported that 'the working classes in his parish [were] generally depressed for scarcity of employment, low wages, and payment in truck', and referred to 'some insubordinate feelings fostered with association at the beershops, and by reading of inflammatory publications'.[29]

Some of the 'insubordinate feelings' of the victims of this second phase of industrialisation in England were sent, or obtained assisted passages, to New South Wales, where settlements like 'Gloucester' and 'Stroud' date from about this time.[30] In an effort to relieve pressure on the rates, vestrymen and overseers in the Stroud Union, formed under the provisions of the New Poor Law in 1834, raised funds to send poor families and individuals to the new colony, now beginning to expand south, west and north, across Sydney Harbour.[31]

It was not all insubordination. One of the men who came on such a scheme in 1839 was a young Randwick labourer named Simeon Pearce. Pearce's fare to Australia was paid by a Sydney butcher. He was a successful and ambitious character and ended up in property development, building a model village (rich merchants on the hill, poor Irish down by the water, others in between) a few miles east of Sydney, naming it 'Randwick'.[32]

3

THE CASE OF THE INDISCREET LANDLORD

The archives don't generally provide much information on the social consequences of Randwick's examplary poverty, but glimpses are provided by a scandal which erupted in 1713.

The scandal became public when two Randwick women, Mary Bennet and Elizabeth ('Lizzie') Robbins called at the house of Edward Field, a magistrate who lived near Stroud, to tell him what they had witnessed 'on the day after Candlemas [February 2]'.[33] They told Field that the chamber of their house 'adjoyneth to a house belonging to Stephen Mills'. Because of its poor state of repair (it was a single house divided by partitions) they were able to see what happened next door. Robbins told Field that she was looking out of the window one afternoon when she saw Mills 'beckon with his hand to Martha Thomas, who went with him into his house'. She then turned to 'the mudd wall through which there is a slitt or chink . . . [but] apprehending that some dishonest or lewd actions were about to be committed between them, she turned from the said chink and would not be a witness to such wickedness'.

Her companion, Mary Bennet, had no such scruples, and immediately took up Lizzie's position at the spyhole. She saw 'Stephen Mills and Martha Thomas in Mills's house alone and heard Mills bid Thomas, "Lye down" '.

'I will not,' she replied. 'Thou shalt,' said Mills, whereupon she lay herself down upon the floor and Stephen Mills let down his britches and turned up Martha Thomas's petticoats and shifts above her belly and then layd himself down upon her and had carnall knowledge . . . in the sight of the deponent and Elizabeth Robbins. She saw Mills several times kiss Martha while he was upon her and asked if he did it not well. About a quarter of an hour or something more, Mills and Thomas continued in the act of fornication. Then he got off her and helped her up and told her that in a quarter of an hour's time he would do it again, whereto she answered and said that he should not, for he had almost killed her already.

On this evidence Field considered that there was a case to answer, and referred it to the chancellor of the diocese.

Sexual improprieties – transgressions of formal and customary sexual *mores* – threaten all cultures and communities. Sexual *mores* are not always the same, but all cultures have them. In early modern England sexual behaviour was policed in two main ways. Most often it was dealt with by the local community. Transgression was stopped by 'a quiet word in a few ears', perhaps by the parson, perhaps by some other respected neighbour. If the transgression went on, the neighbourhood would stage some 'rough music' to shame the culprits, pressuring them to stop it at once or leave. Either way – prevention or removal – a tension which might eventually lead to greater complications was removed.[34]

The other policing agency was the Church. On most occasions, parishioners seem to have been anxious to keep outside authorities from becoming involved in their affairs. They could be excluded only when local opinion was more or less unanimous. Once a case got into the hands of the authorities only concerted agreement among the neighbours that they would all maintain blanket silence could keep a case from going ahead in the Church courts. This happened at Westonbirt in 1716, where the neighbourhood was able to defy the resolute wish of a powerful landlord that a case should be heard in court.[35] Thus when we do come across a case in the diocesan archives it often indicates that a community was factionalised in some way. This appears to have been the case at Randwick in 1713. The witnesses in this case fall clearly into two groups, the supporters of Lizzie Robbins and Mary Bennet, and the supporters of Stephen Mills.

The first witnesses to testify, in May, were Emma Wildey, an 84-year-old Randwick woman who gave her occupation as 'midwife', her son Daniel, a 40-year-old tailor, and John Fryer, another tailor of Randwick. Daniel Wildey had been one of the first to hear Mary Bennet's allegations. 'Last April,' he told the court, 'he saw John Fryer, Daniel Bennet [Mary's husband, later to give evidence that was damaging to her reputation] and [Mary Bennet] talking together in Mr Morse's woods, and heard Mary say that Stephen Mills's prick was as big as her leg.' Her companions asked her how she could know this, and Mary told the story of what she had seen a few days earlier through the chink in her tenement wall, backed up by Lizzie Robbins. Asked what he knew about the two women, Wildey told the court that some years ago his mother had delivered Robbins of a stillborn bastard child. Throughout the case, attendance at church seems to have been assumed by the court to be an accurate measure of respectability. Wildey told the court that he attended Randwick parish church every Sunday, and had never seen either Mary Bennet or Lizzie Robbins there.

Emma Wildey confirmed her son's testimony, adding that Lizzie Robbins' child had been born sixteen years earlier, when Robbins was employed as a domestic servant. She told the court that she had never heard any scurrilous talk about Mills before this incident. John Fryer confirmed that he had heard Mary Bennet's comments about Mills's anatomy in the woods at Standish (a neighbouring parish). The court scribe wrote down Fryer's testimony that Bennet and Robbins were 'persons with little sense of religion for that they very seldom go to church', a subject on which he was an authority 'because he lives very close to Randwick church (tho' in Stroud parish) and constantly attends it'.

The next witness to be called to give evidence was Richard Robbins, Lizzie's husband, another tailor of Randwick, in August. The strung-out nature of the case is worth noting. The incident described by Mary Bennet to the magistrate, Edward Field, in January appears to have taken place in April 1712, a full year before the first witnesses were called into the Church courts. The witnesses in April (the Wildeys and John Fryer) were effectively character witnesses for Mills and against Bennet and Robbins. Richard Robbins told the court in August that he knew the Wildeys and Fryer well, 'and believed them to be of mean circumstances', i.e. they were poor. He said that Mills 'had promised him to make him a pair of shoes [if] he would prevail with Mary Bennet not to give evidence against him'. Wildey, he thought, was not to be trusted because some months earlier 'he had been brought before Mr Field for woodstealing'. Another of Mills's faction, Thomas Chapman, who was later to give evidence for Mills, 'was reported to have two wives, Ann Beard and Jane Bennet'. Mary Bennet's husband, also later to give evidence for Mills, 'hath left the company of his wife for two or three years and . . . [was] reported in the neighbourhood [to be] suspitiously conversing with one Sarah Cratchley'.

Three weeks later a 50-year-old Randwick widow named Sarah Chapman came forward to add to what Richard Robbins had alleged about the character of Mills's witnesses and his attempts to bribe them. They 'were of mean circumstances' and in her observation 'they had been solicited by Mills to give evidence'. Mills, she told the court, 'has very well treated them with good liquor'. A few days earlier, 'she saw Chapman and Bennet the morrow morning after they had given evidence very drunk lying on the ground. She went to move Bennet but could not make him move, speak, nor rise from the ground, where they remained for some considerable time'. This reference to their having given evidence does not refer to their evidence in court, which was not taken until 3 September and 10 January. Clearly, then, the Church officials were conducting other investigations of their own, and the depositions which survive are not the only ones which were taken.

The allegations of the various witnesses suggest why: the sexual scandal involving Stephen Mills, a 'social drama' in Turner's sense, was revealing the extreme irregularity of Randwick's social life. What began as an investigation of a minor scandal became, willy-nilly, an investigation of a community.

Sarah Chapman told the court that she had heard rumours of Fryer's woodstealing activities, 'but knew not the truth'. She knew how to distinguish between fact and rumour. However, she was sure 'that his wife was with child before their marriage' and 'that there [was] a common fame in the neighbourhood that Daniel Wildey had in the lifetime of his former wife had suspitious conversation with her who is his present wife'.

Thomas Chapman was 'reported to have two wives, both now living in Randwick and both with children'. She told the church officials that Mills had attempted to bribe her. 'When Andrew Page [an official of the court] came to Randwick to summon Mary Bennet and other witnesses', she alleged, 'Stephen Mills solicited and promised her any satisfaction if she would keep the said witnesses out of the way, so Page should not meet them. For if he did, it would be all up with him.' Mills bought her 'two pints of ale' (not, apparently, a usual act of generosity on his part), but she refused to accept anything more because 'she believed him guilty'. Asked why, she told them 'that she had seen part of the action between him and the said Martha Thomas'. Having failed to bribe them, Mills had lately taken to 'threatening her and several witnesses against him to send them to gaol for giving evidence', though he did not say how he would be able to make good this threat.

The court was adjourned once more until September, when the witnesses returned to give evidence. Detail was added confirming that Wildey had indeed been recently convicted of the heinous crime of woodstealing, and that Thomas Chapman did indeed have two wives, both of whom had his children, and both of whom were presently living in the village. Given this labyrinthine conjugal underworld it can be suggested that Randwick's Hocktide revels, far from 'reversing' the normal social order, were simply an occasion for celebrating publicly what went on there all the time. From the Church's point of view, the world at Randwick was permanently turned upside down. Once again, the case was adjourned until January.

In January 1713/14, a full twenty-one months after the incident between Stephen Mills and Martha Thomas, the court called Mary Bennet's estranged husband, Daniel, a 25-year-old tailor, to give evidence. By now the court seems to have forgotten the alleged offence between Stephen Mills and Martha Thomas and concentrated exclusively on Mary Bennet's character. Bennet told the court that he had been trapped into marriage with her when she made a false statement to a magistrate that she was pregnant to him, 'whereupon he was obliged to marry her'.

It turned out to be a false pregnancy, and a few weeks after their marriage 'he was in bed with her and asked why she had taken such an oath. She said she had done it to torment [him] and would do it again if she had not done it already'. He was very concerned that his wife refused to go to church, which he attended 'constantly'. Once he 'applied to [her] to goe and avoid the sin of sabbath-breaking and to reform her life and pray to God for grace and repentance'. She replied that 'she would not goe 'til she was mended and would use her own will'.

The last witness was the bigamous Thomas Chapman, who thought he could shed some light on Mary's motive for prosecuting Mills. She had told him 'she did it for spite [because] Mary and her mother lived in a house belonging to Mills, who distrained her clothes for rent'. As for Lizzie Robbins, she 'was guilty of fornication before her marriage and bears evil will because [Mills] took the house of the said Richard and his wife for money they owed him. Elizabeth said he had sued them and she would never forgive him'. Like everyone else who gave evidence, he told the court that he attended church 'very constantly'.

In order to examine the case of the indiscreet landlord, the court had to find witnesses who, by their own standards of respectability, could be trusted at their word. It seems that the court was unable to find anyone with such qualifications at Randwick. Each witness, it appears, was asked to say whether they attended church regularly; this, presumably, was an attempt to assess how seriously they would take giving evidence under oath. All described themselves as 'constant' attenders.

Against this must be placed what can only be described as extremely irregular conjugal habits, at least in the light of prescribed secular and religious law. Thomas Chapman was a bigamist. Daniel Bennet may have been trapped into marriage with Mary, but it appears that he had enjoyed her sexual favours and therefore *could* have been the father of her illegitimate child. At the time of the case he was living apart from his wife, 'in sin with' 'one Sarah Cratchley'. Lizzie Robbins had given birth to a stillborn bastard child sixteen years earlier. Daniel Wildey was a convicted wood-stealer. Stephen Mills was alleged by several witnesses to have successfully bribed those who gave evidence for him with a few pints of ale and the offer of new pairs of shoes. From an orthodox point of view, the case of the indiscreet landlord had carried the Church officials into a sink of corruption, and it must have been very difficult for them to extricate any clear decisions from it. There is no evidence, in fact, that they came to any decision, or took any further action.

Cases like this are of course the stuff of the bawdy-court records. The impression they leave is that sexual irregularity, slander and gossipy defamation were about as common in Gloucestershire neighbourhoods in the seventeenth and eighteenth centuries as they are in comparable neighbourhoods today. This case at Randwick is exceptional only in that the court officials clearly found it impossible to find a single unambiguously respectable witness. This suggests that practical alienation from orthodox social *mores* was a function of wealth and status. The poorest village in Gloucestershire was also its most 'immoral' village. Randwick people almost certainly knew of their reputation with outsiders, and every year at Hocktide they *celebrated* their infamy.

The Stephen Mills case ranged 'low' against 'high'. He was a propertied man, a landlord. The two women who presented the case against him were his tenants, as was the woman with whom he was alleged to have committed adultery. The quality of his cottages is indicated in the 'chinks' and 'slitts' in the 'mudd walls' through which Mary Bennet and Lizzie Robbins claimed to have watched his transgressions. He had distrained Mary's clothes for rent, and taken the Robbins' cottage in payment for a debt. Mary, certainly, and perhaps Lizzie too, were what respectable people (like the overseers of the poor at Newent) called 'saucy jades', even perhaps 'bawds'. But Mills had all the powers of the law on his side, and they had none. Twelve years after this case he appears in the records as a churchwarden at Randwick, presenting a case against another woman for a disturbance during divine service.[36] Mills was a local big man. In however sordid and petty a way, he represented England's propertied and patriarchal elite. He was an officially sanctioned representative of Church and State in the forms of the property laws and the parish.

3

THE LORD MAYORS OF RANDWICK

One Monday early in May, 1784, a gentleman was riding through Randwick, and noticed 'a crowd of people assembled around a horse-pond'.[37] Looking over the heads of the crowd he saw, in the pond, a man seated upon a chair. At first he thought 'the country people were doing justice in that summary way for which . . . English mobs [were] so famous'. He thought they were ducking the man for some transgression of local custom or morality. In fact he was observing 'Randwick Wap', held every year on the second Monday after Easter, in 'Hocktide'.[38] It was a Whitsun festival, sometimes coinciding with May Day, a form of carnival.

The etymologies of these terms – 'Wap', 'Hock', 'Whitsun' – are eclectic and obscure. The accounts in the OED suggest a wide range of dialect meanings and etymologies which drift back through the mists of Norse, Old German, and Old French into what are probably Indo-European root words. They are 'aboriginal' words. This is about what they meant at Randwick in 1784, when the Wap took a common eighteenth-century form – the 'mock-mayoral election'.[39]

The gentleman dismounted and went into the crowd to find out what was happening. This is the account he sent to the *Gentlemen's Magazine*:

> One of the parish is, it seems, on the [second Monday after Easter], elected mock-mayor. He is carried with great state, colours flying, drums beating, men, women and children shouting, to a particular horse-pond, in which his worship is placed, seated in an armchair; a song is then given out line-by-line by the clerk, and sung with great gravity by the surrounding crowd . . . The instant it is finished, the mayor breaks the peace by throwing water in the faces of his attendants. Upon which, much confusion ensues; his worship's person is, however, considered as sacred, and he is generally the only man who escapes being thoroughly souced.

'The rest of the day, and often the week,' he wrote, 'is devoted to riot and drunkenness'.

The informant could not tell him how far back the event went, but another source refers to it in 1703. Samuel Rudder also referred to it in his *New History of Gloucestershire* (1779), adding that the inhabitants of Randwick 'plead[ed] the prescriptive right of ancient custom for the license of the day'. Rudder thought it an appalling occasion, and referred to 'irregularity and intemperance, and many ridiculous circumstances' enacted by 'the meanest of the people'. 'Even the authority of the magistrate is unable to suppress it,' he wrote.[40] The witness of 1784 confirmed that 'the county magistrates have endeavoured, but in vain, to put a stop to the practice'.

What the witness observed was an eighteenth-century expression of an ancient calendrical festival. The earliest reference to it – in 1703 – assumed that it had medieval origins.[41] This is conjectural, but it is supported by what we know of such festivals. 'When Easter fell on 24th April,' writes Charles Phythian-Adams, 'May Day was followed immediately by Hock Monday and Hock Tuesday.' The context at Randwick, an industrial village in one of the districts where we have documentary evidence of early trade union activity, also establishes a plausible link between medieval carnivalesque festivals and a date that was to become the great annual festival of the Labour Movement.

Hock Monday had to do with the 'traditional superiority of husbands over wives'. This 'was reversed totally on Hock Tuesday which, significantly, survived to be the more enduring of the two customs. According to the locality, it was customary for the wives – as a group – to bind or heave into the air those husbands who could be caught, and to release them only on payment of a ransome . . . Criticism of marital mistreatment or impropriety were formally and noisily expressed'.[42] Hocktide carnivalesque, traditionally, was about levelling class and gender hierarchies.

Now this, in a sense, was the practical meaning of the case of the indiscreet landlord, in which a group of impoverished women, one of whom we know 'had a mind of her own', undermined the public reputation of a local 'big man'. That was an *informal* act of 'reversal'. It undercut the pretensions of a local 'big man'. James C. Scott, writing of a twentieth-century Malaysian village, calls it 'Brechtian – or Schweikian – class-struggle'.[43]

We begin to see that a number of themes coalesce in the Randwick Wap. One way to describe what I have in mind is to use the term 'conjuncture' as Pierre Vilar uses it.[44] Several of the themes invoked by the annual Wap would have been part of its contemporary meaning: Randwick's poverty and legendary immorality, for example, would have given the 'reversal' embodied in its Hocktide revels public resonance. Contemporaries would have known without having to think about the matter that Randwick was a clothworking village, the poorest village in a region notorious for its capacity to combine for the purposes of industrial action and moral economy riots.

For these and other reasons, the very notion of 'Lord Mayors of Randwick' would have struck contemporaries as inherently funny (or irritating), striking up absurd comparisons with the pomp and ceremony surrounding Lord Mayors of important places like Gloucester, Bristol and London. It was taken for granted that the squalid circumstances of a place like Randwick excluded them from constitutional life. That such a place should claim a Lord Mayor of its own transgressed the principle, established in the aftermath of the seventeenth-century revolutions, that only property-holders could seek election to high office or vote in elections.

The Hocktide mock-mayoral elections of eighteenth-century Randwick (and everywhere else that they took place) transgressed constitutional principles, as medieval Lords of Misrule had always done. But where in medieval times they had claimed to be *Lords*, in the constitutional context of the eighteenth century they claimed to be *Mayors*. Such occasions were not *only* 'political' in the constitutional sense, but politics were always *part* of the 'normal' contexts that they deliberately, consciously, transgressed. Carnival was always in part 'political', and as such contained an implicit threat to the status quo. To take this further we shall now consider the Lord Mayor of Randwick's Song, or 'psalm'.

5

THE WEAVERS' SONG

Here is the song, or 'psalm':

When Archelus began to spin,
and 'Pollo wrought upon a loom,
Our Trade to flourish did begin,
Tho' conscience went to selling broom.

When princes' sons kept sheep in field,
And queens made cakes with oaten flour,
And men to lucre did not yield,
Which brought good cheer to ev'ry bower.

But when the giants, huge and high,
Did fight with spears like weavers' beams,
And men in iron beds die lie,
Which brought the poor to hard extremes.

213

When cedar trees were grown so rife,
And pretty birds did sing on high;
Then weavers liv'd more void of strife
Than princes of great dignity.

Then David with his sling and stone,
Not fearing great Goliath's strength,
He pierc'd his brains, and broke his bones,
Tho' he was nine feet and a span in length.

Chorus:
Let love and friendship still agree
To hold the bonds of amity.

The witness thought the psalm 'want[ed] . . . some explanation', and left it to his readers to decide what the explanation was.

Let us first examine the claim that the song had never been written down before. Is it possible to test the plausibility of this claim from the form and content of the song? The rhythm and metre are iambic tetrameter. Each line has four feet, and the natural stress is on the second syllable. The effect, drawing on the beat of the heart, is monotonous, incantatory and slightly ominous. The rhythm and rhyme are older than the references to Homeric Greece. Its drum beats a preliterate rhythm.

Assume the witness was telling the truth, and he wrote it down from ear. The quatrains depend on sense: each introduces and completes a new theme and image. It divides naturally into quatrains, and it would not need to be seen written down to order its lines in that way. The themes and images introduced in the quatrains are very simple, and undeveloped. Rhythm, metre, themes and images all make it entirely plausible that the song had never, and had never needed to be written down. It is easy to remember.

It is a weaver's initiation song, reminding each acolyte that his trade is very ancient. Archelus wove when Apollo sang. Weaving is as old as, possibly older than, agriculture: the claim is demonstrated rather than stated. Weavers were not always disdained as inferior beings.

The second and fourth verses, and the chorus, invoke a state of being that Victor Turner calls *communitas*. Recognisable historical epochs are invoked in verses one, three and five.[45] Under normal conditions, writes Turner, 'society is a structured, differentiated, and often hierarchical system of politico–legal–economic positions with many types of evaluation, separating [people] in terms of "more" and "less" '. *Communitas* refers to people in an 'unstructured or rudimentarily structured *comitatus*, community, or even communion of equal individuals who submit together to the general authority of the ritual elders'.[46]

In this case 'ritual authority', represented by his right to 'souce' everybody and not be souced in return, was delegated by the people to a candidate whose suitability for the role had to do with his reputation as one of the least respectable people in an extremely unrespectable neighbourhood: the mock-mayor. Under the authority of this elected Lord of Misrule, they then proceeded to flout as many respectable conventions as they could for a few days.

The first verse of the psalm contains a reminder that clothmaking was a very ancient 'mystery' – as old, at least, as agriculture. This is conveyed in a populist version of classical mythology. Archelus is a spinner and Apollo a weaver. Whilst not inherently improbable – Apollo is supposed to have wandered in poverty for many years, and lived with wolves in a cave on the slopes of Mount Parnassus, which later became the famous shrine of the Oracle at Delphi – the interpretation would have been regarded as tendentious by eighteenth-century classicists. Classical figures are brought down to earth, and made to seem people like you and me, reversing the prescribed orientation.

The third and fourth lines of the first verse – 'Our Trade to flourish did begin,/Tho' conscience went to selling broom' – could be translated into the proposition that economic growth stimulated by the profit motive brought corruption into the world. Greed overcame conscience. Scholars from across the ideological spectrum have never doubted that the West Country clothing industry was capitalist from the outset – back to the fourteenth century – and Gloucestershire and Somerset clothiers anticipated *laissez-faire* ideology decades before Adam Smith. It was given articulate form in a debate on industrial riots printed in the *Gloucester Journal* in 1738–9.[47]

The clothworkers consistently favoured state regulation of wages, on the grounds that the capitalists who ran the industry were motivated by greed. 'Conscience went to selling broom': 'broom', a plant used to make dye, stood, in the psalm, for commerce in all the products of clothmaking, from sheep pastures to tailored articles of clothing. The art of cornering markets was highly developed in this part of England. The meaning of these lines would not have been obscure.

Verse two needs little exploration. It evokes a direct contrast to the exploitation referred to in the last two lines of verse one. It evokes a prelapsarian state in which power and authority did not derive from the cash-nexus: 'And men to lucre did not yield.' This condition 'brought good cheer to ev'ry bower'. It was *communitas*, the world ruled by conscience and not profit.

Verse three reverts to a mythological representation of history, evoking 'giants, huge and high' who 'fought with spears like weavers' beams'. The image is imprecise and open to various interpretations, relative to the mental furniture of the singer or listener. It is not hard to picture feudal knights, the medieval representatives of the horseriding warriors who ruled every agrarian civilisation in the old world. It could also evoke the civil wars: the weaver's view, from the outside, of a war between Roundheads and Cavaliers. By leaving the specificities open, the verse allows stress on the general idea that weavers viewed these struggles between aliens from without, something that may well have been taken for granted, and was certainly taken for granted by the landed ruling classes. The dialectics of luxury ('iron beds') and exploitation ('which brought the poor to hard extremes') are stated in a language anyone could understand.

Verse four returns to *communitas* by expropriating images of the Holy Land ('cedar trees') and endowing them with substance as a place not unlike the Cotswolds, where 'pretty birds did sing', but most unlike them in that 'weavers liv'd more void of strife/Than princes of great dignity'. This evocation of a simple materialist utopia concludes with a contrast between political ideal and historical reality, a contradiction that is reconciled in the final verse:

Then David with his sling and stone,
Not fearing great Goliath's strength,
He pierc'd his brains, and broke his bones,
Tho' he was nine feet and a span in length.

The low and small, David, overthrows the huge and high, Goliath. David overcomes seemingly impossible opposition to restore the rights of his people, and then leads them to many victories in the golden age of the ancient Hebrews. This is what carnival is all about. No oppressor is so powerful that he cannot be overcome. God is not always on the side of the mighty. The first one now may later be last. The meek shall inherit the earth. The song has the genius of simplicity, meaning that it didn't take a genius to understand and remember it. It was a popular political song, a genre tapped by craftsmen with words since the most ancient of days.

In 1784 it would have invoked the victory of brothers and sisters in the North American colonies over the English 'goliath'. The Stroudwater Valleys would have understood the doctrinal planks of the American Revolution, having seen the birth of most of the ideas it embodied. Randwick Wap, like all such occasions, could acquire a contemporary, radical edge. Its message was inherently radical, but every message requires a sympathetic listener. The meanings would vary from generation to generation and year to year.

The chorus invoked the principle of solidarity, the source of radical–

democratic movements throughout history: 'Let love and friendship still agree/To hold the bonds of amity.'

This is not the only possible interpretation of the symbolism of the misrule of Randwick and its mockery of its misrulers. The meanings and their expressions (e.g. 'riot and drunkenness') would vary from person to person and year to year. They would vary from generation to generation. When the households of Randwick were as fully employed as they could wish to be, no doubt the occasion had a different tone than in times of underemployment or poverty. Mary Bennet would have viewed the annual misrule differently from her husband. Popular literacy was being encouraged once again (after the reversal of the Restoration eighty years earlier) in the 1740s. The generation of 1780 probably included more literate members than that of 1720. That would have made a difference: festivals of this sort belonged to the preliterate world. In the nineteenth and twentieth centuries the labouring classes would have to learn forms of understanding and communicating with national and international communities.

The constructions it is possible to put on the case of the indiscreet landlord were numerous at the time, and retelling them nearly three centuries later adds more. Using the law to cut down the men who were supposed to formulate and administer it was a particularly attractive option in the case of the Church courts because it cost nothing, at least to those who had nothing to lose. Interpretations of the meanings of the mock-mayoral elections and of the psalm which inaugurated them also encompass a wide range of possibilities. They might be seen (by participants or observers) as an exercise in outright parody of radical traditions and assumptions. They could be seen as an exercise in self-parody by deferential manufacturing workers who knew about their reputation as the poorest and least respectable people in the country, and who entirely accepted this social assessment. The radicalism of the psalm lay in the fact that it embodied a vision of a golden age in the past, an age which recognised the status of 'princes', but in which princes ploughed and princesses span, like everyone else. Everybody enjoyed the same standards of living. Its radicalism was 'restorationist' as against 'revolutionary'. Classless society lay in the past, not the future. Not until the nineteenth century did the Labour Movement assimilate the masters' doctrines of progress and adapt them to the cause of the worker.

Past or future, the image of classless society was there, in the psalm, for anyone to pick up if they listened closely enough and with the right experience behind them. The evidence for the existence of this message, in forms passed down generation after generation, depended on it being overheard by an informer, or a master, who thought it worth his while to report it to the authorities, and to attempt to suppress it. Only then would it be written down and made accessible to future historians. We cannot, as the historian of commerce and traffic J. A. Chartres stresses, deduce the non-existence of a thing from the paucity of evidence pertaining to it. This is true of all oral, or predominantly oral, traditions. The egalitarian impulse was not the only oral tradition passed on in like fashion. But it was passed on, and as such forms a continuity between the radicalism of agrarian, tributary civilisations and that of modern industrial capitalism.

'Levelling' activities such as those explored here are necessarily present in any hierarchically structured society or situation. Subordinates inevitably explore the limits of their subordination, and in doing so put them under consistent, everyday pressure. Such pressure also provides prescribed authorities with opportunities to exercise institutional sanctions against transgressors, thus constantly redefining or simply re-establishing precisely what limits exist against transgression. Scott calls this radicalism of the quotidian 'Brechtian class-struggle'. It is inarticulate in the sense that its episodes and incidents are (at least overtly) naive, lacking in general theoretical expression. Its protagonists appear to stumble clumsily across invisible social borders, and refer to existing social prescriptions indirectly. Its expressions are like parables, stories with meanings and moralities which change according to circumstances and the angle they are viewed from.

9

'A CONCATENATION OF VICIOUS HABITS'

A season of riots and a public discussion, 1738–41

Gentlemen,
The great advantages which the Art of Printing conveys to the LEARNED WORLD are so well known, that to entertain you with a long Discourse upon that Theme would be a needless and useless Attempt. We shall avoid all Prolixity of this Nature, and beg Leave to acquaint you with our Design at once, *viz.* That we intend to publish a Weekly Newspaper . . . ,*The Gloucester Journal*, wherein we shall insert a just Relation of the most material Occurrences, as well Foreign as Domestic. We also promise you a true Account of the Price of the Several Commodities in the most famous and noted Markets. We doubt not, Gentlemen, but our *Journal* will have the Approbation of all its Readers, and so meet with Encouragement equal to its merits.

Editorial announcement in GJ, 16 April 1736

The mob has already gotten this maxim: that *Adam Left No Will*; they are his sons, and ought to have a share of their father's possessions . . .

Hostile report in GJ, March 1739

Riots, like wars, revolutions and royal scandals, are newsworthy. The *Gloucester Journal* of 16 April 1736 also carried the story of an election tumult at Coventry two days earlier. The polling booths had to be closed after an hour of voting owing to clashes between the Land and Trade parties outside the Town Hall. 'The disorder was introduced and occasioned', the *Journal* reported, 'by a sort of military entry made the day before by a neighbouring lord.' This lord, apparently, 'was pleas'd to put himself at the Head of 1000 Rabble, Horse and Foot, armed with Clubs Sticks and Staves, with Trumpets sounding, Drums beating and Colours flying, to ride thro' almost every street in the most tumultuous and formidable manner'. As they rode and walked, they uttered and sang 'seditious cries of Down with the Rump, down with the Roundheads, no Hanover, down with the King's Head'. Just the sort of thing, in fact, that used to happen in the seventeenth century. As the centenary of the civil wars approached, at least one English lord had still to learn that the English Revolution and Jacobitism were entirely separate subjects. The difference was that in the seventeenth century the factional struggles of the master classes were fought on the battlefield. In the eighteenth century they were fought in the safer space created by newspapers and journals, the instruments and agencies of national public opinion. In eighteenth-century America and France, the printing-press was an instrument of social and political revolution. In England, where the revolution was over, it was a force for moderation, allowing all sides to have their say as long as they had a spokesman who could write the kind of thing a newspaper, given its market ('Gentlemen!'), would want to publish.

The season of riots in 1738–40 was one of the first conjunctures of its type in English history, albeit one that was foreshadowed between 1640 and 1660.[1] By 1740 England had a flourishing national media, in the form of the network of provincial newspapers that emerged after the lapse of Press censorship in 1694. This network greased the wheels of commerce through advertising, diffused innovations and public reforms, provided a means by which the master classes all over England were provided with the same information (e.g. about riots), fostered the rise of nationalism among the middle classes, and generally provided them with a mirror in which to observe and admire their ideological preoccupations. In this sense the riots of 1738–40 were a national phenomenon.

This chapter will concentrate mainly on 'public messages', the loud, clear public expression of ideas and prejudices which were already centuries old, as were the circumstances which had produced them. But before considering the messages, we should recollect Marshall McCluhan's famous slogan, 'the medium is the message'. McCluhan popularised the ideas of Walter J. Ong and spawned a whole range of new disciplines like 'Media Studies', 'Cultural Studies' and 'Communications'. The medium here is the newspaper, which created national public opinion.

Chastened by the Grub Street revolution of the 1640s, the Restoration imposed censorship of the printing-press in 1663. Regular information about what was happening nationally and internationally was available only in the government's *London Gazette*, private correspondence, an expensive subscription to one of the hand-written newsletter services, or word of mouth. Information essential to any kind of political, social and economic power was restricted to an artificially attenuated elite. This happened at a time when interest in and demand for literacy had begun to move deeply into the ranks of society, and when distant events could have very serious repercussions in the localities.

Anyone involved in trade needed news about national and international events. More information of this sort was needed, but so too
were media through which announcements, advertisements and public
issues could be diffused throughout the region. It is no accident that
after the earliest foundation at Norwich, eight years after the lapse of
censorship in 1694, the Western zone provided a significant number
of the pioneering provincial newspapers. Exeter and Bristol had newspapers by 1704, Shrewsbury in 1705 and Worcester in 1710. Even
Cirencester briefly experimented with one in 1716–17. As with all
infant industries, it was a risky business: of 130 provincial newspapers
established before 1760, only 35 survived at that date. One of the most
successful was the *Gloucester Journal*, founded by Robert Raikes and
William Dicey in 1723.[2]

By the time the announcement printed at the head of this chapter
was published, in April 1736, Robert Raikes was the sole proprietor
of the *Journal*. He was looking to expand his market beyond the
immediate trading hinterlands of Gloucester. Survival is one measure
of success, and the impressive volumes of the eighteenth-century
newspapers held today at the Gloucester City Library are testimony
to the initial success of the *Journal*. In the era of Raikes Snr and Jnr it
was one of England's greatest provincial newspapers. Then as now,
to survive, a successful business had to expand. Nine years after the
first edition came out in 1723, Raikes moved into and renovated one
of the most substantial houses in Gloucester.[3] He had imposed his
presence in the county town, the first printer to do so. Early in 1738
he issued a confident handbill announcing that his paper had 'met
with great encouragement from the public, it being of far greater
advantage for advertising of business than any other newspaper on
this side of the country'. 'Correspondents' had been established 'in
the cities of Bristol, Salisbury, Worcester and Hereford, also in the
town of Taunton and other places . . . to make this newspaper more
universal'. It had agents distributing the *Journal* in twenty-one 'divisions' of a region which stretched from Droitwich in the north to
Bristol, Salisbury and Taunton in the south, and from Carmarthen,
Cardiff and Bridgewater in the west to Oxford and Woodstock in the
east.[4] There is no evidence about circulation figures. John Brewer
thinks 250–400 copies per edition is probably about all a provincial
newspaper attained in the 1720s, rising to the high of 2,000 per edition
attained by the *York Chronicle* in the 1760s.[5] If copies could be physically
distributed, the potential market was much greater than this. A good
story and an urgent public debate, well publicised, would increase
circulation. Conceivably (though lack of evidence prevents more than
conjecture) the messages we shall explore in this chapter were purchased by as many as 2,000 households and small businesses (e.g.

taverns). The entire debate was republished in London in the national *Gentlemen's Magazine*. Actual readers could easily have quadrupled circulation figures, through copies kept at inns, taverns, coffee-houses and alehouses.

Riots broke out all over England in 1738–41, but they did not represent any kind of national uprising on the part of the working class. Causes, occasions and consciousness were local. Doubtless word spread from district to district and region to region, but the exploding multitude had nothing like the national press to express its opinions and divisions.

Turnpikes were contentious in the northern hinterlands of Bristol in the 1720s. The problem raised by turnpiking was whether and how to distinguish between long-distance traders and local producers, who thought they should be exempt from tolls. The Kingswood colliers, who kept Bristol's industries going, its food cooked and its parlours warm, felt particularly strongly about this issue. They believed they already put enough of their meagre earnings into the pockets of Bristolians in the matter of provisions – another source of tension. Why should they pay an extra tax for the privilege of supplying the city with a commodity it could not do without? The turnpike issue erupted with explosive regularity after 1727; every time the commissioners erected toll-gates, a group of colliers would ride out at night and tear them down. If arrests were made, they made their indignation known by marching through Bristol's narrow streets armed with cudgels.[6]

In October 1738 colliers from the Kingswood district, east of Bristol, set up flying pickets to prevent coal from leaving the district, conducted a round-up of the colliers' clubs meeting in the alehouses of the district, and marched to the house of one of the mine-owners, a 'Squire Chester'. Finding him not at home, they broke in and confiscated some fine roast beef that the Squire's servants were preparing, lit a fire on the lawn, roasted and ate the beef, and left. These were not the first signs of trouble in the industrial districts of the region. A few months earlier the *Gloucester Journal* reported that 'weavers and combers' in Somerset and Devon 'and several towns in the west . . .'

> lately rose in great numbers on account of the great hardships imposed on them by their masters, who have engrossed into their hands the most necessary commodities of life, such as corn, butter, cheese, eggs, salt, milk, mutton, pork &c.

This rising of colliers was about wage reduction, that of the clothworkers was about truck payments.[7] In the North-East, Newcastle keelmen were threatening similar actions.[8] Middle-men in the food trades were active, and in the late 1730s 'the export of wheat [was] going ahead' in large quantities to 'the Straits, Oporto, France, Lisbon, and Madeira'.[9]

In November the colliers of Kingswood attacked and 'almost destroyed' Safford Lock, east of Bristol. They left a note saying that 'what they had done was nothing; the damage was to come; that at present they assembled in only a small body, but when they came again they would be 1,000 strong'. A week later they fulfilled this promise. They threatened that 'if a bit of coal was carried up the river for the future they would destroy all the locks; for they had as good be hanged as they and their families starve'.[10] In the next edition the *Journal* offered £20 reward to anyone willing to give evidence against the men responsible for £100 damage to Safford Lock.[11]

Other areas of trade were booming. A report in February 1738 stated that 'On Wednesday night last 3,000 quarters of wheat were enter'd at the Customs House for exportation . . . yet it don't rise in price'. The reasons – England became a net exporter of wheat only in the 1710s, and record exports were achieved in the late 1730s following several bountiful harvests – were:

First, what a vast number of acres of woodland have been stubb'd up, ploughed and sowed; and several downs ploughed and sowed; and Thirdly, the present advantageous methods of dressing the land, whereby an acre produces twice as much as formerly, yet we have twenty times as much as we used to have.[12]

Progress was occurring. The next two harvests were to show that the optimism was premature. But as yet food shortages affected only people with not enough work to pay for it; prices were being kept artificially high by government subsidies ('the bounty') to grain exporters. As yet only the manufacturing and labouring classes, excluding those on the land, were feeling the pinch – and becoming restive – as the hard winter of 1738–9 began to take hold.

The clothworkers of Trowbridge and Melksham rose up in late November 1738: 1,500 clothworkers attacked and levelled the mansion, cottages and workshops of a clothier named Henry Coulthurst. A month later the *Gloucester Journal* devoted its front page to 'An Essay on Riots' which blamed the clothiers and the Walpole government, and suggested that riots were not such a bad thing if they served to remind the master-classes of their paternalist responsibilities. In January a Trowbridge clothier began vitriolic defence of the clothiers and the government, viciously and wittily attacking the clothworkers' allegedly idle and debauched habits, and systematically dismantling the complacent self-righteousness of the 'fox-hunting gentry'. His defence occupied the front pages of the *Gloucester Journal* through February, March and early April 1739. Somewhat less dispassionately than the Scarman Report on the English riots of the early 1980s, it presented views on why riots happened, and what should be done to prevent

223

them. At a stretch, we can regard it as an early prototype of the 'condition of England question'. The message of the clothworkers echoed away into the distance as the master-classes squabbled about which of them were best qualified to discipline the poor.

On 22 May 1739 it was reported that Richard Lanham, a clothier of Heytenbury, Wilts, had been fined £10 for truck payments. The magistrate ordered that the fine be distributed among his workers, 'it appearing how daring and bold his offence was, so soon after such a riot committed in the county'. Another article in the same edition of the *Journal* told an exemplary story of self-help. It was the obituary of Mr William Leigh, a carpenter of Warminster, Wilts, who 'by an ingenuity, probity and industry in his business, acquired a very considerable reputation, with an handsome fortune'. He was a man of humble origins risen to prosperity and respectability by dint of his own natural abilities. The article praised his 'singular and extensive charity' which had earned him 'not only the prayers and thanksgivings of the poor and indigent (to whom he was a father) but the esteem of all good people'.[13] Like John Corbet's 'middle ranke' of a century earlier, Lanham was a paternal friend to the poor.

On 10 April 1739 three men were hanged at Fisherton-Anger near Salisbury for their part in the depredations at Melksham. Their confessions, published the same day in the *Gloucester Journal*, concluded four tense months when the Land and Trade parties loudly and publicly debated who knew best how to employ the poor and prevent them from rioting. The three guilty weavers confessed their sins and blamed the clothiers, leaving no doubt in the minds of the readers that they should vote for the country Tory candidate at the next elections in order to sink the labyrinthine Walpolian regime, source of all corruption, including industrial riots. Clothiers and other businessmen should stick to business and leave ruling to landed men with ruling in the blood, the 'fox-hunters' as they were called by the clothiers. Meanwhile, conditions steadily worsened in the depressed manufacturing districts.

The uprisings of early winter 1738 were not directly related to the price of provisions. Wheat was consistently below 6 shillings a bushel between 1714 and 1730, when clothmaking was booming in many districts of the West Country. In the 1730s it was consistently below 5.[14] In August 1739 the *Journal* reported that an abundant harvest was being collected. Prices had recently risen from 4 to 5 shillings, but they were expected to fall following what the *Journal*'s correspondent assumed was going to be a bumper harvest.

But now bad weather was added to the explosive mixture. Prices continued to rise over the following month, the harvest of 1739 was deficient, and the winter of 1739–40 was again exceptionally severe.

Corn mills were frozen up and the price of meal rose. In February 1740 frozen waterways prevented coal shipment and added hypothermia to problems many households in manufacturing and extractive industries were already having with reduced diet.[15] 'This calamitous and rigorous season of cold weather', as the *Journal* described it a week later, prompted Gloucester notables to organise a subscription to relieve the poor, 'to be continued, weekly, during the present rigorous season'. The first collection raised £60.[16] The following week brought news of subscriptions for the poor at Edinburgh, Glasgow, Saffron Walden, Croydon, Allhallows, West Ham, Walthamstow, Sherbourne (Dorset) and Kings Lynn. 'The inhabitants and neighbouring gentlemen of Tewkesbury', wrote another correspondent, had 'not shut the bowells of their compassion' either. Charity was being showered on the poor. They were 'Truly Christian examples,' editorialised Raikes. 'We hope [they] will be followed by all those whom providence has blest with plenty'.[17] By June, wheat was selling at 8 shillings a bushel, double the average price for the 1730s, with no immediate promise of relief.[18]

The earlier riots were industrial disputes, risings of work-people against their immediate masters, mine-owners and clothiers mostly. As the long season of riots drew on, attention shifted firmly away from the industrial masters and towards wholesalers and retailers of food, who became scapegoats. This shift was almost certainly contrived, though probably not in a conspiratorial sense, by an unholy and quite unpremeditated sense of unity between landed and trading masters, who all felt that if there had to be riots it would be better to redirect them at targets other than themselves. In the Western region this policy was fostered in the *Gloucester Journal* and other country newspapers.

In July 1740 the editor of the *Journal* was deluged with reports of rioting throughout the country. At Newcastle keelmen were reported to have burned down the Guildhall, and plundered ships and trows in the harbour.[19] The 'poor people' of Durham had risen 'in considerable numbers', and several were wounded in exchanges with the authorities.[20] Another rising occurred at Norwich,[21] and the 'populace' of the Staffordshire manufacturing districts was in a state of insurrection.[22] At Leek they had prevented the conveyance of flour to Derby, which was also experiencing shortages. The same week four women from Moreton-in-the-Marsh were ordered to be whipped through the town next market-day 'for riotously and unlawfully entering the dwelling-house of Robert Shirley, Innholder, and taking by violence a large quantity of wheat'.[23] We are not told what he was doing with a large quantity of wheat in a time of dearth-prices. In October came a report of the 'misery of the people' at Frome, Somerset. 'Many of the clothiers have turn'd off 100 hands each, and some 500,' reported Raikes' correspondent. Raikes could not resist adding, sarcastically, that this was *'strong proof of the flourishing state of the nation as often boasted of in the Gazeteer'*. The *Gazeteer* was the official government publication.

Dean Forest insurrectionists were busy throughout the summer of 1740, as prices remained high. In mid-July three men 'concerned in a notorious riot and attempt to destroy the dwelling house and Corn Mills of Mr. Joseph Sayer of Redbrook' were convicted at a General Quarter Sessions at Gloucester. The leniency of their sentences, a fine of £5 and surety for a year, suggests that the magistrates were sympathetic.[24] On 30 September it was reported the Kingswood colliers 'rose yesterday on account of the high prices of corn'. They were scouring the countryside from Bath to Bristol looking for millers and innkeepers suspected of hoarding corn. They then attempted to enter Bristol in force, but were prevented by soldiers on the walls. A delegation went in to talk to the mayor, informing him 'that they came with no intent to hurt any man, but for the good of their country'. Their spokesman said 'that for his part he had good bread, good cheese, and good fat beef enough; but that there were hundreds of poor families starving around him'. Leaders often came from among the more prosperous working households, and men with mastery of their skills and occupation were expected to provide leadership for their younger and/or less secure neighbours. The men 'demanded redress for their grievances, by having corn allowed them at six shillings a bushel'. The mayor is supposed to have replied, 'Gentlemen, I'll take care that you shall have Justice done you'. Raikes gives no clue as to which of two possible constructions to put on this. It sounds like a threat of punishment as well as a promise of cheap corn.[25]

By the first week of October 1740 the market price for wheat at Bristol and Gloucester was 8/6d a bushel. 'A detachment of the regiment' was sent by the government to provide 'a strong guard night and day without Lawford's Gate, & another in town, in order to keep the colliers in awe'.[26] It was another week before they went home, still empty-handed. They were the people Wesley preached to. By this time 'divers vessells [had] gone abroad for wheat, & several are soon expected here'. 'The household peck loaf will [soon] look pretty near its usual plumpness,' opined Raikes optimistically.[27]

But the reports of general depression kept coming in. Besides the problems at Frome, the poor were 'starving for want of work at Stroud and other clothing places'.[28] Raikes hoped that the 'J.Ps and surrounding gentlemen [would] take all possible care of them'. In such circumstances every encouragement to charity carried overtones of threat. Riots were a way of keeping speculators in order. A baker of Dyrham, near Bath, had his bread seized in October, and had to pay a fine of 5 guineas for making it under weight.[29] Insurrectionaries at Poole,

Dorset, besieged a miller 'who was lately detected in shipping fifteen bags of flour on board a Norway-man'.[30] In December, Raikes spelled out a message that had been kept implicit, 'that if rich people were oblig'd to bring their corn to market, and not hoard it up in expectation of high prices, bread would be cheaper than at present, and the poor manufacturers and labourers not in that distress which they are in many parts of the kingdom'.[31] He reported evidence from a ship's Master 'just returned from Dunkirk, that notwithstanding the ban on export, there were twelve English ships there loaded with grain'.[32]

The general Quarter Sessions held at Gloucester in January 1741 was 'the largest that has been known for years'.[33] At the end of January Raikes received word from London that 'there never was known such a number of thieves about town as at present'.[34] In February Raikes wrote that 'scarce a post arrives without an account of some tumult occasioned for want of bread'.

> 'Tis to be wished, therefore, that in imitation of our neighbours the *French*, those at the head of affairs would show a fatherly concern for the miseries of their fellow creatures, and acquire popularity by doing some service for the people.[35]

Any mention of imitating the French infuriated Walpolian Whigs and clothiers, who were convinced that cheap French textiles were stealing their markets.[36] The paternalist editor of the *Gloucester Journal* was waving a red rag at pensioners, placemen, tax-collectors, clothiers, dealers, speculators, grocers, shopkeepers, and the great commercial bloc that men like Raikes believed had imposed its evil values on England in the 1720s and 1730s. Any failure to display 'a fatherly concern for the miseries of the poor' on the part of a trader rendered the guilty party open to public odium. Bland mention of a name – 'so-and-so has stopped trying to profit from poor people's misery' – could be taken as a sign that the people should keep an eye on so-and-so to make sure he behaved himself in future. After decades on the outer, the country Tories were making the most of the season of riots.

In March 1739, at the Assizes at Salisbury, the three journeyman weavers of Trowbridge and Melksham, Wilts, were tried and found guilty of destroying Clothier Coulthurst's house and outbuildings, and condemned to public hanging at Fisherton-Anger gallows, near Salisbury. The case by then was a public *cause célèbre*, and on 10 April – the day they were hanged – confessions alleged to have been written by the three men were published in the *Gloucester Journal*. The confessions served as a dramatic conclusion to a vitriolic public debate that had dominated the columns of the newspaper since early December of the preceding year.[37]

A brief report of the rising appeared in the *Gloucester Journal* of 5 December 1738. A crowd of clothworkers attacked Coulthurst's mill-complex, with threats that they would 'kill him, tear down his house and bury him in the ruins'. They 'broke his windows, entered and destroyed his furniture, pulled out the butts in his barrels and got intoxicated on hatfulls of beer'. They went into his workshops and 'threw out a thousand pounds of wool yarn, tore it into pieces and threw it into the river, tore up his account books and stamp'd them into the dirt, and destroy'd his mill'. Finally, they entered the cottages of his tenants, pulled them down from the inside out, and 'spoiled their goods'. The damage was estimated at £500, a figure which was reduced to £400 at the trial in March. No one was injured, but 'the outrages so alarmed the clothiers of Trowbridge, that the next night they ordered the Crier to give publick notice that the journeymen should have full wages and no truck'. The implication of this hasty statement, dictated by urgent circumstances, was that they had not been paying the wages established by Privy Council in 1726.[38] Later discussion tended to blur this basic point of dispute. The rising took place because of illegal practices on the part of the clothiers and the clothiers later issued public denials in order to shift the blame onto the workers.[39]

The longest and fullest confession appeared under the title 'a true copy of a paper written by John Beazer, March 29'. It began with an epigram from St Paul: 'For I have learned in whatever state I am in, therewith to be content.' A sermon-like introduction expanded the theme: 'The Holy Apostle,' it read, 'being exercised in all Christian duties, and an eye-witness of our Lord and Saviour's performances here on earth [*sic*], must, by all means, be allowed to be a sufficient instructor of the important duty of contentment.' The loose ways of Beazer and his confederates had 'unframed the whole course of nature'.

Beazer's life had begun fairly auspiciously. His 'poor parents' went without so he could continue at school until he had 'good learning'. At about the age of 14 he was apprenticed to a local master-weaver. He served his apprenticeship 'lawfully and honestly'. Beazer was a fully qualified man, which was of some importance at a time when apprenticeship rules were beginning to break down. On completion of his apprenticeship he 'married an honest woman' and by 'honest labour and endeavours' he rose through the ranks of his trade to become a master-weaver with two looms and three apprentice boys of his own. For five years after the birth of his 'dear son' he 'lived in good credit, and had the love and esteem of all men'. His behaviour was always 'regular as to outward appearance'; he and his family attended church 'twice a day' and he conscientiously supervised their observation of 'all other performances in regard to temporal ordinances'. Faith gradually seeped out of his 'performances', reducing them to empty gestures. It was not enough to *observe* the proprieties; the observer had to *believe* in them too, and this was where his fall began. 'Not discerning the great goodness of God in *spiritual* performances,' he wrote, 'I unhappily erred, in being too proud of my station.' His fate revealed the roots of his *hubris*, the pride of a poor boy in the process of establishing himself as a master, if not yet of men, then of apprentice boys: 'having all things at my command, I indulged myself too much, and fell into the great sin of drunkenness.' He became 'a *companion of reprobates and fools*'. Eventually his degradation was so great that he was 'even troublesome [to his] parish for sustenance, and so rejected by all men'. Now, utterly shamed, he awaited a hangman's rope to mark the end of his descent into a masterweaver's hell. Drained of piety, drunken and pauperised, he was an object lesson to all who could learn from what had befallen him. The moral was clear. Beazer was a victim of bad faith, bad company and the demon drink.

In keeping with the genre of public confession, Beazer admitted that he was not free from sin, but his confession was not utterly abject. He went on to attack the greater sins of the clothiers, whom he insisted on blaming for the events which had led to his downfall. Before considering what he had to say on this, let us try to view the events through his eyes.

The day the weavers began to gather in the market-place at Trowbridge, Monday 27 November, Beazer was earning a living as a journeyman in the workship of a man such as he had once aspired to be, a master-weaver with several looms, employing journeymen and apprentices. Success and failure hinged very greatly on boom and slump cycles. We are not told how old he was, but he had served his apprenticeship and begun to establish himself as a craftsman at a time when export markets for the Spanish cloth produced in the Trowbridge–Melksham district were declining. Exports began to fall in the 1720s, when Beazer began his apprenticeship.[40] By 1738 the Wiltshire textile industry was in the depths of a recession. The Levant company had large stocks of cloth unsold in the markets of Asia Minor. One Trowbridge clothier claimed that he had sixty looms standing idle in November.[41] Estimates as to the number of workers (men, women and children) kept in work by a single loom vary, but fifteen is a conservative estimate.[42] The circumstances of just one clothier, then, meant something like 900 people looking for work elsewhere, or forced onto the parish rates.[43] The slump was serious, so the riots which broke out when harvest was over and winter began to bite cannot have been entirely unexpected. Beazer's master had enough work in the week of the riots to keep himself and three journeymen weaving, probably for Henry Coulthurst, who the striking weavers believed kept up work by paying short rates and truck.

The weavers began to gather at Trowbridge on Monday 27 November. They sent word to country weavers suspected of working for Coulthurst 'at Ten Pence Halfpenny and One Shilling per Yard' (the statutory rate, set in 1726, was 14 pence) that they 'intended to cut the chain' from the loom if they refused to join the stop-work.[44] According to the clothiers' account,[45] matters began to escalate when 'a certain weaver near Trowbridge, who was not only poor, but destitute of work', was warned by a crowd of journeymen not to take in work from Coulthurst under the standard rate. Tension built up throughout Monday, and the next day the crowd 'reassembled in great numbers' and marched off towards Melksham. Coulthurst heard, or suspected, that they were after him and arranged for messengers to intercept them with promises that he would pay the rates they were demanding. The journeymen demanded that this be committed to paper. They wanted Coulthurst's personal signature, but he had gone to the country with his family the night before, and the signatures of his messengers failed to satisfy them. They marched on to Coulthurst's mill-complex where they were met by one of his employees, 'Mr Aland, a Shear-grinder, who used all possible means to appease them . . . by offering his bond for any sum, or his person as hostage'. They brushed him aside, 'broke open the doors, and drove in the windows, . . . beat to pieces and destroyed great part of the Household Goods, Partitions and Wainscotes, drank, carried out, and spilt, all the Beer, Rum, Wine and Brandy in the Cellars, and staved in all the casks that contained them'. Then they tackled the cottages of Coulthurst's tenants, and left when darkness began to fall, leaving one man, John Crabb, still at work in the upstairs room of one of the cottages. Crabb was captured by 'some honest neighbours', and taken before a magistrate who sent him under escort and cover of night to gaol at Chippenham.

Next day (Wednesday) the weavers gathered on the outskirts of Melksham to demand Crabb's freedom. The magistrate refused the clothiers' request that Crabb be released to ease the situation. The clothiers made a hurried collection and purchased food and beer for the strikers, who were waiting for news about Crabb in the fields beyond the town. This probably ensured that Coulthurst's property was their sole target. They ate the food and drank the beer and then marched through Melksham to make good their promise to 'reduce [Coulthurst's houses and mill] to the condition of the city of Jerusalem, viz. that of them there should not remain one stone upon another'. They began in symbolic style, by 'untiling' the roof. A few hours later

Coulthurst's property was little more than a heap of rubble. The clothiers quickly arranged another collection, and the demolishers were informed that more food and drink was awaiting them in the market-square. After a picnic they again dispersed.

On Thursday they returned to survey their work and marched around Melksham to make sure the point had been taken. Seeing that their work-ban was operating, they were satisfied and dispersed for the weekend. On Monday they 'threatened [the clothiers] with another visit from them, but a detachment of Colonel Harrison's Regiment of Foot, marching into the town about the middle of Sunday night, put an end to their further mobbing'. 'The soldiers . . . were sadly harrassed, having marched one whole night, and half another to our assistance,' the clothiers' spokesman announced.

The second morning of the rising (Tuesday) Beazer's master heard that the journeymen were approaching Melksham, and told his men to take the cloth from his looms and carry it to his house on the outskirts of town.[46] Whether this was from fear or from solidarity with the strike is unclear, probably both, certainly the former. That he had work for himself, apprentices and three journeymen indicates that he had good connections with a clothier, perhaps Coulthurst. The three journeymen remained at their master's house outside town (possibly a farm) until the early hours of Wednesday morning, not returning to their accommodation in town until the strikers had dispersed for the night. Next morning work was laid aside for the rest of the week, and the three journeymen went for a stroll through the streets to see what damage had been done . . .

> and, standing gazing about, the days being short, the tumult of people being returned from Trowbridge, and entered the town of Melksham, to demand the body of John Crab, whom they had left behind the night before. Seeing this hurricane, we did not make haste, but stood looking on; and being to and fro among them, I was in and out of the buildings of Mr Coulthurst; and I must confess I did strike at some of the wainscote, and I think it was a door; but for carrying a hatchet or poult [the allegation which led to his conviction] I was no ways guilty thereof, although two oaths were taken against me.

It was a delicate situation. The Kingswood colliers could rise again at any moment, as could the clothworkers further south in Somerset and Devon. Stroudwater and the Vale of Berkeley were experiencing symptoms of stress, and the soldiers sent to suppress the rising at Melksham might have to be rushed elsewhere, leaving discontented weavers who might decide to tear down the houses and workshops of another local clothier. Fear was in the air. A cooling-off was needed, an enquiry to show the concerned public (including the most concerned, i.e. rioters) that the matter was receiving the attention of the master-classes and that justice was being done.[47]

All three men claimed that corrupt means were used to obtain their convictions and sentences. There is a hint in the state papers that there may have been a conspiracy to ensure exemplary convictions and penalties.[48] Thirteen men were tried at the Assizes in March.[49] Crabb and Richard Rowd *als* Rude were convicted and sentenced to death for 'assembling with twenty other malefactors and beginning to demolish and pull down a dwelling house of Henry Coulthurst'. Nine others were convicted and sentenced to fines of 40 shillings and one year in prison 'for a riot', and for damaging Coulthurst's property inside the buildings; one man, James Stephens, was acquitted. Beazer's conviction was for demolishing the house of one Samuel Stevens, presumably one of Coulthurst's tenants.

Beazer thought he was 'piqued at by the masters of his parish' – because he was known to them, unlike most of the weavers, who were from Trowbridge, but also because he had been in receipt of poor relief. Rowd or Rude denied that he was ever closer to Coulthurst's house than a bridge which lay 30 yards from the clothier's front door. Crabb claimed he would die 'falsely accused' even though he admitted that he was 'not innocent of the crime'. Three oaths were sworn against him: that he had been first into the clothier's house, that he had damaged a particularly valuable clock, and that he had threatened Coulthurst's life. He denied all three of these oaths, without denying that he had taken a leading part in the depredations; the implication being that, in the absence of solid evidence, his accusers had 'fitted him up'. What outraged them was not that they were innocent of participation in the attack, but that the state could convict them only on false testimony. If it had been a fair trial, they implied, they would have got off: a case, perhaps, of professional informers.

The ease with which people were drawn into the 'hurricane', as Beazer described it, was stressed in all three confessions. Crabb was in no doubt that his 'fatal end' was due to his 'relations and false witnesses'. He first 'met with the mob at Trowbridge' and 'by many entreaties and the disappointment of [his] friends . . . [was] induced to accompany them in their desperate design'. The convictions seem to have rested on a prosecution account which envisaged a core of twenty or so ringleaders conducting the demolitions while the rest of the crowd (which reports put at between 1,000 and 1,500) watched.[50] Beazer's account, stressing a confused 'hurricane' in which individuals were 'in and out' of the buildings, puts a different slant on the proceedings, but, like the other accounts, he tells us nothing of the organisation that lay behind the strike.

The only reference to weavers' organisations came in William Temple's final essay on riots, in the *Gloucester Journal* of 10 April 1739. 'The *Manufacturers*', he wrote, 'have stocks raised by their *Clubbing*, sufficient to carry on Prosecutions of any kind, being several hundred pounds capital.'[51] He mentioned it not out of any interest in the clubs, but to suggest that, if they could afford to subscribe to them, the weavers couldn't possibly be as impoverished as the clothiers' critics were suggesting. 'They cannot surely plead Poverty and Incapacity. Why not prosecute, as well as riot and plunder?', he asked.

This is all we are told about grass-roots organisation. Clubs are implied but not described in documents relating to another strike by clothworkers at Stroud in 1755–7.[52] A description of such a club and its mode of operation occurs in the prosecution papers relating to an identical attack on a clothier's mill-complex at Wotton-under-Edge in 1826. They state that 'Regular meetings of the club were and are held and they [i.e. the weavers] there determine on their proceedings. They have a Secretary and they call one of the body King and another General'.[53] The club was organised and controlled by leading master-weavers of the district, and one of its main tasks was to maintain wages against the efforts of clothiers to employ 'weavers of lower scale' to lower wage-rates.

Smaller meetings (perhaps 'chapters' of the general body) met in various alehouses around the town. During strikes 'large meetings' were held 'in the Chipping [market-place] at Wotton'. The General would call for information about strike-breaking and, on receipt of names, parties would march off to pay them a visit. Strike-breakers would have their cloth cut from the loom, and, in cases of especial bitterness, windows and hedges around cottages might be broken. Trials of strike-breakers would be held during the evenings at a local inn, presided over by the King of the Weavers. The General was responsible for organising the attendance of the accused and witnesses. If the clothiers still refused to negotiate, or agree to the weavers' demands, the dispute would enter its second phase: an attack on the buildings of a prominent local mill-owner. This is exactly what happened at Trowbridge and Melksham in 1738.[54] The prosecution of the Wotton weavers in 1826 alleged that 'in all acts of the mob where violence is used the most active of them are strangers which is done to prevent if possible any legal proceedings being taken'.[55]

Eighty years and 50 kilometres separate the strikes at Melksham and Wotton, but in spite of this it is valid to project some of the information relating to the latter into the context of the former. During an earlier strike over wage-rates in 1726 the weavers of the Melksham-Trowbridge districts 'went about with KWG in their caps, signifying that they were King George's Weavers'.[56] It cannot be assumed that their loyalism was unambiguous. The weavers among the defenders of Cirencester in 1643 had been adamant that they were fighting in the name of the king. A contemporary Tory writer interpreted this to mean 'that the majority of Weavers were dissenters and . . . far from having Jacobite sympathies'.[57] But it could also mean that the weavers' 'king' was named George, and that they were deliberately playing with the elite preoccupations of the divided Land and Trade parties. The evidence that plebeian protest movements of all kinds invariably incorporated mockery into their campaigns is obscured by the allusive nature of the references, but it is generally accepted that 'reversal' was an established habit in the mentality of working people in early modern England. In the last chapter we saw an ancient weavers' initiation song used to inaugurate a traditional Lords of Misrule Whitsun carnival, which they called a 'Mock-Mayoral Election'. If nothing else, that conjuncture demonstrated an odd and yet, on reflection, plausible intermixing of traditions. Only 'the meanest of people' were entitled to participate. This meant roughly 70 per cent of the people living in the Stroudwater Valleys.

The first impression obtained from the description of the weavers' club at Wotton is of conservatism: its 'constitutional structure' seems to mirror that of the kingdom of England. It has a king to preside in judicial and ceremonial matters, and a general to see to strategy and organisational matters. It is monarchical as opposed to republican. But weavers would have had an ambiguous attitude with respect to the British army. Soldiers had been used to put down strikes in West of England clothworking districts since 1738.[58] Colonel Wolfe's comment about recruiting strikers at Stroud in 1756 shows that then, as now, the British army recruits best in what were then called 'slumps', and are now called recessions and depressions. Many weavers would have served time in the army. They would be familiar with military discipline. It doesn't follow that they were particularly sympathetic towards what the British army represented. A certain amount of mockery was implied in the notion of the weavers' General, wry (at times grim) humour. Mock-Generals and Mock-Kings come in the same category as a Mock-Mayor and Lords of Misrule. In the 1630s enclosure-breaking industrial workers in the Forest of Dean were led by 'Lieutenant Skimmington'. The juxtaposition of a military rank with a ceremony for shaming cuckolds was a joke which suggested that the king's court and everyone associated with it was dominated by unscrupulous and unpatriotic women. The authorities thought it meant a person, where in fact it meant anyone who could see the joke and agreed and could expand upon its implications. Community structure and associational habits varied greatly from district to district in early modern England, but humour was universal.

Vernacular habits – and clubs – of this type almost certainly had a continuous existence in clothworking districts from the time of the medieval guilds, and at Wotton in 1826 they clearly regarded themselves, and not the capitalist clothiers, as the agents responsible for the maintenance of standards in all aspects of the weaving trade, from apprenticeship regulation to quality control, and, of course, piece-rates.

Just where the three condemned men stood in terms of organisation is difficult to say. Beazer joined the strike late, and in his confession he reflects that his drunkenness had lost him the respect of his neighbours. Reference in the Wotton papers to the employment of 'strangers' (almost certainly 'journeymen' from other districts who would have regarded such employment as a necessary part of their apprenticeship)[59] suggests a routine tactic designed to ensure that 'ringleaders' were never caught and tried. As in all armies, the General Staff (men with tactical and strategic experience) kept to the rear while the battle raged. Men like Beazer, and maybe Rowd (Crabb was caught red-handed), were 'piqued at' by parish overseers, or agents of the clothiers, because they were vulnerable. His confession also suggests that at the time when the strike broke out (Monday 27 November) Beazer was working for reduced rates. Beazer claimed he got caught up in a 'hurricane'. Crabb comes through as a more solid union-man, drawn in, albeit perhaps against his better judgement, 'by many entreaties and the disappointments of [his] friends' when the strike began at Trowbridge.

Once the soldiers arrived, the clothiers' fear subsided a little and they began the business of securing some exemplary hangings. A Tory spokesman writing in the *Gloucester Journal* three weeks later blamed the greed, insensitivity and irresponsibility of the clothiers for what happened, condemned the corruption of the Walpole regime, seemed to applaud the weavers' behaviour, and almost certainly sealed the fates of the three men who were hanged in April. All parties could see the sense in making a few examples, and the cases against Beazer, Crabb and Rowd, none of whom sound remotely like ringleaders, may have been touched up a little. It made sense to 'pique' scapegoats from the ragged edges of the rank and file; quite apart from the difficulty of obtaining witnesses against the big men, it might undercut the authority of the clubs and their leaders by showing that *anyone* who got involved with a mob might be 'piqued at'. The condemned men must have felt very bitter and isolated as they sat in their cells awaiting public execution, and their confessions would have carried hopes of pardon. They were the unlucky ones.

Beazer's confession has three distinct strands. First there is his brief autobiography, interwoven with a second theme, the necessity for 'contentment' and 'subordination'. He ends by warning his 'dear friends the journeymen weavers' that to 'obtain the promise of a blessed inheritance [they must] learn to be content'. This was to be Wesley's theme, of course, but it was in direct contradiction to traditions of household independency which were still strong among the weavers, as among other craft workers. They were also the platitudes of the day, one of the few areas which the landed masters and the clothiers could agree upon; the fate of their medium here lent them a cutting edge. But Beazer left no doubt that he did not include the clothiers among those to whom deference was due. 'Remember,' he told them, 'you have been guilty of covetousness and oppression':

> Your advantage has been unspeakable in the measure, whilst we have been from time to time oppressed. I doubt not but you can form deceit enough to conceal the same . . .

(This was a reference to William Temple's defence of the clothiers in the *Gloucester Journal*, and to denials on oath by clothiers and their favoured employees concerning truck and short-rates.)

> . . . but then remember, it is by purchases of your filthy lucre, and no other. Hence arose such tumults for which we are subject to death . . . Remember this is a truth, that you go perhaps an hundred miles, to merchandise your goods, and have an opportunity to receive your gains; whilst we, poor mechanics, are listening at home to hear good news: but with what sorrows are we filled, when you return, and say with bitter frowns: you cannot afford to give the price you have promised. Then you know that with bitter tears of grief we cry out, *it is hard!* and you answer, *we'll give no more!* So that through compulsion and distress we are compelled to work at your stinted prices, and go home to our families, and eat our morsels so much the smaller.

Beyond his emphasis on Pride, bad company and drunkenness, Beazer laid blame firmly at the door of the clothiers. His confession tells us something about the attitudes of the weavers to their trade, and something about where they saw themselves in the social hierarchy. Egalitarian levelling was probably not a significant issue in their minds. They aimed (as had Beazer) to rise to become an independent householder, and it may be that the traditional goal of a self-sufficient yeoman-freehold (or ownership of a few fields) began to reappear as a realistic goal for successful master-craftsmen during the 'ups' of trade. The 'downs' shattered such dreams, which may explain why some men like Beazer turned to drink for consolation and then fell back even from the modestly successful position that they had managed to attain. Land was still the dream. It endowed status, but above all it enhanced the independence of the household by providing food to feed its members when market prices were high – a circumstance which sometimes (as in the second phase of this season of riots) coincided with trade recession and industrial disputes. Weavers were proud of their trade and its traditions of independence, but the goal was always to gain possession of a little land, still the most important source of independency.

From the point of view of the landed classes and the gentry, and also of the weavers, 'filthy lucre' was a means by which men of inherently low status, buyers of other men's labour and sellers of their produce like the clothiers, were able to adopt the style, power and sometimes even the social substance of gentility. Henry Coulthurst's pretentions, for example, are revealed in the 'Mr' he always appended to his name. In gentry minds this still meant the lowest rank of the gentry, below an esquire. It was unbearable to Tories that men like the clothiers exercised enormous *de facto* power over veritable armies of manufacturing workers. Worse still, their power increased when markets were down and people were clamouring for enough work to subsist on. Clothiers, for whom land was at best a sideline, paid much less to the poor rates than did the yeomanry and gentry, who rightly believed that they had to subsidise the wealth and pretentions of the clothiers during trade slumps. The weavers hated the clothiers for different reasons. In theory at least, the humblest apprentice could aspire to the upper reaches of his trade; by assiduous application he could become a moderately respectable – but not a gentle – man. This was the force of John Beazer's story. Recession and reduced wages (or the hated truck) challenged the myth and substance of social mobility of this sort, undermining the clothworker's self-regard, his role, or aspired-to role, as father, husband and master, as a respectable member of his community.[60] Among the chronically underemployed it caused real physical deprivation. Alcohol was the available comforter.

The tendency of periodic recession to impoverish their workers suited the employers admirably, and not only for economic reasons. They eyed the social gulf between themselves and the gentry jealously. It was as much in their interest to widen the social distance which separated them from the craftworking households as it was to bridge the theoretically wider gap which yawned above them in the ranking system as a whole. Families already established as gentry naturally wished to maintain the exclusiveness of their class. Clothiers should remain subordinate, however wealthy they were. The appointment of clothiers to the Bench, and the long reign of Walpole, challenged the old dependency system based on land, premised on intense suspicion of trade and any fortunes made in it. The gentry kept up a barrage of social insult and contempt, and resisted no temptation to slight the group from which most of the challenges to their social exclusiveness came. Trade was no training for a gentleman. Special social refinement and sensibility were required in human relations and the exercise of authority. Trade might be vital to the well-being of the nation but the thick-skinned toughness it bred was disastrous in a governor. Such views found an unpredictable ally in the deferential manufacturing worker. The worker respected the charisma of gentility and the state structure (since he could not expect to attain either), but he had no intention of honouring his employer, a capitalist middle-man; deference was due only to a 'natural' superior (usually the member of a family which had made money in trade enough generations ago for people to have forgotten the origins of his gentility). The untiling of Mr Coulthurst's roof reflected the weavers' desire to demolish his pretentions. The destruction of his house projected their belief that hard times should be shared out fairly among all members of the trade.

Beazer's confession is probably an amalgam of authentic biography, social stereotype, Tory propaganda, glossed by a journalistic hand. Implied in what was written under his name was the Tory ideal of a craftsman: deferential to established authority, stoic in the face of injustice, trusting in his social betters, ambitious in spiritual terms but accepting of whatever station in life God and the vagaries of secular trends might dictate. The stereotype almost certainly existed inside Beazer's head, and inside those of his fellow workers, whose hatred was reserved for the capitalists who oppressed them, the clothiers.

The voice of the weavers, represented by the hanged men's confessions, was no more than a passing whisper in a media debate that was dominated by two spokesmen for the Land and Trade parties. Their contribution dominated the *Journal* from December to April, and expressed intense hostility between the masters of industry and trade and the landed elite.

From 19 December 1738 to 10 April 1739 more than a third of the *Gloucester Journal*'s columns were occupied by the debate which these events gave rise to. A total of more than 40,000 words were written by several different hands, but the chief antagonists were Thomas Andrews, who wrote as 'Old Commonsense', and William Temple, a Trowbridge clothier, who wrote as 'Philolethes'. Andrews lived in the village of Seend, near Trowbridge, and 'was a stern moralist who paid high poor rates and, perhaps in consequence, was alive to any signs of extravagance among working people; but he rightly placed the causes of their misery not primarily on their tippling habits but on the unfair practices of the clothiers'.[61] Everything Temple wrote, on the other hand, supported Josiah Tucker's contention that in the West of England cloth industry 'the master is placed so high above the condition of the journeyman, both their conditions approach much nearer to that of a planter and slave in our American colonies than might be expected in such a country as England' – and that he expected matters to stay that way.[62]

The first salvo was fired on 19 December, when Andrews' 'Essay on Riots' occupied the whole of the front page. Aware that public opinion was only too ready to see them in a sinister light, the clothiers submitted their own account of the events at Melksham to the following edition, which came out on Boxing Day. On 9 January Andrews once again occupied page one with a long list of 'certain measures proper . . . for the revival of trade, and the effectual relief of the poor manufacturers of England', adding emphasis to his original position that the roots of plebeian rioting lay, firstly, with the fiscal policy of the Walpole regime, and, secondly, with the arrogant and selfish attitudes of the clothiers.

Andrews was a paternalist. 'It is the chief Business of a Government', he wrote, 'to convince the People, that it seeks their *Happiness* in, and above, all Things, because the *Good of the People* is the great End, for which all Government is established.'[63]

A riotous spirit . . . is generally owing to one or more of the following causes: Carelessness in those at the helm, of the true interests of subjects; – negligence in the magistrates in executing the laws; – oppression of the poor by the rich, or those in power; – or, lastly, to a spirit of licentiousness and immorality diffused among the common people.

Andrews did not believe that 'subjects', 'the common people' could be held responsible for their bad habits. Their 'licentiousness and immorality' were symptoms of bad government by trade masters and rulers. Which was the greater evil, to receive starvation wages, or for a clothier 'to have his house, buildings, or necessaries of trade destroyed by a riotous mob'? 'Badness of trade' was bound to be a problem from time to time, but 'the Progress of a Spirit that, wherever it hath predominated, hath always proved destructive of *National Happiness, Liberty* and *Good Government'* had led to 'mutual oppression and mutual destruction' in the industrial communities, class struggle between clothier merchant/industrialists and the households that depended on them for subsistence.

The greatest responsibility lay with 'those at the helm' of government. It was from them that 'the Spirit' which explained all contemporary evils sprang. The government had a direct interest in the encouragement of vice. In order to support 'P[lacemen] and P[ensioners]' public revenue was raised on malt, wine, ale and spirits. The lust for oil to grease the wheels of patronage spread corruption down through the ranks of the social order. 'I was at a *Sessions* held [at] a trading town in *Wilts*, for licensing *Ale-Houses*,' wrote Andrews to illustrate his point. 'One of the Clerks told me a few Days after, with an *Air of Gladness*, that his share of the *Fees* came to between *Three and Four Pounds*.' 'Carelessness in those at the helm' led to a *'supine neglect of Duty*, too! too! apparent in many *Magistrates*, who seem to have little sense of the Concatenation of *vicious habits* and *unruly Actions* with each other.' The proliferation of *'Tippling-Houses, Tipplers, Common-Swearers, Sabbath-breakers, Vagrants &c.'* flowed inexorably from the *'large fees* for Warrants, Licenses, Mittimus's, Orders &c.' which flowed into the pockets of petty clerks, magistrates, all to serve the common end of keeping a corrupt regime in power through the exercise of patronage.[64] 'Thus hath the *Spirit of Rioting* been nursed up in this Nation,' he concluded. 'I pray God, it may not be the Forerunner of *Insurrections* and *Slavery*.'

In addition to 'the hardships which the poor groan under from the *Excises* on the Necessaries of Life and Trade, such as Malt, Beer, Soap, Candles, Leather, Salt, Oil &c.', Andrews pointed to 'another thing which exceedingly *hurts* our Poor'. This was

> The great numbers of People who *live* upon them, and suck their maintenance out of their Labour; I mean, our innumerable *Alehouse keepers, Bakers*, and *petty shop-keepers;* tis plain, these People live, in general, much better than our *poor Manufacturers* do, out of whose earnings the greatest part of their subsistence arises.

'Our *Rivals* in *France* and other Countries', he believed, arranged things more humanely. 'The Magistrates of their great *Trading Towns* make it their business to buy in corn, and other *Necessaries* . . . at the cheapest markets, which they put in a *Store-House*, and deal out again to the *poor Manufacturers* in small quantities, as they want em, at the *Prime Cost*.' In England, already (in the manufacturing districts and the towns) a nation of shopkeepers, the manufacturing classes had to deal out 'the fruits of their labour . . . to a set of *petty Oppressors* who make them pay a good deal more for Things, than they are worth'. This was to become a familiar theme in the pages of the *Gloucester Journal* in the next three decades: the moral economy. It is not clear, however, that the manufacturers would have wanted it this way, except during subsistence crises.

Andrews even went so far as to claim that riots could be a good thing, if understood as symptoms of general corruption, and thus as a stimulus to reform. They 'may be a means of convincing [the people] of the Love which a Government bears to them; and tho' an evil in itself, have the happy effect of *endearing* Governours and Subjects to each other'. Andrews captured the essence of Tory ideology in his follow-up article on 9 January, when he recommended that the Sumptuary Laws be revitalised. It was indeed *old* commonsense to suggest that the Principle of Subordination be represented by a society in uniform, but it summed up the view of the country Tories that wealth and social responsibility could not be assumed to go hand-in-hand. The masters of trade were clear examples of illegitimate and irresponsible use of power. The recent rash of rioting in the West Country industrial districts provided an opportunity for the landed masters to leap at the throats of commerce, the traffickers in commodities and power.

Trade had teeth enough to defend itself – and take the fight to the enemy. On 7 February William Temple published an advertisement in the *Gloucester Journal* promising a reward of a guinea to any clothworker who could provide evidence of malpractice, i.e. truck or short-payments, by any clothier. He also promised to provide work for such persons, should they be laid off for informing against a master, 'and if good *Workmen*, shall be continu'd with a Preference' in his employ for as long as they wished. On 27 February the front page of the *Journal* was occupied by his epic defence of the clothiers. This defence was to occupy the front page of the next four editions, concluding on 3 April, and continuing throughout the trial of the men accused of rioting and damaging Henry Coulthurst's property.

Temple's reply took the form of a 'Letter to a Member of Parliament'. He began gently, thanking his patron for excepting him, personally, from the corruption perceived in the general body of clothiers. He noted the Member's argument that 'the *Histories* of almost all nations . . . very plainly show'd that the *galling Yoke* of Oppression, was the principal cause of Riots, Tumults, Insurrections, and Revolutions in States and Communities'. He understood the classical origins of such arguments. But he was 'heartily sorry to find so judicious a *Senator*' as him to be so mistaken in his analysis. It was 'the Duty of every honest Man . . . to endeavour to remove the Prejudices of Mankind, purge off their errors, and diffuse Truth'. His duty in this case was to 'oppose the Torrent of Injustice and Defamation', to 'clear the Clouds of *Dullness* and *Impertinence*, which the Author of the *Essay on Riots* ha[d] thrown around . . . *Truth*.' Seeing 'the Press spew out such *Incentives* to Tumult and Confusion', he had no choice but to take up his pen.[65]

Andrews was beneath contempt. 'Who is the most worthy animal,' Temple asked, 'an *Hyppolytus* who hazards his neck after a *fox* all his life, or a *clothier* who employs and surveys the work of thousands?' He had two main themes. The first was his defence of the clothiers. Against Andrews' generalisations, he observed that 'there never was a Body of Men of any sort in the World, who all deserved the Epithets

241

of *Just* and *Honourable*'. There were some corrupt clothiers, as there were some corrupt magistrates, politicians and fox-hunting gentry, but the generality, in his view, were honest men. To show his fairness, he cited the case of a clothier whom he called *Tarquinius Superbus*, who used to 'kick, cuff, beat, and abuse his Servants of every rank and degree'. This apparently was a notorious case, which 'gave birth to the *Opprobrium* which is very often, and very unjustly, cast on the Body of Clothiers now'. In fact the allegation that rich clothiers made corrupt magistrates had been a platitude among workers and landed gentlemen since at least the sixteenth century. In an ironic allusion to Andrews' arguments against the magistracy, Temple pointed out that now 'Tarquinius Superbus' was on the Commission for the Peace, he 'has indulged [the clothworkers] in every Fraud and Insolence towards the Clothiers . . . I presume, by way of recompense for his own base conduct'. Temple's prose bristled with violent, contemptuous images, reflecting the resentment he and others of his class felt of the thanks they were given by the public for the great public services they daily engaged in.

His contempt for 'the cause of the Poor' was deep:

> The cause of the Poor is popular [he wrote], and apt to byass many thinking and judicious persons, who have not much to do with them. The World would have quite a different Opinion of the Manufacturing Populace from what, perhaps, they have, if they were acquainted with their *Insolence, Idleness, Debauchery, Frauds* and *Dishonesty*, so well as the Clothiers.

'In the town of Trowbridge,' he wrote in his second article, 'where the Inhabitants have been computed at about 3,000 men, women and children':

> there are near 2,000 Hogsheads of Strong Beer drank in a year publickly, as appears from the excise-books: Yet we have no Market but for Flesh-meat, Roots and Greens; and are no great Thoroughfare from or to any place. To this we may add, that they say there are near 30 or 40 Gin-Houses, where the Poor rendez-vous and debauch themselves with that *infernal liquor*, in spite of the vigilance of the Excise officers; and they are so sincere and faithful in Support of the Means of their *Debauchery* and *Ruin*, that the Officers can procure no Informations against any person for selling those liquors, though it is constantly done.

It was 'beyond all contradiction . . . that the Poor have such high Wages, as furnish them with the *Means* and instruments of Luxury and Idleness'.

Temple could agree with 'Old Commonsense' about one thing: that 'subordination is necessary in the universe: a variety of states and conditions is as necessary to the harmony of the world, as a variety of notes to harmony in *music*'. But 'when once a contempt of *officers*, and licentiousness in *soldiers* arise in an army, thro' want of strict discipline, mutiny and confusion quickly break forth. When contempt of a *parent* or *master* arises in a family, murmurings and discontent, disorder and *anarchy* quickly appear'. There was little here that a Tory could object to, except perhaps the allusion to Hanoverian musical sensibility; Handel seems to have been objectionable to Tory ears, or at least to country Tory ears.[66] And Temple seemed to prefer military analogies to the universal religious contexts suggested in the Tory account. But the argument had a barb in its tail:

When disregard, contempt, fraud and insolence towards masters, are nourished by *superiors*, who will wonder to see riots, tumults, houses pull'd down, and a licentious *rabble* march off with the plunder, and boast they have done no harm.

The *fox-hunters*, self-styled upholders of the moral order, were in fact encouraging and applauding riots – as indeed Andrews appeared to do in his 'Essay on Riots'. But Temple warned:

The mob has already gotten this maxim: that *Adam left No Will;* they are his sons, and ought to have a share of their father's possessions. And nothing was more common in their mouths than, *if they wanted, d–n it, they would take it where they could find it.*

Watch out, Temple warned, insubordination, insurrection and full-scale rebellion were milestones along the same track.

Andrews' complaints about 'truck', too, were no more than hypocrisy:

I would beg leave to ask . . . ,whether some of the [farmers and gentlemen] have never paid their servants in truck? Whether wheat, cheese, bacon, beef and mutton were never sold by any of them to their servants at a market price: and whether they thought they injured their servants by such a sale. *It is a common thing for some persons to bellow out against offences of their neighbours whilst they are guilty of the same criminal conduct.*

Which was perfectly true. Farmers did pay in 'truck'. But no one would have called it that in the farming community, because it was traditional. Temple thought criticisms of this sort were no more than pretexts for the Tories to trot out their (preferably biblical) cliches about the 'oppression of hired servants', express their cosmic moralisms, litter their talk with the odd rumour about an oppressive clothier, or a clothier-magistrate's most recent social *gaffe*, and congratulate themselves for their fine sensibility and wonderful paternalism. Temple had news for the farming community. Your average agricultural labourer was no doubt a fine specimen. But *'the poor in the Manufacturing Countries will never work any more time in general, than is necessary just to live, and support their weekly debauches'*. At least truck might stop them getting drunk. Pay the worker a decent wage, and 'he shall be celebrating the orgies of Bacchus instead of pursuing the *arts of Minerva* . . . If the manufacturer can acquire in two days, by high wages, enough to keep him drunk the other five, you may find him rendezvousing in a tippling-house, or, in summer-time, carousing under a hedge'.

Nor did Temple think that 'badness of trade' had much to do with this thirst for licentiousness. 'In a Plenty, or in a Scarcity; in a Brisk or Dead time of Trade, you find the Poor always poor, especially in the manufacturing towns. So that by reducing wages, you would not only make the poor more laborious, more diligent, more virtuous, and not at all lessen the consumption of provisions and necessaries.' He underlined this point, his major theme. 'The reduction of wages in the woollen manufactures would be a national blessing and advantage, and no real injury to the poor'. *'The clothiers may and ought to keep down the Price of Labour,'* he repeated in his final article.

Andrews had alleged that the clothiers entered into combinations to reduce the wages of the poor manufacturers. Maybe so, Temple wrote, but not in his experience. 'The clothiers of Trowbridge generally leave the reparation they think in justice due to them to the servant's own conscience, or they pay him his full wages and dismiss him,' he wrote. Accept the price offered or be laid off. He admitted that truck (which he personally disliked) and short-payments were routine responses to 'deadness of trade', but poured scorn on the idea that this implied 'combinations . . . to lower the price of weaving, spinning &c.'. It was a matter of common sense. What was a clothier to do, conjure orders from the air? 'The French, the Dutch, the Flemings, the Irish work cheaper than us,' he wrote.

> The chinese have the most extended manufactures in the world; and their manufacturers push themselves into all countries, meerly by their cheapness. The price of labour there is exceedingly low, and the common people very miserable . . . their drivers, like our carters, push them on 'til the poor exhausted creatures drop down and die under the labour of it.

But he was a humane man. He did not believe such measures 'worthy of imitation'; in fact he 'abhorred them':

We are under no necessity of reducing the price of labour in this manner; but we must have *some* regard to the prices given by our neighbouring countries, or they will run away with our foreign trade, and reduce in time the poor manufacturers of this nation to the utmost poverty and misery by robbing them of all their employments.

Temple drew attention to the ingratitude of the manufacturing poor. 'If [they] flock to the [clothing] towns, what is it for?' His answer: 'because they know they can serve themselves by it':

It is trade that has made the common people rich, just as it is pride that has made the gentry poor. In the districts and towns where the woollen manufacture is carried on, proper employment is found for every sort and size of people. The *blind*, the lame, the *impotent* and *aged*, the children find some work adapted to them. Blind persons card, spool or wind quills; the lame do the same, or spin and scribble. Now what an advantage it is to be born under the influence of a *clothier*, who, like the *sun*, scatters life and the supports to it, to everyone around him. What a happiness it is to the poor, to be planted in such a situation.

The weavers warmed by these 'suns' were 'in general . . . the most feeble, weak and impotent of all the manufacturers'. If they would but work even moderately regularly they could earn more than enough in the good times to enable them to live comfortably in the lean. 'I would be understood to speak here,' announced Temple, 'of the *industrious* poor, not the *idle* and *debauched*; not the *drunken punk*, the *tattling gossip*, or the idle, vociferous *fuddle-cap*: such will always be poor, in spite of Providence.' Andrews' wet paternalist rhetoric was no more than 'rant and virulent squint, aimed at the clothiers' and the government. Temple was free of such prejudice. He admired Walpole:

Does not a great man who wastes his spirits, spends his time, and exerts himself for the interest and preservation of his country, deserve reward, as well as the poor man does for his labour? But Old Commonsense never discovers [reveals] his rancour and spite against the present government, but at the same time he betrays his own ignorance and stupidity.

The season of riots had given voice, once more, to a bitter struggle within the ranks of the wealthy that had been going on since the beginning of large-scale manufacturing for national and international markets. Every boom, be it local or national in scope, generated a small cohort of new men who made their money by purchasing and supplying the raw materials and instruments of production, and by

245

serving as agents of the market. As their wealth and real power grew, they desired not only to be rich but also to have their authority legitimised by initiation into the ranks and positions (the magistracy, Parliament, gentility) of formal authority. At this point their ambitions brought them into conflict with longer-established landed patriarchs who believed that formal authority should be theirs alone. Conflicting ambitions were quickly transmuted into fierce emotions of resentment on both sides, and every snub, every social sneer, every foiled ambition, every failure, fed the dialectic of mutual suspicion and hatred which has simmered and sometimes exploded throughout the history of capitalist England.

The vitriolic rhetoric of Temple's long letter, broadcast to the world through the medium of the Press, signified a new lack of compromise, and a new confidence among the mercantile community, a sense that they represented an *alternative* – 'interest' – to the assumed 'virtue' of the old world. Temple's point of reference, over and again, was *self-interest*. Adam Smith, Thomas Malthus and the Utilitarians, and, more recently, the new Right, were to be among the inheritors of this new moral axiom.

Thomas Andrews caught the violent spirit of the conjuncture with his phrase 'a concatenation of vicious habits'. The episode was exceptional in that it gave loud public voice to the anger of the contending parties, but whatever terms we use to describe them – 'Land', 'Trade' and the 'industrial workers' are as good as any – the parties to the conjuncture were permanent, structural features of English culture, and had been throughout the sixteenth, seventeenth and eighteenth centuries. The newspaper coverage alone made the conjuncture different from any that had preceded it, reifying long-standing structural divisions, reinforcing cultural habits that were already centuries old. The episode should be seen as a symptom of a long-standing disease of the English body corporate, a constitutional psychosis, a tendency for everyday class snobbery to flare into uncontrolled fury.

10

LASTING PREJUDICES
Languages of Social Discrimination

1

LANGUAGES OF SOCIAL DISCRIMINATION

William Temple's contemptuous references to the working classes of
the clothworking districts were extreme public utterances of centuries-
old prejudices. In the verse etched on the memorial to Cirencester's
Parliamentarian hero, the clothier Hodgkinson Paine, in 1643, the
language was that of pious paternalism. Tyndale took for granted that
the servant class should be 'as an ox to its master'. The proverbial
culture of the middle rank of the Vale of Berkeley thought the landless
poor should be seen and not heard. John Smyth saw landless cottagers
as 'slaves in nature though not in lawe'. Corbet's 'vulgar multitudes'
were already 'dangerous classes', but could be put to good use under
the guidance of their prudent superiors, the 'yeomen, clothiers and
the whole middle rank'. As numbers increased, concern intensified.[1]
'Where there are very many poor,' wrote another native of the Vale
of Berkeley, Sir Matthew Hale, 'the rich cannot safely continue as
such.'[2] In 1740 a correspondent wrote in the pages of the *Gloucester
Journal* that 'should the multitudes around us, enraged with hunger,
and despairing subsistence, rise to support existence, too feeble would
then be the civil power, and useful then the military only, to put
starving wretches out of their misery'.[3] Compassion was a variable, but
distance and disdain were all-but-universal elements in the ideology of
the middle rank with respect to the landless labouring classes. Only
among the Quakers, resolute believers in 'perfectibility', was this
theme muted. There is no suggestion in what we know of John Roberts
that he looked down on anyone as naturally or inherently inferior to
himself. Another Cirencester Quaker, John Bellers, wrote disapprov-
ingly in 1699 that 'the masters and their workmen are, unhappily, in
a perpetual war with each other'.[4] Marx did not invent the language
of class struggle.

Languages, ideologies and mentalities of social discrimination cover a wide range of abiding human prejudices: class, gender, race, ethnicity, colour, occupation, wealth are just some. They are concerned, not with simple discrimination between different things, but with ranking people in terms of 'better' and 'worse', 'higher' and 'lower', 'pure' and 'impure'. One important task of scholarship in the humanities and social sciences is to scrutinise lasting prejudices like these.[5]

Keith Wrightson's recent work on languages of class in early modern England argues that 'representations of social order' were in flux, in response to 'the social dynamism of the sixteenth and seventeenth centuries'.[6] 'Older paradigms persisted,' he writes, 'albeit in modified form.' But older paradigms 'failed to provide an adequate account of contemporary reality, or to express the shifting alignments of a society undergoing profound, if gradual, social, economic and political change'. Wrightson's conclusions are worth quoting at length:

> The language of 'sorts' filled that gap . . . it could capture the mutability of social alignments and the plasticity of social identities. It could lump together the distinguishable estates and degrees of inherited social theory into broad groupings which prefigured the social classes of the nineteenth century. It could imply alternative conceptions of the fundamental nature of social differentiation, express conflicts of interest, and edge perceptive contemporaries along the path towards a thoroughgoing reappraisal of the structures of society, the basis of social inequality, and the dynamics of social process. In all these ways it has much to teach about the immediate antecedents of the concept of the social class in its English form and about the deep roots of England's ambiguous class identities.[7]

Wrightson's work on 'sorts of people' reopens debate on the subject of class identity and social discrimination in early modern England.

The language of 'sorts' was not the only language of social discrimination in sixteenth-, seventeenth- and eighteenth-century England. Keith Thomas describes another such 'language'. 'In Tudor and Stuart England,' he writes, 'the long-established view was that the world had been created for man's sake and that other species were meant to be subordinate to his wishes and needs.'[8] He refers, in a section on 'Inferior Humans', to an 'abiding urge to distinguish the human from the animal [which] also had important consequences for relations between men. If the essence of humanity was defined as consisting in some specific quality, any member of the species who did not display that quality, was subhuman, semi-animal'.[9] Shakespeare alluded to the prejudice in *Coriolanus*, where Menenius, the two-faced patrician politician, refers to populist tribunes as 'herdsmen to the *beastly* plebians'.[10]

Systems of social discrimination vary from culture to culture, and even within cultures as complex and variable as early modern England. The concept of vertical hierarchy is one of the commonest of the metaphors and myths that have guided social thought across the ages. Its application to humanity, and to relationships between humanity and 'lower' forms of life, probably originates with the adoption of sky-gods. Earthly life, in sky-god myths, is 'low', and the supernatural spirits in heaven are, it follows, 'high'. People who claim to be, or are recognised as, in some way closer to God, or the gods, are bound to be 'high', at least in relation to other beings not so close to the deities. The elevation of sky-gods from the vast constellation of supernatural spirits recognised by general animists involves the elevation of vertical hierarchy as a way of discriminating between people. The stories people heard about the gods created landscapes of the mind. The power of the stories (and story-tellers) was such that imaginary landscapes slipped unnoticed into thought about society, relations with other people. In reality, no one is any higher or lower, closer to or further away from the gods, than anyone else.

All attempts to represent social order are subject to the criticism that they are not social reality itself. Marx's notoriously incomplete discussion of social class stumbled on this boulder. Even 'in England, [where] modern society [was] indisputably most highly and classically developed . . . the stratification of classes [did] not appear in its pure form'. 'Intermediate strata even here obliterate lines of demarcation everywhere.'[11] Even the most carefully formulated languages and ideologies of social discrimination are riddled with ambiguities and obscurities. Languages and systems of social discrimination demand an agnostic approach. My aim in this final chapter is to do no more than highlight a theme and a field of study (social prejudice, languages and ideologies of social discrimination), and suggest some more elements that should be taken into consideration as we try to formulate a lucid account of 'England's ambiguous class identities'. A comprehensive account of the subject does not exist.

The way people interpret, their characteristic ways of seeing, are at least in part a function of where they are located in the social hierarchy. The world-views of John Aubrey and John Smyth of Nibley illustrate a phenomenon of the late sixteenth and seventeenth centuries also stressed by Wrightson: the 'detachment' of the 'better sorts' from the culture and community of their social inferiors.[12] By the middle of the seventeenth century this detachment was developing into intellectual perspectives which systematically assimilated 'social distance' into their mode of analysis. These perspectives, above all 'Political Arithmetic', one of Aubrey's preoccupations, and a distinctive feature of Smyth's bureaucratic procedures as Steward to the Hundred of Berke-

ley, have since become entrenched characteristics of modern administrative and intellectual practices.

I shall identify lasting prejudices which will have to be included in
any satisfactory account of English modes of social discrimination.
These prejudices are embodied in the thought of three men: John
Aubrey, John Smyth of Nibley and William Petty. Readers can decide
for themselves if the opinions and theories they express were and are
exceptional, or if, as I contend, they are emblematic of very widely
held social and cultural prejudices.

2

JOHN AUBREY AND THE ABORIGINES

The word 'aborigines' was first used to mean 'the original inhabitants
of a country' in the sixteenth century, when it was just as commonly
applied to English as foreign natives. Later it came to mean 'the natives
found in possession of a country by Europeans who have gone thither
as colonists', and later still the indigenous peoples of Australia.[13] John
Aubrey used it for the 'indigenae . . . of North Wiltshire, and the Vale
of Gloucestershire' in the period just after the civil wars.[14] Aubrey,
the eccentric and scholarly author of *Brief Lives*, a gossipy catalogue
of the pantheon of Restoration England, grew up in that part of
England, yet did not consider himself to be an 'aborigine or indigenae'.
He traced his descent 'from a certain Saunders *de Sancto Alberico* or *de
Alba Ripa* . . . a companion of William the Bastard, said to have been
brother to the Count of Boulogne and Earl Master of France'.[15] The
Aubreys migrated to Wiltshire only in the time of his grandparents,
and were originally from genteel Welsh stock. It was his 'blue blood',
descent from Norman–Angevin stock, that distinguished Aubrey from
the 'aborigines' of his adopted *countrey*. In his own mind he was
descended from a superior race, one of those invading groups that
had brought civilisation, something incompatible with aboriginal
ancestry, to England.

Aubrey had a distinctive view of English aborigines: the answer lay
in the soil. The culture of aborigines, he believed, was a variable of
soil and topography. 'Civilisation', on the other hand, implied physical
detachment from the primeval landscape. His sense of personal identity involved the assumption that he belonged to an inherently superior
caste, born to rule and shape the future. His literary work – virtually
a *genre* of its own – is usually regarded as empirical to the point of
theoretical incoherence, fragmentary and highly idiosyncratic. In fact
it embodied a tenacious myth of racial superiority. His *Brief Lives* have
remained in print because the pantheon they describe contains men

who are still regarded as founding fathers of modern England. If there was a bible of modern English civilisation, Aubrey's writings would form one of its canonical texts, all the more powerful for the apparent eccentricities of their author. For, as generations of readers have found, Aubrey's writings have a profoundly seductive quality: they are 'light', casually readable; they give pleasure as they inform. Because of his eccentricities it is possible to read Aubrey without the suspicion that a 'serious' message is being conveyed.

Aubrey spent his adult life in the social networks which gave birth to modern scholarship and science. One of his closest friends was William Petty, the originator of a discipline called 'Political Arithmetic'. The aim of this discipline was to facilitate social engineering by means of models based on quantitative social data. It is perhaps unlikely, in view of his humble origins, or even on purely factual grounds, that Petty would have been convinced by Aubrey's simplistic division of the English population into two races. However, all efforts to quantify people involve abstraction, emphasis on certain aspects, even definitions, of the subject. In the hands of administrators, politicians and social scientists who, on the whole, tend to think, like Aubrey, that certain types of people are inherently inferior to others, the spurious objectivity of social statistics can be an instrument of hidden prejudice. They create an illusion of clinical detachment.

The processes of intellectual and social detachment, of greater social distance between the middle and labouring classes, were facilitated by the assimilation of vernacular literacy as a tool of social analysis and description. John Smyth's compulsive habit of recording everything he regarded as of even minor importance in the life of the Hundred of Berkeley testifies to the impact of literacy and numeracy. I have focused in this book on Smyth's words rather than his numbers, but at least a third of his voluminous manuscript collection consists of lists and social calculations. The sorts of things Smyth and his clerks, and parish and other local officials everywhere wrote down regularly as a matter of routine were the sorts of things the Political Arithmeticians used to make their more general statistical calculations in the second half of the seventeenth century. Without the former, the latter would not have had material to work on. There was a class aspect to the evolution of a literacy-based national culture, in the sense that it tended to be acquired first by the upper and middle ranks of society, and only much more slowly by the lower ranks.

3

NUMBERING AND CLASSIFYING: AUBREY AND THE POLITICAL ARITHMETICIANS

Aubrey was present at the birth of a most important phase in the development of the information culture associated with the modern state. His biographer alludes to this when he refers to his subject as part of 'the growing movement to co-ordinate information of all kinds', of which the founding of the Royal Society in 1662 is symbolic. Aubrey was made a Fellow of the Society in 1663.[16] The birth of empirical science and statistics was not just about *coordinating* information, but about *creating* it. 'Political Arithmetic', pioneered by friends of Aubrey like the proto-economist William Petty, John Graunt and Gregory King, was about reducing the land and population to numerical formulae in order to make rational management decisions about its organisation and administration.[17]

In a list of his fourteen closest 'amici', Aubrey described Petty (the author, in 1676, of a book entitled *Political Arithmetic*) as his 'singular friend'.[18] Aubrey's biographer, Anthony Powell, observes of Petty that 'this great man cannot, indeed, be absolved from being considered the progenitor of the multitudinous and equivocal tribe of statisticians . . . Petty was perhaps the first person in England to appreciate the value of 'number, weight, and measure' where 'ratiocination' was concerned'.[19] Aubrey and his friends redefined knowledge for clearly stated instrumentalist purposes. 'Instead of using only comparative and superlative words, and intellectual arguments,' wrote Petty:

I have taken the course (as a specimen of Political Arithmetic I have long aimed at) to express myself in Terms of *Number, Weight*, or *Measure*; to use only arguments of Sense, and to consider only such causes, as have visible Foundations in Nature; leaving those that depend upon the mutable Minds, Opinions, Appetites and Passions of Particular Men, to the Consideration of others.[20]

In the decades following the civil wars, modes of analysis which excluded 'the mutable Minds, Opinions, Appetites and Passions of Particular Men' had an understandable attraction. Whether anything was left of 'particular men' once those things were excluded from the terms of analysis was another matter, as the subsequent history of Ireland (of which Petty performed a 'political anatomy' in the 1650s) has shown.[21]

Aubrey was the bard of this epic moment in the history of modern civilisation, the birth of all the dismal sciences of social quantification. His 'brief lives' include portraits of its most important figures, and

one of his incompleted projects was to be a series on English mathema-
ticians. Overall, the purposes of the movement were to make the
world more *manageable,* by reducing its phenomena to systematically
classified representations. These representations stressed what their
creators regarded as the most significant aspects of the phenomena.
King, for example, used data produced by tax-collectors to categorise
the population of England by income. Such was the blindness induced
by his way of analysing social reality, that he defined a great proportion of the English working population as 'reducing the wealth of
the kingdom'.[22]

Aubrey and his friends were pioneers in the reduction of the world
to highly abstract linguistic and numerical signs, making it possible to
judge people in their absence, and above all in isolation from their
specific locations and circumstances. A minor aspect of this movement
is to be found in the contemporary habit of asking people what they
do for a living, i.e. what their occupation is. The technique was
invented by thirteenth- and fourteenth-century tax-collectors and
government officials. Today it is second nature. In between is the
history of capitalism and the nation-state.

Aubrey belongs to an important phase in the 'languaging' and 'num-
bering', the re-classifying, of people and their communities. He was
not *only* its 'bard'. He was a penurious gentleman, and spent most of
his adult life travelling and concealing his whereabouts from creditors.
The 'brief lives' represent only the surface monuments of his obsession
to reduce the painful transience of his perambulatory experience to
the apparent solidity and certainty of the written word. In this he was
a living symbol of the reasons for the information revolution of which
he was a part. For in the seventeenth century, as never before, movement and transcience were becoming dominant tendencies everywhere. In what was becoming a highly migrant and vagrant, intensely
transient society, the most desperate need was to discover fixed cer-
tainties. Aubrey was (and described himself as) an 'Antiquary', locating himself with reference to the historical landscape through which
he *moved.*

Aubrey's task, by temperament and circumstances, was to record,
preserve and coordinate information about the English past. In the
sixteenth and seventeenth centuries this meant describing monuments
and memorials, and gave great prominence to the genealogies of resident gentry and nobility. The 'aborigines, or indiginae' were mentioned, if at all, as adjuncts of soil and topography. They were seen
not as makers, only as instruments of (or inhibitors of) civilisation.
Aubrey concentrated on the achievements of *invading* civilisations,
including his own. He took it for granted that the aborigines had not

produced anything worth recording except a few quaint and silly customs and superstitions.

Six centuries after the Norman Conquest, after a revolution which many historians have maintained ended feudalism, Aubrey's consciousness took off from the assumption that he was a hereditary member of a super-civilised caste or race, established six centuries earlier by the Norman Conquest. If we want to understand what this meant, we could do worse than compare it with the British conquest of Australia in 1788, and the movements of the Australian Aboriginals two centuries later.[23]

4

ABORIGINES ECOLOGICALLY DETERMINED

'According to the several sorts of earth in England, (and so all the world over)', wrote Aubrey, 'the indiginae are respectively witty or dull, good or bad.' This derivation of native characteristics from soil and topography recurs in other writers on the region, from John Smyth of Nibley in the generation of Aubrey's parents, to Richard Jefferies in the late nineteenth century.[24] Intelligence and stupidity, virtue and vice, were correlatives of landscape. So too was language. 'In North Wiltshire and the vale of Gloucestershire (a dirty claey country) they speak (I mean the *Indiginae* or Aborigines only) drawning.'[25] They spoke the same language as he did, but 'drawning'. The dialect, idioms and proverbs recorded in 1639 by John Smyth of Nibley give us an idea of what Aubrey had in mind, a broader and more drawn out version of the local accent today. They counted 'wone, twa, three, voure, vive', godparents were said to be 'song'd to a childe', mothers called 'Gyn y com y and tyff y the windowes', and children complained 'Moder, gyn will not y washen the dishen'.[26] For someone like Aubrey, such an accent might at times have approached the level of exclusion achieved today by, say, Liverpool Scouse or deep Cornish. For him this meant they lacked precise, clipped locution.

'Drawning' suggests a way of speaking that was only to be expected of the children of generations dragging their feet through their 'dirty, claey countrey'. The reference suggests that in the seventeenth century dialect and accent were already forming codes which identified the class or caste of their users. Temperament also derived from the soil. 'They are phlegmatiq,' he wrote, 'skins pale and livid; slow, and dull, heavy of spirit'.[27] This was also connected with the kind of work they did, rather grudgingly in his opinion. 'Here about is but little tillage, or hard labour, they only milk the cowes and make cheese,' he wrote of the natives of North Wiltshire and the Vale of Berkeley. Land and work having been established in his chain of logic, he took the next step: diet. 'They feed chiefly on milk meates, which cooles their brains too much, and hurts their inventions.' They were none too bright, and unimaginative. Their 'circumstances make them melancholy, contemplative, and malicious: by consequence whereof more lawsuits come out of North Wilts, at least double the southern parts'.

Landscape predisposed its aborigines to certain religious persuasions. 'And by the same reason [i.e. the soil of the country]', he wrote, 'they are generally more apt to be fanatiques: In Malmesbury hundred, &c. – wet claey parts: here have ever been reputed witches.' By 'fanatiques' Aubrey meant Quakers and sectaries, who were represented in every town and village in the region – not in large numbers, but forming a clearly understood alternative to the national Church, an alternative congregation. He did not see them primarily as children of the Protestant Reformation. Rather, he identified them with pagan practices – 'witches'. He spent many days measuring and draughting what he regarded as the remains of a Druid temple at Avebury, and gave more thought than usual to the pre-Christian religion of the aborigines. The link he proposed between pagan 'witches' and Quakers and 'fanatiques' was not made thoughtlessly.[28]

As the Earth shaped their work, diet, intellect, imagination and religious sensibility, so it shaped their physiognomy. 'Their persons are generally plump and foggy: gallipot eies, and some black: but they are generally handsome enough.' He preferred the qualities of the aborigines 'on the Downes . . . where 'tis all upon tillage, or Shepherds: and labour hard, their bodies strong: being weary after their hard labour, they have not leisure to reade, and contemplate of religion, but goe to bed to theire rest, to rise betimes the next morning to their labour.' There was no substitute for hard work. He agreed with what his close friend, the pioneer demographer and statistician John Graunt, had said to him. 'I remember (upon the forsayed reason) that Capt. John Graunt did say, it was observed there were no Anchor Smyths fanatiqs: for it is a mighty laborious trade: and they must drinke strong drinke to keep up their spirits: so they never trouble their heads with curious notions of religion.' Religious affinity too was a function of soil and topography. 'Surely,' he wrote, 'this tract of land inclines people to zeale.'

Aubrey took for granted that closeness to the land inhibited intellect and culture. He explained physical and cultural appearances in terms of landform and soil, and the type of production that it tended to impose on its inhabitants. English aborigines, in his view, were descended from an amalgam of pre-Roman Celts and (later) Saxons, and 'received the knowledge of husbandrie from the Romans'. It was axiomatic that aboriginal cultures were passive, shaped by but not shaping the landscape they inhabited. The shaping function – 'civilis-ation' – belonged to superior invading peoples.

English aborigines had learned nothing that was not introduced to them by superior invading civilisations: 'they were so far from know-ing Arts that they could not build wall with stone'; 'they lived slut-tishly in poor houses'; 'their very kings were but a sort of Farmers'. Between the Romans and the Normans, he wrote, 'there was a mist of ignorance for six hundred years'. Even the representatives of 'the Christian Religion . . . were ignorant enough in those days'. Only with the arrival of his own ancestors did things begin to improve; 'the Normans then came and taught them civility and building: which, though it was Gothique as also their Policy (*Feudalis Lex*) yet they were magnificent'.[29]

'Civility', for Aubrey, was exclusively 'building' on a 'magnificent' scale. Those great 'gothique' churches and cathedrals were signs on the landscape, fingers of 'civility' pointing towards the sky, directing the mind away from lower forms of life. He took for granted that there was a racial chasm between himself and his ancestors and '*indigenae* or aborigines' such as those of his own native localities. They knew nothing worth knowing that had not been taught them by a superior race. They were trapped in the world of the senses, irredeemably ignorant, conditioned in the simplest and most direct ways by their physical environment. The people with whom he identified, and of whom he was an intellectual (Roman) and genetic (Norman) heir, were *shapers* of the world. The subject *indigenae*, by contrast, were simply and directly shaped by it. The distinction between 'high' and 'low', culturally speaking, was for him a fundamentally racial distinction.

Although he condemned certain types of superstition, such as was evident to him in the sectarians (mainly Baptists and Quakers) who were quite liberally sprinkled among the aborigines of his 'dirty, claey' native districts, other types of superstition were desirable. His own pieties were liberal and latitudinarian. After the Restoration he thought about converting to Catholicism. This had nothing to do with his own, private, religious convictions. It was a matter of indifference to him which particular brand of Christianity the English ruling class adhered to, as long as they all agreed to adhere to the same one. Nothing came of it because the English ruling class paused in its recurring flirtation with Rome because it aroused strong opposition from the lower classes and political opportunists who played upon their preju-dices.

In 1673 Aubrey anxiously assured his friend Anthony Wood, whom he suspected of having gone over to Rome, that he 'was no enemie to them', and thought 'a little superstition is a good ingredient in Government'.[30] This did not mean that he thought the Roman heritage was all supersitition, only its ceremonial trappings. It was not hypocrisy. He believed there was a fundamental, genetic, racial divide between the natural rulers and the subjects of the kingdom of England. Religious formalities were a matter of indifference to him. What mattered was that the hereditary ruling class, i.e. the heirs of Rome via the Gallic connection of 1066 (no matter that William the Bastard was a descendant of Vikings), set a good example and presented a united front. Not so long ago a few 'fanatiques' captured and executed the chief representative of the Roman–Norman Yoke in England, Charles Stuart the Elder.

'Aborigines or indigenes', in this account, were 'inferior humans'. The ideas embodied in the myth, and the language used to express it, have affected the ten generations of humanity that separate him from us with an intensity that would have been unimaginable to Aubrey. It is possible to see in Aubrey, and in John Smyth of Nibley too, the beginnings of the perspectives and interests of the modern discipline of Anthropology. The hierarchical ordering of cultures and peoples was an elite prejudice before it was smuggled into Anthropology in the nineteenth century. It is only one ordering principle, one idea among infinite possibilities.

And so it was in seventeenth- and eighteenth-century England, where languages and mentalities of social discrimination were in flux. John Aubrey's naive racialist ethnography was a late expression of an ideology which had its origins in the Norman–Angevin conquests of the eleventh and twelfth centuries. Dividing the English population according to racial categories has shifted in focus during the nationalist era. Leaving aside questions of fact, the dominant assumption after 1660 was to be that, however they might differ among themselves, the English were one nation. In this sense the 'aborigines' won the English Revolution. For all their claims to fine breeding, aristocrats and gentlemen of modern England do not emphasise their foreign ancestry and connections.

The habit of explaining differences of wealth and power, success and failure, in terms of 'genetic' inheritance survives in modern England. It has advocates in the scholarly and scientific communities, though they are a minority. As a mentality the habit is very common in vernacular thought. People 'fail', 'turn to crime', 'fall into poverty', become chronically unemployed, and so on because they are *inherently* inferior, it is said. There is a universal hierarchy dividing people of 'high' and 'low' intelligence, character, initiative and enterprise. It doesn't matter how much is done for the inherently 'low', they'll still make a hash of it. Charity is misplaced. The only thing to do is to make them work as hard as possible. And don't pay them too much, they'll only spend it on drink. These opinions, expressed by William Temple in 1739, are still commonplace in England.

5

SLAVES IN NATURE THOUGH NOT IN LAW

Plain John Smyth of Nibley held a more subtle, historically informed version of Aubrey's master-race ideology. For him, his masters the Fitzhardings, lords Berkeley, perhaps significantly, were descendants of Vikings, trader–warriors as against the refined, chivalric civilisation of feudal mythology. Smyth was a realist. The Berkeleys were one of a very few English aristocratic dynasties with a clear genealogy back to the eleventh century. Knowing the history of the dynasty as he did, he could not entertain any illusions as to their racial or genetic superiority. Careful attention to business had been, and remained, the key to the relative success of the Berkeley dynasty over the centuries. That was Smyth's understanding of the matter. And, in business, the Berkeleys had always depended on the indigenous middle rank, the yeomanry, the masters of the localities.

In his *Lives of the Berkeleys* he traced every detail in the rise and fall of the Fitzhardings, lords Berkeley. The beginnings of the rise of the middle rank went back as far as the reign of the third lord, Thomas I, who 'aliened much of his land in fee' before 1243, loosening feudal relations with the wealthier peasants and laying the foundations of middle-rank aboriginal liberty. Yet at the time it was a sensible business decision. Smyth was less convinced about the acumen of Thomas II, who 'made near 800 gifts in tayl' in the mid-thirteenth century, 'which he thought prudent, fearful of the fall in rents'. The Berkeley demesnes were enclosed before 1289, and devoted to wool production. By the first decade of the fourteenth century the district had a thriving clothmaking industry, providing employment for the landless cottagers who made up at least 30 per cent of the total population of the Vale. The district thrived, and so did the Berkeleys' rent-rolls.

Before the middle rank could achieve pre-eminence in the affairs of the Vale, aristocratic hegemony had to be undermined, and Smyth identified the time and the reason for its decline with precision. 'This antient family . . . was in the dayes of lord Thomas IV (1368–1417) . . . in the highest exaltation that it had before reached unto and enriched with the amplest possessions for support of the honour thereof', he wrote. But

> Henceforth in the lives that follow, it is a kind of misfortune to my labours, that with the life of this lord Thomas ended all that

regularity which for many ages had been observed in the estate
and household affairs of these lords.

With his steward's eye guiding his scholarship in the family muniments, Smyth noted a sudden decline in the 'regularity' of 'the
accounts of their Receivers, Keepers of the Wardrobe, Steward of the
Household, Clark of the Kitchin, Reeves and Baileys of Manors and
Hundreds, and the like accomptants'. The conclusion was inescapable.
'Where noe government or order is preserved, there consumption
follows, if not of all, yet of too great a part of that great man's estate.'[31]
Somehow, in Smyth's view, the lords had lost the loyal, efficient
service of the middle rank.

Later, in the *Description*, written after the *Lives*, Smyth made it clear
that the men of the middle rank who had, prior to the early fifteenth
century, served the interests of the barony so assiduously had not lost
their efficiency. He hints that they lost respect for their lords, and put
their energies more exclusively into the growth of their own wealth,
estates and power. In the fifteenth century, successive lords failed to
keep plundering armies and squabbling retinues away from their
estates in the Vales, in stark contrast to the success of Maurice lord
Berkeley in protecting his tenants in the equally troubled wars of the
1320s. Smyth thought the Hundred had never recovered from the
ravages of the Wars of the Roses. In the 1490s William Marquess
Berkeley capped the century-long debacle by his 'vast havocking of
his patrimony' in return for titles from Henry VII. For the next fifty
years the Hundred of Berkley was within the lordship of the king. In
the time of the Tyndales, the heir to the barony, Thomas V
(1523–1532), 'was a perfect Cotswold Sheppeard'.[32]

By the time Smyth came to the Vale in the latter decades of the
sixteenth century, it was notable for 'the State and eminency of the
yeomanry'. In spite of (or because of) the local presence of what was
still, at least nominally, the most prestigious lordly family in the
region, the 'Hundred [was] allowed preheminence before any of the
other thirty hundreds of the County' because of its sturdy, long-settled
yeomanry.[33] Smyth's neighbours were the very backbone of Corbet's
'middle ranke', and with minor qualifications he identified firmly with
their culture.

Smyth was never in the slightest doubt as to the capacity of the
yeomanry of the Vale to govern and administer it efficiently. Nothing
could be done efficiently and effectively without men like Edward
Tyndale, Richard Trotman, William Bower the Elder and himself, and
unless they were rewarded with greater liberties and honours their
full cooperation could not be guaranteed. Indeed, their opinions on
the matter could be expressed very forcefully, as they were in the

259

writings of William Tyndale. None of them was much interested in claiming Norman–Angevin, or Latin, heritage, as of course their erstwhile lords, the Fitzhardings, were eminently qualified to do. Their philosophy in this matter was summed up in the local proverb, 'follow him that bears the purse'. They were 'aborigines or indiginae', and proud of it.

Ancient Constitution ideology was well established among the middle ranks of Gloucestershire society. Tyndale expressed historical opinions that assumed that the Roman and Norman conquests were catastrophic events in the story of the English. Edward Trotman laboured to produce an abbreviated, accessible version of Coke's *Institutes*. Edward Coke was Lord Chief Justice under James I: 'the whole tenor of Coke's thinking was radically anti-absolutist.'[34] In simple, the final implication of Ancient Constitution ideology was the more diffuse notion that to be of English descent was to be of higher status than to be of invading stock. The Ancient Britons had civilisation before the Romans, and the Anglo-Saxons had it before the Norman–Angevins. Worlds turn on convictions like these.

Ancient Constitution ideology displaced the hereditary absolutism described by Aubrey. Its main principle was 'that the customary laws of the land had survived unchanged since the days of the Ancient Britons. In [Sir John Fortesque's] opinion the fact that none of the nations which conquered England had altered these laws testified to their excellence'.[35] The racial and ethnic composition of the 'Ancient Britons' was a variable, as were the laws ascribed to them. Prejudices against the Welsh, Scots and Irish are also evident in the period. John Corbet was aware of anti-Welsh feeling among the populace at large, and wrote against it. Prejudices do not require critical analysis, only constant, uncritical repetition.

Another lawyer, Sir Robert Cooke, married Theophila, the daughter of lord Henry Berkeley, in 1613. His kinsman Sir Edward Coke attended the wedding at Berkeley. He must have engaged in discussions of business with John Smyth (an Utter Barrister) during his visit, for in 1639 Smyth ascribed to him responsibility for having introduced a new proverb into the Hundred: 'dip not thy finger in the morter, nor seeke thy penny in the water.' This, it will be remembered, was a caution against the investment of capital in large-scale building and navigation projects.

But if Aubrey and Smyth had incompatible conceptions of the constitution of English society, they agreed in their contempt for the lower orders. Social benefit had resulted when the richer, landed peasants were freed from the bonds of serfdom. Lower in the social order the virtues of the decay of feudalism were less evident.

Under the heading *Sports*, Smyth refers to 'the inbred delight, that both gentry, yeomanry, rascallity, boys and children, doe take in a game called Stoball'.[36] Smyth was old-fashioned in his belief in the importance of sports and local festivals as occasions for social intercourse between the ranks. Special social occasions aside, however, Smyth held a very unsentimental view of the underlying causes of social inequality. 'Since slaves were set free,' he wrote, 'there are grown up a rabble of rogues, cut-purses and the like mischievous men.' If bondage was no longer 'lawful, yet surely it is naturall'. 'We find not such a latitude of difference in any creature as in the nature of man,' he wrote. 'The wisest exell the most foolish . . . by farre greater degree than the most foolish of men doe surpass the wisest of beasts.'

> And therefore when comiseracon hath given way to reason, wee shall find that nature is the ground of masterly power, and of servile obedience which is thereto correspondent; and a man is *animum politicum*, apt even by nature to comaund or to obey everyone in his proper degree.[37]

The 'rascality', in his view, was closer in character and ability to 'beasts' than it was to proven 'naturall' superiors like himself and his landowning yeoman and minor gentry neighbours. This prejudice, like Aubrey's, was grounded in the notion of genetic inheritance. But the scale of inherited qualities to which it referred was universal, a function of 'nature'.

Smyth refers to a particularly troublesome colony of the rascality on the marshy warths of Slimbridge manor. It was 'greate and rich in soile . . . Yet few of its inhabitants [were] wealthy, most very poor.'

> The warth and wast of this manor and parish, if enclosed, w[oul]d yield above 1500 pounds per annum, but used as comonly they are and heer I know they are, the waste grounds yield not the fifth part of their true vallue, drawe many poore people from other places, burden the township with beggarly cottages, inmates and alehouses, and idle people: where the greater part doe spend their dayes in a lazy idleness and petite thieveries and few or none is profitable labour.[38]

Smyth's solution was to enclose the land and convert it into yeoman – freeholds. His belief in the efficacy, above all, of household disciplines implied that any of the ejected cottagers (about half of the 90 households registered at Slimbridge in 1650[39]) who decided to stay would be employed as indentured servants of the master class. This would be a more profitable arrangement, and it would bring social arrangements into closer harmony with the 'naturall' distribution of 'masterly power'.

Smyth, the landed lawyer, shared Aubrey's assumption of a causal relationship between land and culture, but the conclusions he drew from it were different. For him, tillage of the 'durty, claey soil' of the Vale was a sacrament, the purest activity in which a man could engage.[40] The further a man's occupation was from this most life-preserving of activities, the lower his character was likely to be. The craft-working squatters at Slimbridge had no title to land. They were 'slaves in nature though not in lawe'. A distinction should also be drawn between farmers whose main occupation was arable husbandry, and those who specialised in pastoralism and arboriculture. The introductory part of his manuscript on the Hundred of Berkeley included a brief section on 'Soile'. 'The Soile' of the Vale was 'for the most part bountefull'. It was 'rich in pasture and meadow, fruitful in procreation of divers and different kindes of trees (wherof I have numbred many hundreds)'. The woods and orchards of the district were 'delighting the beholders with their beautiful verdancy'. But bountiful nature could adversely affect the temperament of the natives. A rich soil, improperly managed, made the natives lazy and unenterprising: 'and that which hath of old beene written seemes true, that the easy and free encrease of fruite doth nourish sloth in the comon people.'[41] People who could get what they wanted from nature did too little work. Agriculturalists were superior to hunters and gatherers because they worked harder for longer.[42]

Animal husbandry was better than arboriculture, but still inferior, morally and socially, to tillage. 'Sloth [among] the comon people' and 'covetousness of . . . owners' arose wherever a 'bountefull' soil tended to 'easy and free encrease of fruite' and the 'abundance of pasture for kyne and oxen'. The more divorced in occupation a man was from direct contact with the soil, the greater his degeneracy. Townspeople, he thought, 'doe but seeke meanes and busy themselves how to deceive and beguile one another, as if it were the perfection of theire trading'.[43] The connection between soil and collective temperament was an important assumption in Smyth's world-view, but he drew from it the opposite conclusion to that of Aubrey. Closeness to the soil bred men of superior quality.

Languages express social tensions. That is not all they express, but, as Lauro Martines shows, not even the most personal poetry can avoid echoes of profound social change.[44] The ways social tensions are expressed in language and culture are not predetermined, and we are dealing with a fluid, mercurial, contradictory ethos: the ethos of meaning. Even individuals, let alone classes of individuals, can hold logically incompatible convictions, often without knowing or thinking about it. All cultures value constancy because they contain and daily confront so many unpredictable inconstancies. Aubrey was a writer by vocation, if not quite by profession. It is dangerous to ascribe the opinions they write down to the authors themselves. 'The poet he nothing affirms,' wrote Philip Sydney. 'And therefore he never lieth.' Trust the tale, not the teller, as D. H. Lawrence put it. If the prejudices Aubrey represented in his private notes on the Northern Division of Wiltshire were experiments in expression, and not necessarily Aubrey's own unconscious prejudices, we must assume he had heard them elsewhere among his peers and contemporaries. Writers have played on public prejudices many times since.

Smyth, by contrast, was a private writer. He wrote the *Lives of the Berkeleys* for Lord George Berkeley. It was a blue-print for survival designed for one reader only. Likewise his *Description of the Hundred of Berkeley*, written to be read only by his trusted clerk, William Archard, and his son and heir, the second John Smyth of Nibley. Between its lines he expressed a personal philosophy they would have known from long, personal association. In this sense Smyth's words are more trustworthy than Aubrey's. With Smyth the distance between the words and the things they describe is not great. Smyth was not playing with words, but trying to sum up what he had learned, his wisdom. Archard and his son knew the Hundred of Berkeley almost as intimately as he did. What could he leave them in written words that he had not already demonstrated in practice, and spoken? Only distillation, and, perhaps, clear statements of deeply held principles.

The wisdom of John Smyth of Nibley deserves further study. His importance from the point of view of this book is that he gave detailed expression to a world-view, most features of which had dominated the minds of settled agriculturalists since the birth of agriculture. Tillage was the axiom. It was more important than anything else because it provided the staple item in the collective diet. Fruit and meat, arboriculture and pastoralism, were lower activities. Traders, lawyers and politicians could not be trusted. The landless were a nuisance, but they could be trained up in better ways in service in the households of the farmers. They could make cloth, dig coal, repair the roads, do the planting, get the harvest in, bring the cows in for milking, see to the menial work. But Smyth had the peasant mentality too. He was not fully distanced from the menial work. He was not a rentier. He lived on his own farm and ate bread made from grain he had grown himself. He was very proud of this fact. The farmer came higher in his estimation than the estate administrator, the barrister, even the lord. 'The owners foot', as the proverb said, 'doth fatt the soile.'

If he had one foot in the world of the independent peasant proprietor, the other was in the expanding world of property litigation, colonial enterprises, trade and industrial projects. He held these contradictory elements together in his life, and formulated them according to a moral hierarchy beginning with the assumption that tillage was best. Like Aubrey, he assumed that some soils, like some people, were better than others. Vernacular nationalism overwhelmed the version of aristocratic exclusiveness expressed by Aubrey. With sustained population growth, a steadily increasingly proletariat and the growth of massive conurbations, the myth of the superiority of agriculture and land as a source of prestige became less and less appropriate as the basis of social discrimination. It has not disappeared from the repertoire of English culture, but it has lost its once unchallenged centrality.

Smyth's world-view embodied change in the status it assigned to the middle rank. In this sense it is classically 'bourgeois'. It was obvious to him that the lords had once been far more important in the affairs of his region than they were in his lifetime. They had declined, and the property-owning middle rank had risen to fill the space they had vacated. One kind of social system had given way to another.

Smyth would not discuss what we would call 'industry' at all. It was his blind-spot, and we must ask why. A likely explanation is that it posed the most obvious threat to the world which held his loyalties, the old agrarian world. Smyth's intuitions in this respect, if such they were, were correct. Land would remain a solid investment of capital, at least in the long run, but it would have to take its place alongside a burgeoning range of profit-producing investments based on the production of commodities and their sale in an extraordinarily rapidly growing 'market'. In 1739 'Old Commonsense' echoed Smyth's agrarian-based moral hierarchy in the debate on riots. The louder and more arresting tones and phrases, however, were those of the spokesman for the traders and industrialists. Smyth's is the characteristic voice of the period before the civil wars. Temple's is that of the eighteenth, nineteenth and twentieth centuries. In between were the generations of Throgmorton Trotman, Oliver Cromwell, John Corbet, John Roberts, William Petty, and the Political Arithmetic branch of the Royal Society. These men, like Smyth and Tyndale before them, were engaged in an intense effort to redraw the lines of demarcation and social discrimination in their society, and between their society and the rest of the world. In acknowledging the vast changes they and all their contemporaries were trying to come to terms with and explain, we should not ignore the lasting prejudices which structured the systems of social discrimination they imposed on their new maps of culture.

NOTES AND REFERENCES

ABBREVIATIONS

Abstracts and Extracts	Thomas Dudley Fosbroke, *Abstracts and Extracts of Smyth's Lives of the Berkeleys* (London 1821)
Atkyns, *Gloucestershire*	Sir Robert Atkyns, *The Ancient and Present State of Gloucestershire* (Gloucester 1712)
Description	John Smyth of Nibley, *A Description of the Hundred of Berkeley in the County of Gloucester and of its Inhabitants*, vol. III of *The Berkeley Manuscripts* (ed. Sir John Maclean, Gloucester 1885)
GCL	Gloucester County Library
GDR	Gloucester Diocesan Records
GJ	*Gloucester Journal* (GCL)
GRO	Gloucestershire County Records Office
GNQ	*Gloucestershire Notes and Queries*, vols 1–10 (London 1881–1905)
Lives	John Smyth of Nibley, *The Lives of the Berkeleys . . . 1066–1618*, vols I and II of *The Berkeley Manuscripts* (ed. Sir John Maclean, Gloucester 1885)
Men and Armour	John Smyth, *The Names and Surnames of all the Able and Sufficient Men in Body fit for His Majesty's Service in the Wars, within the County of Gloucester . . . in the Month of August, 1608, in the Sixth Year of the Reign of James the First* (ed. Sir John Maclean, Gloucester 1902)
'Intensification'	David Rollison, 'The Intensification of Community, Society and Economy in 17th and 18th Century Gloucestershire', Univ. of New South Wales PhD thesis (1981)
Rudder, *Gloucestershire*	Samuel Rudder, *A New History of Gloucestershire* (Cirencester 1779)
TBGAS	*Transactions of the Bristol and Gloucestershire Archaeological Society*
VCH Glos.	Victoria County History of Gloucestershire

vols VI (ed. C. R. Elrington, Oxford 1965);
VII (ed. Elrington, Oxford 1978); IX (ed. N.
M. Herbert, Oxford 1981); XI (ed. N. M.
Herbert, Oxford 1976)

INTRODUCTION: COUNTRY CAPITALISM

1 Joan Thirsk, *The Rural Economy of England* (London 1984), pp. ix/x.
2 Quoted in E. J. Hobsbawm (ed.) *Karl Marx: Pre-capitalist Economic Formations* (trans. Jack Cohen, London 1964), p. 121.
3 W. W. Rostow, *The Stages of Economic Growth: A Non-Communist Manifesto* (first published 1960, repr. Cambridge 1971); Peter Mathias entrenched the notion of England as *The First Industrial Nation* in his *Economic History of England 1700–1914* (London 1963, repr. 1983); Phyllis Deane, *The First Industrial Revolution* (Cambridge 1965), p. 1, has a summary of broad outlines of the 'watershed'; R. M. Hartwell's *The Industrial Revolution and Economic Growth* (London 1971) was influential in propagating the idea that 'over the century 1750–1850 the British economy changed radically, in structure and in rate of growth; (p. 28); E. P. Thompson, *The Making of the English Working Class* (Harmondsworth 1969) shook the paradigm by the sheer power of its moral polemic; Maxine Berg, *The Age of Manufactures, Industry, Innovation and Work in Britain, 1700–1820* (London 1985) observes (p. 15) that the economic historians 'have increasingly taken their definitions away from technology and industry, to concentrate instead on . . . economic growth. They have focused on the "macroeconomics" of the Industrial Revolution [and have] rarely disaggregated their economy beyond the sectors – agriculture, industry, trade and transport . . .'.
4 Fernand Braudel, 'History and the Social Sciences: The *Longue Duree*', in *On History* (trans. Sarah Mathews, London 1980), pp. 25–54.
5 In a recent review, J. C. D. Clark refers to a 'formidable school of econometric and demographic historians who, in a series of major studies since the 1970s, have decisively replaced the idea of a transformative Industrial Revolution located towards the end of the century with a model of incremental, evolutionary change . . .': 'All energy and experiment', *TLS* 21–27 September 1990, p. 1004; and see Clark, *Revolution and Rebellion, State and Society in England in the Seventeenth and Eighteenth Centuries* (Cambridge 1986), pp. 24, 51, 66, 95, and esp. 37–9; Clark does not refer to the most important critique of the 'industrialisation as watershed' model, which is Berg op. cit. (1985); Maxine Berg, Pat Hudson and Michael Sonenscher (eds) *Manufacture in Town and Country Before the Factory* (Cambridge 1983) note that 'the degree of productivity of the machine and the size and extent of the market mark the traditional analytical limits of the economic historians' approach to the phenomenon of "Industrial Revolution" ' and refer to 'an erosion of the classical boundaries within which the question of industrialisation has been enclosed'. They stress three reasons for the new approach: (1) 'the shift to a slow, evolutionary view of capital accumulation and technological change . . . in which the emphasis is placed as much on the culture and organisation of labour as on mechanical innovation'; (2) 'the progress of social history', and (3) 'the theory of proto-industrialisation and the research it has stimulated' (p. 4); David Levine's emphasis on process and proletarianisation seems to me fundamental: 'Production, Reproduction and the Proletarian Family in England,

1500–1851' in Levine (ed.) *Proletarianization and Family History* (Orlando Fla 1984); Levine's *Reproducing Families: The Political Economy of English Population History* (Cambridge 1987) is a wide-ranging, analytical and usefully polemical discussion of 'the process of industrialisation'; Levine, 'Industrialisation and the Proletarian Family in England', *Past and Present*, 107 (May 1985) states (p. 171) that 'by changing our nomenclature from "the Industrial Revolution" to "industrialisation", we are changing our focus from an event to a process'. Levine is aware that E. Lipson wrote that 'a survey of the older English society reveals that the so-called "Industrial Revolution" constituted no sudden break with the existing order. Mercantile England had already evolved many of the capitalist traits associated with modern England' in *Introduction to the Economic History of England* vol. 2 (London 1931): a classic liberal version, grinding the axe of individualism, but nonetheless rich, rewarding, profoundly knowledgeable, and by no means dated. Eric Wolf, *Europe and the People Without History* (Berkeley 1985), brings the orthodox Marxist perspective, in which *industrial* capitalism (domination of the mode of production by the direct organisers of labour and production rather than by merchants) was born c. 1750–c. 1850, into context with the post-colonial world. Alan Macfarlane, 'Socio-economic revolution in England and the origin of the modern world', in Roy Porter and Mikulas Teich, *Revolution in History* (Cambridge 1986), pp. 145–6, is useful.

6 The phrase is Joan Thirsk's, 'Industries in the Countryside' in F. J. Fisher (ed.) *Essays in the Economic and Social History of Tudor and Stuart England in Honour of R. H. Tawney* (Cambridge 1961, p. 70–88.

7 All references to the *Gloucester Journal* are from the all-but-complete set held at the Gloucester City Library. The *Journal's* role in the dissemination of opinion is considered in Chapter 9 of this book.

8 *OED*, p. 3372.

9 Alan Everitt's chapters in Joan Thirsk (ed.) *The Agrarian History of England and Wales, vol. 4, 1500–1640* (Cambridge 1967), remain the outstanding account of the marketing structure of early modern England. Jean-Christophe Agnew, *Worlds Apart: the Market and the Theater in Anglo-American Thought, 1550–1750* (Cambridge 1986), pp. 1–56, is a useful introduction to the cultural ambiguities of commerce in the early modern period.

10 Population trends calculated from 'Bishop Hooper's Visitation of Gloucester', *English Historical Review*, 19 (1904), pp. 98–121 (1551); 'Furney Ms.B', BGAS Library, GCL (1563); 'A Religious Miscellany', BGAS Record Series (1976), pp. 61–104 (1603); C. R. Elrington, 'The Survey of Church Livings in Gloucestershire, 1650', *TBGAS*, 83 (March 1965, pp. 85–99 (1650); Hearth Tax Assessments for Michaelmas 1671, PRO E179/247/14 and (photocopy) GRO D383; Staffordshire County Records Office, Salt Ms. 33 ('Compton Census' 1676); Atkyns, *Gloucestershire* (1712); Benson Survey Book, GRO GDR 285B (1750); 'Parochial List of Dissenters, Families', GRO D1762/4 (1735); Rudder, *Gloucestershire* (1779); and national censuses 1801–31; method and source criticism in Rollison, 'Intensification', Ch. 5: 'Gloucestershire, So Fruitful of Inhabitants', pp. 290–361.

11 Karl Marx, *Capital Volume One* (Harmondsworth 1984) p. 473. William Petty, *Political Arithmetick* (London 1690, but written 1671–2), Ch. 1: 'That a small Country, and few People, may by their Situation, Trade and Policy, be equivalent in Wealth and Strength, to a far greater People, and Territory. And particularly, How conveniences for Shipping and Water Carriage, do

most eminently, and fundamentally, conduce thereunto', seems to be making the same point with less precision: C. H. Hull (ed.), *The Economic Writings of Sir William Petty*, Vol. 1 (Cambridge 1899), pp. 249–67; and for dating of this work, cf. editor's introduction, p. 235.

12 On the affective and behavioural aspects of the processes I have in mind, see the brilliant synthesis of Norbert Elias, *The Civilising Process: State Formation and Civilisation*, trans. Edmund Jephcott (Oxford 1982), e.g. pp. 241–2: 'as the conveyor belts running through his existence grow longer and more complex, the individual learns to control himself more steadily; he is now less a prisoner of his passions than before. But as he is now more tightly bound by his functional dependence on the activities of an ever-large number of people, he is more restricted in his conduct, in his chances of directly satisfying his drives and passions . . . for what is lacking in everyday life a substitute is created in dreams, in books and pictures . . . the battlefield is, in a sense, moved within [the individual] . . . the drives, the passionate affects, that can no longer manifest themselves in the relationships *between* people, often struggle no less violently *within* the individual against this supervising part of himself.' This chapter aims to provide a sketch-map of the 'conveyor belts', but I also wish to draw attention to the subjective and psychological implications.

13 E. P. Thompson, 'Peculiarities of the English', *The Socialist Register*, ed. Ralph Miliband and John Saville, No. 2, 1965. Philip Corrigan and Derek Sayer, *The Great Arch: English State Formation as Cultural Revolution* (Oxford 1985); Clark, *Revolution and Rebellion* op. cit., sees the process from the vantage-point of the state; Thompson's place in the development of 'history from below', and his efforts to 'listen to the inarticulate', are well known; Corrigan and Sayer try to find a middle ground, in which political and social developments are seen as interconnected.

14 Eric R. Wolf, 'Kinship, Friendship, and Patron–Client Relations in Complex Societies', in Michael Banton, *The Social Anthropology of Complex Societies* (London 1966), explains the theoretical framework of the 'corporate kin-coalition'; Keith Wrightson persuaded me that 'corporate' is too strong a word for the Trotman kin-coalition.

15 See Harvey J. Graff, *The Legacies of Literacy: Continuities and Contradictions in Western Culture and Society* (Bloomington 1991), in which Gramsci's 'concept of social and cultural hegemony . . . underlies the analytic and interpretative framework' (p. 11); Graff, *Literacy in History: An Interdisciplinary Research Bibliography* (New York 1981); I have been influenced in particular by Eric Havelock, *Preface to Plato* (Cambridge, Mass. 1963); and Jan Vansina, *Oral Tradition as History* (London 1985).

16 J. Goody and D. Watt, 'The Consequences of Literacy', in *Literacy in Traditional Societies* (Cambridge 1968).

17 Lucien Febvre and Henri-Jean Martin, *The Coming of the Book* (London 1976), and Elizabeth L. Eisenstein, *The Printing Press as an Agent of Change* (Cambridge 1979), esp. Ch. 2 'Defining the Initial Shift . . .', pp. 43–159, are the classic texts on the print revolution; Benedict Anderson, *Imagined Communities* (2nd ed, London 1991), esp. pp. 37–46, reflects on the relations between the print revolution, capitalism and popular nationalism. David Cressy, *Literacy and the Social Order: Reading and Writing in Tudor and Stuart England* (Cambridge 1980); Keith Wrightson's summary of 'Educational opportunity and popular literacy', pp. 184–193 of *English Society 1580–1680* (London 1982); and Margaret Spufford, *Small Books and Pleasant Histories*

(Cambridge 1981), are starting-points for the quantification and effects of literacy in early modern England.

18 Walter J. Ong, *Interfaces of the Word: Studies in the Evolution of Consciousness and Culture* (Cornell 1977), p. 207; Ruth Finnegan, *Literacy and Orality: Studies in the Technology of Communication* (Oxford 1988), esp. Ch. 2, 'Communication and technology', p. 38, identifies 'strong' and 'weak' theories of determinacy in relations between information technology and social change. The passages cited from Ong's writings imply a 'strong' theory of the cleavage between, e.g., preliterate and literate worlds, and between literacy and the world of electronic global communications systems. Finnegan's arguments in favour of a 'weaker' level of determinancy than Ong (and McCluhan) suggest are convincing.

19 Ong, *Interfaces*, op. cit., p. 18.

20 Ibid., p. 18.

21 Ibid., p. 187.

22 J. Goody, *The Interface Between the Written and the Oral* (Cambridge 1987).

23 Paul Ricoeur, 'The Model of the Text: meaningful action considered as a text', in J. B. Thompson (ed.), *Paul Ricoeur, Hermeneutics and the Human Sciences* (Cambridge 1989), p. 213.

24 *OED*, p. 580, 'Country'.

25 Quotes from *OED*. Ann Hughes, *Politics, Society and Civil War in Warwickshire 1620–1660* (Cambridge 1987), p. 112, for a brief discussion of the 'several applications' of the word 'country' among the gentry of Warwickshire. Also relevant is the discussion in Hughes, 'Local History and the Origins of the Civil War', in Richard Cust and Ann Hughes (eds), *Conflict in Early Stuart England: Studies in Religion and Politics 1603–1642* (London 1989).

26 The following are important local studies, and/or reflections on local studies, which have influenced me: Christopher Hill, *Society and Puritanism in Pre-Revolutionary England* (London 1964): Emmanuel Le Roy Ladurie, *The Peasants of Languedoc* (trans. Barbara Bray, London 1978); Victor Skipp, *Crisis and Development: An Ecological Case Study of the Forest of Arden, 1570–1674* (Cambridge 1978); Margaret Spufford, *Contrasting Communities: English Villagers in the Sixteenth and Seventeenth Centuries* (Cambridge 1974); Philip Styles, *Studies in Seventeenth-Century West Midlands History* (Kineton 1978); Keith Wrightson and David Levine, *Poverty and Piety in an English Village, Terling 1525–1700* (New York 1979); R. H. Hilton, *A Medieval Society: The West Midlands at the End of the Thirteenth Century* (London 1966); various articles collected in Hilton, *Class Conflict and the Crisis of Feudalism* (London 1985); E. P. Thompson, *Whigs and Hunters: the origin of the Black Act* (Harmondsworth 1975); Alan Everitt, *The Pattern of Rural Dissent: the Nineteenth Century* (Leicester 1972); Everitt, 'Country, County and Town: patterns of regional evolution in England', *Trans Royal Historical Society*, 29 (1979); Carlo Ginzburg, *The Cheese and the Worms: The Cosmos of a Sixteenth-Century Miller* (trans. John and Anne Tedeschi, London 1980); Edward Britton, *The Community of the Vill* (Toronto 1977); Alan Macfarlane, *Reconstructing Historical Communities* (Cambridge 1977); Macfarlane, *The Justice and the Mare's Ale* (Oxford 1981); Fernand Braudel, *The Identity of France, vol. 1: History and Environment* (trans. Sian Reynolds, London 1989); John Morrill, *The Revolt of the Provinces: Conservatives and Radicals in the English Civil War 1630–1650* (London 1976); David Underdown, *Revel, Riot and Rebellion: Popular Politics and Culture in England, 1603–1660* (Oxford 1987); David Levine and Keith

Wrightson, *The Making of an Industrial Society, Whickham 1560–1765* (Oxford 1991, read in proof 1990); Paul S. Seaver, *Wallington's World: A Puritan Artisan in Seventeenth-Century London* (Stanford 1985); Michel de Certeau, *The Practice of Everyday Life* (Berkeley and Los Angeles 1984); Charles Phythian-Adams, *Rethinking English Local History* (Leicester 1987); David Warren Sabean, *Power in the Blood: Popular Culture and Village Discourse in Early Modern Germany* (Cambridge 1984); Sabean, *Property, Production and Family in Neckerhausen, 1700–1870* (Cambridge 1990).

27 Fernand Braudel, *The Wheels of Commerce*, vol. 2 of *Civilisation and Capitalism 15th–18th Century* (New York 1982), pp. 231–42, provides an account of the genesis of the words 'capital', 'capitalist' and 'capitalism'.

28 Frank Perlin, 'Proto-industrialization and pre-colonial South Asia', *Past and Present*, 98.

29 M. Mollat and P. Wolff, *The Popular Revolutions of the Late Middle Ages* (trans. A. L. Lytton-Sells London 1973).

1 CRADLES OF CHANGE

1 Eric. R. Wolf, *Europe and the People Without History* (Berkeley 1985), p. 2.

2 Francis Jennings, *The Invasion of America: Indians, Colonialism and the Cant of Conquest* (New York 1975), p. 100; Wolf, *Europe*, op. cit., p. 2.

3 'Smyth of Nibley Papers, 1613–1674', consisting mainly of Ms. collections relating to Virginia in the New York public library, *Bulletin of the New York Library*, i, (July 1897), pp. 186–90.

4 Atkyns, *Gloucestershire*, p. 78.

5 Christopher Saxton's Map of Gloucestershire, 1577: British Museum Maps C.7, c.1.

6 All references to occupations in 1608 are to *Men and Armour*.

7 Thomas Fuller D. D., *The Histories of the Worthies of England* (repr. London 1840), vol. 1, pp. 551–2; *Description*, pp. 26–7.

8 'An Act touching the making of woolen Cloth', 4–5 Philip and Mary, excluded 'any towns or villages near the river *Stroud*, in the county of *Gloucestershire*': John Smith, *Memoirs of Wool* (London 1747, facs. repr. New York 1969) vol. 2, p. 99.

9 E. Carus-Wilson, 'Evidence of Industrial Growth on some Fifteenth-Century Manors', in Carus-Wilson (ed.) *Essays in Economic History*, vol. 2 (Cambridge 1962).

10 R. H. Hilton, *A Medieval Society: The West Midlands at the End of the Thirteenth Century* (London 1966), p. 161.

11 *Abstracts and Extracts*, p. 108.

12 In none of Thomas lord Berkeley's manors (Smyth lists 50 belonging to the estate) did he have flocks of less than 300, and 'in some 1,000'. In 1334 5,775 sheep 'belonging to that and adjacent manors' were sheared at Beverstone, a Berkeley manor in the Cotswolds: Smyth, *Lives*, vol. 1, p. 302.

13 Charles E. Boucher, 'The Black Death at Bristol', *TBGAS*, 60 (1938), pp. 31–46.

14 R. Perry, 'The Gloucestershire Woollen Industry', *TBGAS*, 66 (1945), pp. 53–5.

15 Eric Kerridge, *Textile Manufactures in Early Modern England* (Manchester 1985), p. 12, comments that one of the reasons for the decline of the older-established Flemish woollen industry was 'the violent opposition of the

foot-fullers and the coercion their sheer weight of numbers enabled them to practice . . . to compel municipal authorities to deface mills . . .'. Kerridge regards 'this Luddism without the name' as the 'prime mover' in the decline of the old centres where foot-fulling was the norm. A similar fate seems to have befallen the urban production centres of the medieval West Country: by the end of the sixteenth century the once prolific textile industries of towns like Salisbury, Bristol and Gloucester were moribund, and production had shifted to villages and market towns with fast-flowing, perennial streams to run the fulling mills belonging to the leading clothiers: Perry, 'The Gloucester Woollen Industry', op. cit., p. 73, dates the decline of the urban centres, especially Bristol, to 'before the dawn of the fifteenth century, when there is evidence that the weavers of the city made inferior kinds of cloth and were in a depressed condition'.

16 *Abstracts and Extracts*, p. 108.

17 See Joan Thirsk, 'Projects for Gentlemen, Jobs for the Poor: Mutual Aid in the Vale of Tewkesbury, 1600–1630', in Patrick McGrath and John Cannon (eds) *Essays in Bristol and Gloucestershire History* (Bristol 1976).

18 'The Yorkist administration failed completely to cream off higher rents from the developing cloth industry of Bisley, part of the advancing cloth industry known as Stroudwater, in Gloucestershire. In the fourteen-fifties the tenants of Longford's Mill, then a fulling mill and still a well-known cloth factory today, paid the Duke an annual rent of 15 pounds 4 shillings and a halfpenny, and sublet for 66s 8d. From the early fifteenth century to the reign of Henry VIII income from the manor of Bisley remained more or less static and its accounts were a complete farce: tenants names recur unchanged for a century or more, even after 1461 when the manor became part of the royal estates and Edward IV was making a determined effort to tighten up the administration of the royal demesne': J. R. Lander, *Government and Community, England 1450/1509* (London 1980), pp. 12–13. But there may have been method in their madness: 'the subsidy paid by Bisley, the area of the Stroud Valley development, increased thirteenfold (sixty-four pounds as against five pounds)' between 1334 and 1524, whereas 'Cirencester in 1524 paid only rather more than twice the subsidy it was assessed at in 1334': Hilton, *A Medieval Society*, op. cit., p. 86, citing E. Carus-Wilson, 'Evidence of Industrial Growth, op. cit.

19 Ibid.

20 Table 17.2 of J. A. Chartres, 'The Marketing of Agricultural Produce', in Joan Thirsk (ed.) *The Agrarian History of England and Wales*, vol. V, part ii: *Agrarian Change* (Cambridge 1989), pp. 410–11, allows comparison with other counties. Only Devon (45), Somerset (39), Yorkshire (54) and Lincolnshire (37) had more market towns than Gloucestershire (34), and all were much larger counties. As this chapter shows, however, many of Gloucestershire's 'market towns' are more accurately described as 'manufacturing towns'.

21 For the sources and methodology used to estimate the population of Gloucestershire from 1551 to 1831, see Rollison, 'Intensification', Ch. 5: 'Gloucestershire, so Fruitful of Inhabitants'.

22 *Men and Armour*.

23 This is an appropriate place to acknowledge the seminal influence of the work of Joan Thirsk, whose 'Industries in the Countryside', in F. J. Fisher (ed.), *Essays in the Economic and Social History of Tudor and Stuart England, in Honour of R. H. Tawney* (Cambridge 1961) first alerted me to the import-

ance of manufacturing in country districts of early modern England. All of the essays in Joan Thirsk, *The Rural Economy of England* (London 1984), the three volumes of the *Agrarian History of England and Wales* of which she was the editor, and her *Economic Policy and Projects: the Development of a Consumer Society in Early Modern England* (Oxford 1978) are starting-points for the study of early modern England.

24 The introduction of 'cloths of more finely spun yarns . . . dye[d] . . . stammel or scarlet in a new way that made the colour faster . . . the naps were raised by means of the newly invented mosing mills . . . which raised the nap gently . . . When first invented, the new Stroudwaters were sold mainly at local fairs, and not until about 1615 were they regularly sent up to the London market': Kerridge, *Textile Manufactures*, op. cit., p. 33.

25 D. C. Coleman, *The Economy of England 1450–1750* (Oxford 1977), p. 151.

26 'To sell cloths abroad [in the sixteenth century], it was the conventional wisdom that dyeing (and other finishing processes) had better be deferred until they had been taken as far as the international market at Antwerp, where the foreign merchant who bought the cloths might select the colour to suit his customers. Only from the early seventeenth century were consumers on the nearby continent to put aside their prejudices and wear cloths dyed (and finished) in England': G. D. Ramsay, *The English Woollen Industry, 1500–1750* (London 1982), p. 12.

27 Men and occupations in 1608 from *Men and Armour*; for the later periods the data are from the Dursley and Wotton baptism and burial registers GRO P124, IN 1/2 etc. Care was taken to record every entry in the relevant years on a slip of paper; slips were then collated and cross-referenced to avoid duplicating individuals with more than one entry.

28 The presence of dyers and fullers in 1608 shows that some Vale of Berkeley clothiers, like their counterparts (and relatives) in Stroudwater, were finishing cloth in the early seventeenth ccentury. However, what the changing occupational structure reveals is a consolidation of a trend that was already taking hold early in the century. Some Gloucestershire clothiers, it is clear, had already anticipated the motives of Alderman Cockayne's project to ban the export of unfinished cloth in order to increase employment and profitability at home, for which see Charles Wilson, *England's Apprenticeship 1603–1763* (Oxford 1965), pp. 70–8.

29 Dursley Poll Tax Assessment, 14 June 1689, GCL 16527 (43) (Smyth of Nibley Papers); Rollison, 'Intensification', pp. 236–50.

30 Dursley Poll Tax Assessment, ibid.

31 Dursley Court Roll 1654, GCL RX 115.20.

32 Rollison, 'Intensification', p. 240.

33 E. Lipson, *The Economic History of England*, Vol. III: *The Age of Mercantilism*, 6th edn (Oxford 1961), pp. 53–4, where it is also stated that master-dressers sometimes 'kept as many as fifty men and boys'. Robert Reid, *Land of Lost Content: the Luddite Revolt 1812* (London 1986), pp. 43–4, describes the work and character of the shearers' trade.

34 'Generally, in textiles, the finer the article, the more likely it was that the industry making it would be dominated by big capitalists capable of making the bigger outlay on finer materials, expensive dyes and tools.' Wilson, *England's Apprenticeship*, op. cit., p. 66.

35 'The introduction of new fabrics and techniques enhanced the larger master's role', Kerridge, *Textile Manufactures*, op. cit., p. 192; on p. 204 he cites Unwin to the effect that 'the new capital built up was not employed

primarily in trading, but in bringing together a greater number of workmen, belonging sometimes to different branches of manufacture, and thus organising industry upon a larger scale'.

36 'John Wallis, clothier, inoculated for the smallpox, has recovered', *GJ*, 10 May 1743: 'The vestry [of Wotton] proposes to inoculate voluntary poor at parish expense', *GJ*, 22 May 1743; 528 people were inoculated, 4 died, *GJ*, 22 May 1743.

37 A. R. Bridbury, *Medieval English Clothmaking. An Economic Survey* (London 1982), pp. 68–9.

38 Stumpe was the son of a North Nibley weaver who purchased buildings belonging to Malmsbury Abbey in 1540, and set them up as weavers' workshops: G. D. Ramsay, *The Wiltshire Woollen Industry in the Sixteenth and Seventeenth Centuries* (London 1965), Ch. 3: 'Stumpe and his Contemporaries'. Kerridge, *Textile Manufactures*, op. cit. p. 196, questions the scale of Stumpe's 'factory', suggesting that the buildings he used for this purpose, referred to by Leland as 'vaste houses of office' were actually the monastic toilets. 'Neither they nor the little church or chapel can have housed very many broad looms', comments Kerridge.

39 Recent discussions of the process of industrialisation stress 'a slow evolutionary view of technological change . . . in which the emphasis is placed as much on change in the culture and organisation of labour as on mechanical innovation': Maxine Berg, Pat Hudson and Michael Sonenscher (eds) *Manufacture in Town and Country before the Factory* (Cambridge 1983), p. 4.

40 Woodward's story is told in Joseph Stratford, *Great and Good Men of Gloucestershire* (Gloucester 1867), pp. 55–68. Robinson was a cousin of Godfrey Goodman, the crypto-catholic Bishop of Gloucester, and had been Minister at Dursley since 1625. In 1646 he joined the Puritans, publishing *The Peoples Pleas Fully Vindicated*, his 'vindication'.

41 Stratford, ibid.

42 In 1657 a female sectary, Deborah Harding, 'after the priest [Woodward] had ended his sermon, would have given a Christian exhortation to the people, but they fell on her with an uproar, some crying "kill her", others "strike her down", others "tear her to pieces". The magistrates to secure her from the rabble sent her to prison. . . .': *A Collection of the Sufferings of the Quakers* (London 1690), p. 22.

43 GRO D2940/1 contains a parish-by-parish account of references to dissenters and nonconformists in the Vale of Berkeley from the time of Wycliffe and Trevisa; I have mapped references in GRO NC9, 'Licenses for Nonconformist Meeting Houses and to Preachers under the Declaration of Indulgences in 1672': 60 per cent of references are to Stroudwater and the Vale of Berkeley. Similar analysis of references to nonconformists in the Compton Census of 1676 (Salt Ms. 36, Staffs RO; photocopy at GRO); 'Extracts from Thomas Storey's Journal', GRO D1762/9; the 'Parochial List of Dissenters' Families' (1735, 1750), also known as Bishop Benson's Survey, GRO GDR 285B and GRO D1762/4. Rollison, 'Intensification', Ch. 4.

44 From a letter to 'Mr D' by John Wesley, quoted in Humphrey Jennings, *Pandaemonium: the coming of the machine as seen by contemporary observers* (London 1987), p. 50.

45 By the late seventeenth century 'we should probably not be far out if we concluded that about a third of England's textile production . . . was exported . . . At this time textiles made up about four-fifths of total exports': Kerridge, *Textile Manufactures*, op. cit. p. 220.

46 See below, Chapter 6.

47 See below, Chapter 9.

48 Perry, The Gloucestershire Woollen Industry', op. cit., p. 79.

49 Kerridge, *Textile Manufactures*, op. cit., p. 102.

50 Joan Thirsk, 'The Fantastical Folly of Fashion: the English Stocking Knitting Industry 1500–1700', in Thirsk, *Rural Economy*, op. cit., pp. 235–58.

51 This was a long process, and doubtless proceeded unevenly. There is not space to discuss earlier phases here, but we get some idea of what was involved from Lipson's comment 'that dyers, weavers and fullers "will not work on the cloths of others except at an excessive wage" ': this is a citation from 1364, when of course conditions favoured labour, and before the great expansion of the industry in the later fifteenth and sixteenth centuries: *Economic History of England*, vol. 3, op. cit., p. 40.

52 G. D. Ramsay, *The Wiltshire Woollen Industry*, op. cit., Ch. 8: 'Changes in the Organisation of the Wiltshire Woollen Industry During the Seventeenth Century', writes of 'a whole group of large industrialists who flourished in the Avon Valley in this period' (p. 127), of spinners as 'an unorganised mass of sweated labour' (p. 128), of resort to truck when 'credit difficulties' arose (p. 129). Each district differed from every other in topography, manorial and parochial customs, proverbial culture and so on. But the dominance of London merchants in the diffusion of marketing information imposed a similar general pattern of development on all districts in the long run. Development was uneven, but combined.

53 The sample used only inventories in which the occupation of the deceased is recorded. The low probate values for clothiers in the later period suggests that a gap had opened up between men in a small way of business, whose estates continued to register in diocesan probate records, and the big clothiers whose estates were handled by the Archdiocese. It was during the boom of the early eighteenth century that the fathers of the men later characterised as 'gentleman clothiers' made their fortunes, just as a similar wave of successful households came to the fore in the 1640s, the sons and grandsons of the successful 'yeoman clothiers' of the late sixteenth and early seventeenth centuries: E. A. L. Moir, 'The Gentlemen Clothiers', and 'George Onesipherous Paul', in H. P. R. Finberg, *Gloucestershire Studies* (Leicester 1967). Probate samples from GDR, GRO. Albion Urdank, 'The Consumption of Rental Property: Gloucestershire Plebeians and the Market Economy, 1750–1860', *Journal of Interdisciplinary History*, XXI (2), pp. 261–81, includes a discussion of the use of probate inventories in a later period.

54 J. De L. Mann, *The Cloth Industry . . . , in the West of England from 1640 to 1880* (Gloucester 1987), pp. 28, 29, 34.

2 TRAILS OF PROGRESS

1 David Harris Sacks, 'Bristol's "Little Businesses" 1625–41', *Past and Present*, 110, p. 70.

2 F. M. Stenton, 'The Road System of Medieval England', *Economic History Review*, 1, VII (1936), p. 5.

3 Daniel Defoe, *A Tour Through the Whole Island of Great Britain* (Harmondsworth 1971), p. 391.

4 Saxton was employed by Thomas Seckford, Master of the Court of Requests and Surveyor of the Courts of Wards and Liveries: his work was licensed

by Queen Elizabeth: R. V. Tooley, *Maps and Mapmakers*, 7th edn (Dorset 1987), p. 65.

5 John Ogilby 'made the first survey of the roads of England and Wales, the result being published in a folio volume . . . [in] 1675' Tooley, ibid, p. 54. Michael Frearson, a student of St Johns College, Cambridge, who is currently engaged in a study of English road maps and communications in the early decades of the seventeenth century, informs me that road maps of particular regions appear in these decades (personal communication).

6 'Thomas Tyndale', in Oliver Lawson Dick (ed.) *Aubrey's Brief Lives* (Harmondsworth 1978), pp. 461–2.

7 'From the first year of Queen Mary to his death in the eleventh of King James', Henry lord Berkeley spent £260,000, most of it from the sale of assets. Smyth, *Lives*, vol. II, p. 261.

8 Rudder, *Gloucestershire*, p. 21.

9 In the eighteenth century, and probably earlier, cheese was 'a species of provision so considerable, that nothing, except that of live cattle, can exceed it', *GJ*, 15 May 1739.

10 Mary Prior, *Fisher Row, Fishermen, Bargemen, and Canal Boatmen in Oxford, 1500–1900* (Oxford 1982), Ch. 3, part ii, 'The improvement of the river', is a useful survey of the improvement of the Thames below Oxford: the idea seems to have been first canvassed in 1580, and an Act for 'Clearing the Passage by Water from London and beyond the Citye of Oxford' was passed by Parliament in 1607; 'on 31 August 1635 the first barge reached Oxford from London' (p. 122); many of the bargemen of Fisher Row had connections with Lechlade (p. 134, 143, 170, 184, 246). 'The Gloucestershire men carry all by land-carriage to Lechlade and Crickley, and so carry it down the river to London', *GJ*, 15 May 1739.

11 Occupations in 1608 from *Men and Armour*; for 1698–1706 they are from the Lechlade parish registers, GRO P97, IN 1/1. Multiple references to individuals were excluded by the process of analysis. Quotations and further information from *VCH Glos.*, 'The Hundred of Brightwells Barrow' – 'Lechlade'.

12 The important breakthrough in the Thames navigation below Oxford seems to have occurred in the 1630s: 'To compare [John] Taylor's voyages up the river in 1632 and 1641 is to note considerable improvement. On his first voyage Taylor found the river 'unnavigable, scorn'd, despis'd, disgrac'd' with 'weeds, shelves and shoals all waterless and flat'. On his second journey, he admitted that there was hardly any stoppage from Staines upward, except by weirs which had locks to open and shut; only between Cricklade and Cirencester was the river really in a bad condition and that was a portion which no-one had intended to make navigable'; 'Defoe saw large barges as high as Lechlade Quay': T. S. Willan, 'The Navigation of the Thames and Kennet', pamphlet repr. from *Berks Archaeological Journal*, 40(2) (1936), pp. 4–5.

13 *GJ*, 15 May 1739.

14 Prior, *Fisher Row* op. cit.; the rest of this paragraph is based on this source.

15 Ibid., p. 122.

16 Ibid., pp. 134, 143, 170, 184, 246.

17 An illustrative case of such a kin-coalition, the Trotmans of the Vale of Berkeley, is found in Chapter 5, below.

18 J. A. Chartres, *Internal Trade in England 1500–1700* (London 1977), p. 11. 'It is clear that transport lay at the root of trading patterns in this period . . .

[but] the history of sixteenth-century transport remains largely unwritten and, bar Willan's work on water carriage, little of substance exists for the seventeenth century. In this essential area of the subject the familiar problem of lack of information is combined with a paucity of academic interest.' (p. 39). Chartres, 'The Functions of Transport Changes', Part G of Chartres, 'The Marketing of Agricultural Produce' in Joan Thirsk (ed.) *The Agrarian History of England and Wales, vol. V. part II: Agrarian Change* (Cambridge 1989), p. 465, refers to 'the growing integration and efficiency of marketing (which tended to accelerate the natural wastage of markets and fairs between 1640 and 1750)'. Chartres, 'Road Carrying in England in the 17th Century: myth and reality', *Economic History Review* 2nd Series, XXX (1977), p. 77, shows that 'the capacity of carrying services to the capital more than doubled between 1637 and 1715 and perhaps grew as much again by 1750, with a parallel expansion of provincial networks'.

19 See below, Chapter 5.

20 Carriers' locations: *Men and Armour*.

21 Badgers' locations: *Men and Armour*.

22 Hasfield recorded 5 badgers, Upper Ley 3, Uckington and Ashleworth 1 each: *Men and Armour*.

23 The analysis that follows derives from GRO QS Process Book 1, Q/SW6, vol. 1, under the head 'Names of badgers licensed at Epiphany, Easter, Michaelmas 1757, and Epiphany 1758'. The form of entry was as follows: 'Richard Arundell of Stroud Baker, in 50 pounds, Michael Ballard of the same, in 25 pounds, upon condition that he shall not forestall or ingross or do anything contrary to the true meaning of the statutes against Forestallers, Regraters, and Engrossers, or anything contained therein, then this recognisance to be void or also to be and remain in full force' (e.g.).

24 GRO QR/EL Returns for 1785.

25 William Marshall, *Agriculture* (1789), p. 108.

26 Daniel Roberts, *Memoir of John Roberts* (London 1742), p. 42.

27 See Turnpike map in B. S. Smith and Elizabeth Ralph, *A History of Bristol and Gloucestershire* (Beaconsfield 1972), p. 92.

28 Although he reported that Birdlip hill, 'formerly a terrible place for poor carriers and travellers out of Wales &c, [is] now repaired very well': Defoe, *A Tour* op. cit., p. 391.

29 *Gloucestershire Turnpike Roads* (GRO Publications), Doc,. 13/1.

30 Arthur Young, *A Six-Week Tour through the Southern Counties of England and Wales*, quoted in *Gloucestershire Turnpike Roads*, op. cit.

31 Ibid.

32 *GJ*, 19 October 1756.

33 *GJ*, 8 January 1739/40.

34 *GJ*, 14 August 1739; and for a later reference to neglect of Newent's roads by turnpike commissioners, *GJ*, 13 April 1756.

35 All references in this sentence are to *GJ*, May–June 1755.

36 *GJ*, 16 July 1745.

37 For the information in this and the next paragraph, see advertisements and announcements in the *GJ*, 30 May 1724; 11 April 1725; 28 March 1737/8; 6 February 1738/9; 7 July 1741; 14 December 1742; 27 March 1743/4; 1 May 1744; 22 May 1744; 7 May 1745; 22 July 1755; 7 October 1755; 9 april 1759; 21 April 1766; 19 May 1766 and *passim*.

38 *GJ*, 18 February 1745/6.

39 *GJ*, 13 May 1755.

40 *GJ*, 17 October 1755.
41 *GJ*, 18 November 1755.
42 *GJ*, 2 December 1755.
43 *GJ*, 7 May 1745.
44 *GJ*, 30 July 1745.
45 GRO D.1956, 'Holford of Westonbirt Papers'.
46 *GJ*, 27 September 1743.
47 Peter T. Marcy, 'Bristol's Roads and Communications on the Eve of the Industrial Revolution', *TBGAS*, 87, p. 158.
48 GRO QR/EL, Returns for 1785.
49 GRO D1799 ×13, Depositions Sworn Before William Blaythwayt J.P., 1734–41.
50 Richard Wilkinson has estimated that every horse required 'between four and eight acres of land under hay': *Poverty and Progress* (London 1973), pp. 123–6. This rough approximation assumes that the ratio of humans to horses indicated in the Dursley figures was uniform throughout the county. Calculations based on Wilkinson's *minima* – 4 acres of hay per horse per year.
51 Thomas Rudge, *Agriculture of Gloucestershire* (1809), p. 335.
52 Ibid, p. 338.
53 Ibid, p. 338.

3 PROVERBIAL CULTURE

1 William M. Reddy, *The Rise of Market Culture* (Cambridge 1984), p. 1.
2 Marshall Sahlins, *Culture and Practical Reason* (Chicago 1976), p. viii.
3 Milan Kundera, *The Book of Laughter and Forgetting* (Harmondsworth 1986), p. 197.
4 Marshall Sahlins, *Islands of History* (Chicago 1988), p. 29.
5 'Phrases and proverbs of speach proper to this hundred': *Description*, pp. 22–33.
6 Claude Levi-Strauss, *The View From Afar* (Harmondsworth 1985), p. xiv.
7 Thomas Fuller D. D., *The Histories of the Worthies of England* (repr. London 1840), vol. 1, pp. 551–2, cites 'You are a man of Durseley' as meaning 'one that breaks his word, and faileth in performance of his promises'.
8 J. Blunt, *Dursley and its Neighbourhood* (Gloucester 1887), p. 9. Blunt also mentions another reference to sharp-dealing in the cloth industry in the sermons of 'that very plain-spoken preacher old Latimer', who 'preached against racking cloth and filling it up with "devil's dust" ': ibid., p. 13.
9 See above p. 52.
10 Jonathon D. Spence, *The Memory Palace of Matteo Ricci* (London 1985), p. 2.
11 Frances Yates, *The Art of Memory* (Harmondsworth 1969) is the classic account.
12 Spence, *Memory Palace*, op. cit., p. 2.
13 Paul Carter, *The Road to Botany Bay* (London 1987), describes the ways European explorers and cartographers imposed their cultural assumptions on the Australian landscape.
14 Bruce Chatwyn's *The Songlines* (London 1987) is an imaginative meditation, thinly disguised as fiction, on certain theories about how Australian Aboriginal people made sense of themselves and the landscape they inhabited.
15 David Rollison, 'The Bourgeois Soul of John Smyth of Nibley', *Social His-*

tory, 12(3) (October 1987) describes the transitional character of Smyth's world-view, and the fundamental importance within it of a thoroughly individualistic theology.

16 Quoted in 'The Historians of Gloucestershire', in H. P. R. Finberg (ed.), *Gloucestershire Studies*, (Leicester 1967), p. 269.

17 *Description*, p. 42.

18 Ibid., p. 75.

19 Ibid., p. 43.

20 Based on author's count of Cirencester registers of baptisms, burials and marriages, 1560–1637, GRO P 86 IN 1/1.

21 GRO P298a, OV 1/1, and note dated 26 April 1649, OV 2/3.

22 Martin J. Wiener, *English Culture and the Decline of the Industrial Spirit 1850–1980* (Harmondsworth 1985); the quotes in this paragraph are from pp. 4–5.

4 TYNDALE AND ALL HIS SECT

1 Stephen Greenblatt, *Renaissance Self-Fashioning from More to Shakespeare* (Chicago 1980), p. 7.

2 A. G. Dickens, *The English Reformation* (London 1970), p. 59.

3 'There was a persistent family tradition described in a letter from one Tyndale to another written in 1663 claiming that a certain Tyndale came out from Northumberland during the Wars of the Roses into Gloucestershire where he changed his name to Hutchyns for safety, married and only revealed his true name to his children on his deathbed. Be that as it may the fact remains that in the 1500s members of the family, our Tyndale among them, used *both* names as if they wished to keep to their original surname, especially now that the Lancastrians (with whom they had fought) had regained the throne': Lewis Lupton, *Tyndale the Translator*, vol. XVIII of *The History of the Geneva Bible* (London 1986), p. 8. Arthur C. Tyndale, 'The Parentage of William Tyndale alias Hutchyns', *TBGAS*, 73, pp. 208–15, 'explodes . . . the family legend' by showing that the Tyndale family rented 'Milkeshames' farm at Stinchcombe in 1400 (p. 209); this farm, called 'Milsh 'mscourt', was held by Tebota Hochyns in 1478, when a Richard Tyndale held 'a croft called Holderscroft' adjacent to it (ibid.). The Hochyns tenancy was in the possession of Richard Tyndale when he died on 22 January 1506/7, and was inherited jointly by his sons Thomas and William Tyndale *alias* Hochyns. It seems likely that Tebota Hochyns and Richard Tyndale were married, and that Thomas and William were two of their sons, the latter being our man.

4 Anthony Kenny, *Wycliffe* (Oxford 1985), esp. pp. 100–9.

5 Ibid., pp. 65–6.

6 The identification of Tyndale as no more than a disciple of Luther goes back to the polemical opinion of his arch-enemy Sir Thomas More, who referred to him in relation to 'hys mayster Marten Luther', *The Complete Works of Thomas More* vol. 8, p. 585; this has continued to be the conventional view. S. L. Greenslade, *The Work of William Tyndale* (London 1938), p. 27, wrote that 'We cannot be sure that he had developed any constructed theology to replace the old until he went to Germany and came fully under the influence of Luther, whom he probably knew in person.' A comprehensive summary of the scholars who have propagated this theme is to be found in Donald Dean Smeeton, *Lollard Themes in the Reformation*

Theology of William Tyndale, vol. VI of *Sixteenth Century Essays and Studies* (Kirksville, Missouri 1986), pp. 17–25.

7 Smeeton, ibid., *passim*.

8 E.g. he refers to 'Berkeley Castle' as being 'just outside the Gloucester border' (ibid, p. 41) and cites the proverb 'As sure as God's in Gloucestershire' as expressing 'a popular evaluation of the religion of the region'. Smeeton does not claim expertise as a social or cultural historian of the region, and for this reason is unaware of the extreme ambivalence of 'popular evaluation of the religion . . .' etc., which was multivalent, changing over time and surrounded with multiple ironies.

9 Ibid., p. 39.

10 Ibid., p. 42.

11 Letters transcribed by George W. Marshall, 'Notes Relating to the Family of Tyndale of Stinchcombe and Nibley in Gloucestershire', *The Genealogist*, 2(10) (July 1877), pp. 4–5.

12 John Smyth refers to William, Marquis Berkeley's 'vast havocking of his patrimony' in return for titles: *Lives*, vol. II, p. 148.

13 Thomas Berkeley V (lord from 1523 to 1532) 'was a perfect Cotswold shepherd'. A contracted version of the estate reverted to Henry, lord Berkely (1534–1613), on the death of Edward VI 'for default of issue male of the body of Henry VII according to the entail of William Marquis Berkeley': *Lives*, vol. II, pp. 222, 261.

14 Smeeton, *Lollard Themes*, op. cit., p. 42; Lupton, *Tyndale*, op. cit., pp. 9–10.

15 Lupton, *Tyndale* op. cit., p. 10; Lupton describes one of the books as 'Pellican on Old Testament banned in Royal Proclamation July 1546'.

16 Lucien Febvre, 'The Origins of the French Reformation: a badly put question?' in Peter Burke (ed.) *A New Kind of History* (London 1973), p. 60.

17 Smeeton, *Lollard Themes*, op. cit., p. 253, notes another implication of the rising social status of the class, with reference to Tyndale's clothmerchant brother, John Tyndale: 'The merchant-traders, including Tyndale's own brother . . . achieved some protection from ecclesiastical persecution because of their economic and social standing.'

18 Dickens, *The English Reformation*, pp. 56, 267, 369, is the classic expositon of the connection; Smeeton makes the connection with reference to Tyndale and the Vale of Berkeley, *Lollard Themes*, op. cit., pp. 28, 32, 63, 253; as does Lupton, *Tyndale*, op. cit., pp. 13, 17–18.

19 Lupton, *Tyndale*, op. cit. pp. 7–24; Smeeton *Lollard Themes*, pp. 39–42.

20 Vita Sackville-West, *Berkeley Castle* (n.d.), p. 21 writes that Trevisa 'was a friend of Wycliffe, with whose views he was in complete sympathy'; this may be true, but it is not substantiated: Wycliffe had many 'views' and it was possible to sympathise with some of them (e.g. his interest in vernacular translation) yet be completely opposed to others (e.g., his anticlericalism and his view of the sacraments). Where Trevisa stood is not known.

21 John Hollander and Frank Kermode (eds) *The Oxford Anthology of English Literature*, vol. 1 (Oxford 1973), p. 349.

22 Smeeton, *Lollard Themes*, op. cit., p. 39.

23 Smeeton, *Lollard Themes*, op. cit., pp. 37–9; Lewis Lupton writes that Smeeton 'proves a solid continuity of *thought* from Wycliffe to Tyndale', *Tyndale*, op. cit., opp. p. 1, although the degree to which this continuity was a patrimony of his native culture in the Vale of Berkeley remains conjectural. It is conceivable that the Berkeleys protected a degree of anticlericalism on the part of their subjects, although Smeeton (op. cit., p. 41) cites authorities

to the effect that 'neither Trevisa nor his lord was a Lollard'. During Trevisa's lifetime there were no 'Lollards' as such, he being a contemporary of Wycliffe's.

24 K. G. Powell, 'The Social Background to the Reformation in Gloucestershire', *TBGAS* 92, (1973), pp. 115–19.

25 Smeeton, *Lollard Themes*, op. cit., passim.

26 Rollison 'Intensification', Ch. 4; Anthea E. Jones, 'Protestant Dissent in Gloucestershire: A comparison between 1676 and 1735', *TBGAS*, (1983), pp. 131–45, esp. p. 135.

27 Powell 'Social background', op. cit., p. 117.

28 Smeeton, *Lollard Themes*, op. cit., p. 54: When Tyndale left for London a few years later, Walsh gave him an introduction 'to a Walsh relative, Henry Guildford . . . [who] had strong import-export connections in the wool trade'.

29 Derek Wilson, *The People and the Book: The Revolutionary Impact of the English Bible* (London 1976), p. 40.

30 Tyndale, 'Preface to the five books of Moses' in Henry Walter (ed.) *Doctrinal Treatises and Introductions to Different Portions of the Holy Scriptures*, Parker Society (Cambridge 1848), p. 395.

31 Ibid. editor's introduction p. 41.

32 Ibid.

33 Fox, *Acts and Monuments*, (London 1570), pp. 688/9.

34 ibid., p. 666.

35 Fox, *Acts and Monuments* op. cit., p. 702.

36 Thomas Fuller, *The History of the Worthies of England* (repr. London 1860), vol. 1, p. 551.

37 Hockaday Abstracts: 'Coaley', GCL; E. Wraight 'Religious movements from the Reformation onwards, illustrated from the history of the churches, chapels and other meeting places in the Vale of Berkeley', handwritten ms. GRO D2940/1.

38 Ibid., 'Wotton-under-Edge'.

39 J. Blunt, *Dursley and its Neighbourhood* (Gloucester 1887), pp. 52–62.

40 Quentin Skinner, *The Foundations of Modern Political Thought*, vol. 2, *The Age of Reformation* (Cambridge 1979), pp. 71–3.

41 *The Complete Works of Thomas More* (ed. Louis Martz and Frank Manley, 1976), vol. 6, part 1, p. 286. Quoted in David Ginzberg, 'Ploughboys versus Prelates: Tyndale and More and the Politics of Biblical Translation', *Sixteenth Century Studies*, XIX(1) (1988), pp. 54–5.

42 'Tyndale's New Testament and the Gloucestershire Dialect', *GNQ*, CCCCII, refers to the curious orthography of the last edition, published in 1535. It notes that 'Tyndale was a philological reformer, who, after much investigation, had devised a method for bringing the spelling of the English language into exact conformity with its pronunciation . . . and that he adopted this spelling avowedly as representing the pronunciation of the ploughboys of his own county'.

43 See above, Chapter 3 for a detailed account of this culture.

44 Tyndale *The Obedience of a Christian Man*, in Walter, *Doctrinal Treatises*, op. cit., pp. 171–2, 177.

45 See Chapter 6 below.

46 Stephen Greenblatt, 'The Word of God in an Age of Mechanical Reproduction' in Greenblatt, *Renaissance Self-Fashioning*, op. cit., p. 89.

47 Ibid.

48 Smeeton, *Lollard Themes*, op. cit., pp. 123–248.
49 Dickens *English Reformation*, op. cit., pp. 51, 54.
50 Ibid., p. 53.
51 *Description*, p. 23.
52 Tyndale, *The Practice of Prelates*, in Walter, *Doctrinal Treatises*, op. cit., p. 294.
53 For a discussion of the lasting potency of the myth of the Norman yoke, see Christopher Hill, 'The Norman Yoke', in Hill, *Puritanism and Revolution* (London 1968), pp. 58–125.

5 NEIGHBOURHOOD TO NATION

1 Smyth, *Description*, p. 5.
2 Michael Mitterauer and Reinhard Sieder, *The European Family* (Oxford 1988), p. 27.
3 Eric R. Wolf, 'Kinship, Friendship and Patron-Client Relations in Complex Societies', in Michael Banton, *The Social Anthropology of Complex Societies* (London 1966), p. 9.
4 *Description*, pp. 123–4.
5 Will of Thomas Trotman of Cam, 'Clothyer', repr. in F. H. Trotman, *The Trotman Family* (Nottingham 1965), p. 4.
6 W. P. W. Phillimore, 'The Trotman Family', GNQ, II, p. 202; will of 'John Trotman the Elder of Cam, Cloathman' repr. GNQ, V, pp. 201–1; Trotman, *Trotman Family*, op. cit., p. 4.
7 Lewis Lupton, *Tyndale the Translator*, vol. VIII of *The History of the Geneva Bible* (London 1986), p. 8.
8 Arthur C. Tyndale, 'The Parentage of William Tyndale alias Hutchyns', TBGAS, 73, p. 210.
9 GNQ, II, p. 208.
10 Tyndale, *The Practice of Prelates*, in Henry Walter (ed.) *Doctrinal Treatises and Introductions to Different Portions of the Holy Scriptures*, Parker Society (Cambridge 1848), p. 336. Tyndale's injunction had been put into practice at Cam, where the benefice had been purchased by members of the Woodward family, fathers and uncles of the man who became Minister of Dursley in 1645, Joseph Woodward: see *Description*, p. 123.
11 Phillimore, op. cit. 'Trotman Family', p. 202; Trotman, *Trotman Family*, op. cit., p. 5: (Richard Trotman) 'Married Katherine, daughter of Edward Tyndale who was local receiver of rents for the lordship of Berkeley, to which office he was nominated in 1519 . . . He was a brother of William Tyndale whose translations of the Bible brought him to the stake in 1536. Another brother was John Tyndale who was punished for aiding in the circulation of William's New Testament. After the death of Katherine's father in 1546 his widow and son Thomas inherited the estates. Thomas Tyndale was described as 'of Eastwood, Gent' and in 1566 he leased part of the manor of Poole to Richard and Edward Trotman. Katherine on her mother's death became co-heiress with Thomas and when he died in 1571 inherited the estates of Eastwood, which property on her death passed to her son Edward Trotman'.
12 This projects the impression given by the Hearth Taxes of the 1660s back a century: in the Cam/Dursley neighbourhood 680 households were assessed in 1671; of these 287 paid and 393 were exempt on grounds of poverty; 431 households had but one hearth and a further 98 had but two

– these were the categories which tended to be exempt, and can probably be more or less identified with smallholders and labouring poor; I have classified households with 3–9 hearths as 'middle rank': 63 households had 3 hearths, 57 had 4 or 5, and 8 had 6–9: 19 per cent of all households, on these criteria, were 'middle rank': Rollison, 'The Bourgeois Soul of John Smith of Nibley', *Social History* 12(3) (October 1987), p. 324.

13 *Description*, p. 130; Trotman, *Trotman Family*, op. cit., p. 3; *GNQ*, V, p. 15.

14 'Henry Trotman who dyed 18 H[enry] VIII having by deed dated 17 April 3 HVIII purchased the same (messuage, water mill and lands comonly called Mabson's Lands) of Henry Mabson': *Description*, p. 137.

15 *GNQ*, III, p. 200.

16 *GNQ*, II, p. 203.

17 Wills of Richard Trotman and Katherine Trotman repr. in *GNQ*, V, pp. 200–3.

18 *Lives*, p. 802; *Abstracts and Extracts*, p. 191.

19 *Description*, pp. 135–6.

20 Trotman, *Trotman Family*, op. cit., p. 5.

21 *Description*; Lupton, *Tyndale*, op. cit., p. 13.

22 Lupton, *Tyndale*, op. cit., p. 10.

23 Ibid., p. 11.

24 Trotman, *Trotman Family*, op. cit., p. 5.

25 The will of Richard Trotman the Elder of Cam, Cloatman, repr. in Trotman, ibid., p. 4.

26 *Men and Armour*, 'Rodborough'.

27 See above, Chapter 3, p. 69, 'He'll prove a man of Dursley'.

28 *Description*, pp. 135–6.

29 Details from wills of Richard and Katherine Trotman, op. cit.

30 From the award to 'Edward Trotman of Cam the sonne of Richard Trotman of the same place', in Trotman, *Trotman Family*, op. cit., p. 8.

31 J. P. Cooper, 'Ideas of Gentility' in G. E. Aylmer and J. S. Morrill (eds), *Land, Men and Beliefs: Studies in Early Modern History* (London 1983) is the best general discussion of this topic.

32 *Men and Armour*.

33 Will of Edward Trotman of Slymbridge, Yeoman, proved at Gloucester 3 June 1618, abstract repr. *GNQ*, V, p. 205.

34 All references to Trotmans in or around 1608 are from the index and listings of *Men and Armour*, unless otherwise indicated.

35 'Thomas Tyndale', in Oliver Lawson Dick (ed.) *Aubrey's Brief Lives* (Harmondsworth 1978), pp. 461–2.

36 Smyth provides the tenurial history, *Description*, p. 359.

37 *Men and Armour* classifies men as 'short', 'middle' and 'tall'. Of the twenty-two Trotmans for whom this information is given, four were in the smallest category (none descendants of the branches discussed here), twelve were of middle height, and six were in the tallest category.

38 Compton Census 1676, 'Tytherington'.

39 Deduced from the statistically unusual character of the reference.

40 Trotman, *Trotman Family*, op. cit., p. 9: 'The limitation to the Grant is worthy of notice, as it is made to the "heirs" of Edward Trotman and not just to his descendants, as is usually the case . . .'

41 The epitaph, recorded by Smyth in 1639, read as follows: 'Heere lyeth the body of Mr Edward Trotman the Elder, late of Estwood, son of Mr Richard Trotman of Poole Court in Worcestershire, by Katherine his wife, daughter

of Mr Edward Tyndale, Esquire. Hee was born the 5th day of October 1545, and comfortably departed this lyfe the 6th day of June 1633': *Description*, p. 135.

42 This information is also provided in *Men and Armour*, indicated by the abbreviation 'sub'. Arms and armour brought to the musters were also recorded. Twenty years later 'in the fifth year of king Charles were – 404 subsedy men in this hundred'.

43 The practice of writing moral sayings on the walls of the household is described in Rollison, 'The Bourgeois Soul', op. cit.

44 Christopher Hill, 'The Norman Yoke', in Hill, *Puritanism and Revolution* (London 1968), p. 72.

45 See above, p. 95.

46 'Entries in Cam Registers', *GNQ*, V, p. 23; his surname was spelled alternately 'Throgmorton' and 'Throckmorton'. I have retained the name as spelled in the Cam register.

47 Trotman, *Trotman Family*, op. cit., p. 7; *GNQ*, V, p. 203.

48 *Description*, p. 135.

49 The following analysis is based on Throgmorton Trotman's will, repr. in Trotman, *Trotman Family*, op. cit., p. 10.

50 R. V. Tooley, *Maps and Mapmakers*, 7th edn (Dorset 1987), pp. 31–2.

51 See above, Chapter 2, pp. 38–9.

52 Bernard Capp, *The Fifth Monarchy Men* (London 1972), pp. 203–4, 252, 256.

53 'To Mr A[nthony] P[almer]', *The Disputation at Winchcombe, November 9 1653* (Edmund Thorne, Oxford n.d.), copy at GCL, pp. 1, 35–6.

54 See Joan Thirsk, 'Projects for Gentlemen, Jobs for the Poor: Mutual Aid in the Vale of Tewkesbury, 1600–1630', in Patrick McGrath and John Cannon (eds) *Essays in Bristol and Gloucestershire History* (Bristol 1976); D. N. Donaldson, *A Portrait of Winchcombe* (Gloucester 1978), pp. 55–83; it was a town with truculent clubman tendencies, e.g. GRO D45, MI (rent-strike, April 1637); 'The Easter Book of Winchcombe, 1631–37', GRO GDR 141A, in conjunction with *Men and Armour*, pp. 76–79 (62 of 102 men were described as 'labourer'), the 1671 Hearth Tax listing, and the parish registers for 1690–1705 (giving occupations, 142 men being described as 'pauper'), provide illuminating information on a town which was described in 1574 as being in 'a ruinous and decayed state', a condition it seems to have maintained for the following two centuries.

55 Emma Dent, *Annals of Winchcombe and Sudeley* (London 1877), pp. 253–77.

56 Abstract of Samuel Trotman's will, dated 24 May 1684, in Trotman, *Trotman Family*, op. cit., p. 12.

57 Ibid.

58 Ibid.

59 *GNQ*, II, p. 273; the same phrase appears in Trotman, ibid., p. 12.

60 Extracts from the manuscript, 'preserved at Siston Court for several generations, but now [1884] in the possession of Colonel Hibbert of Bucknell Manor, Oxfordshire' repr. in *GNQ*, II, DCCXVI, pp. 273–8; the same excerpt, omitting three sentences, is repr. without a reference in Trotman, *Trotman Family*, op. cit., pp. 12–14.

61 Holford Papers of Westonbirt, GRO 1954; for an account of different kinds of festivities on Holford's manor of Westonbirt, see Rollison, 'Property, Ideology and Popular Culture in a Gloucestershire Village, 1660–1740', *Past and Present*, 93 (November 1981).

62 Correspondence concerning the rebuilding of Dyrham House by William

Blaythwayt, GRO D.; engraving of Badminton House in Atkyns, *Gloucestershire*.

63 *GNQ*, II, pp. 275–6.

64 Information on Tetbury from a pamphlet at GCL, 'The Tetbury Wonder', which lists the persons afflicted and the persons who died; confirmed by examination of Tetbury parish registers, GRO; information on the general malaise deduced from Gloucestershire parish register aggregates at Cambridge Group, and my own aggregates of the Buckland, Dursley and Cirencester registers.

6 'SMALL THINGES AND GRANDE DESIGNES'

Keith Wrightson read a very early draft of this chapter and made a number of important suggestions with regard to Corbet's place in formulating the 'middle-class' interpretation of the English Revolution. A later version was read at a meeting of the Cambridge University Social and Economic History Seminar in November 1990. I would like to thank the members of that seminar, in particular Keith Wrightson and Andy Wood, for their penetrating questions and observations, which drew attention to weaknesses in my argument.

1 *An Historicall Relation of the Military Government of Gloucester from The Beginning of the Civill Warre Betweene King and Parliament to the Removall of Colonell Massie from that Government to the Command of the Western Forces, By John Corbet, Preacher of God's Word* (printed by M. B. for Robert Bostock at the King's Head in Paul's Church Yard, London 1645), hereafter referred to as *Historicall Relation*.

2 R. C. Richardson, *The Debate on the English Revolution* (London 1977), pp. 1–2.

3 Biographical details from 'Biographical and Historical Memoir of John Corbet', in J. Washbourne (ed.) *Bibliotheca Gloucestriensis: A Collection of Scarce and Curious Tracts Relating to the County and City of Gloucester; Illustrative of, and Published During the Civil War*, Part Two (Gloucester and London 1823), pp. iii–viii. The biographical memoir identifies Corbet with Richard Baxter's neighbour: for which see also N. H. Keble (ed.) *The Autobiography of Richard Baxter* (Letchworth 1974), pp. 215–16, 248. In 1662 Corbet refused to conform to the Restoration Settlement, was ejected from a benefice at Chichester and went up to London for some years, where he became a close friend of Baxter. Baxter preached his funeral elegy in 1680.

4 Richardson, *Debate*, op. cit., p. 113.

5 Brian Manning, *The English People and the English Revolution* (Harmondsworth 1976).

6 'John Corbet', in Joseph Stratford, *Great and Good Men of Gloucestershire* (Gloucester 1867), pp. 147–152; Quoted from p. 148.

7 John Morrill, 'Introduction', in Morrill (ed.) *Reactions to the English Civil War* (London 1982), p. 3.

8 *Historicall Relation*, p. 104.

9 Morrill, *Reactions*, op. cit., p. 10.

10 Christopher Hill, 'A Bourgeois Revolution', in J. G. A. Pocock (ed.) *Three British Revolutions, 1641, 1688, 1776* (Princeton 1980), repr. with a 'Postscript' in *The Collected Essays of Christopher Hill, Vol. 3: People and Ideas in 17th Century England*, (Brighton 1986), pp. 94–122.

11 G. E. Aylmer, *Rebellion or Revolution: England from Civil War to Restoration* (Oxford 1987), pp. 44–5.

12 Pierre Vilar, *A History of Gold and Money* (trans. Judith White, London 1984), pp. 39–40.

13 The phrase 'from below' and all hierarchical expressions are relative to specific social arrangements. In Corbet's society (and usage) it meant people who were not from the prescribed – i.e. armigerous – elite. For him the primary agent was 'the middle ranke', the constitution of which is discussed in detail below. The foregoing quotes are from Corbet's *Historicall Relation*, pp. 3–4.

14 Neither the Gloucestershire Diocesan Records (GDR) nor the Gloucester Borough Records (GRO) appear to contain any reference to Roger Corbet. The earliest reference to his occupation as a shoemaker is in *Bibliotheca Gloucestriensis*, which gives no source; Stratford, *Great and Good Men*, op. cit., p. 148, repeats the reference, again without source. F. Hyett, *The Crypt School, Gloucester* (Gloucester, n.d.) writes that Corbet was 'son of Roger Corbet of Gloucester, shoemaker. Magdelen Hall Oxford; matriculated 1636 age 16; B. A. 1639; supplicated for B. D., 1658. Rector of St. Mary de Crypt and Public Lecturer in the City [i.e. of Gloucester]', and transcribes the following entry from the records of the Crypt School: 'Elected Usher 5 Feb. 1640–1 at salary of 13 marks (13/6/9d) p.a.; this increased to 20 pounds "upon condition that he shall leave and yield up the Cure of Crist [sic] Church to Mr Valentine Marshall".' Marshall had been Rector of Eastington, in the gift of Nathaniel Stephens, from 1613 to 1633. Corbet resigned his post at the school in July 1643, when Massey appointed him his chaplain.

15 However, John Allibond used the phrase 'puritannically affected' to refer to the ministers who organised the parliamentary campaign of Nathaniel Stephens of Eastington in 1640: see below, p. 146.

16 Robert Ashton, *Reformation and Revolution 1558–1660* (London 1983), p. 313, describes Gloucester as 'strategically crucial' to Parliament.

17 Stratford, *Great and Good Men*, op. cit, pp. 124–5: 'Mr John Biddle, a gentleman of Wotton-under-Edge, who had been a student at Oxford, was at this time master of Crypt Grammar School, Gloucester. While holding this office, he began to give expression to doctrines which grieved and alarmed the orthodox puritans. It is probable, that from feeling dissatisfaction with the modes in which some of the mysterious truths of the Gospel were taught, his metaphysical mind was led to question the facts themselves.' Biddle and Corbet are bound to have discussed these matters while they were coadjucators of the Crypt School, and Corbet's ideas may have been influenced by Biddle. There was also a class affinity between the two men, who were both sons of the Gloucestershire 'middle ranke'.

18 *Historicall Relation*, p. 3: 'but things more grand and lofty seeme to be turned upon the wheeles of Providence; too high for the imitation of men.' Thus humans could grasp, but not alter, the course of history. The task was to bring human behaviour into harmony with the structures of the universe, the iron laws of mechanical motion set in force by the First Cause. It is not entirely clear how far Corbet had thought through the implications of this ultimately deterministic theory of universal origins and motions.

19 *Historicall Relation*, 'Epistle Dedicatorie', and p. 1.

20 *Historicall Relation*, p. 2.

21 Vilar, *History of Gold*, op. cit., p. 39.

22 While he makes frequent reference to 'Providence', he is careful to avoid

saying that he, personally, believes in it: e.g. *Historicall Relation* p. 6: 'If this collection shall present any thing that comes home to a civill life, or the imployment of a souldier, if it shall bring to minde acceptable services, and cause the people to remember the day of small things, with the power of active and faithfull endeavours, that observe and follow the Divine Providence, I shall not faile of my end.' This expression is compatible with the notion that, while an advanced and sophisticated intellectual like Corbet could live with the notion that there was never any absolute touchstone for knowledge, the common people could not. He may have worked out that 'if God did not exist, it would be necessary (in the interests of good order) to invent Him.' *If* this is so – and it is no more than compatible with Corbet's formulae in the *Historicall Relation* – he later lost this (conjectural) youthful arrogance, and in later (post–1662) writings expressed deep, even mystical piety: see *Great and Good Men*, op. cit., p. 149.

23 *Historicall Relation*, p. 3.
24 *Historicall Relation*, p. 8.
25 Transcribed from the original at Cirencester parish church.
26 *Historicall Relation*, p. 8.
27 *Historicall Relation*, p. 9.
28 *Historicall Relation*, p. 16.
29 *Men and Armour*; R. H. and A. J. Tawney, 'An Occupation Census of the Seventeenth Century', *Economic History Review*, 1, 5(1) (1934) pp. 25–64; John Wyatt, 'Men and Armour for Gloucestershire in 1608', *Gloucestershire Historical Studies*, 8 (1974); Wyatt, 'Trades and Occupations in Gloucester, Tewkesbury and Cirencester in 1608', *GHS*, 7 (1973); Wyatt, 'Occupation and Physique in 1608', *GHS*, 6 (1972); Wyatt, 'How Reliable is Men and Armour?', *GHS*, 9 (1978); Wyatt, 'Industry in Gloucestershire in 1608', *GHS* 10 (1979). Rollison, 'Intensification', aggregated the occupations in *Men and Armour* on a parish-by-parish basis for the entire county, following the procedures laid down by Mr Wyatt.
30 Rollison, 'Intensification'; Tom Arkell, 'The Incidence of Poverty in England in the Later Seventeenth Century', *Social History*, 12 (1) (January 1987) pp. 23–48, reminds scholars that the Hearth Tax listings are not a definitive source, and should not be used uncritically; that is to say, the results yielded by aggregative analysis of lists should be used in conjunction with other records pertaining to the settlements in question.
31 R. H. and A. J. Tawney, 'An Occupation Census', op. cit. Leslie Jeffrey Zweigman, 'The Role of the Gentleman in County Government and Society: the Gloucestershire Gentry, 1625–1649', McGill University PhD thesis, July 1987, Vol. 1. p. 110.
32 The term 'middle rank' is used by Corbet twice, both usages illustrating that it was a term which came naturally: 'neither they of the middle rank, nor the needy were devoted to the examples of the gentlemen' (p. 9) suggests that in his mind the distinction was one of material security, between plebeians who lived moderately well, and those who, from time to time, experienced 'necessity'. The second occasion (p.16) refers to 'the yeomen, farmers, cloathiers, and the whole middle ranke of the people'.
33 *Historicall Relation*, p. 10.
34 Ibid. Corbet's proposition here is confirmed in Baxter's *Autobiography*, op. cit., esp. Ch. IV. Baxter also writes (p. 34) that it was 'principally the differences about religious matter that filled up the parliament's armies and put the resolution and valour into their soldiers, which carried them

on in another manner than mercenary soldiers are carried on'. With regard to prejudices against the Welsh, Corbet assumed they were conventional but does not appear to have shared them, referring to 'an inveterate hatred derived by fabulous tradition [that] had passed betweene the Welch-men and the citizens of Gloucester. Such slight and irrational passages prevail much with the common people in whom opinion beares rule': *Historicall Relation*, p. 27.

35 *Historicall Relation*, p. 6.
36 Allibond–Heylin, 24 March 1640, PRO SP16/448/79, repr. (with omissions) in *GNQ* I, pp. 410–11, and in Morgan, *Memoirs of the Dutton Family* (Gloucester n.d., copy at GCL), pp. 146–7.
37 Victor Turner, *From Ritual to Theater: the Human Seriousness of Play* (New York 1982), pp. 69–70.
38 *DNB*, 'Godfrey Goodman'.
39 See above, Chapter 4.
40 Peter Levi, *The Life and Times of William Shakespeare* (London 1983), pp. 28–9.
41 All citations in this section, except where otherwise indicated, are to Allibond–Heylin, op. cit.
42 Emma Dent, *Annals of Winchcombe and Sudeley* (London 1877), p. 223.
43 Peter Clark, 'The Ramoth-Gilead of the Good: urban change and political radicalism at Gloucester 1540–1640', in P. Clark, A. G. R. Smith and N. Tyacke (eds.) *The English Commonwealth 1547–1640* (London 1979), p. 168.
44 Joan Johnson, *The Gloucestershire Gentry* (Gloucester 1989), 81.
45 Ibid, p. 185; see also P. Clark, 'The Civil Leaders of Gloucester 1580–1800', in Clark (ed.) *The Transformation of the English Provincial Town* (London 1984); Peter Ripley, 'The Trade and Social Structure of Gloucester, 1600–1640', *TBGAS* (1976) pp. 117–23.
46 Sir Robert Cooke – JS of Nibley (February 1642?), GRO D2510/10.
47 Cooke–Smyth, 28 October 1640, GRO D2510/11.
48 Aristocratic honour in the sixteenth and seventeenth centuries, and its milieus, is described, defined and discussed in Mervyn James, *Society, Politics and Culture: Studies in Early Modern England* (Cambridge 1988).
49 Stephens' leadership of the clothmaking sector was long standing. In 1630, writes Brian Manning, 'Nathaniel Stephens, well-to-do Squire and a J.P., and a puritan and an opponent of the Court, put himself at the head of the resistance to Wither and his [Cloth] Commission. Wither reported to the privy council that Stephens encouraged the clothiers and searchers in their laxity, and opposed his Commission; the Merchant Adventurers complained that Stephens interfered with the appointment of searchers and persuaded other J. P.s to obstruct Wither's work'. *The English People*, op. cit., p. 157. 'Men like Nathaniel Stephens . . . sat in the House of Commons, [and] had backed the clothiers against the government and owed their seats . . . very largely to the votes of the clothiers': ibid., p. 162. It is unlikely that the votes of clothiers alone would have got Stephens elected; Manning, unfamiliar with the grass-roots circumstances in counties like Gloucestershire, fails to recognise that many master-craftsmen owned freehold land sufficient to give them a vote, and that many yeomen and craftsman in other trades owed their prosperity, directly or indirectly, to the clothing industry, and would also have supported Stephens.
50 Turner, *Ritual to Theater*, op. cit.; Vilar, *History of Gold*, op. cit.
51 Zweigman, 'Role of the Gentleman', op. cit., p. 212. Stephens, usually called 'of Eastington', was the youngest of three sons to Thomas Stephens,

who, by means of a judicious marriage to the only child of a London merchant, and by the wealth he gathered in his position as Attorney to Prince Henry and Prince Charles, the sons of James I, was able to bequeath to each of his sons a portion sufficient to form the basis of three separate gentry lineages. Nathaniel's older brother, Edward, 'was ancestor to the Stephens's of Sodbury'; the second oldest, John 'was ancestor to the Stephens's of Lypiat (on the outskirts of Stroud); Nathaniel himself was ancestor 'to the Stephens's of Cherington': Atkyns *Gloucestershire*, gives an abstract of the genealogy under his account of Eastington. GRO D547a, E2, 'Stephens Papers', give details of his property at Eastington during the Civil War, including claims for expenses engaged while billeting Parliamentarian soldiers.

52 Of the 70 able-bodied men attending the 1608 muster from the manor of Alkerton (part of Eastington), 42 were clothworkers, including one of the most substantial clothiers in the county, William Clutterbuck, who was accompanied to the muster by no fewer than 10 servants. Of 52 men from the manor of Eastington, 26 were involved in clothmaking. Eastington was a clothmaking *centre*, as the presence of Clutterbuck and four other clothiers (including Edward Stephens, probably Nathaniel's uncle) indicates: *Men and Armour*, pp. 310–11.

53 'The Tracy family of Toddington . . . was engaged in tobacco growing around Winchcombe, [and] one younger member, William Tracy of Hailes, near Winchcombe, was actively associated with the Virginia Company, recruiting men for the Virginia plantation': Joan Thirsk, 'New Crops and their Diffusion', in *The Rural Economy of England* (London 1984), p. 261 and *passim*, and also 'Projects for Gentlemen, Jobs for the Poor', ibid., pp. 287–307. I.e. the key distinction is not between people who were actively involved in trade, and/or who lived in areas which were involved in economic monoculture for national and international markets, and those who were or did not. Rather, it is a reference to the different types of social order and mentality implied in the plantation monoculture, in which hundreds of impoverished labourers left their households at certain times of the year to work together in the fields under the direction of overseers, and the 'domestic' or 'dispersed' production model that predominated in the clothworking districts. In the economic sense clothworkers were no more independent than the tobacco-plantation workers at Winchcombe, both depending on capitalists to provide them with raw materials and to sell what they produced. The whole matter is too complex to describe in detail at this time, except to say that the history and traditions of the clothworking trades, sustained by guilds and clubs in every town, and the physical circumstances of their lives and work in individual household units engendered an inevitable affinity to 'independency', such that it was necessary for them to feel that they were personally in control of the social disciplines which ordered their lives. In a plantation economy the household tends to be reduced to 'sleeping quarters'; in dispersed manufacturing it is a powerful affective unit. Puritanism was strong in the clothworking and urban districts and weak in the Royalist stronghold of northeast Gloucestershire for precisely this reason. It was this relative household autonomy which united the richest yeoman farmer and the poorest clothworker, both of whom knew what 'independency' and 'liberty' meant without having to think about it, even if many of them were never likely to achieve their necessary prerequisite: a yeoman-freehold, or at least a

substantial plot of rented land to provide subsistence in time when markets could not sustain a livelihood in clothmaking (or another trade)

54 R. H. Hilton, 'Winchcombe Abbey and the Manor of Sherborne', in H. P. R. Finberg (ed.) *Gloucestershire Studies* (Leicester 1967).

55 *Men and Armour*, 'Sherborne'.

56 Quoted in Dent, *Annals*, op. cit., p. 229; 'Queen Elizabeth's Progress in Gloucestershire in 1592', *GNQ*, DCCXCVIII.

57 Tracy's great-grandmother was the second daughter of Gyles Brydges, 2nd lord Chandos of Sudeley: Dent, *Annals*, op. cit. p. 223. George Brydges, 6th lord Chandos of Sudeley, was Charles I's main agent in Gloucestershire in the presentation of his Commission of Array in August 1643, and his family were proverbially referred to as 'kings of the Cotswolds': *DNB*, 'Grey Brydges', and see below for what happened when he tried to present the king's Commission at Cirencester, then the centre of clothmaking in the region and the town where the wool and cloth producers met.

58 Pierre Bourdieu, *Outline of a Theory of Practice* (London 1977), p. 79.

59 Marshall Sahlins, *Culture and Practical Reason* (Chicago 1976), p. viii.

60 Sir Ralph (b. 1603) was the youngest son of Sir William Dutton of Sherborne, and though a knight as a result of his court connections, was head of a cadet branch of the family of which John Dutton of Sherborne was the head. He was a Colonel of Horse and Foot in Charles's army, and drowned in a shipwreck while fleeing to France in 1646: P. R. Newman, *Royalist Officers in England and Wales, 1642–60: A Biographical Dictionary* (New York and London 1981).

61 They were 'Fox of Tewkesbury', 'Geery of Elmore, the canny mumping fellow with the red head, whom [Heylyn] sometime knew at Magdelen Hall [Oxford], likewise suspended and deprived', 'Marshall of Elmore', 'Stansfield, a lecturer of Rodborough', 'Guilliam of Hatherley', 'Prior of Sandhurst, an ordinary law-driver, and strongly puritannical', 'Baxter of Forthampton . . . who spares not to excuse . . . the Scots in their holy proceedings', 'Whynnell, our learned lecturer at Gloucester', 'Jones of Tidrington, a man in whose face one may read schism and malice', 'Workman the younger', and 'Stubbes, Sir Robert Cooke's chaplain, of the right strene *cum multis aliis*': Allibond–Heylyn, *GNQ*, I, pp 412–13. He added two laymen 'both strong and rank puritans, Nelmes and Edwards'.

62 e.g. F. D. Price, 'An Elizabethan Church Official: Thomas Powell, Chancellor of Gloucester Diocese', *Church Quarterly Review* (1939), pp. 94–112; and Price, 'Elizabethan Apparitors in the Diocese of Gloucester', ibid. (1942), pp. 37–55; *DNB*, 'Godfrey Goodman'.

63 Patrick Collinson, *The Religion of Protestants: the Church in English Society 1559–1625* (Oxford 1982), *passim*.

64 *Historicall Relation*, p. 17.

65 James, *Society, Politics and Culture*, op. cit., *passim*.

66 *Historicall Relation*, p. 9. As here, there is much in Corbet's analysis, and even in his phraseology, to suggest the influence of Machiavelli: see Bernard Crick's introduction to Crick (ed.) *Machiavelli: The Discourses* (Harmondsworth 1970), pp. 39–41. Whether this similarity of analytic modes and of terminology is due to a reading of the Florentine's writings, or whether it is due to the similarities of social and historical circumstances – i.e. that similar social circumstances will tend to produce similar analyses – is a matter for further research into Corbet's reading habits and education.

Felix Raab, *The English Face of Machiavelli: A Changing Interpretation 1500–1700* (London 1964), provides useful background.

67 *Historicall Relation*, pp. 15–16.

68 *Historicall Relation*, p. 16.

69 *Historicall Relation*, pp. 8, 14.

70 *Historicall Relation*, p. 14.

71 *Historicall Relation*, p. 9.

72 *Historicall Relation*, p. 9.

73 Calculated from the figures for households and freeholders given for every parish in Atkyns, *Gloucestershire*, it should be noted that there were very considerable variations from district to district, ranging from ratios of around 4:1 in the districts around Gloucester, Tewkesbury and Circencester, to just under 6:1 in the Stroudwater/Vale of Berkeley clothing districts and in the Forest of Dean. Freeholders were more numerous in absolute terms, but fewer as a proportion of total population in the more densely populated manufacturing districts.

74 Calculations from GRO 323, photocopy of the Lady Day 1671 listings for Gloucestershire.

75 See William Tyndale, *The Obedience of a Christian Man, and How Christian Rulers Ought to Govern*, in Henry Walter (ed.) *Doctrinal Treatises and Introductions to Different Portions of the Holy Scriptures*, Parker Society (Cambridge 1848): 'The obedience of all degrees proved by God's Word: and first of Children unto their Elders'; 'The obedience of Wives unto their Husbands'; 'The obedience of Servants unto their Masters'; 'The obedience of Subjects unto Kings, Princes and Rulers'; 'The Office of a Father, and how he should rule', etc., pp. 168–203.

76 *Historicall Relation*, p. 9. Richard Baxter's *Autobiography*, op. cit., pp. 26–42, vividly illustrates the contrast that Corbet had in mind. In Baxter's home country further north in the Severn Vale in Shropshire, and in Worcestershire, 'the fury of the rabble' was for the king, 'but when I came to Gloucester,' he wrote, 'among strangers also that had never known me, I found a civil, courteous and religious people, as different from Worcester as if they had lived under another government': ibid., p. 39.

77 Letter dated 21 January 1642(3), repr. in Beecham, *History of Cirencester* (1887, repr. Dursley 1978), p. 9, 288; the reference was to Circencester's position at the head of the Thames Valley, where the main London–St David's thoroughfare entered the Cotswold Hills. Cirencester had been an important road junction since Roman times, when it was a much more important city than either Gloucester or Bristol. Arguably, and in spite of its relatively small resident population (3,000–4,000) it re-assumed this pre-eminence between 1540 and 1660, when its franchise was restored (all householders had the vote) and it became the unchallenged centre of the manufacturing districts to the south, in Wiltshire, and the Stroudwater Valleys to the west. Effectively it was a suburb of London, an extremely lively and conflict-ridden borough where the pastoral (wool-producing) magnates of the North Wolds and their armed retinues, and the clothiers and craftsmen of the clothmaking districts, rubbed shoulders on a daily basis.

78 *Historicall Relation*, p. 8.

79 This was Shakespeare's view in *Coriolanus*, and Machiavelli's in *The Discourses* (ed. Crick, op. cit.) e.g. 'The Populace, misled by the False Appear-

ance of Advantage, often seeks its own Ruin, and is easily moved by Splendid Hopes and Rash Promises', pp. 238–42.

80 *Historicall Relation*, p. 8 (emphasis added).

81 Letter from John Gifford, 'Cisseter the 16th August 1642', in *Bibliotheca Gloucestriensis*, op. cit., vol. 1, repr. in Beecham, *Cirencester*, op. cit., pp. 287–8.

82 Ibid.

83 *Historicall Relation*, p. 8.

84 Populist sectarian disputation raised its head at Gloucester in July 1644, as soon as Massey had cleared the county of Royalist garrisons. Both sides of the dispute are documented in Robert Bacon, *The Spirit of Prelacie Yet Working, or Truth from under a Cloud in a Relation of that Greate and Publicke Contestation had in Gloucester, July 1644* (Giles Calvert, London 1646), and John Corbet, *A Vindication of the Magistrates and Ministers of the City of Gloucester from the Calumnies of Mr Robert Bacon* (Robert Bostock, London 1646). Bacon implied that the ministers of Gloucester, led by Corbet, had him suppressed and ejected from the city 'because the people had such recourse to me, and their congregations where he and the rest of the Ministers taught . . . were like to Pharoes fat kine' (p. 4), i.e. his sermons attracted much greater crowds consisting of the poorer sort. In his reply Corbet states that at Gloucester they 'had greate experience of 'the vain boastings of secretaries' (p. 18) and implied that Bacon's doctrines were 'antinomian' (p. 26). He refers to Bacon's populist rhetoric ('he did alwayes ground into something extraordinary, beyond that which the people had been formerly taught, even concerning the substance of fundamentall doctrine: every mindfull hearer took it for a new way, especially his own favourers, & then of prodigall preachers . . . began to be rolled on every tongue': (pp. 7–8). Corbet saw himself as representative of 'the Elect' (p. 17). Bacon was given a horse, taken to Sudeley with Massey's soldiers, and given an escort of two men as far as the Parliamentarian garrison at Warwick. For Massey's victories of May 1644, see *Historicall Relation*, pp. 93–103, and *Eben-ezer: A Full and Exact Relation of the Severall Remarkable and Victorious Proceedings of the Ever-Renowned Colonel Massey, Governor of Gloucester, from May 7 to May 25 1644. In which time he took these severall considerable garrisons of the Enemie in Gloucestershire and Wiltshire, namely Wesbury, Little Deane, Newnham, Beverstone-Castle, Malmesbury and Chippenahm* (John White, London, 4 June 1644).

85 *Historicall Relation*, p. 25. Of the siege of Cirencester he writes that 'the souldiers of the Earle of Stamford's regiment had acted the best part'; and after the siege 'the *common* souldiers [were] quite off the hinges, either cowardly or mutinous' (emphasis added, ibid., p. 20).

86 *Historicall Relation*, p. 31.

87 *Historicall Relation*, p. 21.

88 *Historicall Relation*, p. 22.

89 Ibid.

90 *Historicall Relation*, pp. 40–1.

91 *Eben-ezer*, op. cit.

92 *Historicall Relation*, pp. 63, 131. In late 1643 'the enemy swarmes in every corner, except the country [i.e. the in-shire] of the city and Whitstone Hundred' (p. 87). Whitstone Hundred was clothier country, and housed the garrison at Nathaniel Stephens' house at Eastington. In the weeks following, the Royalists 'wasted the hill country whilst we secured the

Vale'. Beverstone Castle was taken because 'the gaining of it would free the clothiers of Stroudwater from the bondage and terrour of that government' (p. 97). 'Most of the gentlemen fled their houses' during the engagements (p. 121). 'Yate Court within ten miles of Bristoll' was relieved 'to secure the neighbourhood being a well-affected people' (p. 129): it was clothier country (*Men and Armour*, pp. 215–17).

93 *Historicall Relation*, p. 118.
94 *Historicall Relation*, p. 125.
95 *Historicall Relation*, p. 138.
96 The quote is from *Historicall Relation* p. 140.
97 *Historicall Relation*, p. 100. Corbet himself does not labour this point, which I have drawn out from passages in his descriptions in order to underline his (and Massey's) underlying assumptions.
98 Aylmer, *Rebellion*, op. cit., p. 50.
99 With respect to certain fighting engagements, Corbet does occasionally mention the role of local people as distinct from soldiers. During a skirmish at Brockthorpe in February 1644 a lieutenant 'was inforced by the enemy to engage himself, *and many willing people of the neighbourhood* in that weak hold'; in the engagement 'we lost three inferior officers, seaven and thirty common souldiers, *and many country men*. Similarly, 'at that season the governour had commanded to Stroud, another guard of fifty musketiers *to support and strengthen* the place *in its own defence*': *Historicall Relation*, p. 89 (emphasis added). Parliament's was a popular cause in Gloucestershire; but for military resistance and victory, implacable resolution was necessary. Taking his text as a whole, Corbet is quite clear that such resolution was the quality of a small minority. In other words, Corbet's account is in fact more sensible than much decontextualised quotation has made him seem.

7 CUNNING MAN AND QUAKER

I am grateful to John Morrill and Colin Davis for their comments on early drafts of this chapter.

1 All references in this chapter are to *Some Memoirs of the Life of John Roberts Written by his Son Daniel Roberts*, 2nd edn (Sam Farley, Bristol 1747). There is an incomplete undated ms. copy, entitled 'Life of John Roberts' at the GRO (D.1829), handwritten on paper watermarked 1707, which may be in Daniel Roberts' hand. The manuscript version, while earlier than any of the printed versions, is word-for-word the same, which suggests that the *Memoir* was circulated in manuscript before it was printed.
2 These words are ascribed to the Bishop of Gloucester, John Nicholson: *Memoir*, pp. 3, 52.
3 He appears in the Hearth Tax listings for Siddington St Mary as living in a four-hearth household, GRO D.383.
4 *An abstract of the Sufferings of the People Called Quakers . . . Taken from Original Records and other Authentick Accounts, Vol. 1 1650–1660* (London 1667), p. 173.
5 Ibid., pp. 167–73.
6 Ibid., pp. 172–3.
7 *A Collection of the Sufferings of the Quakers* (London 1690), vol. 1, p. 216.
8 Ibid., p. 221.
9 Ibid., pp. 222, 223, 224, 225.
10 *Memoir*, pp. 3, 52.

11 Humphrey Carpenter, *Jesus*, 'Past Masters' series (OUP 1980), p. 1.

12 *Memoir*, p. 27.

13 e.g. Alan Cole, 'The Quakers and the English Revolution', in Trevor Aston (ed.), *Crisis in Europe 1560–1660, Essays from Past and Present* (London 1965).

14 Richard T. Vann, *The Social Development of English Quakerism 1655–1755* (Harvard 1969), p. 73.

15 The list is in a manuscript ledger held at the GRO, D.1340 A1/A2.

16 Cole, 'The Quakers', op. cit., p. 341; Vann, *Social Development*, op. cit., pp. 49–69.

17 *Memoir*, p. 3; Cole, 'The Quakers', op. cit., p. 342.

18 As some scholars have claimed of the early Quakers; see Cole, 'The Quakers', op. cit., p. 342.

19 Carpenter, *Jesus*, op. cit.; Ian Wilson, *Jesus: the Evidence* (London 1984).

20 'Andrew Sollace' is the first name on the list of subscribers to *The Petition of the Inhabitants (of Cirencester) . . . presented to his Majesty at Oxford, February 28 [1643]* (Oxford 1643).

21 *Memoir*, p. 4. Daniel Roberts' quiet stress on his family background underlines the transfer of something like 'honour' to bourgeois families, although of course John Roberts, in becoming a Quaker, opted out of the 'gentry race' by becoming anti-Establishment. Mervyn James describes the kinship dimension of 'honour' as follows: 'The steadfastness of the man of honour, manifesting itself in a "faithfulness" to his freely given word, was of the essence of the social dimension of honour. Only one obligation went deeper than this: that of the lineage, the family and kinship group. For this, being inherited with the "blood", did not depend on promise or oath. It could neither be contracted into, nor could the bond be broken. For the man's very being as honourable had been transmitted to him with the blood of his ancestors, themselves honourable men. Honour therefore was not merely an individual possession, but that of the collectivity, the lineage': Mervyn James, *Society, Politics and Culture: Studies in Early Modern England* (Cambridge 1988), p. 325. As I show, however, John Roberts did break the family and kinship bond, explicitly and wilfully, in favour of 'the light within'. 'Honour' then became an *individual* quality. The concept remained the same (as the surprising ease with which these words of James could be applied as a description of Roberts shows), but its locus changed. Quakers like Roberts were extremely radical, as I show, in their explicit rejection of the 'concentric circles' of traditional loyalty: family, household, neighbourhood and 'country' in every sense all took second place to 'self', the 'inner light'.

22 *Memoir*, pp. 7–9.

23 Ibid.

24 John Bossy, *Christianity in the West 1400–1700* (Oxford 1985), Ch. 8.

25 The Quaker ledger 'Christian and Brotherly Advice' (GRO D.729), compiled some time after 1690, when the movement gradually became 'routinised', testifies to this qualification: the 'Heads' include advice on 'Children' (pp. 43–59), 'Families' (pp. 135–8), 'Love' (p. 167), 'Marriage' (pp. 169–84), 'Orphans' (p. 241) and 'Servants' (p. 365). However, the careful compilation of 'advices' (the categories were continually added to by different hands) suggests a felt need for careful, unambiguous guidelines which, it might be suggested, would not have been required a century earlier, when the family was the taken-for-granted *sine qua non* of all social life.

26 Cole, 'The Quakers', op. cit., p. 342, citing M. E. Hirst, *The Quakers in Peace and War* (London 1923), pp. 527–9.

27 *Memoir*, p. 4.

28 The simplicity of Daniel Roberts' text indicates careful and self-conscious preparation. One long paragraph (*Memoir*, pp. 3–5) covers the events of 1643.

29 *Memoir*, p. 16, where Roberts lists these as symbols the Restoration Church shared with the 'Papists'.

30 *Memoir*, p. 5.

31 Michel de Certeau, 'What Freud Makes of History: A Seventeenth-Century Demonological Neurosis', Ch. 8 of *The Writing of History* (trans. Tom Conley, New York 1988).

32 Giles Fettiplace, Lord of the Manor of Coln St Aldwyns, and governor and leader of the defence of Cirencester in 1643, became a Quaker somewhat later than Roberts, and used to ride to Meetings at Cirencester in his coach and six. The famous Quaker political economist, John Bellers, regarded by both Marx and Owen as a pioneering writer who espoused the labour theory of value, was from Cirencester and married Fettiplace's daughter, becoming himself Lord of the Manor of Coln St Aldwyns in 1701: Leslie Stephen, *Cirencester Quakers* (Cirencester 1973). Cole, 'The Quakers', op. cit., p. 347, gives as a reason why 'they so often stood aloof from political movements' that 'the conditions for the re-emergence of an independent popular movement did not exist: the yeomen and artisans of the old order had been decisively defeated, and the modern working class movement had not yet been born'. As I have already suggested, there are other indices of connections between the radical movement of 1642–3 (or, indeed, 1639–40) and the Labour Movement in the eighteenth century, which appeared in precisely those parishes and districts that John Corbet identifies as the outposts of Parliamentarian resistance during the first civil war (John Corbet, *An Historicall Relation of the Military Government of Gloucester from The Beginning of the Civill Warre Betweene King and Parliament to the Removall of Colonell Massie from that Government to the Command of the Western Forces, By John Corbet, Preacher of God's Word*, London 1645), e.g. pp. 88–9; refs to Painswick and Stroud, which in turn suggests that the shape of the war, locally, was determined not by strategic military exigencies, but by the predetermined loyalties of neighbourhoods, which in turn had to do with the variable political–economic contexts in which different neighbourhoods operated. The Quakers became strong in precisely those districts which the defenders of Gloucester selected to defend as their outposts (see Chapter 1 above): for a comprehensive account of these, see e.g. 'Extracts from Thomas Story's Journal of Quaker Meetings in Gloucestershire, 1693–1733', GRO D.1762/9. I am not suggesting the continuities are simple to explain – e.g. Quakers tended to come from the 'employer class', which on the face of it hardly qualifies them as founders of the Labour Movement – only that there is too much circumstantial evidence that they existed, to deny them.

33 Elfrida Vipont, *George Fox and the Valiant Sixty* (London 1975); Hugh Barbour, *The Quakers in Puritan England* (New Haven 1964), p. 85, writes that 'the Quakers were strongest in Gloucestershire, Somerset and Dorset, an area that needs more study . . . Gloucestershire had been Lollard country, and there was some tradition of Puritanism, which had spread from Bristol and Plymouth'. As indicated, this last observation is wrong. It is just as

accurate to say that 'Puritanism' spread to Bristol and Plymouth from the rural areas of counties like Gloucestershire. Norman Penney (ed.) *The First Publishers of Truth* (Philadelphia 1907), pp. 104–11, transcribes contemporary accounts of the foundations of Meetings in Gloucestershire, though the information given in this source is not exhaustive.

34 *Memoir*, p. 5. The *Memoir* actually dates this in 1665, but this is clearly incorrect. Richard Farnsworth, the instrument of Roberts' conversion, was in Banbury gaol in 1655: Penney, *First Publishers*, op. cit., p. 167, records '1655 . . . Richard Farnsworth was . . . imprisoned long at Banbury in Oxfordshire'. And, as we have already seen, the Restoration authorities identified Roberts as a likely source of resistance in 1660, when he was arrested at Quaker Meetings at Cirencester.

35 *Memoir*, p. 5.

36 Vipont, *George Fox*, op. cit., p. 19.

37 Ibid.

38 It takes an effort of imagination to reconstruct the impact of women travellers like the two who came to Cirencester enquiring 'after such as Fear God', and of the courage that was required by women to engage in such travelling. To put it mildly, they were putting themselves in jeopardy by doing so. Nor were Quaker women necessarily in an apparently subordinate position to the 'patriarchs' of the movement like Farnsworth and Roberts. Theophila Townshend was a particular thorn in the flesh of the Establishment in Gloucestershire in the 1670s and 1680s. For details of her activities see *A Collection of the Sufferings*, op. cit., pp. 224–5, where she is described as a 'preacher'.

39 Penney, *First Publishers*, op. cit., p. 278.

40 As I note below, John Roberts identified strongly with the Old Testament prophet Daniel, naming his eldest son and memorialist after him. Quakers like William Dewsbury similarly identified with the archetypal opponent of 'the great Beast of Nebuchadnezzar': Cole, 'The Quakers', op. cit., p. 345.

41 This paragraph is based on Wilson, *Jesus*, op. cit., 'Jesus the Jew', pp. 57–70, esp. p. 63.

42 The novels of Anita Mason, *The Illusionist* (London 1983) and *Bethany* (London 1981), are of some interest in this respect, as highly plausible fictional evocations of the kind of activities I have in mind.

43 Here a reader may consult another fictional evocation, Bertolt Brecht, 'The Experiment' (written through the eyes of a fictional servant of a fictional Francis Bacon), in *Tales from the Calendar*, (trans. Yvonne Kapp, London 1966).

44 *Memoir*, pp. 5–6.

45 Ibid. Elizabeth Braithwaite Emmot, *A Short History of Quakerism, Earlier Periods* (New York 1923), p. 106, says that Farnsworth, like Roberts, was 'a man of good education'. Vipont, *George Fox*, op. cit., p. 16, describes him as 'well-educated' and 'thoughtful'. A lot of instinctive prejudices, derived from centuries (millennia) of understandable Establishment propaganda designed to discredit authority that is not licensed from above, i.e. which derives from popular experience, have to be short-circuited in order to see the rational side, but above all the 'quiet' assurance of men like Farnsworth, who were as far from 'ranting' as it is possible to be. No doubt King David was none too pleased when the *Nabi'im* Isaiah voiced the universal suppressed knowledge that he had arranged for one of his

generals to be placed in the front line because the king was committing adultery with his wife. The major problem with *Nabi'im* and wizards is not their magic, but their truth-telling.

46 Beecham, *History of Cirencester* (1887, repr. Dursley 1978), 'The Baptist Chapel', pp. 139–40.

47 In conversation with the Bishop of Gloucester, Roberts put it like this (*Memoir*, pp. 24–5). 'I was a long Time seeking Acquaintance with the Living GOD amongst the dead forms of Worship, and enquiring after the right Way and Worship of GOD, before I could find it; and now, I hope, neither thou nor any man living shall be able to persuade me out of it . . . In Oliver's days . . . The Common Prayer Book was then become (even among the Clergy) like an old Almanack, very few regarding it in our Country. There were two or three Priests indeed, who stood honestly to their principals, and suffer'd pretty much; but the far greater number turn'd with the Tide: And we have Reason to believe, that if *Oliver* would have put Mass into their Mouths, they would have conform'd even to that for their Bellies.'

48 Vann, *Social Development*, op. cit., p. 3.

49 The Society of Friends also used print and literacy to reinforce the Quaker sense of community, and to unify what would otherwise have been a highly dispersed 'congregation'.

50 County studies have shown that the gentry as a class never lost control of the English provinces. Leadership personnel sometimes changed after the defeat of the King's Party, but the class remained at the helm. Thus the English Revolution was not a 'middle-class' revolution in any plebeian sense. The middle ranks, as John Corbet assures us, were the rank and file. Quakers like John Roberts were in the vanguard of the rise of the English middle classes, constantly raising the question 'who fought?' in the minds of gentlemen who, at the outset, had been, in Corbet's words 'detestably neutral', but who qualified as regional officials under Cromwell on the grounds that there was no evidence that they had been Royalist, nor was there any that they had actually opposed the cause of Parliament.

51 John Bellers, for example, advocated a European state: Leslie Stephen, *Cirencester Quakers*, op. cit.

52 'And after this time he patiently bore the Cross . . .': *Memoir*, p. 6. I stress 'patiently' since he was clearly asked to bear a cross of some kind in the previous decade. What changed after 1655 was his manner of bearing it, i.e. 'patiently'. This was where he crossed the line from doubt to faith. Patience means willingness to wait, and confidence that what one is waiting for will eventually arrive. His 'conversion' by Farnsworth implied no funda-mental change of outlook, only a shift of emphasis, a reduction in the degree to which human instrumentality was seen as a factor, abandonment to the will of the deity. Quaker 'silence' was an aspect of this patience. It involved clearing the mind ('meditation') to receive a message, to be a human conduit for that message. It is only possible to be patient if one has faith that useful and important messages would arrive in due course. The human mind being what it is, meditation does in fact have an effect like this, 'subconscious' priorities which are suppressed coming to the surface. Modern science of course applies 'Occam's Razor' to this process, arguing that it is not necessary to explain the insights gained by such disciplines in supernaturalist terms.

53 *Memoir*, p. 6.

54 *Memoir*, pp. 17–22.

55 *Memoir*, p. 22.

56 *Memoir*, p. 23.

57 Strictly speaking, these are Daniel Roberts' words, of course. If this distinction is rigorously adhered to, and on the assumption that Daniel wrote his account before 1710, it confirms that the radical spirit of Quakerism survived into the second generation, that the 'quiescent', 'introversionist', 'routinised' stage had not yet been fully reached.

58 *Memoir*, p. 33.

59 Ibid.

60 *Memoir*, p. 23.

61 *Memoir*, p. 25 (during his second dialogue with the Bishop, whom he then asks, 'if thou dids't not think thy Religion worth venturing thy Throat for in *Oliver's* days, I desire thee to consider it is not worth cutting other Mens Throats now for not conforming to it').

62 *Memoir*, p. 28.

63 Quoted in Robert Nelson, *The Life of Dr George Bull, Late Bishop of St Davids, with the History of those Controversies in which he was Engaged* (London 1713), p. 53.

64 *Memoir*, p. 29.

65 *Memoir*, p. 26; one of these occasions took place in 1681, as reported in *A Collection of the Sufferings*, op. cit., p. 221.

66 Nelson, *Life of George Bull*, op. cit., p. 61.

67 Ibid., p. 54.

68 *Memoir*, p. 36.

69 Keith Thomas, *Religion and the Decline of Magic* (Harmondsworth 1978), see the index: 'cunning men and women'.

70 The 'ancient . . . Widow Hewlings' killed by Jenkins the hangman during the incident at Cirencester in 1670 is described as 'an useful woman in the neighbourhood, a skilful Midwife, and ready to do good to all': *A Collection of the Sufferings*, op. cit., p. 216.

71 Thomas, *Religion*, op. cit., p. 292, and 'The Magical Profession' pp. 291–300; for a discussion of the derivation of 'wizard', Ibid., see pp. 209–10, and *OED*, p. 3805.

72 Ibid., p. 292.

73 Bull was in the Bishop's entourage when it stopped for refreshment – and discussion – at Roberts' farm, the occasion of their third dialogue. No doubt with a twinkle in his eye, Roberts 'offer[ed] the Cup to Priest Bull' who 'refus'd it, saying it was full of Hops and Heresy'. Roberts replied, 'as for hops I cannot say much, not being at the brewing of it; but as for heresy, I do assure thee neighbour Bull, there's none in my beer . . . Here thy lord bishop hath drunk of it, and commends it; he finds no Heresy in the Cup'. No doubt this left Bull a little sulky. 'The Bishop then took his Leave, and went not to George Bull's, at which he was very much offended.' It is possible to see the kind of expression that might have been present on 'Priest Bull's' face from the contemporary portrait that hangs in the Great Hall of Exeter College, Oxford.

74 *Memoir*, p. 13. There is a shorter account of the help lady Dunch gave Roberts in *A Collection of the Sufferings*, p. 221, which tells us that this episode took place in 1681.

75 *Memoir*, p. 13.

76 *Memoir*, p. 15.

77 Roberts rode through a blizzard to her house a few days later to inform her of a Meeting. 'How can you expect I should go out in such weather as this,' she exclaimed. 'You know I seldom stir out of my Chamber; and to go so far [about 5 miles] may endanger my Health.' Roberts implacably left it up to her, and of course she rugged up and came along in her coach, Roberts riding alongside through the elements. Once there, she was extremely fidgety during 'Silence', Daniel (who was there) reports, but she was mightily impressed with the discussion, and became 'ashamed' of her former 'restlessness', 'proclaiming [that she was] a very Fool'. She attended several more Meetings after that, and Daniel was 'fully persuaded she was convinced of the Truth' before, 'going up to London' shortly after, 'she was taken ill and died': *Memoir*, pp. 16–17.

78 The seminal article on this is L. Stone, 'The Educational Revolution, 1560–1640', *Past and Present*, 28 (1964).

79 Mark Curtis, 'The Alienated Intellectuals of Early Stuart England', *Past and Present*, 23 (1962), pp. 25–43; Roger Chartier, 'Time to Understand', in Chartier, *Cultural History: Between Practices and Representations* (Oxford 1988), pp. 127–51.

80 Roberts once threatened the Bishop of Gloucester that 'If thou should'st come to my House under a Pretence of Friendship, and, in a Judas-like Manner, betray me hither to send me to Prison, as I have hitherto commended thee for thy Moderation, I should then have Occasion to put thy Name in Print, and cause it to stink before all sober People': *Memoir*, p. 34.

81 Ibid.

82 *Memoir*, pp. 37–8.

83 *Memoir*, p. 38.

84 *Memoir*, p. 39.

85 *Memoir*, pp. 47–8.

86 *Memoir*, p. 49.

87 *OED*, p. 1168.

88 James, *Society, Politics and Culture*, op. cit., p. 365, Quote from H. Walter (ed.), *Doctrinal Treatises . . . by William Tyndale, Martyr 1536* (Cambridge 1884), pp. 393–4.

89 Victor Turner, *The Ritual Process* (Chicago 1969).

90 Eric Hobsbawm, 'Introduction: Inventing Traditions', in Eric Hobsbawm and Terence Ranger (eds) *The Invention of Tradition* (Cambridge 1984), pp. 1–14.

8 COMMUNITY AT THE BORDERS

1 James C. Scott, *Weapons of the Weak: Everyday Forms of Peasant Resistance* (New Haven 1985), p. xvii.

2 Michel de Certeau, *The Practice of Everyday Life* (Berkeley 1984), p. ix.

3 C. Hugh Holman et al., *A Handbook to Literature* (Indianapolis 1972), quoted in Tom Wolfe, *The Purple Decades* (Harmondsworth 1983), p. xi.

4 Eric Wolf, *Europe and the People without History* (Berkeley 1985), p. 6.

5 *VCH Glos.*, vol. XI (Oxford 1976), p. 224.

6 Ibid. Randwick wood today 'conceals an ancient fortified camp, and a long barrow', p. 224.

7 Hooper's Visitation (1551), Whitgift's Enquiry (1603), Parliament Survey (1650), Compton Census (1676), Rudder's *Gloucestershire* (1779), 1801

Census, 1831 Census. Rollison, 'Intensification', Part Two: 'Demographic Intensification'.

8 *VCH Glos.*, vol. XI, p. 227.

9 *Men and Armour*, pp. 308–9, reports 23 weavers, 4 fullers and 1 dyer under Oxlynch manor, which included Randwick. Most of these were almost certainly from Randwick, because the other parts of the manor, in the Vale, were agricultural.

10 *VCH Glos.*, vol. XI. p. 227.

11 Alan Everitt, 'Nonconformity in English Country Parishes', in J. Thirsk (ed.) *Land, Church and People: Essays Presented to H. P. R. Finberg* (London 1970).

12 *VCH Glos.*, vol. XI, pp. 228–9.

13 Compton Census 1676, Photocopy of 'Salt Manuscript 33', p. 441, GRO.

14 *VCH Glos.*, vol. XI, pp. 229–30.

15 John Wesley, *A brief account of the late tryall . . .* (Bristol 1748).

16 W. E. Minchinton, 'The Beginnings of Trade-unionism in the Gloucestershire Woollen Industry', *TBGAS*, 70 (1951), pp. 126–41; Minchinton, 'The Petitions of the Weavers and Clothiers of Gloucestershire in 1756', Ibid., LXXIII (1954), pp. 216–27; John Rule, *The Experience of Labour in 18th Century England* (London 1981), pp. 159, 161, 162–3; Rule, *The Labouring Classes in Early Industrial England, 1750–1850* (London 1986), 257.

17 Beckles Wilson, *The Life and Letters of James Wolfe* (New York 1909), pp. 302–11.

18 Rollison, 'Fiery and Active Constitutions', Ch. 3 of 'Intensification', and below, Chapter 9.

19 The 1766 uprising has been most intensely studied, because E. P. Thompson referred extensively to it in 'The Moral Economy of the English Crowd in the Eighteenth Century', *Past and Present*, 50 (1971), pp. 76–131. Dale Edward Williams, 'Morals, Markets and the English Crowd', *Past and Present*, 104, pp. 56–73, critiques Thompson's account. Adrian J. Randall, 'The Gloucestershire Food Riots of 1766', *Midland History*, X (1985) is a useful account. Randall notes that 'riots were far from unusual in 18th-century Gloucestershire' (p. 72). None of these accounts looks closely enough into the *routine* life conditions or the habitually class-structured and class-conscious circumstances of the clothworking settlements, and consequently they fail to observe (or in Williams' case denies) any long-term or 'structural' continuities.

20 This estimate is based on analysis of PRO E179/247/14 (1664) and GRO D383 (1972), in conjunction with C. R. Elrington (ed.), 'The Survey of Church Livings in Gloucestershire, 1650, *TBGAS*, 83 (March 1965). The Randwick Hearth Tax listings do not give lists of exemptions, perhaps because the collectors knew no one would demand them for this particularly notorious village. I have estimated them by comparing the number of households listed in the 1650 survey with the numbers listed in the Hearth Tax records. The conjectural nature of the result is less significant than the fact that it confirms everything else we know about Randwick from other sources.

21 *VCH Glos.*, vol. XI.

22 Atkyns, *Gloucestershire*, 'Randwick'.

23 *VCH Glos.*, vol. XI, p. 228.

24 Adam Smith, *The Wealth of Nations* (ed. Andrew Skinner, Harmondsworth (Pelican English Classics) 1974), Ch. 1: 'Of the Divison of Labour', pp.

109–10. Clearly the pin-makers of Randwick did not keep the profits of their labour, since the workhouse was leased to a 'manufactory' at Gloucester. Smith seems to have exaggerated the productivity of the Gloucester pin-makers: Smith states that each worker could produce 4,800 pins every day. Extraordinary dexterity and stamina, since lost to humanity, are implied in the ability to produce an average of 6.7 pins per second over a 12-hour day. His figures stretch credulity, to put it mildly. I am grateful to Barry Smith for drawing attention to this anomaly, which seems to have escaped the attention of two centuries of commentators on A. Smith's famous illustration of the advantages of the division of labour in manufacturing.

25 David Levine, *Reproducing Families: The Political Economy of English Population History* (Cambridge 1987) is a brilliant synthesis of evidence leading to this conclusion.

26 'To the honourable the Commons of Great Britain in Parliament Assembled. The humble petitioner of the Clothiers and makers of Woollen Broad Cloth in the several counties of Gloucester, Wilts and Somerset & on behalf of themselves and all others concerned in the same trade, 1774', Ms. at GRO.

27 Rollison, 'The Bourgeois Soul of John Smyth of Nibley', *Social History*, 12 (3) (October 1987).

28 'Report from W. A. Miles Esq. on the Condition of the Handloom Weavers in Gloucestershire', *Commons Papers* (1840), Vol. 20, pp. 406–13.

29 Ibid., p. 418.

30 Irene Wyatt (ed.) *Transportees from Gloucestershire to Australia 1783–1842, BGAS Record Series* (Gloucester 1986).

31 In 1837 Bisley parish assisted 68 people to emigrate to NSW. A year later Painswick overseers instituted a similar scheme. Minchinhampton sent 40–50 people the same year, and in 1839 offered financial help to families willing to emigrate to New Zealand or the United States. Eighty members of the Shortwood Baptist congregation were given assisted passages between 1838 and 1840. *VCH Glos.*, vol. XI, pp. 23, 80, 201, 217.

32 *Australian Dictionary of Biography*, vol. 5, pp. 419–20. I would like to thank Kate Schlink and her colleagues at the Randwick (NSW) Local History Society for information about Pearce and his 'model village'.

33 The depositions on which the following account is based are GRO, GDR 2081, Consistory Court Depositions: Mary Bennet *alias* Carsway (23): 10 April 1713; John Fryer of Stroud, Taylor (27): 30 May 1713; Edward Field of Pekinhall (Paganhill) (43): 10 January 1713/14; Daniel Wildey of Randwick, Taylor (40): 30 May 1713; Emma Wildey of Randwick, widow (84): 30 May 1713; Richard Robbins *als* Butcher of Randwick, Taylor (43): 13 August 1713; Giles Mills of Randwick, Taylor (49): 3 September 1713; Thomas Bennet of Randwick, Taylor (30): 3 September 1713; Mary Roebuck *als* Baker (15) and Elizabeth Robbins *als* Butcher, wife of Richard Robbins, both of Randwick: 10 April 1713; Thomas Chapman of Randwick, Taylor (30): 10 January 1713/14; Daniel Bennet *als* Carsway of Randwick, Taylor (25): 10 January 1713/14. With the exception of the magistrate, Edward Field, all witnesses signed their depositions with marks. Christopher Hill, 'The Bawdy Courts', Ch. VIII of *Society and Puritanism in Pre-Revolutionary England* (London 1964) contains useful information about the work of the courts in an earlier period, as does Martin Ingram, *Church Courts, Sex and Marriage in England, 1570–1640* (Cambridge 1987).

34 Martin Ingram, 'The Reform of Popular Culture', and 'Ridings, Rough

Music and Mocking Rhymes in Early Modern England', in Barry Reay (ed.), *Popular Culture in Seventeenth Century England* (London 1985), discuss aspects of this nexus. My only criticism of Ingram's work is that his research tends to focus on quieter more conformist villages, and that his generalisations are less applicable to industrial districts.

35 Rollison, 'Property, Ideology and Popular Culture in a Gloucestershire Village, 1660–1740', *Past and Present*, 93 (November 1981).

36 GRO, GDR 2083.

37 *Gentlemen's Magazine* (May 1784), repr. *GNQ*, vol. V, pp. 34–6: except where otherwise indicated, all references and quotes in the following account are from this source. *VCH Glos*, vol. XI, p. 225, also refers to the occasion: 'A custom known as Randwick Wap formerly provided the chief holiday of the village year. On the second Monday after Easter a "mayor" of Randwick was elected and carried in procession to a pool south of the church where a song which alluded to the local weaving trade was sung. In the 19th century an unofficial fair was held at the time and the ceremony was often accompanied by riots and drunkenness. The custom, for which a medieval origin was claimed, was recorded c. 1703 (Bodleian Library, *MS Rawlinson B323 f. 158*), and in the 1770s (Rudder, *Gloucestershire*, p. 619), and in spite of efforts to abolish it, continued until 1892.' Bob Bushaway, *By Rite: Custom, Ceremony and Community in England 1700–1880* (London 1982), p. 153, mentions 'Randwick Mop' and there is a brief reference to the occasion in Robert Malcolmson, *Popular Recreations in English Society 1750–1850* (Cambridge 1973), p. 81.

38 Rudder, *Gloucestershire*, 619.

39 John Brewer, 'Theatre and Counter-theatre in Georgian Politics: the Mock Elections at Garrat', *Radical History Review*, 22(19) pp. 7–40; Malcolmson, *Popular Recreations*, op. cit.

40 Rudder, *Gloucestershire*, p. 619.

41 *VCH Glos*. vol. XI, p. 227.

42 Charles Phythian-Adams, *Local History and Folklore, a New Framework* (London 1975), p. 28.

43 Scott, *Weapons*, op. cit. de Certeau, *The Practice*, op. cit.

44 'Broadly speaking, the conjuncture means "the totality of all the conditions" in which a problem or an event is located. The historian, like the man of action, must constantly define this "general conjuncture", since even the apparently most remote facts may influence the understanding of a given moment.' We should also bear in mind Vilar's warning that 'the concept should be used with care (especially by those using it for the first time). It should, above all, not be used for effect. To say "this can be explained by the conjuncture" is like saying "the storm can be explained by meteorology", i.e. it is a purely verbal explanation. It is often better not to use the term while showing some understanding of the concept, and locating a problem in its broadest context': Pierre Vilar, *A History of Gold and Money 1450–1920* (trans. Judith White, London 1984), pp. 39–40. I use the term not to explain but to describe, though of course the two can amount to the same thing. I am using all the facts related in this chapter in an attempt to *evoke* the meanings that 'coalesced' in the Randwick Wap, and thus to explain a public 'symbol' or 'conjuncture'.

45 The provenance and meaning of the 'psalm' is necessarily conjectural – necessarily, because earlier versions referred to in the sources were said to be exclusively oral, and therefore, by definition, not recorded before

1784. I have had discussions with a number of scholars on this subject. Dr Paul Turnbull of James Cook University has studied Freemason songs of the eighteenth century, and sees similarities of form and content between Freemasons' songs and 'The Lord Mayor of Randwick's Song'. This tends to confirm my own view that the psalm is an old weavers' initiation song adapted, in the eighteenth century, to new contexts. The similarity between this and certain Freemason songs would therefore be explained by the provenance of all such forms in oral and associational craft guilds and 'clubs'. I also consulted Alan Howkins of the University of Sussex; Howkins agreed that the psalm is what the sources claim it to be: a literate 'fixing' of an older oral form. On the literature relating to 'carnivalesque' and 'the world turned upside-down' in medieval and early modern European mentalities, Peter Stallybrass and Allon White, *The Politics and Poetics of Transgression* (London 1986), pp. 1–26, provide an excellent introduction; general influences on the interpretation that follows include Lucien Febvre, *The Problem of Unbelief in the Sixteenth Century: The Religion of Rabelais* (Harvard 1982); Michael D. Bristol, *Carnival and Theatre: Plebeian Culture and the Structure of Authority in Renaissance England* (New York 1985); Victor Turner, *From Ritual to Theatre: The Human Seriousness of Play* (New York 1982); Craig Calhoun, *The Question of Class Struggle: Social Foundations of Popular Radicalism during the Industrial Revolution* (Oxford 1982); M. M. Bakhtin, *Rabelais and his World* (trans. H. Iswolsky, Cambridge Mass. 1968); Bertolt Brecht, *Poems 1913–1956* (various trans. London 1976); Ivan Illich and Barry Sanders, *The Alphabetization of the Popular Mind* (Harmondsworth 1988), esp. Chs 1 and 2 'Words and History' and 'Memory'; Albert Lord, *The Singer of Tales* (Harmondsworth 1965); and, above all, Ernst Bloch, *The Principle of Hope*, 3 vols (trans. Neville Plaice, Stephen Plaice and Paul Knight, Oxford 1986). David Phillips' gentle suggestion to me that I had imposed rather than extracted my interpretation from the psalm caused me to reconsider my theoretical and methodological approaches, and to try alternative readings; he is undoubtedly right in his perception that in practice not every hearer or reader of the verses would have drawn as systematic and unified a reading as I have drawn from them, and readers should be reminded of this necessary caution; 'reading' is always in part a function of variable experience and context; there is no such thing as unambiguous historical evidence. In the light of the burgeoning literature on the carnivalesque as a continuous presence in the mentalities of preliterate cultures, or cultures on the borders of preliteracy and literacy like that of eighteenth-century Randwick and of the context which I have indicated in this chapter, I remain convinced that the interpretation that follows not only was possible, but represents a permanent undercurrent in the consciousness of the manufacturing classes of early modern England: a consciousness that indicates awareness that the dominant, inequalitarian ruling-class ideologies of their society were grounded not in unquestionable (mainly religious, but increasingly the political–economic ideology usually called *laissez-faire*) axioms, but in *power*, that is to say, variable combinations of inherited status and wealth. This is a simple but very potent and subversive (though of course not necessarily revolutionary) insight.

46 Victor Turner, *The Ritual Process* (Chicago 1969), pp. 94–7.

47 J. De L. Mann, 'Clothiers and Weavers in Wiltshire during the Eighteenth Century', in L. S. Pressnell (ed.) *Studies in the Industrial Revolution* (London

1959), pp. 75–8; Mann, *The Cloth Industry in the West of England from 1640 to 1880* (Gloucester 1987), pp. 109–10.

9 'A CONCATENATION OF VICIOUS HABITS'

1 Pre-Civil War newsbooks are not a source I have mined, so I cannot be certain that the preoccupations of the late 1730s were not also those voiced by the Press a century earlier, albeit in seventeenth-century language, which was generally more earthy and mundane than eighteenth-century public rhetoric. Sixteenth-century social historians will be quick to point out that preachers made reference to fraught social relations in sermons. Lollards had interpretations of social relations in England that foreshadow the sermons of Puritans and the comments of sectaries like the Quakers, brilliant exploiters of the medium of the Press in the second half of the seventeenth century. Quakers like John Bellers wrote disquisitions on dealing with the poor, as did the erstwhile Puritan, or associate of Puritans, Sir Matthew Hale. All foreshadow the substance of this chapter, and all took it for granted that in most times and in most places the poor meant 'the manufacturers', households that depended on being paid wages to process some raw (or pre-worked) material into a commodity for the market. The rhetoric of Press commentators in 1738–9 is described below. The newspapers of the eighteenth–century Press explosion are closer to their modern counterparts, though they clearly represent a development of earlier experience.
2 Lionel Cranfield, *The Development of the English Provincial Newspaper 1700–1760* (Oxford 1962), chs 1–3; Cranfield, *A Handlist of English Provincial Newspapers and Periodicals* (London 1961), pp. 5 and 8. Copies of the *Cirencester Flying Post* are held at the Gloucester City Library.
3 Margaret Richards, *Ladybellegate House, Gloucester and Robert Raikes* (Gloucester Records Office publication, 1978).
4 GCL, NV 26.1.
5 John Brewer, *Party Ideology and Popular Politics at the Accession of George III* (Cambridge 1976), p. 144.
6 For the activities of the Kingswood colliers in 1737–8, see *GJ*, 21 February 1737–8, 16 May 1738, 23 May 1738, 17 October 1738, 29 October 1738 and 12 December 1738. See also the very interesting 'Collier's letter to the Turnpike', GRO D15/2.
7 *GJ*, 17 October 1738 (colliers); 23 May 1738 (clothworkers).
8 *GJ*, 16 May 1738.
9 *GJ*, 21 February 1737/8. The *Journal* printed reports on wheat exports in every edition of 1738.
10 *GJ*, 29 November 1738.
11 *GJ*, 12 December 1738.
12 *GJ*, 21 February 1738/9.
13 *GJ*, 22 May 1739.
14 Food prices taken from my long-term series prepared from W. G. Hoskins, 'Harvest Fluctuations and the English Economy 1620–1759', *Agricultural History Review*, 16 (1968), pp. 15–31, and (for this period) from prices at Gloucester market, given in every edition of the *Gloucester Journal*. The annual prices are averages of prices in February, May, September and late November. Nett national export figures cited in this study are from T. S. Ashton, *Economic Fluctuations in England 1700–1800* (Oxford 1959), 183.

15 *GJ*, 5 February 1739/40.
16 *GJ*, 12 February 1739/40. Cases of private charity were also reported, e.g. 'the frosty weather being like to continue and no coals to be purchased here, Henry Guise Esq. out of his great humanity, gave yesterday 200 bushels (which he had preserved for his own use) to numbers of distressed families in the city' *GJ*, 19 February 1739/40.
17 *GJ*, 12 February 1738/9.
18 Local grain prices were published in each edition of the *Journal*: transcribed, analysed, graphed and trends compared with export figures, local riots and expenditure on poor relief, 1723–1780, in Rollison, 'Intensification', pp. 139–41, 264–76.
19 *GJ*, 8 July 1740.
20 Ibid. David Levine and Keith Wrightson, *The Making of an Industrial Society: Whickham 1560–1765* (Oxford 1991), *passim*, and esp. pp. 375–427.
21 *GJ*, 22 July 1740.
22 Ibid.
23 *GJ*, 29 July 1740.
24 *GJ*, 22 July 1740
25 *GJ*, 30 September and 7 October 1740.
26 *GJ*, 7 October 1740.
27 *GJ*, 14 October 1740.
28 *GJ*, 28 October 1740.
29 *GJ*, 22 October 1740.
30 *GJ*, 25 November 1740.
31 *GJ*, 6 January 1741.
32 *GJ*, 2 December 1740.
33 *GJ*, 20 January 1741.
34 *GJ*, 27 January 1741.
35 *GJ*, 10 February 1741.
36 John Smith, *Chronicon Rusticum – Commerciale, or Memoirs of Wool* (1747, repr. New York 1969), vol. 2, *passim*, is a very useful compendium of contemporary public commentary in the period that concerns me here. The anti-French theme recurs and intensifies. Irish competition was another routine preoccupation, but commentators seem to have felt more confident that it would be easier to stamp out than the French. The general impression that I derive from this material is that many English people in the cloth trade wanted the government to fight France, i.e. point potential English rioters at someone outside England, ideally the French. There is also a hint that they thought the English would win such an encounter, possibly because they thought English rioters were fiercer than their French counterparts. This belief was proved untrue in 1789.
37 The following based on articles in the *GJ*, 19 December 1738, 9 January 1738/9, 30 January 1738/9, 13 February 1738/9, 24 February 1738/9, 6 March 1738/9, 13 March 1738/9, 3 April 1739 and 10 April 1739. Modern dating is used throughout the text, with the new year beginning on 1 January.
38 J. De L. Mann, 'Clothiers and Weavers in Wiltshire during the Eighteenth Century', in L. S. Pressnell (ed.) *Studies in the Industrial Revolution* (London 1959), pp. 66–71, discusses the circumstances and issues which led to the fixing of wage-rates.
39 Mann, ibid., has a judicious account of the issues and complexities of the industry that lay in the background of the public debate of 1739.

40 J. De L. Mann, *The Cloth Industry in the West of England From 1640 to 1680* (Gloucester 1987), p. 38.

41 Mann, 'Clothiers and Weavers', op. cit., p. 72.

42 Mann, *The Cloth Industry*, op. cit., appendix 3, pp. 316–18, cites contemporary estimates, which vary from 14 to 28 persons per loom.

43 'To the author of the Gloucester Journal', a letter which occupied the front page of the edition of 30 January 1738-9, was rather more sanguine about this subject, playing down the effects of 'a dull season of trade', and emphasising the role of 'those idle and immoral Wretches, that generally turn out the Ringleaders of such assemblies'. 'In the Clothing Trade', he wrote, 'as in other employs, the Value of Labour has its ups and downs, according to the Demand there is for it.'

44 *GJ*, 10 December 1738.

45 Ibid.

46 'Confession', *GJ*, 10 April 1739.

47 Tony Hayter, *The Army and the Crowd in Mid-Georgian England* (London 1978) is an excellent study of the use of soldiers against the civilian population in this period and these places. He shows that practice made perfect. As Tory prejudices against the use by governments of standing armies against their own people were overcome by periods in office, they became more adept at handling revolting common people.

48 Mann, 'Clothiers and Weavers', op. cit., p. 72, n. 5, cites PRO SP36/47, a 'letter from a Chippenham Justice to Lord Harrington, one of the Secretaries of State, thank[ing] him "for the kind part you have acted in this affair" '. Mann comments: 'In fact, the Government may even have used influence to secure a verdict against the rioters.'

49 This and the following information from Gaol Calendars for the Western Assizes, March/April 1739, PRO Assi 23/6, pp. 2–3.

50 'To the Author of the Gloucester Journal. An Exact and particular relation of the horrid and cruel Devastations committed by the Mob at Melksham', signed by Coulthurst and thirteen other clothiers, reported that the crowd which gathered to try and obtain the release of Crabb was 'not less than 1500'.

51 *Conclusion of the Case . . .* , *GJ*, 10 April 1739, p. 1, col. 1.

52 W. E. Minchinton, 'The Beginnings of Trade-unionism in the Gloucestershire Woollen Industry', *TBGAS*, 70 (1951), pp. 126–41; Minchinton, 'The Petitions of the Weavers and Clothiers of Gloucestershire in 1756', ibid., 73 (1954), pp. 216–27.

53 This and the following is from papers relating to the prosecution of striking weavers in the parish papers of Wotton-under-Edge at the Gloucester City Library, handwritten manuscript headed 'Gloucester Epiphany Sessions 1826: The King against Charles Owen, William Lewis and John Brown', p. 2.

54 Ibid., p. 5.

55 Ibid., p. 4.

56 Mann, 'Clothiers and Weavers', op. cit., p. 69.

57 Ibid.

58 Hayter, *The Army*, op. cit.

59 The best account of 'journeying' as a liminal stage between apprenticeship to a craft and mastery is R. A. Leeson, *Travelling Brothers* (London 1980).

60 Hans Medick, 'Plebeian Culture in the Transition to Capitalism' in Samuel and Stedman Jones (eds), *Culture, Ideology and Politics: Essays for Eric*

Hobsbawm (London 1982), stresses the importance of respectability and its measurement by consumption relativities in plebeian culture. No doubt this was true for some clothworkers. Beazer's phrase referring to the fact that he had 'lived in good credit, and had the love and esteem of all men' meant something broader than this, being 'regular as to outward appearance', obeying the laws and attending church regularly.

61 Mann, *The Cloth Industry*, op. cit., p. 110.

62 Josiah Tucker, *Instructions to Travellers* (1751), quoted in John Rule, *The Experience of Labour in 18th Century England* (London 1981), p. 158; Mann, 'Clothiers and Weavers' op. cit., p. 66, makes the same point.

63 'An Essay on Riots; their *Causes* and *Cure*. With some Thoughts on Trade, and a Method of Relief for the Miseries of the poor *Wiltshire* Manufacturers', *GJ*, 19 December 1738.

64 Andrews' account brings to mind E. P. Thompson's description of a 'predatory' social system in which the fruits of 'ground level' exploitation rose rapidly through society to 'the higher regions', where it 'accumulated in great gobbets . . . Real killings', Thompson concurs, 'were to be made in the distribution, cornering and sale of goods and raw materials, in the manipulation of credit, and in the seizure of offices of State': 'Eighteenth-century English Society: class-struggle without class?', *Social History* 4 (1979), pp. 133–66; J. G. A. Pocock, 'Virtue Vs Commerce in the Eighteenth Century', *Journal of Interdisciplinary History*, 3 (1972–3), pp. 119–34, and Thomas Horne,'Politics in a Corrupt Society: William Arnall's Defence of Robert Walpole', *Journal of the History of Ideas*, 41 (1980), pp. 601–14, provide useful analysis of elite political and ideological conflict at the time of the riot.

65 For some of the contemporary connotations of these references, see Pat Rogers, *Hacks and Dunces: Pope, Swift and Grub Street* (London 1980), Part 2: 'The Plagues of Dulness'.

66 An extremely sardonic account of a performance of Handel's 'Israel in Egypt' appeared in the *GJ*, of 10 April, 1739, in the column next to John Beazer's confession.

10 LASTING PREJUDICES

1 For quantitative estimates of the increasing proletarian proportion of the population, see David Levine, *Reproducing Families: The Politcal Economy of English Population History* (Cambridge 1987), Ch. 2: 'Agrarian capitalism and rural proletarianization', esp. pp. 40–41.

2 Matthew Hale, *A Discourse Touching Provision for the Poor* (London 1683), p. 2.

3 *GJ*, 18 October 1740.

4 John Bellers, *Essays about the Poor, Manufactures, Trade, Plantations and Immorality* (London 1699), quoted in Marx, *Capital Volume One* (Harmondsworth 1984), p. 553.

5 Sociological debate on class and status, broadly flowing along parallel channels laid out by Marx and Weber, is extensive. In this context 'class' means classification according to relativities of wealth and power, the social relations of production (cf. Marx, *Capital Volume Three*, Moscow 1986, pp. 885–6). 'Status' questions relate, for the purposes of this analysis, to culture. The ways cultural messages are transmitted and reproduced (information technology) relate to the mode of production fairly directly. Words and

ideas are more open to becoming divorced from reality. Yet, however divorced from reality, they can be repeated, disseminated so often that they become of the taken-for-granted belief system (prejudices).

6 Keith Wrightson, ' "Sorts of people" in Tudor and Stuart England', ms. of public lecture given by Wrightson at the University of Adelaide, September 1991, p. 2; more generally see G. Stedman Jones, *Languages of Class* (Cambridge 1983).

7 Wrightson, 'Sorts of People', op. cit., pp. 30–31.

8 Keith Thomas, *Man and the Natural World: Changing Attitudes in England, 1500–1800* (Harmondsworth 1984), p. 17.

9 Ibid., p. 41.

10 Harry Levin (ed.), *Coriolanus* II, i, lines 87–90; and cf. II, i, lines 236–49, in Alfred Harbage (gen. ed.) *The Complete Pelican Shakespeare: The Tragedies* (Harmondsworth 1969), pp. 414–15.

11 Marx, *Capital Volume III*, op. cit., p. 885.

12 Keith Wrightson, *English Society 1580–1680* (London 1982), esp. pp. 226–7.

13 *OED*, 'Aborigine'.

14 *Aubrey's Natural History of Wiltshire* (first printed 1847; repr. Trowbridge 1969), cited in the 'Introduction' by K. G. Ponting, opp. title page; Anthony Powell, *John Aubrey and his Friends* (revised edn, London 1988), p. 38, quoting from Aubrey, *Essay Towards the Description of the Northern Division of Wiltshire* ('Put together', writes Powell, 'between 1659 and 1670'); Oliver Lawson Dick, *Aubrey's Brief Lives* (Harmondsworth 1978), pp. 46–7.

15 Powell, *John Aubrey*, op. cit., p. 21.

16 Ibid., p. 66.

17 Petty 'attempted the first Essay of Political Anatomy' in *The Political Anatomy of Ireland* (London 1691), in C. H. Hull (ed.) op. cit. pp. 121–223; the book was conceived in the months following his appointment as Physician-General to the Army in Ireland in 1652. He applied the principles of physical anatomy to the land of Ireland in order to render more efficient the distribution of forfeited lands to English soldiers: Lord Edmund Fitz-Maurice, *The Life of Sir William Petty, 1623–1687* (London 1895), pp. 21–55; 'The war was over,' wrote FitzMaurice. 'The division of the spoils was about to commence. "As for the blood shed in these contests," Dr Petty afterwards wrote, "God best knows who did occasion it; but upon the playing of the game or match the English won, and had amongst other pretences a gamester's right at least to their estates". He had not been concerned in the original quarrel, and he now simply regarded himself as a servant of the state called upon to perform a definite duty': ibid., pp. 43–4.

18 Powell, *John Aubrey*, p. 248.

19 Ibid., p. 261.

20 Petty, 'Preface' to *Political Arithmetick*, written 1671–2, published London 1690, in Hull op. cit., p. 244; for a powerful critique, see Peter Linebaugh, 'The Thanatocracy and Old Mr Gory in the Age of Newton and Locke', mimeo (1983).

21 Petty, *Political Anatomy*, op. cit.

22 D. V. Glass, 'Two Papers on Gregory King', in D. V. Glass and D. E. C. Eversley, *Population in History, Essays in Historical Demography* (London 1965), provides a useful introduction to King's approaches and methodology.

23 Paul Carter, *The Road to Botany Bay* (London 1987) describes the ethnocentric

cartographic and bureaucratic sensibilities of English explorers and sur-
veyors of Australia, and how these shaped the ways they perceived and
divided up a continent.

24 Richard Jefferies, *Hodge and his Masters* (1880; repr. London 1979), Ch.
XI: 'Fleeceborough – A Despot'; Jefferies' ecological determinism serves a
distinctly nostalgic purpose, intended as it is to praise a type of associational community that was just beginning to decline. His model was
Cirencester.

25 Powell, *John Aubrey*, op. cit., p. 38; Dick, *Aubrey's Brief Lives*, op. cit, p.
46; Ponting, 'Introduction', has 'drawling'.

26 See above, Chapter 3.

27 Except where otherwise indicated, all quotations are from the passage as
cited in Powell, *John Aubrey*, op. cit., and Dick, *Aubrey's Brief Lives*, op. cit.

28 There is some slight documentary back-up for Aubrey's belief that this
district had a reputation for witches. The Tetbury burial registers for this
period contain two tantalising references, one for 12 March 1675/6 ('A child
of Witch Warrand, buried'), the other for 1 May 1689 ('A child of Witch
Comleys, buried'). These are the only two references after the Restoration.
The others are for a resident of Gloucester (GDR 40, Presentments and
Detection Causes, 24 December 1576); an accusation in the same book that
the Minister of St Mary de Lode 'useth sorcery' (again 1576); a detection
for suspicion of witchcraft against Margaret Roades of Cirencester (GDR
87, 13 February 1599/1600); and a presentment 'for using charmes' against
Alice Lewes of Minsterworth in the Deanery of the Forest (GDR 203,
1639ff). I owe these references to Brian Frith. It may be of some significance
that the last three of these cases all refer to Aubrey's region – i.e. Cirencester and Tetbury – and that both towns were noted centres of Quaker
activity after the Restoration.

29 Powell, *John Aubrey*, op. cit., p. 275; *Aubrey's Natural History*, op. cit., p.
2.

30 Aubrey-Wood, 23 February 1673, quoted in Powell, *John Aubrey*, op. cit.,
p. 147.

31 *Lives*, II, vol. 36–7.

32 *Lives*, vol. II, p. 222.

33 *Description*, p. 5.

34 Ibid.

35 J. P. Somerville, *Politics and Ideology in England, 1603–1640* (New York 1986),
p. 88.

36 *Description*, p. 10.

37 *Description*, p. 43.

38 *Description*, p. 328.

39 This figure is a conservative estimate, derived from *Census 1650* and *Hearth
Tax 1671* (Slimbridge); the former gives 90 families, and the latter lists 33
tax-paying households. 115 able-bodied men were listed in *Men and Armour*,
of whom 44 were weavers, fullers or tuckers, and another 10 were tailors
or shoemakers.

40 John Walter, 'The Social Economy of Dearth in Early Modern England', in
John Walter and Roger Schofield (eds), *Famine, Disease and the Social Order in
Early Modern England* (Cambridge 1991), p. 75, notes that 'the impoverished
repertory of English folk tales lacks those tales, common in other early
modern European societies, in which peasant culture confronts the
dilemma of too many mouths to feed and in which supernatural salvation

so often took the form of a superabundance of food'. Walter contrasts this lack with the French peasant world described by Robert Darnton, in 'Peasants tell tales', pp. 9–72 of *The Great Cat Massacre* (Harmondsworth 1984). Many of the proverbs discussed in Chapter 3 (above), and of course John Smyth's elevation of tillage in particular, and farming in general, as 'the only vocation(s) wherein innocence remaineth' (*Description*, p. 43), tend to support Walter's view, and that of many other commentators since Laslett, that dearth and famine were less intense problems in early modern England than they were elsewhere, e.g. in contemporary France. They were nevertheless intense, above all in Smyth's lifetime (1567–1643). Smyth's sacramental view of tillage, and of hard-working agricultural self-sufficiency, was probably the conventional wisdom of the yeomanry. As such it may have contributed a great deal to increasing agricultural productivity to meet the challenge of rising numbers.

41 *Description*, p. 4.
42 Marshall Sahlins, *Stone Age Economics* (London 1974), is a critical examination of this aspect of modern myths of progress.
43 *Description*, p. 42.
44 Lauro Martines, *Society and History in English Renaissance Verse* (Oxford 1985), e.g. p. 71, and *passim*.

INDEX

aborigines, 70, 71, 73, 250–1, 254–8
absolutism, 10, 13, 17, 74, 147, 175, 191, 260
Act of Uniformity, 110, 112
agriculturalists, 262, 263
agriculture, 93; culture and, 23, 72–4, 261–4; freehold farms, 153, 154, 167
Allibond, John, 136–8, 140–2, 146
Ancient Constitution, 7, 260
Ancient and Present State of Gloucestershire (Atkyns), 116
Anderson, Benedict, 69
Andrews, George, 60
Andrews, John, 90
Andrews, Thomas, 238–46 *passim*
animal imagery, 77–8
annalistes, 127
anthropology, 67, 257–8
apprenticeships, 228, 229, 235
arboriculture, 262
Archard, William, 263
aristocracy, 47, 133, 258, 264
Arminianism, 169, 181, 191
Arnold, William, 60
artisans, 47
Arundell, John, 35
Asgrave, Hugh, 105
Atkyns, Sir Robert, 21–2, 56, 116, 204
Aubrey, John, 77; aboriginal culture, 9, 250–1; political arithmetic, 252–4; world-views, 249–50, 258–64
Audlam, John, 177
Aylmer, G. E., 125, 162

'badgers' (carriers), 2, 52–5
Baptists, 180, 181
Barkesdale, Clement, 111–12
Bathurst, Thomas, 58

bawdy-court case, 205–11
Baynham, James, 89
Beard, Ann, 207
Beazer, John, 228–9, 231–2, 235–8
Bell, John, 88
Bellers, John, 247
Bennet, Daniel, 207, 209–10
Bennet, Jane, 207
Bennet, Mary, 205–10, 217
Berkeley, Lord George, 161
Berkeley, Lady Katherine, 87–8
Berkeley, Sir Maurice, 141–2, 153, 161, 259
Berkeley estate/family, 47; cloth trade, 22, 24–7, 36–7; Corbet and, 141–2, 153, 161; culture, 3–4, 67–83; Smyth's studies *see* Smyth, John; *see also* Trotman, Thomas (and family); Tyndale, William
Berkeley Manuscripts, 100
Bible (Tyndale's work), 4, 5, 89, 154
Biddle, John, 126, 128, 146
Black Death, 25, 78
Blaythwayt, Sir William, 116
Boleyn, Ann, 91
bourgeois civilisation, 15, 181, 264
bourgeois revolution, 56, 175
bourgeoisie, 41, 119, 159
Bower, William, 78–9, 80
Bower, William, the Elder, 78, 259
Braudel, Fernand, 3, 17, 21, 69, 125
Brayne, Richard, 101–2
Brewer, John, 221
Bridbury, A. R., 37
Brief Lives (Aubrey), 250, 252–3
Bristol, 25
broadcloth-making, 35
Brydges, George, 112, 126, 155–6

Brydges, Gyles, 144
Brydges, Sir John, 138
Bull, George, 168–9, 183–9 *passim*, 192–3
Bull, William, 94
Byron, Sir John, 173

Calvinism, 39, 113
Cam, John, 177
capital accumulation, 75, 76, 78
capitalism, 203, 215; class formation, 62–3; country, 1–18, 43, 51, 78; development, 56, 83, 174
Capp, Bernard, 110
Careless, William, 188–9
carnival (at Randwick), 196, 204, 209, 211–13, 216, 234
carriers, 2, 51–3, 60
Carter, Giles, 106
Carus-Wilson, E., 23–4
censorship, 220, 221
census data, 32–4
Chapman, Sarah, 208
Chapman, Thomas, 207, 208–10
charity, 225, 226, 257
Charles I, 10, 13, 40, 138, 145, 147, 157, 257
Chartres, J. A., 51, 218
Church courts, 206–10, 217
Cirencester, 40
civil wars, 10, 27, 56; Corbet's analysis, 123, 126–7, 131–7, 139, 145, 148–55, 157–8, 160–2; Robert's experience, 168, 169, 171, 173–5; Trotmans and, 111–13
civilisation, 250–1, 253, 256; bourgeois, 15, 181, 264
class, 119; Corbet's perspective, 148–54; formation, 62–3; one-class society, 181; Quakers, 166–9; social discrimination, 9, 247–64; *see also* feudalism; middle-rank; proletarianisation; proletariat; ruling classes; working class
class struggle, 148, 247; Randwick study, 11, 199–218; riots, 11–12, 219–46
classless society, 217
cloth industry: heresy and, 5, 85–90, 92–4; internal trade, 51–63; proverbs, 69–70; Randwick study, 200–2; riots, 223–4, 227–39, 241–2, 244–5; Trotman family, 6, 101–3,

119; Tyndale family, 86–90, 92–4; *see also* weavers
clothmaking, large-scale: development/origins, 21–7; occupational patterns, 32–7; population history, 39–43; Puritan discipline, 37–9; structural impact, 43–4; urban development, 27–32
clustering process, 32, 52
Clutterbuck family, 153
coach travel, 59–60
coal industry, 39, 60, 118, 222–3, 226, 231
Coke, Sir Edward, 107, 141, 260
Cole, Alan, 167
Coleman, D. C., 32
collective consciousness, 77–82, 174, 176
Collinson, Patrick, 146
commerce, 3, 55–6
Commission of Array, 155, 156
commodity production, 55–6
commonwealth, 8, 17, 92, 109, 113, 124
communitas, 191, 196, 203, 214–16
communities (imagined), 69
community at the borders *see* Randwick study
Company of Haberdashers, 108, 110
Company of Merchant Adventurers, 109
congregation, 91–2, 154, 172–3, 180–1
Congregationalists, 8, 90, 110, 112, 146
'conjunctures', 125, 127–8, 172, 212, 246
Cooke, Sir Robert, 107, 133, 138–41, 142–3, 145, 147, 260
Cooke, Sir William, 139
Cooper, Richard, 35–6
Corbet, John, 6, 9, 10, 200, 247, 260, 264; approach and methodology, 123–8; class perspective, 148–54; historiography, 128–31; nationalism, 158–63; Short Parliament, 136–48; social analysis, 131–6; social structure, 155–8; theology of, 124, 126–7, 129–30, 135–6, 152, 153
Coriolanus (Shakespeare), 137–8, 149, 248
Coulthurst, Henry, 223, 227–8, 230–1, 232, 237–8, 241

countrey (district), 4, 7–9, 16–17, 69, 250; Corbet's, 142, 152–3, 162; Trotman's, 98, 100, 112; Tyndale's, 5, 86, 90, 92, 94–5
country (definition), 16–17
country capitalism, 43, 51, 78; language, 12–15; nation-states, 15–18; study background, 1–12
Court of Wards, 174
Crabb, John, 230, 231–2, 235
Cratchley, Sarah, 208, 210
Crew, Arthur, 36
Cromwell, Oliver, 8, 154, 164, 168, 176, 178, 180, 184–5, 264
Cromwell, Thomas, 85, 106
culture, 196; aboriginal, 70, 71, 73, 250–1, 254–8; agrarian, 23, 72–4, 76, 77, 82; carnivalesque, 196, 204, 209, 211–13, 216, 234; collective consciousness, 77–82, 174, 176; oral, 3–4, 13–16, 71–4, 81–3, 191, 218; preliterate, 12–14, 73, 81–3, 191, 218; secular, 90–1, 92, 184; vernacular *see* vernacular culture
culture, proverbial, 3–4; cloth trade, 69–70; collective consciousness, 77–82; dialect, 68–9; language-landscape, 67–8; local imagery, 70–2; oral, 81–3; political–economic changes, 74–7; proverbs, 72–4
'cunning' man (Roberts), 168–70, 183, 187–92 *passim*

Dashwood, Sir Robert, 116
de Certeau, Michel, 199
Defoe, Daniel, 46, 57
dependency system, 167, 171, 175, 237
Dewsbury, William, 172
dialect, 3–4, 15, 67–83, 94, 254
Dicey, William, 221
Dickens, A. G., 84, 92, 94
Didson, John, 89–90
diocese probate inventories, 41, 42
discipline, Puritan, 37–9
Dissenters, 201
Dissolution, 75, 85, 94, 144
division of labour, 204
domestic production, 32, 35, 37
Dostoevsky, F. M., 195
'drawning', 254
Dunch, Lady, 188–9

Dutton, John, 139, 140, 141–2, 144, 147
Dutton, Sir Ralph, 145–6

Ecclesiastes, 65
ecological determinism, 254–8
economic function, population history and, 39–43
Edward II, 24, 47
Edward VI, 5
'elders', 91, 92, 96, 154, 171, 172–3
elections (Short Parliament), 6, 136–48
elites, 63, 71–2, 83, 211, 220, 257
Elizabeth I, 144
empirical-rational techniques, 169, 188, 190, 191–2
empirical reasoning, 187, 189, 195
empiricism, radical, 8, 81, 127, 129
Engels, Friedrich, 163
English Revolution, 4, 8, 45
English Revolution (Corbet's view), 6; approach and methodology, 123–8; class perspective, 148–54; historiography, 128–31; nationalism, 158–63; Short Parliament, 136–48; social analysis, 131–6; social structure, 155–8
enlightenment, 169, 180
Europe and the People Without History (Wolf), 21
Everett, Thomas, 36
exports, 17, 223, 229

factory system, 18, 32, 36, 70
family, 7, 8; loyalty (Quakerism), 171–3; *see also* household; kin-coalitions
Farnsworth, Richard, 8, 168, 177–8, 179–80, 182
Feast of Fools, 11
Febvre, Lucien, 86
feudalism, 47, 62, 91, 104; Aubrey on, 254, 258, 260–1; clothmaking and, 24, 27; Corbet on, 138–9, 144, 149; and culture, 74, 78
Field, Edward, 207
Fifth Monarchists, 110–12
Fish, Simon, 89
FitzHarding lords Berkeley *see* Berkeley estate/family
flying wagons, 56, 57, 59
folk wisdom, 72–4

food and drink proverbs, 79
food supply, 222, 223, 225, 226–7
foreign trade (cloth), 41, 42
Forest of Dean, 39, 47–8
Fortesque, Sir John, 260
Fox, George, 177–8, 180, 181
freeholders, 151, 152, 153, 154, 236, 261
Fryer, John, 207
Fuller, Thomas, 22, 69, 89

Gentlemen's Magazine, 211, 222
gentry, 47, 74, 87, 119, 170, 237; role (Corbet's view), 124, 133–4, 137–9, 149, 151–2, 161
George, James, 193–4
Gloucester, 39, 40, 41–2, 47–8
Gloucester Journal, 2, 58–60, 221, 247; riot reports, 215, 219, 222–8, 233, 235, 238–41
God, 8; communion with *see* inner light
Goodman, Bishop Godfrey, 137
Goody, J., 14–15
Goodyeare, Thomas, 177
Graunt, John, 252, 255
Great Rebellion, 174, 185, 191
Green, Edward, 23, 70
Greenblatt, Stephen, 84, 91–2
guilds, 24
Guise, Sir Christopher, 56

Hale, Sir Matthew, 77, 170, 200, 247
Halford, John, 77
Hallowes, Sarah, 35
Haynes, William, 59
Hearth Tax, 35–6, 133–4, 151–2, 203
Helme, Carnsew, 110, 111, 112
Henry II, 138
Henry, VII, 5, 99, 259
Henry VIII, 91, 99, 138
heresy, 5, 85, 87–90, 92–4
Heylyn, Peter, 136, 137, 138, 146
Hickes, George, 114
Hickes, Sarah (*née* Trotman), 114, 115–16
Hill, Christopher, 123–4, 125, 174
Hill, Isaac, 36
Hilton, R. H., 24
historical materialism, 127
Historical Relation (Corbet), 123, 127, 128

historiography, 174; Corbet's view, 128–31; localism and, 45–6
history (written texts), 13–15
Hobsbawm, E. J., 196
Hodges, Thomas, 133
Holder, Christopher, 177
Holford, Sir Richard, 114–16, 118
Holford, Susannah (*née* Trotman), 114–16
Hooper, William, 27, 29
horse stealing, 61
House of Lords, 174
household, 7, 8, 35, 67, 147, 151; marriage imagery, 79–81
Hugh Holman, C., 199
Hundred of Berkeley *see* Berkeley estate/family
Hungerford, Sir Anthony, 104
'husbandmen', 134
husbandry, 27, 71–2, 262

iconoclasm, 13, 51, 97–8
Illich, Ivan, 68
imagery, local, 70–3, 83
independency, 152, 154, 167, 169–71, 201, 204, 236–7
'indiscreet landlord' case, 205–11, 212, 217
industrial action, 42, 201–2, 213; riots, 215, 222–5, 227–38; strikes, 21, 233–5
industrial relations, 42, 201–2, 212, 213, 233
industrial revolution, 199
industrialisation, 1–2, 205
industrialism (symbolic exclusion), 82
industry, 24–5, 264
information, 220–1, 252, 253
information technology, 12
inheritance (and bequests), 99–102, 105, 109–10
inner light, 9; Roberts' discovery, 8, 168, 172–7, 179–80, 182–3, 189–90
intensification: concept, 2–3; cultural *see* culture, proverbial; of internal trade, 51–63; kinship dimension *see* kin-coalitions; of traffic *see* traffic (and trade)
internal trade, 51–63
internationalism, 113

James, Mervyn, 196
James I, 260

Jeffries, Richard, 254
journeymen, 235, 236

Kerridge, Eric, 36, 41
kin-coalitions, 51, 69; Roberts, 169–73;
  Trotman, 5–7, 11, 87, 98, 106–8,
  113–19; Tyndale, 86, 87
King, Gregory, 252
King George's Weavers, 233–4
Kingswood colliers, 39, 60, 118,
  222–3, 226, 231
Knight, Daniel, 36
knights/knighthood, 87, 124, 134,
  138, 139
Kundera, Milan, 65

Labour Movement, 212, 217
laissez-faire, 215
land, 216, 237, 246; culture and,
  261–4; ecological determinism,
  254–8; freehold, 151, 152, 153, 154,
  236, 261; see also yeomen
landless persons, 63, 93, 154, 156,
  161, 175, 204, 247, 263
landscape: aborigines and, 254–8; and
  language, 4, 67–8; local, 4, 47, 77–8;
  local imagery, 70–3, 83
language: and landscape, 4, 67–8;
  social discrimination, 9, 247–64;
  written, 12–15
Lanham, Richard, 224
Laslett, Peter, 181
Laud, William, 137
Lawrence, D. H., 263
leadership, 158–63, 226
Lechlade (occupational data), 48–51
Leigh, William, 224
Leland, John, 23, 99
Lenthall, Mr Speaker, 113
Levi-Strauss, Claude, 67–8
Levine, David, 174
Leyes, John, 60
licences, 54–5
literacy, 69, 217; see also language
local: imagery, 70–3, 83; landscape, 4,
  47, 77–8; studies/history, 15–17;
  topography, 46–8
localism, 45–6
Lollards, 56, 85, 86, 88–9, 92, 201
London, 46, 48, 50–1
London Gazette, 220
Lord Mayors of Randwick: carnival,
  211–13; Weavers' song, 213–18

Luther, Martin, 5, 85, 92
Lutheranism, 88

Mabson, Henry, 99
McCluhan, Marshall, 220
magnate class, 147
make-work schemes, 25, 93
Malthus, Thomas, 246
Mann, J. De Le, 41
Manning, Brian, 123–4
Manning, Sam, 60
manufacturing, 17–18, 78, 82, 203;
  districts, 2, 21–44, 142–4, 146–8,
  150–1, 153, 157; occupational
  specialisation, 28–9, 31;
  occupational status categories,
  133–5, 150–1; traffic see traffic (and
  trade); see also cloth industry;
  clothmaking, large-scale
maps, 26, 47–8, 52, 57, 109, 112
market towns, 28–9, 31–2, 55, 57, 61
marriage (as merger), 98–100, 114–18;
  see also kin-coalitions
marriage imagery (proverbs), 79–81
Marshall, William, 55
Martin, William, 36
Martines, Lauro, 262
Marx, Karl, 1, 3, 128, 163, 184, 195;
  on class, 148, 158, 247, 249; theory
  of manufacturing, 17, 78, 203
Marxism, 127, 148, 158
Mary I, 23, 88
mass production, 75
Massey, Edward, 124, 127, 159, 160–2
Master, Thomas, 165
master-race ideology, 249–51, 254–8,
  260–3
Masters, Sir William, 156
media, 11–12, 202; development and
  (role), 219–22; Gloucester Journal
  (role), 215, 219, 222–8, 233, 235,
  238–41; Temple-Andrews debate,
  241–6
memory, imagery and, 71–3, 83
Men and Armour, 39, 53
mentalité theory, 8, 43; localism,
  45–6; preliterate culture, 81–3
Mercator, Gerard, 109, 112
Mercurius Aulicus, 136
metaphors, 67, 70, 73–4
Methodism, 39, 201
methodological individualism, 129
middle-rank, 9–11, 15, 36, 91, 251,

258–9; culture *see* culture, proverbial; family merger *see* kin-coalitions; landed *see* yeomen; *see also* Corbet, John; Roberts, John; Trotman, Thomas (and his family); Tyndale, William

Middlemore, Giles, 55

Mills, Stephen, 205–11

Mitterauer, Michael, 97

Monmouth, Humphrey, 88

moral economy riots, 7, 201–2, 213, 240

More, Sir Thomas, 85, 89, 90, 91

Morrill, John, 124

mortality rates, 76–7, 117–18, 204

Morton, Sir William, 124

muster-lists, 22, 29–30, 32–4, 41, 52, 54, 103, 133–4, 150

Nabi'im, 169, 178, 179, 188

nation states, 6–7, 15–18, 45, 63, 68, 94–5, 175

nationalism, 6, 13, 15, 17, 68–9, 220, 264; Corbet, 158–63; Trotman, 113; Tyndale, 94–6

neighbourhood, 7, 8, 152–4, 161, 181, 188

'neo-separatism', 146

New History of Gloucestershire (Rudder), 212

New Poor Law, 205

newspapers, 202, 220–2, 227

Niblett, Samuel, 54

Nicholson, Bishop, 166, 182–7, 192

Nietzsche, Friedrich, 195

nobility, 47, 124, 134, 151–2

nonconformism, 56, 110, 175, 201

Norman-Angevin framework, 63, 95, 134, 138, 250, 257, 260

Oath of Allegiance, 164

Oath of Uniformity, 165

Obedience of a Christian Man, The (Tyndale), 89, 91

occupational: data, 48–50, 201; patterns, 32–7; specialisation, 27–31, 36–7; status categories, 133–5, 150–1

Olliver, John (blacksmith), 36

Olliver, John (tanner), 36

'one-class society', 181

Ong, Walter J., 3, 14, 220

oral culture, 3–4, 13–16, 71–4, 81–3, 191, 218

overseas trade (in cloth), 41, 42

Page, Andrew, 208

Paine, Hodgkinson, 132, 247

Palmer, Anthony, 110, 111, 112

Papists, 190

Parable of Wicked Mammon (Tyndale), 89

parish registers, 35, 36, 42–3

parish relief, 204, 229

parishes, 29–30, 37, 38

Parliamentarians, 10, 56, 173–4; Corbet's analysis, 127, 131–2, 136, 139, 145, 148, 155, 157–8, 160–2

paternalism, 111, 158, 223–4, 244–5, 247

patriarchy, 4, 74, 78–9, 80–1, 118, 145, 211, 246

patronage, 85, 87, 88, 239–40

Pearce, Simeon, 205

peasants, 153, 167

people (sovereignty), 16, 17

perfectibility, 176, 190, 196, 247

Perkin, Harold, 181

Petty, William, 250, 251, 252, 264

Phillips, Francis, 35

Phillips, John, 36

Phythian-Adams, Charles, 212

Piers Plowman, 88

pin-makers, 204

Pitt, John, 59

political arithmetic, 249, 251, 252–4, 264

political-economic changes, 74–7, 127–8, 136–48, 162–3

Poll Tax, 35

Poor Law, 205

Poor Rate, 204

population: data, 3, 22–4, 27–30, 54, 61, 93, 117–18, 201; history, 39–43

postmodernism, 129

poverty, 23, 40, 76–7, 247; Randwick, 203–13, 217; riots and, 225–7, 242, 244–5

Powell, Anthony, 252

Poyntz family of Acton, 75, 87, 88

Practice of Prelates, The (Tyndale), 98

prejudice (social discrimination), 9, 247–64

preliterate cultures, 12–14, 73, 81–3, 217

Presbyterianism, 38, 90, 136, 174, 181
prices, 224–6, 227, 244–5
Prince, John, 36
Prior, Mary, 50
production: control, 40–2; domestic, 32, 35, 37; factory system, 18, 32, 36, 70; location, 7–8, 17–18; mass, 75; role of, 21–44
professionalism, 191
proletarianisation, 35, 41, 43, 63
proletariat, 9, 10, 11, 131–2, 150, 155–61
property, 92, 211, 213; culture and, 261–4; *see also* land
Protestantism, 7; Corbet's, 10, 138, 146, 154, 158; Roberts', 167, 169–70, 172, 186; Trotman and, 97–8, 110–12; Tyndale, 89–90, 93, 94, 154; *see also* Reformation
protoindustry, 6, 201
proverbs, 3–4, 67, 69–70, 75, 89; in agrarian culture, 72–4, 76–8, 82; in oral culture, 72–4; sexual, 78–81; *see also* culture, proverbial
public opinion, 220
Puritanism, 88, 90, 170, 175, 180, 191; discipline, 37–9; Fifth Monarchists, 110–12; *see also* Corbet, John; Trotman, Throgmorton
Purnell, John, 35, 36
Purnell, Thomas, 35
Purnell, William, 35

Quakers, 7, 8–9, 247; conversion of Roberts, 177–81; inner light, 173–7; kinship loyalty, 171–3; persecution, 164–6; social composition, 166–9; testimony of truth, 182–7; *see also* Roberts, John
Quinton, William, 80

racial superiority, 249–51, 254–8, 260–3
radical empiricism, 8, 81, 127, 129
radical individualism, 7, 8, 166, 171–3
radicalism, 217, 218
Raikes, Robert, 221, 225–7
railways, 61, 62
Randwick study: background and data, 199–203; carnival, 211–13; poverty, 203–5; social relations, 205–11; Weavers' Song, 213–18
rank, 91; aristocracy, 47, 133, 258, 264;

knights, 87, 124, 134, 138–9; nobility, 47, 124, 134, 151–2; *see also* class; feudalism; gentry; middle-rank; yeomen
rational empiricism, 169, 188, 190, 191–2
Read, Lady, 116
Read, Sir James, 116
reasoning, empirical, 187, 189, 195
Reddy, William M., 65
Reformation, 4, 5, 13, 17, 23, 27, 45, 47, 83, 85–6, 88–90, 111, 138, 154, 172, 186
regional: localism, 45–6; topography, 46–8
religion: aboriginal, 255, 256–7; Church courts, 206, 207–10, 217; Corbet's, 124, 126–7, 129–30, 135–6, 152–3; heresy, 5, 85, 87–90, 92–4; Trotman's, 97–8, 108–9, 110–12; Tyndale's, 5, 8–9, 26, 85, 90–2, 112, 186; *see also* Baptists; Methodism; nonconformism; Presbyterianism; Protestantism; Puritanism; Quakers; Reformation
Renaissance, 71
Restall, John, 60
Restoration, 38, 110, 112–13, 164–5, 175, 183–4, 185, 250
revolutionaries: Puritan (Corbet), 123–63; Quaker (Roberts), 164–96
Ricci, Matteo, 71
Richard III, 99
Richardson, R. C., 123
Ricoeur, Paul, 15
riots, 11–12, 43; Beazer, 228–32, 235–8; *Gloucester Journal* (role), 222–8, 238–41; Kingswood colliers, 222–3; media role, 219–22; moral economy, 7, 201–2, 213, 240; Temple-Andrews, 241–6, weavers' activities, 229–38
ritual authority, 215
road system: maintenance, 58–9, 61–2; topography, 46–8; turnpikes, 48, 56–61, 222
Robbins, Elizabeth, 205–10
Robbins, Richard, 207–8, 209
Roberts, Anthony, 165, 167
Roberts, Daniel, 165–70, 173, 176–7, 182–3, 186, 195
Roberts, John, 247, 264; Bull and, 187–94; conversion, 177–81; family,

169–73; inner light, 173–7; Quaker
persecution, 164–6; social
composition of Quakers, 166–9;
testimony of truth, 182–7; his
wizardry, 187–96; yeoman status,
7, 8, 167, 169
Roberts, Lydia (*née* Tyndal), 170, 172
Roberts, Nathaniel, 165, 167
Robinson, John, 38
Rowd, Richard, 232, 235
Royal Society, 252, 264
Royalists, 10, 56, 111–13, 173–4;
Corbet's analysis, 126–7, 131–2,
135–7, 139, 145, 148, 155, 157–8,
160–2
Rudder, Samuel, 42, 48, 212
Rudge, Thomas, 61–2
ruling classes, 63, 95, 132–3, 216,
256–7
rural capitalism, 1–18, 43, 51, 78
rural clothmaking, 35–8, 40, 42–4
rural industry, 24–5

Sahlins, Marshall, 65
Sanders, John, 114–18
Sandys, Sir William, 76
Saxton, Christopher, 26, 47–8, 52, 57,
112
Sayer, Joseph, 226
scandal (indiscreet landlord), 205–11,
212, 217
Scarman, Report, 223
Scott, James C., 199, 212
Seamore, Sir John, 133
secular culture, 90–1, 92, 184
self-interest, 246
self-sufficiency, 46, 53, 204, 236
Settlement Laws, 175
sexual *mores* (indiscreet landlord
case), 205–11
sexuality (proverbs), 78–81
Shakespeare, William, 137–8, 149, 158
shepherds, 27; Short Parliament, 6,
136–48
Ship Money, 139, 140, 147, 154
Shirley, Robert, 225
Short Parliament, 6, 136–48
Sieder, Reinhard, 97
Skinner, Quentin, 90
smallpox epidemic (1711), 117–18
Smeeton, Donald D., 88
Smith, Adam, 204, 215, 246
Smith, Henry, 35

Smith, Humphrey, 177
Smith, William, 35
Smyth, John, 7, 10, 51, 139–41, 173,
204; Berkeley estate, 5, 25, 36, 67,
249–51, 258–9, 263; dependency
system, 171, 175; muster-lists, 22,
52, 54, 103; proverbial culture, 3, 4,
9, 22–3, 67–83, 94, 254; social
discrimination, 247, 249–51, 254,
257–8; Trotmans and, 97, 99–100,
103–6, 119; world-view, 8, 258–64;
yeoman status, 76, 258–9, 261
social analysis (Corbet), 131–6
social composition (Quakers), 166–9
social conflict, 43, 137, 147
social controls, 79, 143, 175
social discrimination, 9; aborigines
(and Aubrey), 250–1; ecological
determinism, 254–8; languages of,
247–50; political arithmetic, 252–4;
Smyth's world-view, 258–64
social engineering, 251
social mobility, 237
social order, 91, 248–9, 260–1
social relations (Randwick study),
205–11
social structure (Corbet's view),
127–8, 152, 155–8
social tensions and language, 262–3
socialisation, 93, 146, 202
society, English (development), 46
Society of Friends, 8, 165, 168–9,
171–2, 176, 177, 191
Solliss, Andrew, 169, 172, 174
Solliss, Mary, 169
Spratt, George, 36
stage-coach travel, 59–60
state (role), 46
Stenton, F. M., 46
Stephens, Edward, 133, 141, 145–6
Stephens, James, 232
Stephens, John, 171–2, 195
Stephens, Nathaniel, 133, 136, 140–3,
145, 147, 154, 160
Stevens, Samuel, 232
Stokesley, John, 85, 100
strikes and strike-breaking, 21, 233–5
Stroud, 42–3, 54–5
Stroudwater, 22–4, 26, 29, 42–3
structural impact (clothmaking), 43–4
structure/culture dichotomy, 12
Stubbes, Henry, 110
Stumpe, William, 37, 70

subordination, 241, 243
Sumptuary Laws, 241
Sydney, Philip, 263
Symons, Edward, 193

'Tarquinius Superbus', 242
Tawney, A. J., 134, 151
Tawney, R. H., 134, 151
taxation (and traffic), 61
technology, 12, 36, 37, 40–1
Temple, William, 233, 238, 241–6, 247, 258
testimony of truth, 182–7
Tewkesbury, 40
Tewkesbury, John, 88–9
thaumaturgy, 187, 189, 192
Thinne, Sir John, 101
Thirsk, Joan, 1, 41, 75
Thomas, Keith, 187–8, 189, 248
Thomas, Martha, 205, 206, 208–9
Throckmorton family, 75, 87
Throgmorton, Sir Thomas, 78, 101
Thurston, John, 36, 177
Tilladam, John, 36
Tillotson, John, 65
Tippets, William, 36
topography, 46–8
Tories, 240–1, 243
Tracy, John, 138
Tracy, Sir Robert, 138–40, 141–3, 145–6
Tracy family, 87
trade, 238, 246; internal, 51–63; traders, 51–4; *see also* traffic (and trade)
trade unions, 201, 212, 233
traffic (and trade), 2–3; capitalist development, 62–3; commodity production, 55–6; localism, 45–6; occupational data, 48–50; road maintenance, 61–2; road system, 56–61; Stroud-centredness, 54–5; topography, 46–8; trade intensification, 50–1, traders, 51–4
transport *see* traffic (and trade)
Trevisa, John, 88
Troteman, John, 99
Troteman, Richard, 99
Trotman, Samuel, 102–3, 107–8, 113–6, 118, 119
Trotman, Thomas (and his family), 4, 9; background/career, 98–9; family and business, 99–102, 107–8; kin-

coalition, 5–6, 7, 11, 87, 98, 106–8, 113–19; Samuel's expansionary policy, 102–3, 113–14; theology, 97–8, 108–9, 110–12; Throgmorton's vision, 108–13; yeoman status, 6, 97, 98, 102–7
Trotman, Throgmorton, 7, 108–13, 119, 171
Trouthyman, Henry, 99
Tucker, Josiah, 238–9
Tunstall, Bishop, 88–9, 91
Turner, Victor, 136, 148, 196, 208, 214
turnpikes, 48, 56–61, 222
'two societies' debate, 11–12, 219–46
Tyndal, Thomas, 170
Tyndale, Edward, 5, 85–7, 98, 100, 106, 170, 259
Tyndale, John, 5, 86, 88–9, 100
Tyndale, Katherine, 98, 99, 100
Tyndale, Thomas, 99–100
Tyndale, William, 10, 247, 260; career/background, 87–9; heresy, 87–90, 92–4; influences on, 84–6; nationalism, 94–6; theology, 5, 8–9, 26, 85, 90–2, 112, 186; Trotman family and, 98–100, 106–9, 114, 119, 170; vernacular culture, 4, 5, 15–16, 94–6, 154, 196; yeoman status, 5, 86–7, 91, 92–3

unemployment, 40, 43, 76
urban development, 27–32

Valiant Sixty, 177, 180
Vann, Richard, 166, 167
vernacular culture, 13, 67, 84, 91, 235, 251, 257, 264; Tyndale's work, 4, 6, 15–16, 94–6, 154, 196
vertical hierarchy, 249
Vilar, Pierre, 125, 212

Wadman, Hannah (*née* Trotman), 115–16
Wadman, Robert, 115–16
wages, 42, 215, 222, 228, 230, 233, 237, 244
Walpole government, 118, 223–4, 235, 237, 239, 245
Walsh, Sir John, 85, 87, 88
Warcup, Mary (*later* Trotman), 113
Warne, Edith (*née* Trotman), 102
Warne, Thomas, 102
Wars of the Roses, 5, 74, 99, 129, 259

waterways, 48, 49–51, 62
Watts, Anne, 100
wealth, 78, 93, 245–6
weavers, 5, 21, 41; industrial action, 21, 200, 224, 227, 229–38; occupational data, 32–5, 150–1, 201; organisations, 233–5; Short Parliament, 6, 136–48
Weavers' Song (Randwick study), 11, 213–18
Web, Francis, 108
Webb family, 51, 69–70, 99, 153
Wentworth, Lord, 101, 104
Wesley, John, 39, 201, 226
Whitefield, George, 201
Wiener, Martin, J., 82
Wildey, Daniel, 207–10 passim
Wildey, Emma, 206–7
William the Bastard, 250, 257
William the Conqueror, 47
Williams, John, 36
Wilson, Ian, 178–9
Winstanley, Gerard, 82
Winter, Sir William, 161
Wittgenstein, Ludwig, 191–2

wizardry (of Roberts), 8, 168–9, 178–9, 183, 187–96
Wolf, Eric R., 6, 21, 97, 201
Wolf, James, 43
Wolfe, Colonel James, 21, 23, 201, 234
women Quakers, 178, 188
Wood Anthony, 256
Woodward, Joseph, 35, 38–9, 110
Woodward, Mary, 35
working class, 251; class struggle, 11, 199–218; riots/debates, 11–12, 219–46
Worthies of England (Fuller), 22, 69
Wrightson, Keith, 174, 248, 249
written language, 12–15
Wycliffe, John, 15–16, 84–5, 88, 92

yeoman, 18, 41, 69, 134, 153, 236, 237; Roberts family, 7, 8, 167, 169; Smyth family, 76, 258–9, 261; Trotman family, 6, 97, 98, 102–7; Tyndale family, 5, 86–7, 91, 92–3
York Chronicle, 221
Young, Arthur, 58, 62

JAN 2 4 1994